3.95
905
B&N

DATE DUE			
NOV 15 82			
OCT 26 83			

We Have Eaten the Forest

We Have Eaten the Forest

THE STORY OF A
MONTAGNARD VILLAGE IN THE
CENTRAL HIGHLANDS
OF VIETNAM

Georges Condominas

TRANSLATED FROM THE FRENCH BY

Adrienne Foulke

PHOTOGRAPHS, MAPS, AND DIAGRAMS BY THE AUTHOR

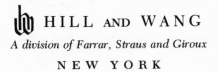 HILL AND WANG

A division of Farrar, Straus and Giroux

NEW YORK

English translation © 1977 by Farrar, Straus and Giroux, Inc.
Originally published in French as *Nous Avons Mangé la Forêt de la Pierre-Génie Gôo,* © 1957 by Mercure de France, Paris
FIRST AMERICAN EDITION, 1977

Published simultaneously in Canada by McGraw-Hill Ryerson Ltd., Toronto

Printed in the United States of America
DESIGNED BY HERBERT H. JOHNSON

Library of Congress Cataloging in Publication Data

Condominas, Georges.
   We have eaten the forest.
   Translation of Nous avons mangé la forêt de la pierre-génie Gôo.
   Bibliography: p.
   Includes indexes.
   1. Mnong (Indochinese tribe) 2. Sar Luk, Vietnam—Social life and customs.   I. Title.
DS539.M58C63 1977   309.1'597'03   77-887

CONTENTS

ILLUSTRATIONS

PHOTOGRAPHS

MAPS, DRAWINGS, CHART

Preface to the English-Language Edition

Some twenty years separate the first French edition (1957) from the present English translation of this chronicle of Sar Luk; meanwhile, it has appeared in Italian, German, and Russian. In those intervening years, several attempts were made to bring out an English-language version, but they came to nothing. Except for one—the first, as it happens, which dates back to 1962. But this initiative is singular in that it is a "pirated" edition ascribable to the United States Department of Commerce, which acted for political and military reasons rather than out of any deep scientific concern, and did so without consulting either me, the author, or the original French publisher, Mercure de France.

With some cynicism (or unintentional humor?), the persons responsible for this infringement of international copyright laws and the most elementary rules of common courtesy sought to minimize their infraction by announcing that they had translated only "a large portion" of the book, including "the Introduction, all the text (10 chapters), and the Glossary." Which is to say, the entire book except for the indexes! When, by signaling the fact that the indexes had been omitted, these persons tacitly demonstrated that they found them important, it is likely that they did not suspect they were, actually, at one with the "torpedoed" author, who considers the indexes anything but mere appendices; rather, they are a second part of the book, complementary to the first—the text proper— and very important indeed.

The concept that governed the writing of this book I have set forth in the Introduction. Of course, the presentation of events in chronological order can arouse the interest of the reader who is not a specialist and who is responsive to elements that would make this chronicle more closely resemble a literary work: description of a milieu, portraits of individual people, biographical information, interlaced accounts of action and stories. On the other hand, to reconstitute reality with a maximum of detail risks distracting the anthropologist who would be looking only for a fuller presentation of certain specific areas in the Mnong Gar documentation provided here. Hence the multiple indexes.

The Index of Geographical and Ethnic Group Names follows a standard form. The Index of Plant Names is slightly expanded because of the place plants occupy in the life of these Montagnard "forest eaters."

In setting up the Index of Personal and Clan Names, I have included all the relevant details about each individual, my purpose being thereby to flesh out their portraits in terms of their own actions or words as well as the social constellation in which they lived. Furthermore, when, for example, a confrontation occurs between two individuals, recourse to the personal-name index better enables the reader to situate them in relation to one another and, at least in part, to understand the underlying reasons for their confrontation. Also, certain situations recur, and the detailed data in the index make it possible for one to place them in analogous contexts, and to distinguish some constants in the Mnong Gar pattern of personal relations.

Lastly, in the Subject Index I have attempted to group under headings all the information about the Mnong Gar that is to be found in the text except data included in the other indexes. Most often I have presented the data under headings that accord with a logical order closely akin to indigenous concepts (e.g.: Souls and Body). Exceptions to this arrangement have been made only when the indigenous classification would have required of the reader actual preliminary study (e.g.: Animals). Another mode of presentation has been to subdivide by time sequence (e.g.: Agrarian Rites), rather than to follow the usual alphabetical order. Finally, some entries follow yet another order, going from the general to the specific (e.g.: Trade). By means of this rather innovative styling of the Subject Index I hope to have provided researchers with an overall view of each subject which, by turning to the references cited, they can reconstitute in its entirety. Thus, the agronomist who is uninterested in reading about rites or stories of love and death will be able, thanks to the heading "Agriculture," to reconstruct the Mnong Gar's methods and techniques for clearing the ground for planting according to their own calendar. Additionally, for the linguist let me note that the vocabulary supplied in the Subject Index, together with that in the Index of Plant Names and the Glossary, puts several hundred Phii Brêe words at his disposal.

On several occasions, readers undoubtedly influenced by the popularity of Oscar Lewis's books have asked me why I made no use of a tape recorder. In each instance, my answer has been very simple: at the time of my study (1948–50), the lightweight battery-powered tape recorder did not exist, and that is the only type that would have been practicable in an altogether isolated forest village remote from any source of electricity. And even if such equipment had been on the market, I would not have been in a position to buy it, given the fact that no funds whatever were made available to me; indeed, I was obliged to play the beggar in Ban Me Thuot in order to obtain one camera, which was the sum total of my research gear.

On my return to Sar Luk, in 1958, the director of the Ecole Française d'Extrême-Orient supplied me with a Nagra. This high-precision machine rendered substantial service, notably in collecting music and oral literature, and also in conducting interviews on specific predetermined topics. But in the sort of research I wanted to do it could not have been as useful to me as one might assume. In many situations, the presence of a recording device would have risked modifying people's behavior. The Mnong Gar had no writing, and so it did not disturb them to see me write; whereas the tape recorder, by not merely reproducing sounds but also recreating through voice inflection an important part of an individual's personality, risks modifying the attitudes of the person who expects to be reheard and to rehear himself. Actually, this is why one is obliged to work with a very small number of people, as Oscar Lewis, with incomparable talent, has done.

Because I have had the opportunity in another book to give a full account of my field research,* here I may simply add that the effort required for the work carried out in Sar Luk was such that I have never been able to repeat that experience elsewhere. I have utilized only a part of the documentation gathered among the Mnong Gar; this fact, together with the fear of forgetting a part of my knowledge of the Phii Brêe, has subsequently deprived me of the means and the time to really immerse myself to a comparable extent in the language of groups I have since studied.

What has become of the Mnong Gar? After an absence of eight years, I went back to Sar Luk, in 1958, on a very short visit. This was four years after the Geneva Agreements had confirmed the independence of Vietnam, and naïvely I was expecting to find the Mnong freed of the problems colonial domination creates. No such thing. The Geneva Agreements had divided Vietnam in two; the southern half had been handed over to those who had not fought against the colonial administration and who therefore felt that to make their patriotism credible they must show them-

---

* *L'Exotique est quotidien* (Paris: Plon, 1965). In this book, the reader will also find examples of the Mnong Gar's tribulations under the French colonial government and, in the final chapter, a survey of the Diemist regime's actions in their regard. The Afterword to the new edition, which appeared in 1977, gives more details on what the American period entailed for them.

selves hypernationalistic by imposing their concept of "Vietnicity"—by force if need be—on minority groups that were too weak to resist.

My meeting with the people of Sar Luk was a sorrowful one. Many of my friends—Baap Can, Truu, Kroong-the-Short, among others—had died during my absence. Two days after my arrival, the eldest son of Bbür, my first Mnong Gar friend, died at the age of ten. . . . Above all, there was nothing but recriminations against the odious attitude of the military and civilian officials of the dictator Ngo Dinh Diem toward the Montagnards: the South Vietnamese were treating them with disdain, taking every un- fair advantage of them, fining them if they wore their loincloths, ridiculing their customs. This was in line with what I had heard elsewhere: promi- nent among the dictator's plans was to forbid the Moï ("savages") to wear their traditional garb, make sacrifices, speak their own language. . . . In a word, Diem wanted to make their culture totally disappear, to uproot every trace of their ethnicity—hence the word "ethnocide," which I derived from "genocide," being at that point reluctant to use the term that denotes a physical massacre. But I did not doubt, even then, that the former would lead, sooner or later, to the latter.

My 1958 visit to Sar Luk was to be my last. When, in August 1962, I was able to return to that general area, it was already too late. The pre- ceding April, a National Liberation Front unit carried out a bold raid in the Fyan region, starting in the Daak Kroong Valley. Following that raid, the Diemist army sent a large-scale expedition to clear the valley of all its inhabitants, thereby removing all popular support for the revolutionaries. And so it was that on the Fyan Plateau I found the pitiful wreckage of a population that, with the worst kind of brutality, had been hounded by the soldiery from the land of its ancestors. The fears I had felt for the fu- ture of the Mnong Gar at the time of my 1958 visit to Sar Luk were as nothing to the reality I now saw: haggard people, "uprooted" in the true sense of the word, torn forcibly from a land the smallest corner of which they knew and with which they were accustomed to commune as if that land were human; they had been transplanted to terrain where they knew nothing of the religious taboos or those (probably more numerous) having to do with planting, moving about, etc., all of which were being drummed into their ears; they were prisoners, not shackled in irons but broken by illness and despair, in what the organizers of their death delicately termed "refugee camps."

It was these men to whom I owed the best of myself, and I may be forgiven if I find it hard to linger over this account. All the more so because, after I had waited four years to return, I learned that Srae, whose marriage I described (see Chapter 5), had been tortured by an American sergeant. I wanted to get to the bottom of this, and to interview him in Mnong. However, the valley's having been thoroughly cleared out had not completely satisfied the new masters; they had set up two Special Forces camps, one in Phii Ko', the other in Daa' Mroong, in order the better to control the countryside, which had been, additionally, decreed a Free Strike Zone. I could not avail myself of one of the helicopters that serviced the Special Forces camps without passing as a friend of the people who were maltreating the Mnong; a severe rheumatism prevented my making long marches—what's more, made it impossible for me to run, a dangerous inability in a forest area subject to random bombing; the distance between Dalat and Phii Ko' was long, not to mention the difficulty in getting through the observation posts on the rim of the Lang Biang Plateau. I ran into a similar block when I tried to get through via Ban Me Thuot: the little buses could not even reach the former Poste du Lac. In short, not only had the Mnong been decimated in 1962, when they were driven from their territory by the Army, and been further reduced by the consequences of their forcible removal (malnutrition, epidemics, loss of their zest for life); now they had but two alternatives: they could take to the bush and thereby preserve their liberty, but they would be obliged to endure bombardments and grave consequences should they be captured—all this without being able to lead their traditional way of life; or they could submit to the orders of foreign masters and accede to being penned in the Special Forces camps where, depending on age and sex, they were transformed into beggars or docile hirelings.

How could an ethnic group surmount such an ordeal, especially when it was to last almost twenty years? The devastation caused by highly sophisticated bombs; the ravages wrought by epidemics that sweep through camps where people have been dumped who in the literal sense of the word have been uprooted and who have lost the will to live; the forced dispersal that cuts young people off from their culture and even alienates them from it (because of the arrant scorn displayed by those around them); a countryside pitted with bomb craters and laid waste by defoliants . . . The balance sheet is catastrophic. The most terrible of wars did not spare the Mnong Gar. It is my hope that their compatriots on the plains, the Vietnamese, will be able to help survivors of the holocaust preserve whatever still exists of their ethnic identity, as they have done for other minority groups in the North, and thereby enrich a common national patrimony. I should like to think that this book might aid them to that end, and that it not be reduced to a mere collection of records.

If until now the ethnographer has been considered the historian of the subproletariat of the Third World, I hope that henceforth he may be deemed above all the historian of the different ethnic communities of reunified nations.

Paris, February 1976

Introduction

Hii saa brii . . . ("We ate the forest of . . .") followed by a place name is how the Mnong Gar, or *Phii Brêe* ("the Men of the Forest"), designate this or that year. These slash-and-burn seminomads of the Central Highlands in Vietnam have no method whereby they log the passing of time other than by referring to the wooded areas they clear and burn off in succession to make their annual plantings.

Thus the same year will be given a different name by each village, for in that period each will have "eaten" a section of its own domain. When a community has, successively, leveled all the forests covering its territory, the people return to an area they had cleared ten or twenty years earlier. Once more they identify the year as the one in which they again ate that particular forest. So the same term serves to denote two years separated by one or two decades. If people wish to avoid possible confusion, they can be more specific and mention the site on which their village stood in a given year, for the location of hamlets is also changed if they are too remote from the fields under current cultivation or if they have been struck by an epidemic. One can avoid confusion also by referring to some unusual event that took place during the year in question.

In the village of Sar Luk, "We ate the Forest of the Stone Spirit Gôo" designates the year 1949—or, more exactly, the agricultural season that ran from the end of November 1948 to the beginning of December 1949. In the present book, I propose to recount events that took place in Sar Luk in the course of this single agricultural cycle. Obviously, the first chapter deals with things that happened a month before the preceding calendar year ended. This would never disturb the Mnong's sense of time, for it is conditioned by the continual unfolding of their days and labors. The mind of the Man of the Forest, unlike ours, is not clouded by the all-powerful presence of numbers.

For this account of a Mnong community, I have taken unedited material from notebooks I kept during my stay in Sar Luk. A structural portrait of Mnong society will be prepared and presented elsewhere. But meanwhile it has seemed of interest to picture different aspects of their group life with concrete examples drawn from their everyday reality. For example, here I do not make any theoretical statement about the Mnong Gar *Tâm Bôh* but describe a specific Exchange of Buffalo Sacrifices—one performed by two individuals, Baap Can and Ndêh—and I place it in the context of daily life. Similarly, I have not traced the schema of a typical Mnong Gar marriage; rather, I have related how the wedding of Srae and Jaang took place, including minor incidents that accompanied it.

A single observation does not suffice to give representative value to the description of an institution. But Mnong Gar culture is both geographically confined and very homogeneous. These facts alone limit the amount of indispensable data to be collected about each of its institutions. In the course of my long stay in Sar Luk, I did assemble notations sufficient to validate statistically the synthesized description that will be included in ethnological studies now in preparation.* May I add at once that the variants I present in this book do not depart from the norms which emerge from the categorized data.

By studying a human group and deriving from a mass of observations the schema and the movement of its social structure, one can trace a portrait in depth of that society. But it is a theoretical one—an X ray, so to speak. The wealth of notations for each given category of facts allows one to establish a coherent system representative of the society under study— what one might call a pattern of it. This is absolutely essential work, without which there is no true science of ethnology. Yet in conjunction with such a task it seems to me of great interest to present purely ethnographic documentation which, because it offers concrete examples, reproduces the play of institutions in their episodic context. It also serves to illustrate how one's theory of the institution differs from actual life; in a word, it shows the flesh—and also the garments—that cover the skeleton. One's concern may be with institutions, with structured wholes, yet one cannot forget that these are perceived and felt—i.e., lived—by human beings, by individuals with differing faculties and ways of behaving. Within the context their culture imposes, people act partly under the influence of personal motivation, partly in response to external circumstance. Here I would like to show not the cultural pattern but rather how it is made manifest in the pulsations of real life. In this entirely documentary account, the reader will notice some contradictions in explanations supplied

---

* See the studies listed in the Bibliography and Supplementary Bibliography in the back matter of this volume.

by my various Gar informants, or differences between the explication and the actual performance of a particular ritual. Formulas and prayers, too, not only present internal variations but also are used in varying ways.

The publication of raw data seems to me useful from another point of view. In constructing the schema of an institution, for this or that reason one perforce makes a choice among the supporting facts. But if all the facts are presented as sequentially observed, conceivably another specialist may attach importance to data that in a systematic study would have been discarded.

An ethnographic work has still another advantage. It restores *in vivo* relationships between individuals belonging to complementary categories: the connections between brothers, between brother and sister, uncle and maternal nephew, etc. Lastly, the play of a given institution can sometimes be conveyed more vividly by descriptive detail than by statement of fact. For example, in Chapter 3, which relates a grave infraction of a taboo, the reader will see how important material proof is to the Mnong Gar, who do not consider mere suspicion of guilt to be sufficient; in Chapter 9, it will be seen how the division of an inheritance is actually carried out by the family.

I shall no doubt be reproached for alluding to my own presence at events I describe. But my purpose is not to paint an exotic canvas or to construct some sort of prehistoric ethnography. Rather, it is to render reality as it was lived while being observed. My aim is to offer documentation, so it would be unscientific to eliminate—with the excuse that I was accepted by the society which was the object of my study—modifications in behavior, however minute, that were caused by my presence. It is self-evident—but perhaps worth emphasizing—that to be able to collect this material I had to be present while the events documented were taking place. I did the maximum, I believe, to ensure that my presence had the minimum possible effect on the normal life of the Mnong Gar village in which I lived. I always worked directly, without the intermediary of an interpreter. For that matter, my entire staff consisted of one Mnong Rlâm servant, who was unwilling to stay more than three months among the Men of the Forest. After he left, I replaced him with a native of Sar Luk, thus reducing the elements alien to the community to one.* However, even when observations are made under such conditions, one cannot eliminate from the account of what was observed facts that were modified by the presence, no matter how discreet, of the researcher. He is intent

---

* For details about the research methods, see G. Condominas, "Rapport d'une mission ethnologique en 'Pays Mnong Gar (pays montagnard du Sud-Indochinois)," *Bulletin de l'Ecole Française d'Extrême-Orient* (Hanoi), Vol. XLVI (1952), Fasc. No. 1, pp. 303–13; or, for more details, G. Condominas, *L'Exotique est quotidien, Sar Luk, Viêt-Nam central* (Paris: Plon, 1965).

on scientific investigation, but nonetheless shares the nature of his subjects of study—he remains a man among men. Although I discarded the
habitual or "normal" comportment of my fellow Frenchmen and tried to
blend into the Mnong world, the Men of the Forest could not see in me
anyone other than a member—individualized, of course—of a social category belonging to a global structure into which colonialism had projected
them. Certainly, never before had it occurred to a *Phii Brêe* to confide in
a European as some did in me, and never before had a white man been
asked to come at the time of the planting rites to insert the drinking straw
in the jar and invoke the ancestors together with "the holy men in the
forest and in the village." Had I been a simple Man of the Forest—just
another villager—I would not have been asked to do this. The holy men
asked me to pray because they believed my words would increase the
chances of the prayers' being heard. And if they attributed to me an
"elephant-soul" rather than a "buffalo-soul," that (if one wishes to in-
terpret scientifically this detail of religious ethnography) was because of
my socioeconomic position and because the Mnong Gar were already in-
tegrated into a far vaster sociological entity than the restricted one to
which they belonged at the time their country was conquered.

At first glance, their customs may appear picturesque or exotic, as if in
an almost immutable way they reproduce a tradition rooted in the night of
time—as the Mnong Gar indeed believe—but the Men of the Forest are
nonetheless men. What is more, they are men of the twentieth century
and are involved in a socioeconomic system that embraces the planet. For
them, this involvement is translated into the payment of taxes, labor on
plantations or roads, the superimposition of a monetary system on their
barter economy, the regulation of their lives within the framework of a hierarchical colonial administration, the introduction of writing and medical
care, and military service in the Army or the Garde Montagnarde.

The object of this book is to present firsthand raw data about life in a
present-day Mnong Gar village. It deals with a village because the tribe's
traditional political unity does not extend beyond this horizon and because
it is through the medium of the village that one can sense the people's ad-
aptation to modern life. It utilizes documentation obtained during the unfolding of a complete year-long agricultural cycle because this span represents the most complete time unit available.

Simple raw materials, in a word, with no attempt on my part to establish a sociological structuring or to compromise the material with literary embellishments.

Paris, May 1955

·🌷·🌷·🌷·🌷·🌷·🌷·🌷·

A Guide to Mnong Gar Pronunciation

The transcription used here is the one recommended by the Dalat Commission on August 1, 1949.*

Consonants:

k, g, t, d, n, p, b, m, l, and *s* are pronounced approximately as in English, but without aspiration (an example of an unaspirated consonant is the *p* in "spot")

h indicates an aspiration in all positions (for example, *hiu* [house]; *boh* [salt]); when it follows *p, t,* or *k,* it indicates that they should be aspirated (an example of an aspirated *p* is the *p* in "pot")

jj, dd, bb, and *nn* are the preglottalized equivalents of *j, d, b,* and *n* (preglottalization is a closing of the glottis before emission of sound)

c is somewhat like English *ch,* but without aspiration

j is somewhat like English *j*

ng is like the *ng* in "sing"

ny is somewhat like the *ny* in "canyon"

r is always pronounced with the tip of the tongue

' signals a glottal stop (like the middle sound in English "oh-oh!")

Vowels:

A doubled vowel indicates a long as opposed to a short vowel; for example, *maang* (rice basket) as opposed to *mang* (night)

a is like the *a* in "mama"

e is like the *e* in "pen"

---

* See G. Condominas, "Enquête linguistique parmi les Populations montagnardes du Sud Indochinois," *Bulletin de l'Ecole Française d'Extrême-Orient* (Hanoi), Vol. XLVI (1954), Fasc. No. 2, p. 580.

ê is like the *a* in "may"

i is like the *ee* in "meet"

o is like the *a* in "ball"

ô is like the *o* in "rose"

u is like the *oo* in "too"

ö when short resembles the *u* in "but"; when long (*öö*) it is somewhat
like the *u* in "hurt"

ü does not exist in English; it is somewhat like the French *u* or German *ü*

We Have Eaten the Forest

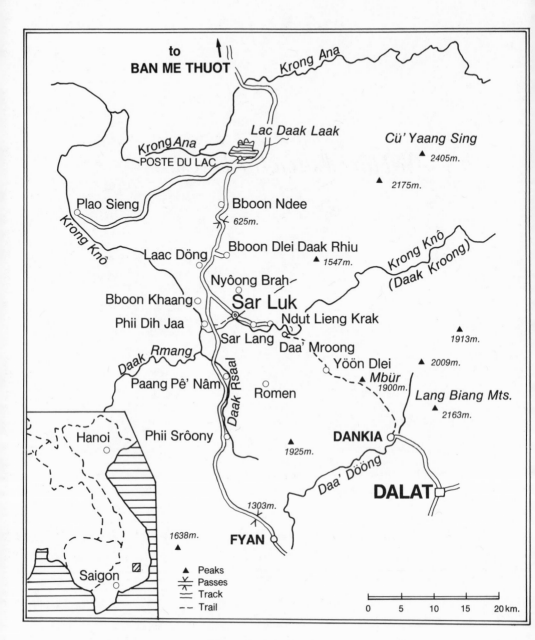

to
BAN ME THUOT

Krong Ana

Krong Ana
POSTE DU LAC

Lac Daak Laak

Cü' Yaang Sing
▲ 2405m.

▲ 2175m.

Plao Sieng

◦ Bboon Ndee
⊁ 625m.

Bboon Dlei Daak Rhiu
▲ 1547m.

Krong Knô

Laac Döng

Krong Knô
(Daak Kroong)

Nyôong Brah

Sar Luk

Bboon Khaang ◦

Ndut Lieng Krak

▲ 1913m.

Phii Dih Jaa

Sar Lang

Daa' Mroong

▲ 2009m.

Daak Rmang

Paang Pê' Nâm

Yöön Dlei

▲ Mbür
1900m.

Lang Biang Mts.
▲ 2163m.

Romen

Daak Rsaal

Phii Srôony

DANKIA

Hanoi ◦

▲ 1925m.

Daa' Dööng

DALAT

1303m.

▲ 1638m.

FYAN

Saigon ◦

▲ Peaks
⊁ Passes
≡ Track
-- Trail

0   5   10   15   20 km.

Mnong Gar Country

1

The Mnong Gar, or Phii Brêe ("The Men of the Forest"). Sar Luk

AT whatever point one approaches the coast of central Vietnam, one sees, in the background, an unbroken line of heights rising toward the east which in certain places along the littoral extend into the sea as mighty promontories. These elevations belong to the Chaîne Annamitique, which, on its seaward side, rears up like a steep wall above narrow but extremely fertile plains that the Vietnamese wrested some centuries ago from their then southern neighbors, the Chams. On their western, inland flanks, the mountains do not drop abruptly. They descend in a series of plateaus toward the Mekong. This great river, which rises in Laos and eastern Thailand, flows through Cambodia, and, its flood waters controlled by the reservoir-like action of Tonle Sap (Great Lake), rolls on until it branches out to form the vast Mekong Delta.

What strikes the traveler moving westward from the coast is the great contrast between the people of the plains and those who live in the mountains inland. The plains, narrow as they are, support a very dense population, people who are the heirs of ancient civilizations. Although the Sinicized Vietnamese completely absorbed Champa, vestiges of that brilliant culture are scattered throughout the countryside, bearing witness to the profound influence of Hinduism. The moment one nears the mountains, however, the landscape changes entirely. Irrigated paddies and well-to-do villages give way to forest and jungle. This vegetation covers the immense area of mountains and plateaus which extends from the coastal plains to the banks of the Mekong. It is sparsely inhabited by a handful of tribes belonging to what is culturally the oldest stratum of the Indo-Chinese peoples. In Vietnamese, they are known as Moi, meaning "savage." They acquired the pejorative name because of their reputation for ferocity, anarchic independence, nomadism, and the possession of magic pow-

3

ers. Such sinister fame has been aggravated by reports of the world these people live in, which is said to be inhabited by wild beasts and infested with deadly fevers and malefic spirits.

Mnong Gar Country

The Mnong Gar, or *Phii Brêe*—"the Men of the Forest," as the Kudduu call them—are established on both banks of the Middle Krong Knô, which is the southern branch of a tributary of the Mekong, the Srepok. (The Mnong name for the Krong Knô is Daak Kroong; the Rhade term may be translated as "the Male River.") The Daak Kroong has its source among the peaks of the Chaîne Annamitique. It descends in torrents through very rugged terrain over which the Mnong Cil roam (called "the Up-stream Cil" by the Mnong Gar). It then meanders widely through what Gar and Cil call its "plain"—actually, a narrow alluvial strip bordered on the north and south by a double series of moderately high, fairly parallel mountain chains. Downstream from the village of Phii Dih, the Krong Knô forces its way through a granite ridge before reaching Bih country. Here it joins the Krong Ana (for the Rhade, "the Female River"), which along its route has drained the overflow of Lake Daak Laak. After this now imposing current crosses Rhade territory southwest of Ban Me Thuot, the administrative capital of the Southern Montagnard Country, it takes on the Cambodian name Srepok and flows on to empty into the Mekong at Stung Treng.

The Mnong Gar inhabit the plain of the Daak Kroong and the small mountain chains bordering it on the north and south. On the north, their territory stops at the edge of the fertile Daak Laak basin, which the Mnong Rlâm and their neighbors to the west, the Bih, cultivate as ir-rigated paddies. To the southeast and south, a long, curving chain of high mountains encircles the Gar country and separates it from the high pla-teaus of Lang Biang and Upper Donnaï Province, where other rice growers live—the Laac around Dalat, and the Kudduu around Fyan.

Two tribes, the Cil Koon Ddôo' and the Cil Bboon Jaa, exhibit a marked tendency to overstep the boundaries of their own territory on the heights of the southern section of the big chain, and to edge toward Gar country; the Cil Bboon Jaa have even bought from the people of Phii Ko' the section of the latter's terrain that lies south of the Daak Kroong.

Lastly, let me note that the Men of the Forest are in direct touch, on the east, with the Upstream Cil, who are established on the upper reaches of the Daak Kroong; and on the west, with the Mnong Pröng, who inhabit the area situated to the south of the Daak Kroong, down-stream from Phii Dih.

Perpendicularly to the axis of the Male River, a track crosses Gar country from north to south. Passing through Poste du Lac and Fyan, it connects Ban Me Thuot to the road built by the French that runs from Dalat to Djiring and on from there to Saigon. The track crosses the Daak Kroong at Phii Ko', where there is a temporary bridge, and traverses the southern Chaîne Annamitique via a pass 1303 meters above sea level. To reach Dangkia and Dalat, the Gar also have a traditional footpath at their disposal. This path runs straight toward Mount Mbür, scales it to a height of almost 2000 meters, then descends to the Lang Biang Plateau, which is no more than 1500 meters above sea level.

Gar country is very mountainous, one undulation following upon another. Even the so-called "plain," which lies 500 meters above sea level and at its widest point is less than eight kilometers as the crow flies, bristles with hills. Vegetation in the "plain" hardly differs from that in the "mountains," except that there are more numerous swampy areas such as are found ordinarily only in the valleys below. Otherwise, forest, bush, and bamboo stands cover the entire Gar country. Only areas cleared for current crops—the *miir*—and the savannas of lalang grass (*Imperata*) which succeed them permit one to glimpse a span of horizon. Then one is able to see compact masses of full-grown timberland. This is the habitat of the Spirits and, for that reason, is never touched by the rice planter's axe.

To move about this region, people use the track—passable for vehicles in the dry season—which runs from north to south, and from which a small fork turns off at Bboon Dlei Laac Yô', crosses the territories of Paang Döng, Sar Luk, Sar Lang, and Ndut Sar, and ends at Ndut Lieng Krak. In 1949, this small fork was extended as far as Daa' Mroong.* Before the French–Indo-Chinese War, this track was the only relatively usable vehicular route in existence between Ban Me Thuot and Djiring or Dalat. Its economic importance vanished in 1946, with the construction of the road that connects Djiring and Ban Me Thuot via Kinda. However, the Mnong still like to use it to reach the villages it serves, because the track is wide and therefore offers a measure of protection against wild animals. But since these villages are few and constitute only a small part of Mnong country, of necessity the traditional paths that do connect villages are still the most heavily traveled. They are narrow, and whenever possible they run along valley floors; people either ford the streams or cross via rude bridges—most often, simply a tree trunk thrown over the current, although sometimes a smaller horizontal limb serves as a sort of handrail.

As for the Daak Kroong, numerous stretches of the river are navigable by canoe, but they are separated by rapids, so that for long trips the river

---

* It was on this occasion that the prehistoric lithophone of Ndut Lieng Krak was discovered. (See *L'Exotique est quotidien*, Ch. 33.) I may point out that formerly this segment did not start out from Bboon Dlei but from the Phii Ko' ferry and ran along the river. Because it required maintaining numerous bridges, it was abandoned in 1948.

is seldom used. In no way, certainly, does it constitute a barrier. None-theless, since 1933 it has served as the administrative boundary between two provinces—Darlac, on the north bank, and Upper Donnaï, on the south. This senseless division cuts the Mnong Gar tribe in two. Whereas members settled in even the most remote areas to the north of the Daak Kroong need make only a long one-day walk to reach Poste du Lac, to which they administratively belong, the people to the south of the river, or about a third of the tribe, must make an onerous three-day journey to reach Dran, which is the official seat of their province.

Sar Luk

This village of a hundred and forty-six inhabitants, which I chose as my field of study and where I came to live in September 1948, occupies a central position in the middle valley of the Krong Knô. Sar Luk is situated fifty-five kilometers south of the nearest "civilized" locality, Poste du Lac, which was garrisoned at the time by a detachment of the Garde Monta-gnarde under the command of a young French civil servant. In the dry season, it was easy to reach Sar Luk from Poste du Lac via the big track and its Bboon Dlei Laac Yô' turnoff. You had to travel only seven kilome-ters along the fork to reach Paang Döng, then the government-run Frontier School, and, next, Sar Luk. The colonial administration consid-ered Paang Döng and Sar Luk to be one village: Bboon Rcae.*

The first time I arrived at the Middle Daak Kroong was in May 1948. At the edge of the forest and brushland I saw, ahead and to the right, the village of Paang Döng tucked between track and river. A hundred meters farther on, to the left, the thatched roofs of the Frontier School rose above a high barricade of tall, pointed posts. Immediately after passing in front of the school I came upon a rather startling sight: tumbledown huts, their thatched roofs caved in, stood on a raised stretch of ground overgrown with grass and brush. This was—or used to be—Sar Luk. A severe epidemic had recently ravaged the village. The inhabitants had abandoned it and gone to live in their field huts or in emergency huts built on the edges of the *miir*. In August, the Spirits acquiesced in the choice of a new village site, and Sar Luk was rebuilt beyond a big bend in the river, a kilometer from the school.

On leaving the school behind, you traverse a wide cleared space where the *tram* cooliest pasture the horses of the canton chief and his deputy. Next, you cross a government-built bridge, its floor made of thick logs

---

* Actually, Bboon Rcae was the name of a third village, whose territory adjoined that of Paang Döng, but it had disappeared. For many, the official term "Bboon Rcae" eventually erased any recollection of the two original names of the agglomeration. I met Mnong Laac who took my Mnong surname—Yoo Sar Luk—to be my real name.

† Corvée workers employed as messengers to deliver government orders.

covered with a woven bamboo matting, walk through a large grove of bamboo, then an expanse of timberland. From this you emerge to find before you the new Sar Luk of August 1948.

Actually, immediately on leaving the forest, you enter a broad rectangular clearing through which the track runs lengthwise. A path shoots off it, straight to the rear of the village. For Sar Luk turns its back on the timberland and is squeezed in between track and river. To get the best overall view of the village, you have to move a way up the Daak Kroong. Perched on a cliff, the buildings are tiered on a gentle incline; some thirty meters from the first row of houses, the land slopes sharply to the bank of a broad stream flowing below. This is the Daak Mei, whose confluence with the Daak Kroong serves as the villagers' watering place. Inundated during periods of high water, this lower level will be used as a garden. The tall parallel lines of long thatched roofs rise above the treetops and the swaying sacrificial posts and pole masts. To the left, near the edge of the cliff, a bulky construction resting on stilts rather spoils this vista. It is the house of the ethnologist—namely, me.

The striking thing about the exterior appearance of Mnong Gar dwellings is their length—in Sar Luk, two are almost forty meters long—and their massive roofs. Actually, all you see is roof. On either side of a ridgepole three to four meters high, a double thickness of thatch pitches down to within sixty centimeters of the ground and thus conceals the greater part of the low bamboo-wattled walls. The roof is rounded off at either end of the house. Doors are low, narrow openings cut in the front wall. A rattan arch supports the edge of the roof, permitting one to pass in and out. Beneath the lalang-grass overhang, chicken coops are stashed against the side of the house, near the doorways. Like oblong boxes and fashioned variously of wood or wicker, the cages are entirely closed and so narrow that the chickens have no room to move about.

An open space in front of each dwelling separates it from the house opposite. Generally, this is quite clean and well kept. Now and then the grass is cut back, and some people even sweep the area once a day. However, during the rainy season these yards, as one may call them, inevitably turn into quagmires. Close by the houses of *kuang*—men of substance and power—spiny trunks of bombax tower straight and tall. The upper sections are carved and crowned with decorated bamboo stalks. These trunks have been used as ritual pole masts in past buffalo sacrifices. Others older still have become fine, tall trees, living witnesses to the prestige of the men who planted them. Sometimes an immense decorated bamboo, perhaps twenty meters high, stands in front of a *kuang*'s house to complete this ritual setting. Also, before a *kuang*'s doorway there may be a small veranda of plaited bamboo mounted on low posts. This, too, would have been built on the occasion of an important sacrifice.

But what you find in larger numbers in these yards are huts built on

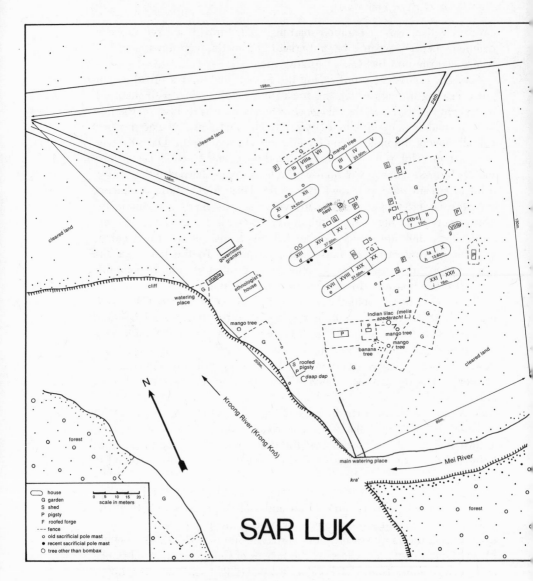

Map of Sar Luk drawn in February 1950
by Messers. P.-F. Antoine, Caco, Ribo, and Schmid

Letters in lower-case italic indicate the respective locations of the long houses (*root*) from the upper to lower village; the position of a house is not determined by any hierarchical classification whatever.

Roman figures designate the order of succession of houses (*hih nâm*) established according to the same principle but dated as of August 1948, when the village was rebuilt. In the keyed listing below, only those houses without the asterisk remained as they had been when built a year and a half before.

*long house (*root*) moved but without internal modifications
**root* reduced by two granaries, or households. One was re-formed: the widow of Kroong-Troo (*Jaa-Ntöör*) remarried; because the new husband was also named Kroong (belonging to the *Rjee* clan, however, and erstwhile husband of Mae-Kroong, deceased), their household, VII, still has the same name—Kroong-Troo. The other household, VI, was absorbed by V and XII.
***long houses reconstructed at the close of the weeding season; resident households are grouped differently than they were in their previous *root*.

***a
Ib. Kröng-Aang
VIIIa. Yôong-the-Mad
VII Kroong-Troo (remarriage of the widowed Kroong-Mae and Troo-Kroong)

**b
III Bbaang-Aang (Bbaang-the-Stag and Aang-of-the-Mincing-Step)
     Wan-Rieng
IV   Brôong-the-Widow (*Cil*)
     Laang-the-Widow
V   Jieng-Taang (widow of Taang-the-Stooped)
     Tôong-Mang (Tôong-the-Cook)

c
XI   Truu, the canton chief
XII The *Rjee* (Mhoo-Lang, old Troo, Brôong-the-Widow, Kroong-Sraang)

d
XIII Baap Can
     Can-Groo
     Srae-Jaang
XIV Kröng-Jôong
     Kroong-Aang (Kroong-Big-Navel and Aang-of-the-Drooping-Eyelid)

XV   Tôong-Jieng
     Krae-Drüm
XVI Mbieng-Grieng
     Tôong-Wan

e
XVII Choong-Kôong
XVIII Bbôong-Mang (Bbôong-the-Deputy and Mang-of-the-Jutting-Jaw)
XIX   Kraang-Drüm
XX   Bbaang-Jieng (Bbaang-the-Pregnant-Man). Bbieng-Dlaang

***f
IXb Tôong-Mang (*Rjee-Bboon Jraang*)
c   Wan-Ngaa
II   Chaar-Rieng

***g
VIIIb Poong-the-Widow

***h
Ia   Bbaang-Lang (Bbaang-the-One-Eyed)
X   Tôong-Biing

*i
XXI Troo-Jôong
XXII Wan-Jôong (*Mok-Rtung*)
     Kraang-Dlaang

tall, thin stilts—similar to those in the *miir*—and, especially, low, squat pigsties inside small enclosures of closely set staves. A few fruit trees— mango or banana—and relatively low termites' nests add to the decor of the yards, which all day long are alive with the traffic of people, dogs, pigs, and poultry. The water buffaloes appear only for a moment in the evening, when the young men who have gone to round them up in the forest bring them back to the narrow corral where they are kept at night. To the buffalo corrals characteristic of all Mnong villages must be added buildings peculiar to Sar Luk—i.e., stables, for the canton chief and his deputy each has a horse. The stables are completely closed, boxlike con- structions in which the animals have scarcely room to move about. This is a necessary precaution, because the horses' very strong odor attracts tigers. Fear of tigers likewise accounts for the fact that a wide area sur- rounding the village is cut back and kept clear of brush.

House Interiors

Inside, the houses are very dark. You need several seconds for your eyes to adjust enough to see distinctly. Then you find yourself in a large room more or less unencumbered except at the back. Here an immense low plat- form of planks or wattling extends along the back wall from one end of the house to the other, and projects into the room for a third of its width. Large jars are aligned on the platform, standing against the wall. Above them, one or two rows of small neckless jars—*yang dâm*—are suspended from individual rattan supports. Obviously, the number of jars varies ac- cording to the wealth of the master of the house. This large room, or *wah*—I will call it variously the common room or the visitors' room—is closed off at either end by huge rice granaries mounted on four or six sturdy posts. These extend the two rows of posts that support the roof in a direction parallel to the ridgepole.

Each such granary occupies one third of the width of the house. To the rear, occupying another third, is the low platform. The section of the plat- form that is adjacent to the granary serves as pallet for the master and mistress of the house; a plank or a heap of baskets, chests, and so forth separates this sleeping area from the common room. The remaining third, to the front, is free space containing only a cupboard or, worse, encum- bered by piles of firewood; however, the wood is always carefully stacked and secured by tall stakes, so that this area can function as a sort of pas- sageway by which people easily circulate from one end of the house to the other. Except at either end of the long house, the granaries stand two by two and back to back; abreast of the one near the outer house wall is the *nal* door, the "private" or "family" door.*

---

* See plan on facing page.

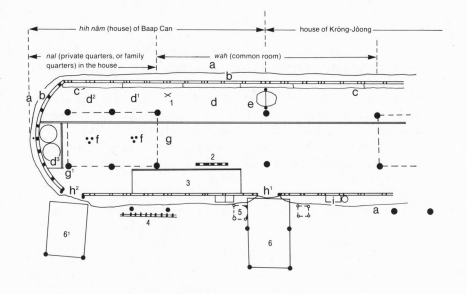

Plan of Baap Can's hih nâm
*showing the arrangement of the ritual decor
prepared for the buffalo sacrifice*

a) edge of the roof (*tieng jaa,* or "the tail of the lalang grass")
b) wall (*par hih*)
c) "the head of the pallet" (*buung bic*) and planks on which the large jars are aligned
d) low platform (*ndrôong bic*). Old Krah sleeps near the suspended drum
d¹) sleeping area of Baap Can, Aang-the-Long, and their children
d²) sleeping area of Can, Groo, and their baby
d³) small low platform on which grain silos are placed, thus keeping them from contact with the ground
e) suspended drum (*nggör*)
f) hearths (*bôong nhaak*)
g) granary (*nâm*)
g¹) granary post, which is anointed "to summon the Spirits in the belly of the Paddy" (*khual Yaang ndül Baa*)
h) doors (*bbang*)

h¹) main entrance, the door to the common room (*bbang wah*)
h²) private, or family, door (*bbang nal*)
i) chicken coops (*tum ier*)

Ritual constructions:

1) place under the roof where the small altar is suspended (*ndrööng Yaang*)
2) jar barrier with its central stake (*nggaar, ndah yang*)
3) secondary low platform, used only for buffalo sacrifices and removed after the celebration (*ndrôong lôong jöng*)
4) the two bombax sacrificial posts (*ndah blaang*) behind their ritual barrier
5) ritual stall (*naang rah*)
6) main ritual veranda, roofed (*naang röng wah*)
6¹) secondary ritual veranda, not roofed (*naang röng nal*)
7) giant-bamboo pole mast (*ndah rlaa*)

The women do their cooking in the area beneath the rather low granary floor on open hearths constructed of three cylinders cut from the compact earth of termites' nests. Needless to say, in such cramped quarters the air is terribly smoky. Indeed, when meals are being prepared simultaneously for all the families occupying such a multiple dwelling, smoke fills the entire house, including the common room. And if visitors have arrived or if the weather has turned cold, a good wood fire will have been started here, too, in front of the low platform, and will be giving off generous amounts of smoke.

Each granary belongs to an independent family. When the family group includes only the couple and their still young children, they make do with a single granary on four posts, with a single hearth beneath. But if the family group includes other adults—a recently married daughter, for example, or widows (the mother or sister of either wife or husband)—the granary is built on six posts and covers two hearths, one used by the mistress of the house, the other by her adult dependents.

Thus, each family's domicile is determined by its granary. The term denoting someone's residence is *hih nâm* (house-granary), in contradistinction to *root,* which denotes the whole long house containing several *hih nâm.* Each household has its *wah;* that is, one half of the common room, the other half of which belongs to the neighbor co-occupying the long house. In fact, the only visible boundary between the two homes is marked by two vertical columns that rise by the main door, which is used by members of both households as well as by guests. The *nal*—a family's private quarters, so to speak—in which the granary is the prominent feature, is bordered by the passageway in the front and in the rear by that portion of the low platform that serves for sleeping and miscellaneous storage. The private door is used by all persons living in one end of the long house.

A Mnong Gar house seldom, which is to say almost never, shelters a single household. (In Sar Luk, the case of Poong-the-Widow is an exception.) Generally, several families connected by blood or simply by friendship group together to construct and occupy the same dwelling. In these circumstances, the building can attain a length of nearly forty meters, as, for example, the long house shared by Baap Can and Kröng-Jôong, which contains four granaries, or that of Taang-the-Stooped, which contains five.

Mnong Gar Economy

Here I will confine myself to the broad outlines of the *Phii Brêe* way of life, which will be dealt with more fully later in this book, and examined in even greater detail in a series of ethnological studies.

Like most Proto-Indo-Chinese, the Mnong Gar are seminomadic cultivators who practice the slash-and-burn method of agriculture, whereby a section of forest is cleared, the debris and brush remaining is burned, and rice is sowed in the field thus enriched by wood ash. The field (in Vietnamese, the *rây;* in dialects of the Mon Khmer language family, the *miir*) is abandoned after one harvest or, in rare cases, after two. The cultivators return to an old field after a cycle of from ten to twenty years, during which period they will have planted all the other territory belonging to their village. If the *miir* under cultivation is far away, the village may be moved; such a displacement inevitably occurs when an epidemic has caused several deaths. The *rngool* (village sites) that have been temporarily abandoned may be recognized by the presence of fruit trees or vegetables—varieties of eggplant, for example—but especially by the rows of bombax, which are memorials of buffalo sacrifices.

In addition to their work in the fields, the Mnong Gar practice various crafts with great skill. Every man knows how to repair his own tools, and in each village two or three men are renowned for their ability to forge from imported bar iron sabers, bush hooks (*wiah*), lances, hoes, and so forth, which other members of the community order from them. But, like most Montagnards, it is in basketry that the Men of the Forest demonstrate their greatest mastery. Using bamboo and rattan, the men make numerous types of baskets and receptacles of many kinds that are widely used. The women, who are responsible for household chores (pounding rice, cooking, etc.) and the less strenuous field work, are generally excellent weavers. The talent of the mistress of the house produces the clothing worn by her household: tunics, loincloths, skirts, and blankets. Cotton and indigo are cultivated in recently abandoned rice fields; wild plants are gathered in the forest for the dyes used to tint the fringes and small decorative bands on clothing.

Trade is based chiefly on a complex barter system.* Merchandise is evaluated and priced by various methods of assessment: so many jars, pigs, skirts—and, for very valuable items, buffaloes. Today, currency in the form of the Indo-Chinese piaster plays a role also. Negotiations are always conducted in the presence of at least one go-between, who accompanies the vendors through the village. I might point out that while Gar men successfully raise poultry and pigs, it is thanks to the blankets woven by their wives that they are able to procure the buffaloes needed for important sacrifices from their rice-growing neighbors, the Laac in the Lang Biang and the Rlâm in the Poste du Lac area. Also, it should be noted that today markets in Dalat and Ban Me Thuot play an important role. There Vietnamese and Chinese merchants sell the Gar salt, imported fab-

---

* For more details, see G. Condominas, "Aspects of Economics among the Mnong Gar of Vietnam: Multiple Money and the Middleman," *Ethnology,* Vol. II, No. 3 (1972), pp. 202–19.

rics, new jars, etc. The Gar's major sources of currency for these transactions are the tea and coffee plantations, the Army, the Garde Montagnarde, and the French colonial government, which not only pays its agents (canton chiefs and others) and the temporary workers it recruits in piasters but also, and most importantly, requires that taxes be paid in currency.

To conclude this rapid sketch of Mnong Gar economic life, let me point out that side by side with the district government staff established by the French there coexists a traditional social organization in which the three "holy men in the forest and in the village" (*croo weer tööm brii tööm bboon*) enjoy a special prominence in the community. It is their responsibility to control land tenure, to assign plots for planting, and also to preside over and lead religious ceremonies related to the Soil and the Paddy. Finally, I may mention the important place in Gar society occupied by the *njau*—the shaman, the magician—whose income is appreciably increased by the consultations he grants the sick.*

Clothing and Adornment

Mnong Gar dress includes the same items of clothing worn by other Proto-Indo-Chinese in Vietnam. For all, the most characteristic is the *suu troany,* or loincloth (the langooty of the explorers, the *kpin* of the Rhade). It consists of a long strip of cloth that is slipped between the thighs, wound around the waist, and carefully tied off so that the more highly decorated end falls free in front. This male garment, which leaves the legs and hips completely bare, is often all that men wear during the day; normally, however, it is complemented by a short, sleeveless tunic. In the evenings, the men like to protect themselves against the mounting chill by draping themselves in ample blankets as they sit in their yards, talking with neighbors. During the day, the same blanket is used as a sling to carry an infant on one's back; at night, it serves as a cover for sleeping.

The women wear a skirt made of a large indigo rectangle, the two flaps of which close over in front and are secured around the waist with a narrow belt. Their bosoms may be bare or covered with a tunic, generally long-sleeved. Clothing of foreign manufacture is being worn more and more frequently. The women gladly buy black calico skirts and white cotton blouses, but it is primarily the men who shop for European clothing—vests, shirts, jackets, or topcoats. They care little for short pants and less for trousers.

Both men and women wear their hair in a chignon. Today, however,

---

* For more details, see G. Condominas, "Schéma d'un *mhö*', séance chamanique mnong gar," in "Chamanisme et possession en Asie du Sud-Est et dans le Monde Insulindien," *Asie du Sud-Est et Monde Insulindien, Bulletin du Centre de Documentation et de Recherche,* Vol. IV (1973), Fasc. No. 1, pp. 61–70.

young men and older men who have served in the French armed forces
cut their hair short, "European fashion." For important occasions, the
men fancy covering their heads with a turban—either a white one woven
by their wives or, if they are rich, one of imported black satin. On ordinary days, they are most often bareheaded. There is, however, one style
of European headgear that has been resoundingly successful with the
Gar—the Basque beret. They prefer to wear it inside out, so that the
much appreciated label with its gaudy colors can be suitably admired.
One often sees the military forage cap; for a long time, Bbaang-the-Stag,
with a martial air that seemed somewhat comical to me, wore a splendid
officer's kepi that had been stripped of both stripes and visor.

Men and women deck themselves out with a wealth of bracelets and
necklaces. Women wear strands of small beads, like a diadem, in their
hair, and large pins of varying shapes in their chignons. A wooden comb
sheathed in tin is the equivalent adornment for their male companions; on
important occasions, the comb is embellished with a double red pompon,
the loose threads of which are interwoven with the wearer's chignon.

Both men and women pierce their ears; the men insert ivory plugs in
the lobe perforations, the women, discs of soft white wood. Being light in
weight, these must be made to fit snugly so that they will stay in place.
Because the integument of the lobe tends to stretch, the women are
obliged to replace the rounds with ever larger ones. You see old women
with overstretched and flaccid lobes that they allow to sag almost to their
shoulders for fear that when they must substitute still bigger discs, the
thin layer of flesh will tear and give way.

What strikes most Vietnamese and Europeans about the physiognomy
of the Moi is their mutilated teeth. The Mnong Gar are particularly given
to the practice of breaking or filing the upper teeth down to the gums, filing the lower teeth into points, and painting the whole with a brilliant
black lacquer.

The profile of a Man of the Forest, like that of any other Montagnard,
would be incomplete were one to fail to add a pipe, a basket, and a bush
hook (*wiah*). Both men and women smoke pipes, but in addition the
women chew a sort of pipe cleaner—a slender bamboo twig frayed at one
end to collect all the tobacco juice when passed through the bowl and
stem of the pipe (both made also of bamboo). The women regularly wear
these "tobacco excrement sticks" (*möng ê' jju'*) planted in their hair. A
man is hardly ever without his pipe. If it's not in his mouth, it is stuck in
his chignon or, more likely, in his loincloth. What the men do often put in
their hair is a little angled knife made entirely of iron, handle included. At
a distance, it could be taken for a feather, and when the individual wearing it has an angular face—for example, Krah, Baap Can's slave—this little
knife thrust in his hair makes him resemble a Sioux.

The two other characteristic implements of the Central Highlands are the pannier (*sah*), secured by two straps of braided rattan and carried on the back, and the bush hook (*wiah*), which is every Montagnard's inseparable companion. Its short, broad blade is set in a bamboo handle a meter long; the knob into which the shoulder of the blade is inserted has been curved at a right angle with the handle, so that a man can balance his *wiah*, its blade turned upward, on his shoulder, although, obviously, when walking he must hold on to the handle.

Kinship

I will not go into this rather complex subject at length here, but will give only the few indications that are indispensable to an understanding of events and behavior described in the following pages.*

The Mnong Gar family structure rests principally on the *mpôol*, a term translated here as "clan."† The clan is the group of individuals who claim descent from a common ancestor through the maternal line; in fact, both the clan name and a family's possessions are handed down not from father to children but from mother to children. For example, the Rjee belong to this particular clan because their mother, not their father, is a member of it. Members of the same *mpôol* may not marry or have sexual relations. In fact, if they belong to the same generation, they are considered to be brothers and sisters; if they come from two successive generations, they are held to be fathers-mothers and children, or uncles-aunts and nephews-nieces; if they belong to two generations separated by a third, they are considered to be grandparents and grandchildren. This obtains no matter how far in the past the first common female ancestor is found by tracing genealogical lines. Two individuals who from our Western point of view could not lay claim even to the title of cousin here address each other as "brother" and "sister" and "mother" and "child," and so forth.

Personal Names

It is habitual to call a married man by his own name followed by the name of his wife. For example, Kröng-Jôong: Kröng is married to Jôong; inversely, she is called Jôong-Kröng. If a man has children, he is very often

---

* See G. Condominas, "The Mnong Gar of Central Vietnam (Les Mnong Gar du Centre Viêt-Nam)," in G. P. Murdock (ed.), *Social Structure in South-East Asia* (New York: Wenner-Gren Foundation for Anthropological Research, Viking Fund Publications in Anthropology, No. 29, 1960), pp. 15–23; and especially the very stimulating paper by F. G. Lounsbury, "A Formal Account of the Crow- and Omaha-type Kinship Terminologies," in W. H. Goodenough (ed.), *Explorations in Cultural Anthropology: Essays in Honor of George Peter Murdock* (New York: McGraw-Hill Book Company, 1964), pp. 351–93.

† Murdock uses the term "matriclan."

referred to by the name of his eldest child preceded by the term *baap* ("father of"); thus, Baap Can, or Father of Can. When two brothers are known to be mutually supportive—acting as a team, so to speak—or if both enjoy a shared success in life, their two names are coupled in a dual appellation suggesting a single entity. Thus, Taang Truu denotes Baap Can and his younger brother, the canton chief; Ngkoi Bbaang is the dual name of two men who from our point of view are only first cousins.* Some people, women as well as men, are more familiarly known by their own name followed by a nickname, which often has been bestowed upon them in childhood. For example, Kroong-Big-Navel and his wife, Aang-of-the-Drooping-Eyelid (they may be addressed also as Kroong-Aang and Aang-Kroong); or Jôong-the-Hernia, Bbaang-the-Stag, etc.

The Jar

As will become evident in the course of this book, the jar plays an important role among the Mnong Gar, as it does among all other Proto-Indo-Chinese. Sometimes I shall use the word "alcohol" in reference to its contents, but *rnööm* is, in fact, merely a rice beer that can in no way be compared to our brandies or even to our wines and apéritifs. The wort (*coot*), with a base of rice flour and bran, is set to ferment for several days—or, at the most, for somewhat more than a month—in a jar (*yang*) that is hermetically sealed. The jar is opened a few moments before its contents are to be served. A small amount of *coot* is removed for purposes of anointment if a sacrifice is involved. The jar is stuffed with leaves or lalang grass so as to keep the bran at the bottom. The receptacle is then filled to the brim with water, from a dozen to several dozen liters, depending on the size of the *yang*. The *rnööm* is now ready, but before it is drunk it must be consecrated. You insert a drinking straw (*gut*) in the jar, while reciting a few verses and taking care that a few drops of water fall on the ground. You drink by sucking on one end of the straw, the other end of which touches the bottom of the jar. The liquid you ingest is mixed with alcohol as it passes through the fermented *coot*. You may yield your place to another drinker only if you have imbibed two measures of *rnööm* or, if it is a drinking contest, a number—always even—equal to the number drunk by the man who has preceded you. In other words, you move on when the attendant who is stationed on the other side of the jar has been able to pour into it twice the contents of the fire-worked tube, buffalo horn, or plastic glass which he fills from a container of water at his side.

---

* For convenience, I have joined the names of married partners by a hyphen; when thus coupled the two names designate a single individual. The allied names of two brothers appear as separate words since the dual form does not exist in French or English.

Thus, as each drinker takes his turn, the *rnööm* loses more and more of its potency until, after several hours, it becomes a quite inoffensive drink.

The courageous reader who perseveres to the end of this book might take the Mnong Gar for hopeless drunks. But I should like to point out that most of the days reported on here are holidays. And I know very well that the Men of the Forest are not alone in wetting their whistles on the occasion of a marriage or funeral. Not only is the alcoholic content of their strongest drink much lower than that of the apéritifs our countless wineries produce, but also the occasions on which they consume it are far fewer than with us. A jar is opened only to honor the Spirits or a "foreigner"—i.e., anyone, including other Montagnards, who does not live in the given village. There must be a reason for drinking other than the mere desire to drink something that is not water. The Mnong Gar have nothing comparable to the venerable customs to which our so-called civilized contemporaries pay homage several times a day—wine with every meal, cocktails before dinner, the pick-me-up, the after-dinner liqueur, or one-for-the-road. The Mnong Gar would not dream of drinking alone; to initiate a round of drinking—to offer anything like a cocktail party, for instance—without a religious purpose, they would find inconceivable.

2

Baap Can's Alliance. An Exchange of Buffalo Sacrifices

IN the light, chill morning fog, Sar Luk awakens to the dull, rhythmic music of pestles. In every yard, women are hulling the day's rice. Working in groups of two or three around each mortar, they hold their pestles vertically and raise and lower them in a continuous, rolling motion. The operation is suspended briefly to allow one of them to winnow the grain. She pours the contents of the mortar into a cone-shaped winnowing basket, which she shakes vigorously—right, left, right—so that the husk separates from the grain. Then, tossing the rice up in the air several times, she sends the light husk flying. The partially hulled rice is returned to the mortar and the pounding resumes, the entire operation being repeated until the rice is white. The men, meanwhile, armed with brooms of *rhôong* bristles (a Graminaea), sweep out the houses. Baap Can leaves this task to his eldest son and old Krah, his slave. He himself only putters about before settling down to smoke his pipe. Today he has cause to be prouder of himself than ever—he, Taang-Aang, of the Rjee clan, known throughout Gar country as the Father of Can (Baap Can). In a few days, he will sacrifice two large male water buffaloes, bringing to twenty the number of these great animals that he will have sacrificed in his lifetime. Who among the Men of the Forest is the *kuang*, the powerful one, who can claim to have achieved such a score? And today they must go out into the bush to fetch back the giant bamboo (*rlaa*), which five days hence will be erected for the *Tâm Bôh*, the Exchange of Sacrifices that Baap Can and the former canton chief, Ndêh, of Ndut Lieng Krak, will jointly offer to increase their prestige and, with a flourish, seal a ritual alliance based on their long-standing friendship.

Baap Can claims to be a hundred years old. I would say he is fifty-five, sixty at the outside. His face is wrinkled, and his high forehead is crowned by graying hair which he wears in a chignon, but the skinny old fellow is still hale and hearty. Certainly, he is the most important man in the valley. It is not that his material wealth is so enormous (his collection of big jars is incomplete, and I have been told in confidence that he owes six buffalo "heads"); it's rather that over the years he has known how to build up considerable prestige and to advance members of his family to positions of pre-eminence.*

In Baap Can's early youth, years when the French were first exploring this region, Sar Luk was a miserable hamlet of exactly two wretched houses. But Taang had character. Even before the death of his father, he had taken his family's destiny into his own hands. He may have lacked jars and buffaloes then, but he possessed great tenacity and a fund of peasant shrewdness. Early on, he proved himself a good cultivator and, above all, an excellent intermediary—a first-rate fixer. People frequently had recourse to his skill with words, not only to sell valuable property but also to settle lawsuits and arrange matrimonial or sworn-friend alliances. His marriage to the beautiful Jaang, of the Bboon Jraang clan, did not bring Taang into a rich family. However, his young wife possessed those two essential qualities that, when united in the mistress of a Gar household, assure a well-to-do future for the ménage she has founded: courage and skill as a weaver. Jaang brought three children into the world, two of whom survived: Can, born around 1921, and Aang-of-the-Drooping-Eyelid, about four years his junior. After the death of his first wife, Baap Can not only managed to remain on good terms with his sisters-in-law but even got them to take care of his children, who gave over to their aunts their portion of the inheritance. Baap Can did not remain a widower long, and married Aang-the-Long, daughter of a shamaness in the village of Phii Ko'. This second marriage allied him with the Ntöör clan, the principal landowners in Phii Ko', where he lived for some years with his new family-in-law. Thanks to Baap Can, his wife's younger brother, Bbaang-the-Stag, the holy man in the village and a very active youth, became the runner for the canton chief. Aang-the-Long's aunt, Yôong-the-Mad, was rich. However, in a few years, this witty woman (she owed her nickname to the whimsicality she exhibited on any and all occasions) lost the fortune he husband (Kroong, of the Sruk clan) had left her at his death. Aang-the-Long gave Baap Can five children, of whom only three lived: a girl, Jaang (about thirteen or fourteen at the time of my stay in Sar Luk), Choong-of-the-Big-Belly (five), and Dür (two).

Baap Can had an older sister, Jôong-the-Healer. He always contrived to have Jôong live in the same long house with him and share his common room, except for the period of his sojourn in Phii Ko', where she refused

---

* The genealogy of Baap Can and the Rjee clan appears in the chart on facing page.

Genealogy of the *Rjee* in Sar Luk and in Sar Lang

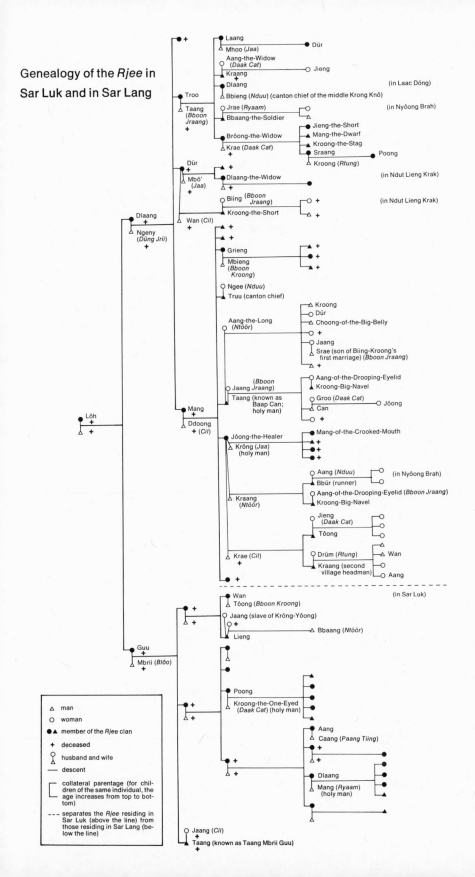

Legend:

△ man
○ woman
●▲ member of the *Rjee* clan
+ deceased
⚭ husband and wife
— descent

⌐ collateral parentage (for children of the same individual, the age increases from top to bottom)

--- separates the *Rjee* residing in Sar Luk (above the line) from those residing in Sar Lang (below the line) to follow him. Jôong had been married three times and widowed twice. By her first husband, who was of the Cil clan, she had had two sons: Kraang-Drüm, now deputy headman of Bboon Rcae, and Tôong-Jieng. By her second husband, a Ntöör, she had had two more sons: Kroong-Big-Navel and Bbür-Aang, the latter now a canton runner living in Nyôong Brah, his wife's village. In her third marriage, she had a daughter, Mang-of-the-Crooked-Mouth, by Kröng, a holy man in the village and a member of the Jaa clan. Baap Can strengthened the influence he wielded over his older sister by insisting that one of her sons—Kroong-Big-Navel, as it happens—"follow the daughter of the mother's younger brother," which is to say, marry Baap Can's daughter Aang-of-the-Drooping-Eyelid. This cross-cousin marriage followed an established tradition, but for other reasons it did not work out. After some delinquencies on the young woman's part, in order to avoid a definitive separation Kroong and Aang left Baap Can's "granary" to join that of Kröng-Jôong, which was nearby. For her part, Jôong-the-Healer was always a very authoritarian mother, and to be sure of keeping one of her sons with her permanently, she arranged to marry Tôong to the daughter of a slave, Jieng, of the Daak Cat clan. Jieng brought with her to her new home her mother and her brother, Kraang-the-Bladder. The granary of the young ménage is adjacent to that of Kröng-Jôong. Crossing their common room, we enter the house of Grieng-Mbieng, sister of Jôong-Kröng, Baap Can, and Truu. Like her older sister, Grieng has always been dominated and guided by their brother Baap Can. Since none of the children born of her marriage to Mbieng-the-Lame, from Ndut Trêe Pül, survived, Grieng and her husband took in some of Mbieng's relatives who, like him, belong to the Bboon Kroong clan: his nephew Tôong and Tôong's wife, Wan (a Rjee from Sar Lang); his niece Dloong-the-Widow and her baby; and lastly, his nephew Ndoong and his grandniece Ngaa. Thus, Baap Can has managed to regroup in his long house the granaries of his elder sister, her second son, and his younger sister.*

The only personage in Sar Luk capable of rivaling Baap Can in strength of character and social position is none other than our hero's brother, Truu-Ngee, ten years his junior and today the canton chief. Actually, Truu was reared by Baap Can and owes his present position to him. Truu first acquired official status during the 1920's, when the French recruited Gar militiamen to consolidate the pacification of the Krong Knô Valley. Baap Can had been chosen, but because he had a large family and especially because he was not one bit eager to experiment with a post in the service of conquerors who were an absolutely unknown quantity, he designated his brother to replace him. Then a very young man, Truu was

---

* See *d* XIII, XIV, XV, and XVI on the map, pp. 8–9.

terrified at the prospect of going far from his village to live among the *Praang* (French), but he had to obey. Just as he had been obliged to obey the year before, when Baap Can decided to give him in marriage to Ngee, the only daughter of a rich Sar Luk family. By joining the militia, Truu learned how to handle the extraordinary weapons the Europeans brought with them; he was fed, dressed, and paid by them, and he traveled. In a word, for a long period he lived outside the limited frame of village life, over which his older brother meanwhile exercised growing control. At last, crowning a career of "work with the white men," in 1943 Truu was named canton chief of Upper Krong Knô, and thus moved into the highest governmental post a Mnong Gar could, prior to 1949, hope to attain. Henceforth, he could assert himself in relation to his older brother. Since Baap Can had their two sisters, Jôong-Krông and Grieng-Mbieng, under his thumb, Truu fastened on their "little mother," old Troo (sister of Taang Truu's mother) and her children: Brôong-the-Widow, Bbaang-Jrae, Dlaang-Bbieng, Kraang-Aang, and Laang-Mhoo. Kraang married Aang, the daughter of Taang-Jieng-the-Stooped, who rules the adjacent house, and he was deputy headman of Bboon Rcae until his death, in June 1948. Bbaang-Jrae, a former infantryman, lives in Nyôong Brah, his wife's village. On the other hand, Dlaang followed her husband, Bbieng, who is canton chief of the Middle Krong Knô, to Laac Döng. So, only two of Troo's daughters and their families live with their old mother in Sar Luk in the canton chief's house and share his common room. One daughter is Laang, who is married to the widower Mhoo, of the Jaa clan (the son of Jôong-Wan, who resides in the large neighboring house, and the nephew of the holy man Kröng-Jôong); the couple has a year-old baby, Dür. The other daughter, Brôong, is the widow of a leper; her children are Jieng-the-Short (five years old), Mang-the-Dwarf (six), Kroong-the-Stag (thirteen), and the lovely Sraang. Sraang is married to Kroong, the son of Bbaang-Jieng-the-Pregnant-Man, a holy man and the sworn friend of Truu; the young couple has a daughter, Poong, who is the same age as Dür. Truu and Ngee never had children of their own, and so they adopted a niece and a nephew of Ngee's—Jaang Bibuu (the daughter of Ngee's brother) and Kraang-the-Dogtooth, aged about fourteen and seventeen, respectively.*

One cannot speak of Rjee clan notables without mentioning Kroong-Biing, called Kroong-the-Short, who is one of the most powerful Gar personalities it has been my privilege to know. Very small, thin, and slightly stooped, he has the fine features of a bird of prey, enlivened by a glance that sparkles with wit and malice. His knowledge is immense. Let some business matter or party bring him near a jar, and immediately a group

---

* See *c* XI and XII on the map, pp. 8–9.

forms around him to listen to this inexhaustible teller of tales, this incomparable singer of judicial maxims or love couplets. Perched on his stool, he embellishes his discourse with long chanted quotations; his delivery is rapid, although interrupted by asthmatic coughs. Even when the matter submitted to his judgment or the story he is telling has a serious side, Kroong-Biing knows how to interpolate words that spark laughter. He is an initiator of fashion. He is also a man whom people fear. Kroong-the-Short is the "brother" (we would say first cousin) of Baap Can and Truu, and came originally from Sar Luk. Now he lives in Ndut Lieng Krak, where he followed his second wife, Biing, of the Bboon Jraang clan. All their children died young, but together they have brought up the children Biing had by her first husband: Jrae, now married to a militiaman; and Srae, who is seventeen years old and currently a student in the Groupe Scolaire Antomarchi in Ban Me Thuot. The couple also has living with them the half sister of Kroong-Biing, Dlaang-the-Widow, and pretty Grieng, a young slave of the Daak Cat clan. For many years, Kroong-Biing served as deputy to the then canton chief Ndêh, of Ndut Lieng Krak, until an unfortunate affair caused both men to be relieved of their posts in 1943. They were replaced by Truu and Bbôong-Mang.

Bbôong's appointment did not mean that the office of deputy canton chief passed from the Rjee clan, because his wife, Mang-of-the-Jutting-Jaw, belongs to this *mpôol*. She is a "distant sister" of the three *kuang* (formerly also guaranty for their parents' debts). The couple lives in the village house nearest the watering place. They have lost all their own children, and so are bringing up Bbôong's nephew Chung, a student in Ban Me Thuot. They share their visitors' room with another of Bbôong's nephews, Choong-Kôong, a former infantryman who was recently discharged from the Army. The other part of the long house accommodates Bbaang-Jieng-the-Pregnant-Man, the holy man of the Fire Sticks, who lives with his son Bbieng-Dlaang and his son-in-law, Kraang-Drüm, the eldest son of Jôong-Krông and currently deputy headman of Bboon Rcae.*

So, to make the position of Baap Can quite clear, here is a recapitulation of his situation and the network of his family connections:

Taang-Aang (or Taang Truu), more usually known as Baap Can, is head of the Rjee family in Sar Luk. He is the ranking holy man in this village, the other two being Krông-Jôong, the husband of Baap Can's older sister, and Bbaang-Jieng-the-Pregnant-Man, a friend, who has performed the Exchange of Buffalo Sacrifices with Baap Can's brother, Truu, and with his first cousin Kroong-Biing. These two men and Baap Can and Ndêh are the most important men in the whole valley. Furthermore, Truu is now canton chief, and Kroong-Biing was formerly deputy chief. In 1949, a

---

* See *e* XVII, XVIII, XIX, and XX on the map, pp. 8–9.

District Council will be established by the French colonial government, and both men will be appointed members. In the context of traditional Gar social organization, Kroong-Biing is a well-known judge, as is Baap Can himself. When the Tribunal Court in Poste du Lac * is enlarged, the government will recruit both "brothers." The present deputy canton chief, Bbôong-Mang, married a Rjee—i.e., married into Baap Can's clan. The present canton runners are, respectively, our hero's son Can; Bbür-Aang, his maternal nephew; and Bbaang-the-Stag, his wife's youngest brother and the holy man in Phii Ko'. Lastly, the deputy headman of Bboon Rcae (the administrative amalgamation of Sar Luk and Paang Döng) is Kraang-Drüm, the eldest son of Baap Can's sister Jôong-Kröng and the son-in-law of Bbaang-the-Pregnant-Man—hence, nephew, son, and son-in-law of the three holy men in Sar Luk. And let us remember that Bbieng, chief of the neighboring canton of Middle Krong Knô, married Dlaang, a "sister" (first cousin) of Baap Cans'.

In point of fact, however, one must be careful not to exaggerate the importance of such a network of family connections in creating an individual's social role. For example, Baap Can's maternal nephew Tôong-Jieng could claim the same ensemble of relationships, yet Tôong-Jieng is anything but a *kuang*. Let me also point out that the social positions I have just enumerated are essentially government functions that derive from a new administrative cadre established by the French colonizers and imposed by them on the indigenous social structure. The one traditional political function—and the only one to have existed previously—is that of holy man. Yet what substance could the *croo weer* of a wretched hamlet have? Only one thing testifies to a man's accession to power and offers manifest proof of his status as a *kuang*: sacrificed buffaloes. And among buffalo sacrifices, one in particular enhances the prestige of the man who can afford it. This is the *Tâm Bôh*, the Exchange of Sacrifices a man offers a partner of matching wealth who, through this ritual, becomes his *jôok*, his sworn friend and ally. The more of such connections a man possesses, the greater his renown. Unquestionably, men who "work with the French" acquire by virtue of their administrative duties authority and material benefits that facilitate the purchasing of buffaloes and the initiating of ritual alliances. But they are considered true *kuang* only by reason of their *Tâm Bôh* rather than because of the governmental status that enabled them to carry out these sacrifices.

Nevertheless, the existence of a large group of relatives who enjoy administrative status is not without value for Baap Can, and it consolidates even his personal authority. For his connections with them are not con-

---

* This court was established to deal with all legal matters concerning the Montagnards. —*Trans.*

fined to family ties. As these men advanced socially, all of them reinforced their familial bonds with Baap Can by offering him a sacrifice, to which he responded with gifts, and this system of ritual exchange plays on the family level the same role as does the *Tâm Bôh* on the extra-kinship level.

Prestige is not acquired once and for all. It must be maintained, reinforced, and extended from year to year by new buffalo sacrifices and, if possible, by new alliances. Since Baap Can had a great liking for Ndêh, and since the former canton chief was a *kuang* on a scale equal to his own, some years ago he proposed that they perform an Exchange of Sacrifices. After the customary demurs, repeated several times, Ndêh agreed. Thereupon, Baap Can asked his brother-in-law Bbôong-Mang-the-Deputy to act as his go-between (*ndraany*). This tall, solidly built young fellow is a fine, resourceful speaker and very capable indeed of taking on the functions of witness, guide, and master of ceremonies, which is what the role of *ndraany* requires. Bbôong's reputation in these respects is already established, for Krŏng-Jôong had already had the deputy act as go-between in his most recent Exchange of Sacrifices.

As the preceding year's crop yield had been good, Ndêh and Baap Can agreed they would perform their *Tâm Bôh* before the next harvest. They did not change their plan when the terrible epidemic struck Sar Luk and forced the inhabitants to abandon the village and rebuild it a few months later on the present site. However, Baap Can's brother-in-law—and next-door neighbor—was ready for his *Tâm Bôh* first. Just one month after people had resettled in the new Sar Luk (the day after I also settled in, as it happens), Krŏng-Jôong immolated the two buffaloes that his *jôok*, Choong-Yôong, headman of Sar Lang, offered him in exchange for the two victims Choong had received from Krŏng two days earlier. It was a magnificent celebration, and Ndêh and Baap Can decided not to delay too long in offering their own. Ten days later, on October 3, Baap Can recruited his two *rnôom*—his male and female servants for the sacrifice. To put it more exactly, he consecrated their arrival in his house by offering the sacrifice of a chicken and a jar of rice beer.

As his female *rnôom*, he had chosen Dloong-the-Black, the fourteen- or fifteen-year-old daughter of Yôong-the-Mad and therefore Baap Can's wife's "sister" (first cousin). The girl's duties will be to see to the cooking; she will also prepare the rice beer, embellish certain parts of the ritual decor with multicolored threads, and gather firewood. The tasks devolving on the male *rnôom* demand great talent and skill. He must fashion all the ritual constructions for the sacrifice, which will attest to his ability to cut, carve, paint, and assemble the various elements. It is also his responsibility to plait all the wicker pieces that will be used in the course of the celebration and embellish them with black motifs against a light background. Further, he must take care of the necessary tools and, if need be, actually forge them. To ensure the complete success of his ceremony, Baap Can went as far afield as the village of Bboon Khaang to engage Kröng-the-Stutterer as his male *rnôom*. This young man of thirty or so suffers from such severe dysphasia that he might be taken for a simpleton— he is actually unable to enunciate one full syllable—but in fact he is the most gifted bachelor in the entire region. Wood carving, fine basket weaving, ironwork—he excels in everything. And not only is he very hardworking; he is also blessed with an equable temper and high spirits. He enlivens every party, and not even the stupidest teasing he must endure because of his infirmity can dampen his ebullience. Since he cannot express himself in words, Kröng-the- Stutterer mimes the stories he wants to tell with irresistible talent, and in spite of his inability to take part in a discussion, he does not let himself be easily bested.

The same evening his two *rnôom* were anointed, Baap Can set out for Ndut Lieng Krak to so inform his future ally and reach an agreement with him about the date of their double sacrifice. This was not the sole purpose of his going, however. Baap Can wanted to take advantage of this obligatory trip—the first step toward a further increase in his prestige—to carry out a long-pondered plan that, in his view, would assure the extension of his family—ergo, of his own power. He was eager to arrange the marriage of his daughter Jaang to the stepson of his "brother" Kroong-Biing. At first glance, this scheme would appear to present no problems, but actually it conflicted with certain plans of Baap Can's younger brother, Truu, and were it to work out, it would be a terrible blow for the canton chief. Did this fact make his project all the more important to the old man? Impossible to say, but this much is certain: he was fiercely determined to carry it out.

Baap Can has always been a good father. As we have seen, he did ev- erything in his power to be able to keep the children born of his first marriage with him, although responsibility for them would normally have reverted to his in-laws. Now his greatest ambition was to assure a solid future for his second daughter, Jaang, the eldest of the children he had had by his second wife, Aang-the-Long. He calculated that the surest way of achieving this was to contrive to marry her to Srae, the son of Biing-Kroong's first marriage. This seventeen-year-old boy is one of the few Mnong Gar who have won admission to the Groupe Scolaire in Ban Me Thuot. The chances are excellent that when Srae completes his studies he will obtain a government post—an abundant and regular source of income. Furthermore, Srae comes from a rich family, which is an additional guarantee of his making a good start in life. Only one big threatening reef might cause Baap Can's project to founder. Several months earlier, Truu had approved of Srae as his son-in-law-to-be. The young man had taken a lively fancy to Truu's adopted daughter, Jaang Bibuu. He resolved to marry her, and to this end confided in his stepfather, Kroong-the-Short. The latter had judged it a very respectworthy idea, and the two men had gone to Sar Luk to feel out the terrain. The reception they got from Truu was most favorable. In fact, Truu could not dream of a husband more suitable for his adopted daughter than Srae. Being a student, Srae could someday replace him as canton chief with no difficulty, since the French colonial government intended in the future to appoint only men who could read and write to such posts. Meanwhile, his son-in-law could act as his administrative secretary. So Truu had given his assent. But there remained the formalities of presenting the official request through a matchmaker and the exchange of gifts. Neither was a pressing matter, since Srae was still pursuing his studies in Ban Me Thuot.

One can readily imagine the quandary into which Baap Can's démarche plunged Kroong-Biing. However, he was only the father—what's more, the stepfather—and the primary thing was to obtain the consent of young Srae's mother and of his maternal uncle. Here Baap Can was moving on particularly sure grounds, for Srae's mother, Biing, belonged to the Bboon Jraang clan, as had his first wife and, by extension, the children she had borne him: Can and Aang-of-the-Drooping-Eyelid were Bboon Jraang also. Beyond doubt, Baap Can reminded Biing-Kroong and her brother, Kraang-Jieng, that on one occasion he had already exchanged the magic plant of the Paddy with the Bboon Jraang clan; also, that he has always maintained excellent relations with his former in-laws. Likewise, he must have emphasized that, in marrying Jaang, Srae would find a clan brother and sister in his young wife's own family. And lastly, given his legalistic turn of mind and his litigious talents, he must have been able easily to demolish the objection that the earlier understanding with Truu might raise: Truu's agreement could not be taken into consideration because it had never been sanctioned by any ritual act.

Three days later, Kroong-the-Short, Biing, Srae, and the Bboon Jraang of Ndut, conducted by Ndêh, arrive late at night at the house of Bbôong-Mang. Handing him the proposal bracelet, they appoint him go-between. Bbôong-the-Deputy betakes himself to Baap Can's house and, in accordance with the rules, submits the proposal to him. Obviously, it is accepted. Bbôong then summons his guests, who arrive promptly, bearing the traditional gifts: a necklace, a white hen, and two *ding paa* (fireworked bamboo tubes containing a preserve of bamboo shoots and cured buffalo hide). Baap Can breaks open a jar and kills a chicken to anoint the foreheads of the affianced couple with its blood. The whole affair is carried out with dispatch and maximum discretion. Apart from those present, no one is informed. The next morning, it is explained to me that the entire village was asleep—and who would have dared awaken anyone? To my great surprise (at the time, I knew nothing of the background of this affair), Baap Can is most insistent in persuading me that Truu had been sleeping like a log and that he, Baap Can, had called him several times to no avail. However, it was readily apparent that Truu was furious. Although he was surely wide awake by afternoon, he did not attend any of the ceremonies that took place in Baap Can's house in the late afternoon. In line with tradition, Baap Can returned their gifts to the Bboon Jraang, then offered "the rice that announces the harvest" to his friend Ndêh. Truu remained shut up in his house and appeared in his yard only at sunset. He did not even pretend to try to hide his foul humor.

Two days later, on October 8, Sar Luk celebrates the rite of the Paddy posts (*nyiit ndah*). On this occasion, each "granary" makes its sacrifice and libation in turn, with the three holy men presiding; the administrative chiefs and other *kuang*, whom everyone eagerly invites, also make the rounds of the village. However, Kröng-Jôong is suffering from a headache (a diplomatic indisposition?) and has arranged for his stepson, Kroong-Big-Navel, to replace him. At the house of Bbaang-Jieng-the-Pregnant-Man—the sworn friend of Truu—Baap Can arranges, in turn, to have his son substitute for him. However, when we reach the house of the Bboon Jraang, Baap Can comes to officiate in person, for this concerns the family of his former wife and, now, the clan of his future son-in-law. Darkness has fallen. The rites have been completed, and Baap Can is tranquilly drinking from a jar. Suddenly, Truu bursts into the house. He is quite evidently reinvigorated by all the alcohol he has consumed in the course of this day which has been replete with ceremonies. No sooner is he inside than he gives full rein to his rage. From where he is sitting, Baap Can replies angrily, and "the two brothers issued from the same belly," the two most influential personages of Sar Luk, exchange vigorous insults. In all the village, there is only one man who can stand up to the canton chief—Baap Can. And there is only one who dares talk back to Baap Can—Truu. This evening, the two brothers abuse each other violently. Aang-of-the-Drooping-Eyelid arrives in tears. She tries to calm her uncle and father, but the most she can do is stand between the two *kuang* and bawl her head off. Jaang has heard the vociferous dispute, and has come on the run. She weeps softly at her half sister's side.

There is a lull. Then Truu lets loose with a stinging blow, and his elder brother, wild with fury, howls at the outrage. Baap Can's two daughters cling to him and beg him to be calm. At last, he closes the incident by chanting:

> *"To the handle of the lance,*
> *To the fallen trunk of a dead tree,*
> *I lead to marriage. . . ."*

During the fierce quarrel between two brothers, two *kuang*, the people present had scarcely dared breathe. It took a long time for the atmosphere to return to normal.

Now that the difficulty had been thrashed out in such spectacular fashion, order was restored. Baap Can and the family of his wife conducted Jaang to the house of her future in-laws for a visit of several days. And in public Truu never spoke about Srae's marriage again.

The village has resumed its customary routine, except that feverish activity has reigned in Baap Can's house ever since the *rnôom* were recruited. The young man in particular has an immense amount of work to complete, although it is true that Can, Srae, and especially old Krah—an excellent carver—are giving him substantial help. Essentially, his task is to build the structures, furnishings, and decorations required for the sacrifice. First, a low platform is made of plaited strips of heavy bamboo, a smaller replica of the one that runs along the back wall of the house. This second platform extends the length of the front wall, from the door of the common room to approximately the second granary post. Outside, a small veranda (*naang röng*) extends the threshold of the private door. (The veranda before the door to the common room was put up for Kröng-Jôong's *Tâm Bôh* and only its roof needs to be rebuilt.) Also, a fine tree must be found, from which various planks will be cut with a *wiah*, then painted with geometrical motifs and stylized representations of familiar scenes. The largest two will be placed the length of each low platform as decoration. Another will be suspended to serve as a sort of rack to accommodate visitors' blankets. Still another and smaller one will be attached to the purlins of the roof on the front, and will serve as a shelf for guests' *wiah*. Thinner boards will be used to build the small altar (*ndrööng Yaang*) suspended beneath the roof at the rear of the house and, especially, the ritual barrier. The central stake of the barrier will be carved at the top and decorated with two tiny horns and a long stalk of bamboo embellished with two palm leaves. This jar stake (*ndah yang*) reproduces in miniature the sacrificial post to which the animal victim is tethered. Because Baap Can is offering two buffaloes, two such posts will be set up. Accordingly, the men will have to look for two very straight bombax (*blaang*) trunks. The tops will be carved, and to each will be affixed a long stalk of bamboo decorated with a miniature hut—it represents the hut of *Yaang Baa*, the Spirit of the Paddy—and armed with two large palm wings that are prolonged by a cluster of wood platelets. When the wind blows, these will rattle noisily. The bombax poles, which are prepared well in advance of the ceremony, will be planted about a meter from the edge of the roof, between the two verandas and close by the strong barrier that will prevent the buffaloes' turning around them. In addition, between these poles and the principal veranda a ritual stall (*naang rah*) will be built; this is a narrow platform about two meters high, supported by four giant-bamboo uprights, the tops of which have been frayed to form a sort of plume. Once everything is ready, including the various utensils, decorated wickerwork, and assorted tools, there remains only the expedition into the forest to search for the lofty sacrificial pole mast.

When a visitor approaching a Mnong Gar village glimpses from a distance two or three immense masts with arms of palm towering above the housetops, he knows he is about to enter a *kuang* village, where only recently two or three inhabitants have been in a position to make a grandiose buffalo sacrifice. To seek out, cut down, and transport the giant bamboo—the most spectacular element in the ritual decor of the sacrifice—is an act of considerable importance, and it calls for great precautions of a magical nature. Such a search for the giant bamboo (*pôong rlaa*) was carried out on October 22, 1948.

That morning, Baap Can's go-between (*ndraany*), Bbôong-Mang-the-Deputy, who is the organizer and director of this *Tâm Bôh*, donned his fine red administrative chief's tunic. As a finishing touch to this elegance, he was carrying a small Rlâm bush hook; the tip of the blade is curved.

We are all assembled at Baap Can's house. When we are ready to set forth, but before we actually cross the threshold, Bbôong-the-Deputy takes ashes from the hearth and scatters handfuls in the air outside, while he recites:

> "Roedeer on the plain, do not bell, for me;
> Pruh *grass on the plain, do not climb, for me;*
> *I fear the taboo. . . .*
>
> *I sow ash in the wind:*
> *May evil omens melt like salt,*
> be lost like ashes in the wind."

If the roedeer were to bell along our path or if we were to come upon *pruh* grass, whose root has protuberances shaped like horns, we would be obliged to retrace our steps and remain briefly in the village before setting out again in another direction. Now that the precaution of throwing the ashes has been taken, we can leave without fear. Bbôong-Mang heads the column. Baap Can is armed with his saber and little Tôong-the-Stutterer (son of Yôong-the-Mad) carries a small basket, but the rest—Can and his two brothers-in-law, Kroong-Big-Navel and Srae, and the sacrifice servant—are equipped with *wiah*. Kröng-the-Stutterer, who brings up the rear, plays a yodeling-like tune on his powerful horn. The music not only lends a festive note to our expedition but also attracts the goodwill of the Spirits; also, it is thus that one must act, in accord with ancient instructions handed down "from the time of the Ancestors."

We have no sooner struck out along the track to the *miir* than Bbôong-the-Deputy tears off the end of a branch of *rkôong,* a shrub (Euphorbiaceae?). He fans the air before him with it, at head level, as if he were chasing invisible flies. He spits on it seven times, and at the eighth, he asks the leaves to keep the roedeer from belling and to keep our path clear of the horned *pruh.*

Five minutes later, at nine-thirty, we pass a group of people resting on the banks of the Daak Dieng Krae. They have come from Upper Donnaï and are on their way to Poste du Lac. Soon after, we catch up with Baap Can's wife, her daughter, and the female *rnôom* and her sister, who are going out to the fields to harvest. We walk along together as far as the *miir,* where we leave them. Passing beyond the fields, for some minutes we skirt the fences that protect them, continue eastward along a fine path until, around ten o'clock, we leave it for another, smaller trail running due south.

Soon we come to a delightful clearing in the midst of the bush. Papayas and several clumps of banana trees surround an abandoned thatched hut, which was once the shelter of a leper; he had been banished from the village, and has since died. As long as lepers are relatively able-bodied, they continue to live in the village, but the day comes when their dreadful disfiguring disease makes them helpless and the danger of contagion also becomes very great. Then the unfortunate sufferer is isolated in a hut outside the community. His wife or his sister brings him food and cares for him. Very often, she is devoted enough to share his exile, as was the case with the man who had lived in this hut.

The leper's little shack stands on the bank of a broad stream. We wade across, and as we climb up the far bank we see that there is no path. We will have to chop our way with our *wiah* through tall *tieng kau* reeds (*Arundo madagascariensis* Kunth) extending as far as the foot of a hill, which is covered with a dense growth of bamboo and bushes. Bbôong-Mang takes the lead in opening up a passage, but he soon has enough of it and surrenders his place to the *rnôom.* In this humid, overgrown terrain, bloodsuckers reign supreme, and in serried ranks attack the legs of intruders. As we start chopping our way up the side of the hill, Bbôong leaves us to clear his own path; he reaches the top well before us. Krông-the-Stutterer's problem is to lay out an almost straight path up a very steep incline, but he has lagged behind to poke around in a badger hole—with no results.

We finally reach the splendid stand of giant bamboo which we had chosen from a distance. Immediately an argument breaks out between Bbôong and Baap Can, which is interrupted by mystifying squeaks from Krông-the-Stutterer. In the end, however, it is the latter's suggestions that carry the day: we will cut down the tallest, straightest *rlaa.* It is sur-

rounded by several others, unfortunately, but the trunks of the trees on
the edge of the stand are crooked.

The boy has hung the little basket he was carrying on a branch. From it
Baap Can takes a wicker box decorated with a geometric pattern and filled
with broken saffroned rice. He throws a handful over the stand of *rlaa,*
and Bbôong-Mang instantly follows suit. They beseech the Spirits:

> *"O Tree Spirit,*
> *O Bombax Ancestor,*
> *and thee, O Liana;*
> *I serve thee, O giant bamboo* Rlaa.
> *I have recruited a* rnôom *to serve thee,*
> *thee, O* Rlaa *of the first beginnings.*
> *The alcohol is in the jar; that is why I summon thee.*
> *I eat meat in order to serve thee,*
> *I drink alcohol in order to serve thee,*
> *I slaughter two buffaloes,*
> > *two male buffaloes in order to serve thee.*
> *I sow the saffroned rice,*
> *crooked* Rlaa, *stand up straight,*
> *crooked* Dlei, *stand up straight,*
> *then I shall be happy.*
> *I shall serve thee tomorrow, and in the days thereafter;*
> *I shall serve thee alone."*

Baap Can takes from the basket a packet of wort wrapped in leaves. He
gives some to Bbôong-Mang, who anoints the feet of several *rlaa* with it,
and Baap Can himself anoints the foot of the one to be felled:

> *"I bless the Tree Spirit, the Bombax Ancestor;*
> *do not speak to me in anger,*
> *do not crush me with thy wrath.*
> *One chicken I have served thee,*
> *and one jar of alcohol,*
> *one chicken, whose blood I shall collect in the village below."*

Now Bbôong-Mang takes from the basket a still smaller one decorated
with black motifs. It contains cooked glutinous rice, which he distributes
to the sacrifice servant, to Can, the young boy, the two sons-in-law of the
master of the séance, and to me. Then Bbôong anoints the *rlaa* that will
be felled, carefully spreading the cooked rice over the trunk:

> *"With this cooked rice I serve thee,*
> *O tree coming from the Spirits,*
> *O Bombax coming from the Plain,*
> *I serve thee, O* Rlaa.
> *I erect the pole mast;*
> *I eat meat; therefore I summon thee;*

I drink alcohol, therefore I summon thee.
May I eat meat at each Rite of the Straw,
may I eat the flesh of goat on each site of a village freshly abandoned;
may I cut bamboo tubes on each site of a village newly rebuilt.
O Rlaa, I serve thee;
do not speak to me in anger,
do not crush me with thy wrath. . . ."

The *rnôom* seizes his bush hook and attacks the huge ramified thorns that protect the base of giant bamboos. When he can get at the chosen *rlaa*, he prunes it in turn. The other members of the expedition rest meanwhile, and smoke their pipes, except for Srae, who sets about building a fire. He sparks it with a flint, for, they tell me, one may not carry a brand into the forest as one does when going to work in the fields. By way of commentary on this explanation, Kroong-Big-Navel sings for me:

"Rub the firewood with the withe of the small rattan palm,
whittle thin the withe of the large rattan palm,
then open your ear to the word,
for we are going to loll about in the forest."

Some of the men pass the time eating glutinous rice. Bbôong-Mang has gone off to gather some red blooms of the wild banana.

When Kröng-the-Stutterer has finished his pruning, Can severs the foot of the *rlaa*. It does not fall, for the short, leafy branches that crown the entire stand are intermingled and support it. Kroong-Big-Navel comes to Can's rescue, and together they tug on the base. Once the giant bamboo is lying on the ground, the four young men lop off the top branches. One of them measures the trunk with a stalk of *dlei* bamboo one and three quarter meters long. The felled giant proves to be eighteen and a half meters in length.

We start back at eleven-forty. First, the *rlaa* is eased lengthwise down the steep path the Stutterer had cleared on his way up. At the foot of the hill, Srae and Can swing the future pole mast onto their shoulders. The immense trunk sways so that their gait becomes perforce a hop-skip. When they reach the stream, infinite precautions must be taken so that nothing strikes the middle section of the giant bamboo. The two brothers-in-law will carry this heavy burden the whole way to the village.

En route, Kröng-the-Stutterer has cut two big hands of bananas that will be used in "the exchange of food." As we approach Sar Luk, we meet Nyaang, of Nyôong Brah, who has come to fetch Sieng-Aang. One of the buffaloes Sieng had purchased for the anointment of the Paddy sacrifice has strangled itself.

Just outside the village and hard by our right, we hear the "pep . . . pep" of a prowling tiger. It is out of the question, Bbôong tells me, to try to catch a glimpse of him; the bush hereabouts is impassable, and we would not get near the beast without alerting him.

In Sar Luk, the *rlaa* is simply deposited on the ground in Baap Can's yard. Everyone goes home without waiting for him, Kroong-Big-Navel, and the *rnôom* to return.

Early in the afternoon, around two-thirty, Baap Can's house is cleaned. The sacrifice servant climbs up to empty some baskets of rice into the granary. In the adjacent common room, Kröng-Jôong is casting some ankle rings for his daughter. Ever since Sieng-Aang, of Nyôong Brah, who is a clever metalworker, visited the village not long ago, all the girls in Sar Luk have been seized by a passion for these rings. But they are unaccustomed to this type of jewelry and have been hurting their ankles, so now they must protect them with wads of leaves.

Two jars of rice beer have been hung from the barrier inside the house, the larger suspended from the central carved post. They have already been opened and filled with water. A small basket with geometric designs has been set at the base of the large jar; it is three quarters full of hulled rice. An egg is being hard-boiled on the hearth.

Baap Can and Bbôong-the-Deputy squat before the medium-size jar, at the foot of which a young chicken and a Mnong bowl filled with wort (*coot*) have been placed. The master of the house passes the chicken and the drinking straw (*gut*) to his go-between, and kisses his hand. The latter responds in kind, and as he inserts the *gut* into the jar, he prays:

"The alcohol of one jar, one chicken, one pig, these I offer thee,
    O double Ngör bamboo, I offer them to thee,
    O triple Ngkaar bamboo, I offer them to thee,
    O Dlei bamboo, bowed by the wind,
O Rlaa bamboo of the Valley of the Daak Kroong, I offer them to thee.
    I do as did my Uncle, younger brother of my Mother;
    I do as did my Uncle, elder brother of my Mother;
    I do as did my Grandfathers,
    I do as did my Ancestors.
If tomorrow and the day after tomorrow I eat meat, may I later eat meat again;
If tomorrow and the day after tomorrow I drink from the jar, may I later drink from
    the jar again. . . ."

Bbôong slits the chicken's neck above the wort in the Mnong bowl while Baap Can continues to pray.

Kröng-Jôong is summoned from the adjacent common room and Bbaang-the-Stag, brother-in-law of Baap Can and holy man in Phii Ko', is fetched from his home. The four men leave the house and squat in a row along the full length of the *rlaa*, all on the same side, their backs turned to Baap Can's house. Bbôong offers the bowl of *coot* mixed with blood to his companions. Each takes a pinch and anoints the future pole mast. He begs for the giant bamboo's mercy, using the same incantation that was recited before the tree was felled. Bbôong leaves his companions praying to the *rlaa* and goes to bless the sacrificial posts, the ritual barrier and stall, the halters, the heavy stakes that support the stack of firewood, the carved jar posts, the blanket rack, the jars, the drum, the gongs. To each object he anoints in turn, he declares that the sacrifice and libation are meant also for it.

Baap Can and Kröng-Jôong rejoin Bbôong-Mang, and the three men come in to squat before the big jar. Baap Can hands a *gut* to each of his assistants, and the three men kiss each other's hands. The go-between takes a bit of blood-steeped wort and anoints the white rice in the small decorated basket; the two others imitate him. This is "the anointment of the white rice to be shared between the villages" (*lêer phei pa' phei bboon*):

> "I give the day in back,
> I plant the day in front.
> May the pointy winnowing basket not tear,
> may the pitted mortar not split,
> may the young men and young women not spill the grain.
> Heartily let us eat meat,
> heartily let us drink from the jar.
> In our village we lead you by the hand;
> in our forest we give you this rice."

While reciting their formulas, Kröng-Jôong and Bbôong-Mang have inserted their drinking straws, but only after carefully sprinkling a few drops of jar water on the earth by brushing the surface with the end of the straw before thrusting it to the bottom. Then, seizing the bowl of wort and blood, Bbôong walks to the private door. He stands with his back to it, so that he faces the last granary post, which he anoints as he chants a prayer. This is "the summoning of the Spirits in the belly of the Paddy" (*khual Yaang ndül Baa*). In effect, he is invoking, one by one, all the Higher Spirits:

> "O Spirit of the Earth,
> O Spirit of the Soil,
> O Spirit of the Environs,
> O Spirit of the Leaves,
> O Spirit of the Foliage,
> O Spirit of the Threads,
> O Spirit of the Spinning Wheel,
> O Spirit of the Plain,
> O Spirit of the Valleys.
> Watering Place, I summon thee also;
> Lalang Grass, I summon thee also;

Anointing the giant-bamboo pole mast . . .

. . . and the sacrificial posts

Water Hole where the buffaloes wallow, I summon thee also. . . .
   When I eat a pig, I offer thee a ham;
   when I eat a buffalo, I offer thee a shoulder;
   when I eat a chicken, I offer thee a breast;
when I eat a goat, I cut its throat for thee, O Spirit. . . .
When I use a gong, keep it from splitting;
when I use an earthen pot, keep it from cracking;
when I use a crossbow, keep the string from snapping;
when I lead one who is younger, when I lead one who is
   older, keep them from sickness, keep them from re-
   turning ill to their homes. . . ."

The prayer, which is very long, is a haphazard succession of entreaties in verse form and of poems enumerating the Place Spirits, with the name of the territory each inhabits always mentioned.

When his go-between set out for the belly of the Paddy, Baap Can stepped up onto the large low platform to deposit a bowl filled with rice beer and another with cooked rice, on which he has laid a hard-boiled egg and a banana, on the little altar that hangs beneath the roof at the rear of the house. He recites:

". *. . The Gods command,*
   the Spirits watch,
   the Powerful Ones listen.
When I seek a buffalo, may I find a large male;
when I seek a jar, may I find one that is black;
when I cultivate a plot of land, may I reap a hundred basketfuls. . . ."

Finally, both jars are opened simultaneously, but a very bureaucratic order is observed in the drinking. I drink from the first, Truu from the second; I give up my place to Kröng-Jôong, and the canton chief relinquishes his to his deputy. It is three thirty-five before Baap Can's family can at last have its midday meal. As usual, the group is divided into two: on one side, Can, his wife, and the male *rnôom;* on the other, Aang-the-Long and her children, Jaang's fiancé, old Krah, and the female *rnôom.* Today Baap Can does not wish to eat. The chicken has been braised and is now distributed among all present.

While drinking, people talk of this and that. Baap Can, however, is preoccupied with drawing up the list of guests he should invite. Before his go-between and Bbaang-the-Stag, his wife's brother, he details the "debts of meat" (*nool poec*) he must repay. He snaps a twig and lays one piece in front of him; this represents the haunch he received from Sieng-Aang, of Nyôong Brah, when the latter "drank" in honor of the Soil. Next to it, he lays another bit of twig; this is the shoulder offered him by Wan-Yôong, of Paang Pê' Nâm, on the occasion of another sacrifice. . . . Baap Can has been thinking about this matter for the last few days. Such gifts of meat must be repaid in kind. Therefore, a man takes advantage of the first sacrifice he makes to settle this type of debt, for under no circumstances must he leave it as a burden on his children.

The old man hands over a little basket of rice to his go-between. Bbôong-the-Deputy makes the rounds of the village, distributes a handful of rice to each householder, and announces the date of the sacrifice. Baap Can, meanwhile, has cut some thread into lengths of fifteen or twenty centimeters. He ties three evenly spaced knots in each; each knot stands for one day. He has thus "knotted the thread of days" (*kuat rsei nang*). He divides these threads among various people with instructions to carry the rice that has just been blessed to each of his invited guests who live at a distance. Tomorrow, Bbaang-the-Stag will leave for Bboon Jaa and Paang Pê' Nâm, Kroong-Sraang and Wan-Jôong for Laac Döng and Bboon Khaang; Can and Srae will go this evening on horseback to Ndut Sar and Sar Lang; tomorrow morning, Baap Can himself will carry his rice of invitation to Nyôong Brah.

In all the Rjee households, the women and young men are busy cutting into strips the buffalo meat that Sieng-Aang brought from Nyôong Brah late this afternoon. This came from the animal that had strangled itself in the forest; Sieng had been obliged to carve it up before he could offer it as a sacrifice to the Spirits.

It is almost seven in the evening when Kröng-Jôong in turn opens a jar. He offers his neighbor and brother-in-law, Baap Can, "the rice beer in response to the rice of invitation" (*rnööm bööm phei*). Kröng has poured a bowlful of the beer and placed it on the shelf supporting his row of large jars. He squats before the bowl and, facing the back wall, utters the same prayer that Baap Can had offered earlier before his altar. Then he rejoins Baap Can at the foot of the opened jar. A small decorated wicker box containing the rice of invitation has been placed nearby. Kröng hands his brother-in-law the drinking straw and a pinch of wort. An exchange of hand kissing follows. Baap Can inserts his *gut* in the jar. Kröng anoints the rice in the box, Baap Can the ground only. As they perform this series of ritual gestures, the two men pray:

> "O Rice of Invitation of the Powerful Ones,
> Today I offer thee the alcohol of a jar as unction;
> come drink with us,
> come eat with us. . . ."

And the drinking begins.

An hour and a half later, the same ceremony is carried out at Bboong-Mang's; although he is Baap Can's go-between, he is also responding to the latter's rice of invitation.

It is almost nine o'clock when Can and Srae heave into sight, breathless and visibly shaken. They do not take time even to stable their horses; they order the young men who had gone out to meet them to see to that. From their shouts for torches and the few words exchanged on their arrival, we understand that the two travelers have just been attacked by a tiger.

They had started their rounds with Sar Lang. As is proper, the people there had responded to their rice of invitation by opening a jar of *rnööm*. They had tarried only as long as necessary not to leave their hosts with unseemly haste, and in one gallop they had covered the two or three kilometers that separate Sar Lang from Ndut Sar. There, also, a jar is broached in their honor. However, they do not linger. Not that they fear any untoward encounters. Can is well armed, for Truu had lent him his old Lebel and two cartridges. But when they borrowed the horses of the canton chief and his deputy, the young men had promised to be back in Sar Luk the same evening. So, confident in their armed might and with their courage powerfully reinforced by all the rice beer they had imbibed, they braved the night.

Ndut Sar is linked to the track by a fairly wide path. They have not advanced a hundred meters when suddenly Can's horse—he was riding ahead—begins to kick, and Srae's mount takes off like an arrow. Guessing what is up, Can slips from his horse, holding the reins in one hand and gripping his rifle in the other. The enormous hulk of a tiger emerges from the bush. Can loads his rifle and presses the trigger. . . . Nothing. The wild animal is approaching slowly. Can jiggles the breech, and tries a second time to fire. Nothing. The cartridges are too old, and they don't go off. The tiger leaps on the hindquarters of the horse, which kicks sideways. Can grasps his rifle by the barrel and with all his might brings it down on the beast's muzzle once, twice. The animal roars in pain and runs off. The young man jumps on his nag and rejoins his companion, who has halted a little way up the path. With no further interruption, they reach Sar Luk none the worse for this adventure except that the horse Can was riding has a deep claw wound in one flank.

October 23

It is Truu's turn to offer the beer of response to the rice of invitation sent by his elder brother. While we are drinking from his little neckless jar, a coolie *tram* casts bracelets for his daughter.

At nine-fifteen, a small happening: a panic-stricken doe with her fawns races through the lower part of the village. I manage to shoot her as she tries to swim toward the far riverbank. Meat for the entire village.

Srae leads the two buffaloes that will be offered Baap Can's *jôok* down to the river and washes them. Krah and Kröng-the-Stutterer are decorating the giant bamboo. Dloong-the-Black, the female *rnôom*, is down by the watering place with the canton chief's daughter. The girls are giving each other Mnong-style shampoos, using water in which rice has been rinsed.

Baap Can delivers his invitation to the teacher in person. Back from the school, where obviously his visit has been acknowledged by a jar of rice beer, the old man busies himself dispelling the baleful effects of the tiger's attack. He is not content with a simple exorcism; he is determined to revenge himself on the beast by means of a powerful curse. This double operation calls for a young chicken, a jar of rice beer, an empty *yang dâm;* simulacra of two flat gongs (two tiny discs carved from a calabash), a pair of elephant tusks, and a rhinoceros horn (all wooden miniatures two to three centimeters long); and pieces of charcoal. Also required: the worn handle of a bush hook minus the blade, and an internode of bamboo that has been used to cook wild vegetables, this "pot" now filled with ashes. The jar of *rnööm* is attached to the small inside barrier. Can and Srae squat before it. Standing and facing the two young men, Baap Can passes the miniatures and the tube of ashes, into which he has stuck the headless *wiah* handle, back and forth above their heads eight times. With each passage, he counts aloud and after enumerating what he is offering, he declares:

> ". . . I pay the fine of this trial;
> I settle my ransom with the Spirits:
> these flat gongs I give up to them,
> these copper bowls I offer them.
> May I stay alive. . . ."

Then, preceded by Bbaang-the-Stag, who has armed himself with a *wiah*, Baap Can carries the gift miniatures and the other materials of the imprecation ceremony to where the path and track meet. He lays everything on the ground, spits on the charcoal go-betweens, describes his offering again, and recites the same wishes as before. Rising to his feet, he takes up the bamboo tube of ashes and the headless *wiah* handle and hurls them into the bush, shouting:

> "May you die, may you rot;
> may the lancets of others pierce you;
> may the bush hook, when you meet it, fell you;
> may the lance, when you meet it, strike you low;
> may the rifle of Yoo, when you meet it, shoot you dead.
> This is my curse.
> Why do you hate our light?
> Why do you behave so ferociously toward our soul?

Why do you force us to hold a trial? . . .
This cooking tube I send to you.
These ashes I throw to you.
This headless wiah *I give to you.*
May you die, may you be killed, you, you Thing!"

The two men return to the village, reciting:

> "Return to your home,
> to your own village,
> to your own forest,
> to your own flowing water. . . ."

Back by the jar, Baap Can slashes the chicken's crest and brushes it
eight times over the foreheads of Srae and of Can, who holds the drinking
straw. When the son inserts his *gut* into the jar, the father begins to pray.
Then eight times Baap Can lays a *wiah* blade on which he has spat against
the foreheads of the two young men. As he performs these various ritual
gestures, he enumerates what he is offering in the exorcism, and expresses the wish:

> ". . . that our body be cool,
> that we sleep deeply,
> that we snore loudly.
> May the thread not break,
> may the snare not give way,
> may the kite be enmeshed in it. . . ."

The deputy drinks first, followed by Bbaang-the-Stag. To my immense
pleasure, for once I am not offered the drinking straw. They count on
seeing me repeat my morning's exploit, this time killing not an animal
which is harmful only to the crops, like the doe, but one that attacks livestock and even men; they designate it fearfully by tensing one hand in the
shape of a clawed paw. In the course of the imprecation rite, this wish has
been voiced several times.

While they are drinking, two Cil Bboon Jaa bring Baap Can a European
shirt and two bottles of Vietnamese brandy from the market in Dalat. Our
Powerful One had ordered them for his celebration.

Finally, toward a quarter to six, Bbaang-the-Stag and Baap Can decide
they will set out to deliver the rice of invitation, the former going to
villages in Upper Donnaï, the latter to Nyôong Brah. Only Bbaang-the-
Stag actually got off, for before dark, a half hour after leaving us, Baap
Can reappeared. He had turned back, very likely because he was still
greatly disturbed by yesterday's incident with the tiger and also was concerned that his own curses might be construed as a defiance by the Other.

As evening falls, the headman of Sar Lang arrives at Kröng-Jôong's
house. He is Kröng's *jôok*, for they performed the Exchange of Sacrifices

together last September. Choong-Yôong has come to inform his friend that he is about to commence harvesting. In his honor, Krông opens a jar, which they consecrate together. An hour later, the holy man in the village breaks open yet another jar, this time for people who have arrived from Nyôong Brah and will be spending the night with him.

October 24

Since five-thirty this morning, the drum and the *cing* have been sounding from Baap Can's house. The Spirits are being awakened and kept on the alert so that they will be ready for the festivities now in preparation.

Krah and Krông-the-Stutterer are putting the finishing touches on the sacrificial posts. While the *rnôom* sculptures a highly stylized squatting man at the top ends of the bombax, the old slave is carving two pairs of "bee's wings" to surmount the sculptures. The wings are fashioned of two thin pieces of mottled wood in the shape of a half circle and mounted on a slender crossbar. The Stutterer will complete this first phase of the decoration by carving out of soft wood the figures of four life-size turtledoves; tomorrow these will be affixed to the bee's wings.

Around ten-thirty, Baap Can finally does get off. He takes all the necessary precautions. That is to say, before leaving his house, he throws several handfuls of ashes to the wind:

> "*I sow the ash so that [the roedeer] may not bell,*
> *so that the* pruh *grass in the plain may not break,*
> *so that the stump in the plain may not fall,*
> *so that the rhôong and* r'aa *plants may not bar our path.*
> *I must go*
> *to bring the announcement of the day in back,*
> *to plant the announcement of the day in front.*
> *Take the tin from your ears.*"

In the afternoon, a veritable hairdressing salon is set up on the cliff, a short distance from where Krông-the-Stutterer is sculpturing his birds. Young Chaar, appointed official barber, gives numerous young men who present themselves for his scissorly ministrations a haircut *à la française.*

In the evening, Bbaang-the-One-Eyed offers *rnôöm* in response to the rice of invitation. It is dedicated to the two partners in the *Tâm Bôh*—to Baap Can, in the person of his elder son, and especially to Ndêh, who is represented by his emissary, Taang-the-Soldier, of Ndut Lieng Krak. The wives of the erstwhile canton chief and of the One-Eyed are "sisters," but the chief reason Ndêh is invited is that he has engaged the One-Eyed's younger brother Nyaang to be his *rnôom.* Although this is a poor household, the crowd is large and the atmosphere very jolly. Bbaang-the-One-Eyed makes no attempt to hide how proud he is to offer this very special hospitality. The ex-infantryman is a great talker; he tells about his exploits, and in particular describes for us his sea voyage—four days he spent aboard a "warship." What astonished him most on this sea adventure, he says, was the fish he saw—"enormous, some of them as big as huge male buffaloes." Admiring comments from his listeners. A few moments later, he informs us that he had been very sick, that he could not stir from his hammock, that he threw up the whole time. But, he adds, no sooner had he set foot again on dry land than his illness completely disappeared.

It is raining. At Baap Can's, they are beating the flat gongs. But Kröng-the-Stutterer prefers the One-Eyed's house; it may lack music but not drink. Despite his speech difficulties, with his immense gift of mimicry, Kröng, as always, enjoys a great success.

October 25

Today Baap Can's guests are to arrive. Starting at seven in the morning, his go-between, Bbôong-the-Deputy, sees to the magic protection of the *kuang*'s residence, where a large number of foreigners will be assembling. Bbôong works alone. Armed with a hoe, he opens a furrow near and parallel to the main door. In it he buries a pair of pincers, some small shells called *kiep mêem*, some tubers of magic plants (the plant of Coolness and another called *Rlööp*), and some potsherds. As he does this, he asks:

> "O pincers, shut tight the mouths of the rich, of the
>   powerful, of the slaves, and of the caak;
> O kiep mêem shell, shut tight the mouths of the rich,
>   of the powerful, of the slaves, and of the caak;
>   this is what I command you to do, O kiep mêem.
> O magic plant of Coolness, keep our bodies cool, our
>   sleep deep.
>   O magic plant Rlööp, strike down and devour, artfully thin.
>   Stick like glue, O glutinous rice.
> I command you to watch over all foreigners, all things,
>   twenty, thirty;
> I command you to watch over all that comes from Ndut
>   Lieng Krak;
> I command you to watch over all the village below."

What remains of the magic plant of Coolness he cuts into small pieces. He places them in a hollowed buffalo horn, which he hangs from the wall near the door.

The protection of the threshold now complete, he performs a ceremony to protect the door itself. Two long pieces of firewood, stripped of bark, are placed on either side as a frame. Two pipe cleaners are passed through the stem of a well-seasoned pipe, stuck in a ripe red pepper, and attached to the frame. The two lengths of wood threaten any soul-eating sorcerers (*caak*) who might presume to cross the threshold if the fiery bite of the pepper or the bitterness of the tobacco dottle were to fail to drive them off.

> "Do not enter, Sorcerer. I have already placed here the tobacco excrement, I have already placed here the red pepper. See this split wood. If you come, I shall strike you down with it. . . . Do not enter my house, my granary. May I drink and eat heartily."

Yesterday's rain has washed clean the big plaques of bamboo for the adornment of the giant pole mast. So now they must be repainted. The black paint is made by moistening powdered charcoal with water; the red paint is made with the bark of the *tii* (*Careya sphaerica*).

Inside the house, everything is in readiness, even to the banana leaf that has been laid athwart the door. The major remaining outdoor tasks are to ornament the long bamboos that must be attached to the crest of each bombax and, above all, to complete the elaborate dressing of the *rlaa*.

All day long, the drinking in Sar Luk has been uninterrupted. Taang-the-Soldier has continued to make the rounds, and in each of the four households visited, his arrival has been honored by a jar.

In the early afternoon, Kröng and Jôong, who had accompanied their *jôok* to Sar Lang last evening, arrive back home. Soon thereafter, the Bboon Khaang guest turns up. Then, around five, Bbaang-the-Stag and the headman of Bboon Jaa, the latter accompanied by two men. They are followed shortly by Baap Can, his wife, and three couples from Nyôong Brah. On reaching Sar Luk, each group goes directly to Baap Can's and takes its place on the big low platform in the rear. When, at last, the master of the house enters, there is no exchange of spoken greetings or handshaking (a custom we French recently introduced, as well as, alas, the military salute). However, as soon as Baap Can has set his burdens down, he distributes a pinch of tobacco among all his guests. Village people present in the room receive their share of the hospitality also. Soon other guests arrive, coming from Paang Pê' Nâm, Düng Jrii, Sar Lang, and Paang Döng.

The atmosphere becomes lively. The guests are numerous and are acquainted with most of the Sar Luk people, who flock to meet friends come from far away. As each Sar Luk villager enters, he begins—if he thinks of it—by offering a pinch of tobacco to each foreigner. People have so many things to tell each other that the visitors' room of Baap Can and Kröng-Jôong is soon buzzing.

Finally, around seven o'clock, Baap Can, the senior guest (Wan-Yôong, of Paang Pê' Nâm), and Mang-Master-of-the-Ivory (headman of Bboon Jaa) join Bbôong-the-Deputy. Crouching on the banana leaf by the door, the deputy holds a live chicken before a small neckless jar for "the blood anointment of feet" (*mhaam jöng*). It is Wan who inserts the drinking straw, as he and his companions ask in unison that everything go well, that the celebration take place amid joy and concord:

"*We are about to anoint the feet of the guests with the
blood of a chicken and a jar of alcohol.
May the roedeer not bell,
may the* pruh *grass put forth no root,
may the* rhôong *and* r'aa *plants not bar our way.
May we have cool bodies,
may we sleep deep,
may our snores be loud.
The* kuang *sell,
the guests arrive.
May the pointy winnowing basket not tear,
may the pitted mortar not split,
may the young men and the young women not spill the grain.
Let us drink, let us eat heartily.
May the magic plant of others travel far.
I command all of you here present
to eat heartily of the chicken,
to drink heartily of the alcohol;
all of you here present, may your bodies be cool.
Do not argue, do not squabble among yourselves;
do not insult, do not revile each other.*"

Bbôong-Mang slips the blade of his knife into the chicken's beak and cracks it. Holding the fowl by its body and bleeding beak, he anoints the foot of Wan and of Master-of-the-Ivory, who then join the other guests on the low platform, where their meal is served them. All the foreigners crowd toward the door, each to present his foot to the witness-director of the celebration. They are mindful not to forget the babies. Each mother loosens her blanket slightly, slips her infant onto her rump, and leans down so that the deputy can mark the nursing child's foot with blood. When everyone, men and women, old and young, has been blessed in this fashion, Bbôong gives the chicken to one of the young men guests, who roasts it, cuts it up, and divides the pieces among the guests.

After the meal, the foreigners—the men only, that is—assemble on the low platform and call for a winnowing basket for "the weighing of the hulled rice" (*weh phei*). A handsome one, spanking new and decorated with geometric designs, is fetched. Baap Can and his go-between join the foreigners. Each guest has taken from his traveling basket a Vietnamese bowl, a little bag containing hulled rice, and a small quantity of food.

Each transfers his rice from his bag to the bowl, then pours it into the winnowing basket, and adds to this gift the egg or packet of salt he has brought. Baap Can admires the things offered him. When all the male guests have poured their offerings into the winnowing basket, the master of the house goes through an exchange of hand kissing with each, and Wan, the eldest man present, launches into a long harangue. He retraces the history of the feast, remarks that Baap Can has been very kind to invite him, and, obviously, in passing sings his host's praises. Wan concludes his address with a short prayer:

> *"Today you, Baap Can, my older brother, you have given*
> *us rice, you have invited us to come eat meat: for*
> *you are about to make the Exchange of Sacrifices*
> *with Ndêh, the former chief of the canton.*
> *May you have a cool body,*
>> *sleep deep,*
>> *snore loud.*
> *May the younger brothers and the older brothers*
>> *catch no sickness and return in health to their*
>> *homes;*
> *may no one stumble on a stone,*
> *may no one step on the stump's horn. . . ."*

At the end, he kisses the hand of Baap Can, who returns his courtesy. All the other male guests recite similar prayers, each of which is followed by hand kissings.

Baap Can responds to Wan's speech with another discourse, delivered—as befits one who is a *"Kuang* of Justice"—at a dizzying speed. He also narrates the history of this *Tâm Bôh* and sets forth the reasons that led him to invite all those who are now gathered around the winnowing basket. He does not forget Bbieng-Dlaang, the chief of Laac Döng Canton, who has unfortunately been prevented from coming. And like Wan before him, he concludes with a prayer:

> *"I have summoned you to eat meat, to drink alcohol,*
> *to speak together.*
>> *May the thread not break,*
>> *may the snare not give way,*
>> *may the kite be enmeshed in it.*
>> *On leaving, may you reach the forest;*
>> *on turning homeward, may you come safely to your village.*
>> *May your body be cool. . . ."*

More kissing of hands. Seated on the smaller platform to the front, six young men are beating rhythmically on their flat gongs.

Baap Can, his go-between, and all his male guests descend from the low platform and squat before the inside ritual barrier, to which two jars are attached. The larger—a costly jar worth the price of four buffaloes—which is fastened to the central sculptured post, contains "the beer of response to the white rice" (*rnööm bööm phei*). The smaller jar is destined for the holy men in Sar Luk. At the foot of the big jar, where the foreigners and their host are gathered, Can cuts the throat of a chicken and collects its blood in a Mnong bowl filled with *coot*. The master of the house and then his go-between perform the mutual kissing of hands with each guest, who then inserts a drinking straw in the jar (one *gut* for each village represented).

The same ceremony but without the chicken sacrifice is enacted at the foot of the small jar with the two other holy men (Kröng-Jôong and Bbaang-the-Pregnant-Man) and Truu acting as partners of Baap Can and Bbôong-Mang. The presence of the canton chief is an innovation owed to the new social order now prevailing, and is accompanied by yet another novelty: when the little jar is opened by the headman of Bboon Jaa, it is I who drink first, then Truu, then his deputy, who cedes his place to Kröng-Jôong, then to Wan, of Paang Pê' Nâm.

This first great drinking bout, which opens the celebration, lasts late into the night.

October 26

As on the preceding days, the village is awakened early by the roll of Baap Can's suspended drum. But even before daybreak, some young men come out of his house and mill feverishly around the buffaloes, which are being readied to be led to the house of Baap Can's ally. Actually, the youths do little more than pass decorations to Krah and Srae, who are taking care of one buffalo, and to the *rnôom* and Can, who are seeing to the other.

Only the head of the victim is adorned. First, two tubes of giant bamboo, the upper sides frayed into plumes, are placed on its horns. The circle begun by the great arc of the horns is completed by a triple hoop of heavy rattan. Then, using the brown bark of a liana which has been cut into very long bands, they wrap the whole—horns, tufted bamboo tubes, and rattan hoops. In constructing this big circle, the men start at the base of one horn, unroll a strip of the liana bark to the base of the other horn, passing it across the animal's forehead; they twist it around the horn, and repeat the whole motion in the opposite direction. They continue this back-and-forth wrapping motion until the animal's forehead has completely disappeared under the liana strips. The buffalo now looks as if it were wearing a helmet surmounted by a great aureole. To the horizontal diameter of this halo the men attach a small board; it is painted with "*sraa* leaf" motifs and both ends are carved in the shape of a crook. Behind this board, the men thrust into the liana bands a generous quantity of *tria'* leaves, which cascade like flowing horse tails to the ground. (Sometimes this adornment is completed by inserting in the tufted bamboo tubes either branches of the *sraa* palm or long, flexible stalks of heavy rattan, the middle section of which has been pared thin and embellished with multicolored threads and tapered white feathers.) Can and the *rnôom* have spent in all twenty minutes to prepare their buffalo. They strengthen the trace ropes. The lead, passed through the nose ring, is doubled and reinforced by being slipped through the trace ring. A second heavy rope is attached by a slip knot to first one, then the other horn.

This work has been performed amid the liveliest excitement. The four leaders of the action shout for a knife, for a length of liana; one will scold the youthful aides, another will berate the buffalo. Baap Can is very nervous and tries to give advice to his *rnôom,* who pays him no mind. The men dart here, run there, shouting in the early-morning light and the fog, which still clings to the booming river at the foot of the cliff. The master of the house urges his people to finish quickly; the sun will soon come up, bringing with it the heat.

Finally, at five minutes past seven, all is ready. Guided by young men holding the longes, the two buffaloes move off at their majestic pace; their heads, surmounted by magnificent vegetal diadems, are pulled up and back by the tug of the reins on their nostrils. The male sacrifice servant leads the march. In a moment, he will protect the procession's advance by blowing on *rkôong* leaves. Even if, this precaution notwithstanding, the roedeer were to begin to bell, the marchers would not retrace their steps. They would simply halt and wait for the animal to stop belling. Ten young men follow the buffaloes. Between the time the victims arrive in Ndut Lieng Krak and we ourselves reach the village, we are forbidden to sleep. A person who sleeps risks having his buffalo-soul attacked by buffalo-souls in the allied and rival village.

Bbôong-Mang makes the rounds of Sar Luk, shouting to the people in each house to hurry. He returns to Baap Can's to give the order of march. Actually, only the foreigners set out at the same time as he; they are the only ones ready. Sar Luk people have a great deal to do first. Not only must they prepare their baggage—that is, get out their best finery and arrange it in their panniers—they must also clean their house, cook their morning meal, not to mention dressing the children, who, naturally, are never on hand when their parents want them. Comes the time to set out, and someone notices that he has forgotten an article of clothing or that a child has disappeared. No sooner has he got under way than some other hitch makes him turn back. What with all this, people do not leave the village together but set off at intervals in small groups.

The go-between marches ahead and alone. Outside Sar Luk, shortly before reaching the first bridge, he tears off a little *rkôong* branch and blows on it to chase away bad omens that could conceivably appear on our journey. Before he throws the *rkôong* branch back into the brush, he wraps it in lalang grass. The track is wide, but nonetheless we advance Indian-file. The line stretches out endlessly, yet is still connected with the village because little groups of late starters constantly join the march. After twenty minutes, Bbôong decides to make a long halt to allow the laggards to catch up with us and to consolidate our file of sixty-five people. Happily, the sun is a member of the party; it quickens and brightens the colors of our rather carnival-like procession. People have not donned their finest clothes for the trip, and our attire is somewhat variegated. Their "Sunday best" is folded and packed in the panniers the women carry. What the marchers are wearing is a bizarre and very colorful mixture of Mnong and imported European and Vietnamese garments; not one person is wearing a costume all of one style. There is even one umbrella, belonging to Mang-Master-of-the-Ivory, whose getup is among the uglier. Like all the Cil Bboon Jaa, he wears only imported Western clothing: today, *cai quan* (Vietnamese trousers), a European-style shirt and vest, a Basque beret, the leather headband of which he has turned inside out, and a towel which he has draped around his shoulders like a kind of neckpiece. Each item is indescribably filthy, which serves to accentuate the look of ethnic debasement one notices in the Cil Bboon Jaa, whereas the Gar have none of it even when they do deck themselves out in mixed clothes. It is interesting to try to imagine what a procession such as ours would have looked like thirty or even twenty years ago, when imported goods had not yet penetrated these regions to any great extent. But it is pointless to mourn the passing of the picturesque: for the Mnong time has not died and they have not, thank God, been dumped in reservations for the benefit of camera-carrying tourists.*

The procession starts out again and weaves its sinuous way along the twisting track. Anyone at the head of the line who turns at no matter what point to look back sees no end to the motley crowd as it advances single-file. The men are armed with *wiah* or sabers and even guns (Truu and his deputy). The women carry panniers or small babies. The young girls hold each other's little finger as they walk; the children frisk about off the beaten path. People chatter and laugh; some young men win passing attention by singing a few songs. As we near the edge of the forest that marches up the pass of Poot Rloo, from which one can glimpse Sar Lang, Bbôong-Mang points out to me another mountain called Noor. Wan, the

---

* Since this was written, in 1954, conditions have worsened grievously. A partial discussion of the ravages caused by United States military action may be found in my address "Ethics and Comfort: An Ethnographer's View of His Profession," *Annual Report, 1972 American Anthropological Association* (1973), pp. 1–17. See also my preface to this edition.

oldest man present, recites for my benefit some lines from a prayer that is related to Noor; it is simply the juxtaposition of the names of four mountains.

At eleven-thirty—an hour and a half after we set out—we reach the *miir* of Ndut Lieng Krak; the track crosses the full length of it. We halt by two streams that flow near its farther border. The village stands some fifty meters ahead but because the terrain is uneven it is still out of sight. Baap Can and Aang-the-Long are forbidden to bathe for the duration of the ceremonies, but everyone else clambers down to wash, the women going to one stream, the men to the other. After these ablutions, they unpack their new—or simply clean—clothes. The women wrap their prettiest skirts around their waists and don Mnong tunics or white calico blouses. As for the men, they definitely ruin what remains of my pleasure in local color. They do, indeed, discard their traveling clothes for the newest attire they possess, but, by preference, they choose European garments. Bbôong-Mang abandons his *suu troany* for a pair of khaki pants; to display his wealth, he wears under his vest—khaki also—two shirts and one pullover; over this he slips a raincoat that the heat will eventually force him to remove; to round out his Western garb—acceptable enough had it not been so exuberant—he adds wool socks, a pair of sandals (given him by me a few days earlier), a Basque beret, a pair of dark sunglasses, and an Army rifle. Truu likewise has dressed in Western style and kept his gun, but also, in a refinement of elegance, he now sports a monstrously filthy necktie. Tall Wan-Jôong finds Army-issue long underwear more to his taste than a Mnong loincloth, beautiful as that may be. Wan-Yôong, the senior guest, has changed into a splendid *suu troany*, but alas he has also pulled on a pair of dreadful Army boots; at the end of his long, bare legs, they look indescribably forlorn.

Our young men who had left this morning to bring over the buffaloes Baap Can is offering his *jôok* arrive now from Ndut. They are coming to bathe in the stream, for they have finally managed to capture—that is, to take down—the little pannier suspended from the giant-bamboo pole mast. Kröng-the-Stutterer was the one to perform this exploit. It means that we may now enter the allied village. Soon we hear the music of flat gongs approaching; the orchestra halts behind a fold of earth, so that the players and we are invisible to each other. They will not stop playing until long after we have entered the village.

Kröng-Jôong's daughter brings Baap Can and his go-between a small decorated basket containing glutinous rice. The master of the celebration squats before it, praying for good health:

> ". . . *The powerful ones pull in harness;*
> *the foreigners arrive.*
> *Clearing the forest, we transport the stumps;*

fishing by the little dam, we follow our ancestors;
exchanging children,
exchanging lovers, we follow the daughter of the
    maternal uncle.
May the pointy winnowing basket not be torn. . . ."

When the prayer is finished, Bbôong-the-Deputy takes the pointy basket and gives everyone a small handful of glutinous rice; it is eaten on the spot. As the go-between is making his distribution and cracking his habitual jokes, three young girls from Ndut pass by, each bowed under the burden she carries. They know us all, but they walk by with lowered eyes and do not say a word. "They are intimidated because there are so many of us," Truu tells me.

Baap Can's gongs, which a young boy has carried this far on his back, are now unwrapped. Each of the six *cing* is entrusted to a young man. We are now ready to approach the village. The go-between marches at the head of the line; the *kuang* of Sar Luk and other villages follow, then our *cing* players, and then all the rest of Sar Luk, women and children included. The Ndut orchestra sallies out to meet us. When it comes abreast of us, the players halt on our left, waiting for all of us to pass so that they can follow, thus bringing up the rear.

The people of Ndut have assembled by Ndêh's house. The former canton chief sits in the middle of his roofed veranda, surrounded by his guests and the more prominent members of his village. Each man has before him a tiny heap of food offerings. The ritual veranda is too narrow to accommodate all the heads of household in Ndut, so the less rich are clustered around it on both sides.

Our procession approaches to the sound of the two flat-gong orchestras. The men of Ndut rise to welcome us. At that moment, the splendid parade of Sar Luk *kuang* and their guests breaks up. With lowered heads, every man in it bears down on the people of Ndut, snorting *"Kuî! Kuî!"*— this in a very nasal voice, in imitation of a charging buffalo. The people of Ndut respond with the same cries. This is the *tâm ge'*, a term denoting how buffaloes fight. Then each local man takes the hand of a new arrival who has been assigned to him as partner for the duration of the festival, and leads him to his serving basket, which is filled with food. Our gongs, meanwhile, led by Kröng-the-Stutterer, perform their ritual circuit. Beating steadily on their *cing*, the players turn several times around the great pole mast, then around the ensemble formed by the buffaloes and the sacrificial posts to which they are tethered, then around the veranda where the *kuang* of both villages and their guests are now installed; lastly, using Ndêh's private door, the players enter the house, where they have been preceded by the musicians of Ndut, who earlier had brought up our rear and who had gone into the house by the main door.

Most new arrivals halt a few steps from the veranda, where the men are offering the ritual exchange of food. This tightly packed mass includes chiefly women and children, but also a few men who had been overlooked when partners from Ndut were assigned. Bbôong-Mang immediately notices this. He guides each solitary Sar Luk man to a Ndut villager who has also been left alone, and the partners go to squat, two by two, on either side of a serving basket of foodstuffs. On the far side from where we entered the village, the young women and children of Ndut Lieng Krak form a compact, curious mass; they are silent, but their eyes devour the scene before them.

The performance that had begun upon our arrival continues with multiple "exchanges of food" (*tâm siam*). Each man from Ndut offers his Sar Luk partner a bottle of *rnööm* and a serving basket of food (a heap of glutinous rice topped by a few bananas and, among the better-off, by an egg or even a bit of pork). Then, picking up a tube (or a glass) of rice beer, he lifts it to his guest's lips, praying:

> "While cutting the meat, do not hurt your hand;
> while drinking the rnööm, do not get a bellyache.
> May you eat pork at every Rite of the Straw;
> may you eat goat at every village site newly abandoned;
> may you cut the bamboo tubes at every village site newly rebuilt.
> May you tomorrow and the day after tomorrow again eat meat;
> may you tomorrow and the day after tomorrow again drink alcohol. . . ."

The person who receives the offering murmurs more or less identical prayer couplets, and drinks. In turn, he fills the tube with rice beer and lifts it to his host's lips, reciting the same prayer. Then the Ndut host takes a big fistful of glutinous rice, on which he places a peeled banana or preferably, if he has it, an egg or some pork. He cups his hands and raises the food to the lips of his guest, repeating the same prayer. The guest nibbles a few grains of rice and slips his hands under his host's to receive the food. Meanwhile, the wife of the Ndut man goes to find his partner's wife and leads her to where the two husbands are carrying out their exchange of food. When the men have finished, the guest hands over to his wife the food and the bottle of *rnööm* he has received, and she puts them in her pannier.

Lôong-Rau, Ndêh's go-between, receives Bbôong-Mang-the-Deputy, his opposite number from Sar Luk. He offers Bbôong drink not from a glass but from a fine buffalo horn with a rattan handle and decorated with multicolored threads and red pompons. Truu is the guest of the village headman, who goes so far as to honor his bureaucratic superior with the offer of a chair; unfortunately, it is rather wobbly. Bbaang-Jieng-the-Pregnant-Man, our third holy man, and Mang-Master-of-the-Ivory, headman of Bboon Jaa, both have the same partner, my friend Kroong-Biing. As for our *rnôom*, he is circulating among the guests in high spirits and carrying, suspended from his shoulder, a very beautiful, meter-long tube. It is made from an internode of giant bamboo, carved along its entire length, and adorned with colored threads. This magnificent vessel has been presented to him, as custom requires, by his colleague in Ndut. It is filled with rice beer, which one sips through a straight drinking straw, the upper end of which scarcely extends beyond the mouth of the tube.

It is almost one o'clock in the afternoon when Lôong-Rau sets a *yang dâm* of rice beer on the veranda, between the door and the roofed section. It is meant for his colleague from Sar Luk, I am told, "to repay him for his pains in blowing on the *rkôong* leaves" and is called "the *rnööm* to fan the go-between's sweat" (*rnööm prah rhaal ndroany*). The beer is drunk without ceremony or prayer of any sort.

Presently the two allies rise and Ndêh hoists Baap Can on his back, setting off an explosion of laughter. This, however, is a ritual act; on ordinary occasions, one must not carry a person on one's back for the fun of it, but in this instance one does so "in accordance with the teaching of the Ancestors." Ndêh crosses the threshold, sets his friend down, and leads him by the hand to the low platform at the rear, near the granary. The two go-betweens enter next, but they pause at the foot of the column facing the main door; here is where the chicken and the small neckless jar for "the blood anointment of feet" have been placed. As the two men pray to the Spirits that the celebration may be joyful and that there be no illness, Bbôong-Mang inserts the drinking straw in the *yang dâm* and brushes the head of the chicken with its broken beak over the feet of all those who have come today from Sar Luk, including our guests and the young men who earlier accompanied the sacrificial buffaloes. Soon the music of the two gong groups is almost drowned by chatter and laughter, as the joyous crowd pours into the house. The gaiety barometer soars, and the celebration begins to resemble a village fair. The crowd's holiday mood, primed by even the little drink consumed so far; the festive appearance of the visitors' room, embellished with ritual decorations and a row of twenty-five jars of rice beer reaching from one granary to the other—all this, with its vast promise of drinking and revelry, would smooth away the dourest frown. After the anointment of feet, each new arrival follows his Ndut partner, who guides him to the jar he has opened and filled with water before our arrival.

When the anointment-of-feet ceremony has been performed for all, the two go-betweens join the two friends on the low platform. In the center of the space around which the four men sit, the mistress of the house places a winnowing basket with geometric designs. It contains a huge flat pastry made of fermented rice flour—the basis for making *rnööm*—and a Mnong bowl filled with wort; the wort has been taken from the large ancient jar attached to the carved post of the inner ritual barrier. Baap Can hands Bbôong-Mang, who is seated on his left, a large Vietnamese bowl filled with white rice. The go-between holds it above the pastry, then presents it to Lôong-Rau, sitting opposite him; this is "the weighing of the hulled rice" (*weh phei*). Lôong-Rau repeats the gesture to Ndêh, on his right. Then the four men, each supporting the bowl with both hands above the pastry, announce that they are performing the reciprocal offering of fermented rice (*tâm triu ndrii*), that they will kill two buffaloes; they pray that all may enjoy good health and that understanding prevail for the duration of the celebration. They place the big bowl of white rice in the winnowing basket. Each man takes a pinch of wort and anoints the pastry. This will be removed by Aang-the-Long, while Ndêh's wife will take the bowl of hulled rice. Baap Can's guest from Düng Jrii presents his "weighing of hulled rice" to Ndêh, for the former canton chief too had sent a messenger to invite him. During this ceremony, close to the four men on the platform, the women are eating.

Suddenly a vast hum fills the house. Paired hosts and guests are praying by the jars as the guest inserts the drinking straw. The four principals step down from the platform and squat before the jars attached to the ritual barrier. The go-betweens take their position before the left jar, the two friends squat before the large ancient jar attached to the central post. (The jar on the right has already been opened by Kröng-Jôong, Baap Can's brother-in-law, who received it from Ngee-Ddôong, Ndêh's elder brother.) The former canton chief passes a straw to Baap Can and another to his *jôok*'s future son-in-law, Srae-Jaang. They insert the straws and pray. In substance, they say that they are offering two buffaloes and a large jar of rice beer so that everyone may enjoy good health and that all may go well.

Lôong-Rau stands up and we follow him in "the leading to the water of the jars" (*lâm daak yang*). Even if he takes only a mouthful, everyone must taste the *rnööm* in each of the twenty-five jars. The ceremony begins with the jar attached to the last post of the neighboring granary and ends with those placed beneath the granary of our host, with a detour to the low platform to sample the *yang dâm* the former canton chief offered before the *tâm triu ndrii* ceremony to Bbaang-Jieng-the-Pregnant-Man and his son-in-law. The procedure is that one stands and sucks up several swallows of rice beer through the straw the man standing opposite has just offered; after drinking, one hands this *gut* to the person behind and, in turn, accepts the straw offered by the man in front of one. In this way, all the straws pass from hand to hand as people file by. Normally, Ndêh's go-between would be followed by Baap Can's go-between, then by the two friends themselves, the other *kuang*, and finally the other men and the

women and children of both villages. Because of my presence, this traditional order has been slightly changed: I come immediately after Lôong-
Rau, Truu follows me, then Bbôong-the-Deputy, and the others without
further change.

When everyone has filed by the jars, each person returns to his own jar
and the serious drinking begins. The crowd fills not only the immense visitors' room of Ndêh and his neighbor but also the areas beneath the two
granaries—the spot preferred by the women—where, for lack of space, a
few jars have been placed. It is difficult to move about in the two *hih
nâm*. At least two people are by each jar; of two partners, one is drinking,
while the other awaits his turn, pouring water into the jar the while. (Actually, often a child or adolescent is responsible for seeing to it that the
level of the rice beer is maintained.) Everyone is talking, the drinker included. The foreigner drinks first; he must ingest a certain number
(always equal) of measures, after which he relinquishes his place to his
host, who must consume the same quantity. Then the guest returns to the
straw, and the game begins anew until they break off and relinquish their
places to another pair of drinking enthusiasts. Generally, the quantity to
be consumed is quite large, so a drinker can now and then offer a glass or
a bamboo tube that he has filled with the help of the straw to someone
else in the group. Even at ordinary times, "the exchange of drinks" has
nothing to do with a sacramental act; it is, above all, an opportunity to
gossip and joke. When the effects of the alcohol are felt and if the partners
have a modicum of wit, the tippling bout is augmented by a singing contest. One readily imagines what a tremendous hubbub can reign in a
room where some hundred and fifty people are jammed together and
where couples, or trios, or even quartets cluster around each of twenty-
five aligned jars.

At such a celebration, the quantity of alcohol consumed and the clamor
invite trouble, and possible discord must be headed off. It is the go-
between, of course, who is responsible for policing the affair. After two
hours of steady drinking, Lôong-Rau rises to his feet, picks up the horn
fitted with a handle, fills it with rice beer, and offers it to Bbôong-Mang.
His partner refuses to take it and does not stir from his place on the low
platform. So Lôong approaches Mang from Bboon Jaa; he also declines
the honor, declaring that he does not feel he is worthy to accompany the
go-between in his address. Lôong then appeals to Wan-Yôong, the senior
guest. Wan protests:

"Bbôong-the-Deputy's the man to perform such a task, not a poor man
like me."

"But Bbôong-Mang has refused."

"Well, anyhow, I don't know how to do it."

There is nothing for it; all Lôong-Rau can do now is to fall back on

Kroong-Ngee, the headman of Ndut, and he, being a good sort, agrees.*
The go-between climbs up on the low platform, positions himself so that
he can be seen by the entire audience, and brandishes his saber
(sheathed), from which he has hung a young chicken by its feet. With all
his might, he bawls the harangue called the *praang baal:*

"Eh, you, all of you! Children and young fry, oldsters and graybeards,
listen carefully to what I say. Do not quarrel with each other, do not
squabble among yourselves. Do not strike each other, do not lay about
you with sticks or clubs. Drink heartily, eat heartily, sing, strike the
bossed gongs and the flat gongs. . . . Let everything be beautiful and
joyful. But if someone does not listen to my instructions, I—I myself—
will take action against him. Anybody who tries to pick a quarrel or to
fight, I—I myself—will take action against him. . . ."

The headman of Ndut, meanwhile, is circulating among the crowd with
the drinking horn. He offers the upright straw inserted in it to each guest,
and each takes a small sip of *rnööm*. On the platform, Lôong-Rau is punc-
tuating every word of his harangue with a sweep of his saber, the
wretched chicken flapping its wings and clucking in despair. Kraang-
Drüm walks up to the go-between and brusquely wrenches the chicken
free. People from Sar Luk shout their approval, for this means that the
bird, which will be cooked, reverts to them. The entire episode lasts
perhaps ten minutes, and in no way interferes with the revelry.

Night has already fallen when, around seven-thirty, Lôong-Rau leaves
the house carrying a small rattan box with geometric designs that contains
saffroned rice. The go-between clambers up onto the ritual stall which
stands between the main door and the sacrificial posts to which the two
buffaloes sent over this morning by Baap Can are tethered. He squats on
the narrow, high-perched stall and throws handfuls of saffroned rice into
the air above the roof of the house, then over the two victims standing
peacefully by their posts. He summons the Spirits:

> "O Spirit of the Earth,
> O Spirit of the Soil,
> Spirit of the Environs,
> Spirit of the Leaves,
> Spirit of the Foliage,
> Spirit of the Threads,
> Spirit of the Spinning Wheel,
> Spirit of the Plain,
> Spirit of the Valley,
> I summon ye all.
> And thou, Spirit of the Door,

---

* I should point out that the headmen of Bboon Jaa and Ndut Lieng Krak, as well as Wan,
of Paang Pê' Nâm, are holy men in their respective villages.

> *Spirit of the Pallet,*
> *Spirit of Daybreak,*
> *Spirit of Moonlight,*
> *Spirit of Sunset,*
>   *I summon ye also. . . ."*

Numerous verses, varied and profoundly sonorous, follow. The scene, which is lighted only by a resin torch, is most appealing.

More grandiose poetry still is recited three quarters of an hour later: "The Song to the Buffaloes" (*Tong Rpuh*). Maang-Ddôong, the son-in-law of Ndêh, grasps a bamboo tube containing rice beer taken from all the jars. A small pine torch held by a friend lights his way as he slips between the edge of the roof and the sacrificial posts, climbs up onto the ritual stall, and sits down between the two victims. A group of young men and women who are connoisseurs of songs from bygone days accompany him. They crowd in between roof and stall, the better to hear. The tapering flames of their resin torches cast a bright glow over the singer, who, clasping his fire-worked bamboo tube, sits firmly ensconced on the ritual stall. They illuminate also the heads of the buffaloes surmounted by their splendid vegetal haloes, and the manifold designs on the sacrificial posts; in the darkness, they disclose the massive shadows of the buffaloes, the elongated shadows of the ritual decor, which is at once light and musical. As the flames flicker in the wind, the shadows shift; they change form and size, now concealing, now revealing men and objects that seem to dance with them. Maang pours a few drops of rice beer on the forehead of Master Krae, one of the two beasts offered by Baap Can. His voice rises softly at first, grows louder, then modulates as he sings one after another of the mythic poems that retrace the deeds of the First Men, the Great Ancestors:

> *". . . We tether the stone-buffalo there far below, splendid;*
> *we tether the eggplant-buffalo there far below, splendor;*
> *we tether the bitter-herb-buffalo there far below, Pöt Taang;*
> *we tether the bamboo-shoot-buffalo there far below, open*
>   *to us.*
>
> *Enter, you who serve, admirable* rnôom;
> *enter, you who serve,* rnôom *of great beauty,*
> *serve soup to the Magpie, offer alcohol from the* ntaang *jar;*
> *serve soup to the Blackbird, offer alcohol from the libation horn;*
> *serve Yee, accomplish your task by fashioning the headdress*
>   *of pheasant feathers;*
> *and Yoong, by planting the thick tufted tubes;*
> *and Yee, by planting the leaves of the sraa palm. . . ."* *

---

* It is extremely difficult to convey in translation the beauty of these esoteric songs. The musicality of the original language and the exceptionally skillful use of the resources it offers,

As he sings, Maang now and then pours a few drops of rice beer on the buffalo's forehead; responding to his voice, Master Krae finally lies down. But Ndêh's son-in-law has no success with Master Joong. After a half hour, wearying of the struggle, the young man hands his bamboo tube over to a girl nearby, and she is able to charm the second buffalo into lying down. Then we all troop inside to rejoin the clamorous revelry, abandoning to the night the two magnificent beasts and the vast decor created for their immolation.

October 27

Very early, the suspended drum and the *cing* resound at Ndêh's house, rousing anyone who might still be asleep. As early as six-thirty, people are drinking from the several jars. In fact, many did not close their eyes all night long, or drowsed only for a moment; in particular, the two *jôok* aspire to stay awake throughout the night. Some Sar Luk people stole and ate two chickens belonging to the master of the house; this was meant to prove their fighting spirit.

A large antique jar attached to the last post of the granary—the one before the private door—is opened, and the rice beer is siphoned off through a straw into an enormous metal pot. Dduu-Phaang, a holy man in Ndut, cuts the throat of a chicken above a Mnong jar filled with wort from this jar. He carries the bowl outside to anoint the foreheads of the two buffaloes. Then, standing before the last post of the granary, while he chants "a summons to the Spirits in the belly of the Paddy," he blesses the granary wall with the blood-drenched wort.

Outside, the two animals are on their feet. Armed with a saber, Bbôong-Mang approaches the one on the right, leaps forward, and with swift, heavy blows, severs the tendon above its rear hocks. The animal falls back on its hindquarters and tries vainly to kick. It lurches against its neighbor, whom Maang-Ddôong, Ndêh's son-in-law, attacks in turn. Maddened by pain, the two buffaloes manage to keep themselves upright on their bleeding stumps; they flounder around the stakes to which they are tethered, stagger into each other, and splash the onlookers with mud soiled by dung and blood. Holding his saber in both hands, Maang brandishes it over his head, the tip pointing down. He thrusts, and strikes the

---

as well as the vast mythological context that the verses evoke in a condensed form, contribute to their beauty. To explain the mythology adequately here would require a long and tedious commentary that could only smother completely the affective response aroused in the Mnong listener by these sonorous songs. I have had occasion to discuss the subject in connection with another mythic Mnong Gar song dedicated to the Flood.

Here I will simply note that the first poem deals with fruitless endeavors by the first men to perform a great sacrifice. Not yet having buffaloes at their disposal, they tried to sacrifice vegetables. The second deals with the tradition established by the first *rnôom,* who served the mythic beings and ancestors—the Magpie and the Blackbird, Yee and Yoong.

side of the first buffalo; despite the animal's lurching, he is able to drive his saber in up to the hilt; he probes around, searching for the heart. The animal falls on its right side, unfortunately thus spilling its blood on the ground. Old Krah kills the second buffalo; people rush up to tamp grass into the wounds from which blood is spurting. The first victim is bellowing in its death throes; the female *rnôom* comes on the run with a gourd and pours water on its bloody nostrils, for at all costs the animal must be prevented from groaning.

The two buffaloes are dead. The mistress of the house comes out bearing "funeral offerings" (*njat rpuh*), which she places on the heads of both victims: large Vietnamese bowls, skirts, a short loincloth embroidered all over (this is made specially for the *Tâm Bôh*), and a spinning wheel. Retrieving the wheel, she turns the handle above the head of one of the victims and recites:

> "Do not be afraid, do not flee,
>   O Souls of the Buffaloes, Souls of the Jars.
>   Do not be in fear of me,
> so that in the future I can again eat meat, again drink alcohol. . . ."

She has placed a valuable *yang dâm* between the belly and thighs of each buffalo. While she officiated thus, her son-in-law was cutting the long strands of *tria'* leaves that formed part of the decoration on their horns.

Inside the house, the *kuang* use glasses to dip rice beer from the big metal pot; they drink, while the holy man, facing the granary, continues to pray.

A young man from Sar Luk, Kraang-Dlaang, cuts off the tails of both beasts. Bbôong-Mang is anxious to adorn his drumsticks with them, so he directs the operation, insisting that the other man cut off only the hairy tips. Other young men cut off the testicles; when braised, these are a great treat for the children, who compete for them among themselves. What remains of the genitals is wound around the wooden horns of the sacrificial posts. A wide gash is made in the groin of each animal and the viscera are removed; some boys carry them forthwith to the river to clean and cook.

The holy man's prayer ended a few moments after the buffaloes' death. The *kuang* continue to drink. Now the women go to eat on the rear platform, where serving baskets of rice and large bowls of steaming vegetables have been set out. Each woman pours water from a gourd over her right hand before she steps up on the platform for her meal.

Nhee-Pöt suddenly turns up. Last evening, he could not leave Düng Jrii, because his wife had fallen ill. He brings me two eggs, and two more for his friend Bbôong-the-Deputy. Among other things, he tells us that their canton chief, an "eater of goods" (belonging to people under his jurisdiction), was preparing to leave for Dran, the district capital, and had threatened to have him summoned there.*

The execution of the sacrificial victims is the major event in this celebration, yet in fact it is soon over. The merrymaking continues apace. Kröng-the-Stutterer, in top form as always, challenges Ndêh's young female *rnôom* to a drinking contest. The girl can hold her beer no less well than he, and the competition, which proceeds with paired liters of rice beer, does not daunt her in the slightest. For a long time, the outcome is uncertain.

At nine-twenty, the *kuang* emerge onto the small roofless veranda built in front of the private door. They squat around a large metal pot and a winnowing basket in which various objects have been placed: several fireworked drinking tubes, a pot of *rnööm*, a big serving basket of glutinous rice, a large bowl of cooked tripes chopped into small pieces and covered with traces of some other rather suspect matter. The big metal pot contains a greenish soup garnished with sliced rounds of innards; a young man heightens the flavor of this dish by tossing in diced red pepper and fragrant herbs.

The exchanges of food (*tâm siam*), identical to those made upon our arrival, are repeated to the recitation of the same prayers. But whereas yesterday the *tâm siam* took place between separate couples, this morning only Ndêh offers drink and food to all the *kuang*, one after another, including those from his own village, and in turn receives the same from them. First, Ndêh honors his *jôok*. He lifts a tube of *rnööm* to Baap Can's lips, then places in his cupped hands a huge fistful of glutinous rice on which a helper has laid three morsels of entrails none too carefully cleaned. Baap Can kisses the rice and pretends to take up a few grains between his lips; he prays together with Ndêh as he receives the gift of food, which he passes on to his second son, who has come to watch the scene. In turn, Baap Can offers his *jôok* a tube of rice beer and a handful of rice with tripes. Ndêh then makes the rounds of the other *kuang*, and each man reciprocates his courtesy:

> ". . . *Let us eat chicken together,*
> *let us drink rice beer together.* . . ."

The ethnologist takes part in the ceremony, obviously, and shares the meal of tripes that follows. Taken aback by the strange taste of this dish and slightly uneasy about the broth, I say as much, whereupon Kroong-Biing succinctly enlightens me: "It's just buffalo shit," he says. And, in fact, only the large intestine is voided in the river; the contents of the

---

* To be sent to what, by Montagnard standards, was such a large and distant city would amount to exile. —*Trans.*

paunch and the rest are tossed into the huge metal pot and cooked in
water as *"tripes à la mode mnong,"* so to speak.

People eat, drink, and joke. Truu loves to get under the skin of his
"brother" Kroong-Biing and the latter's *jôok*, Mang-Master-of-the-Ivory,
with whom Kroong is soon to make an Exchange of Sacrifices. Speaking
loud enough for the gallery to hear, Truu says to me, "You know, Yoo,
they're really powerful men. They're going to sacrifice three buffaloes
apiece." Kroong-the-Short merely laughs and says, "He's lying." But not
the headman of Bboon Jaa; he will not let the matter rest: "Don't listen to
him, Yoo. He's telling stories. There's not a word of truth in what he says,
not a word!" Each time Truu repeats his teasing charge, Mang leaps up
and protests vehemently. This somehow leads to their explaining to me
how the *kuang's* nicknames are assigned. The headman of Bboon Jaa, for
example, is commonly known as Mang-Master-of-the-Ivory. The explanations spark a series of rhymed jokes that sometimes really do poke fun at
the *kuang* who bears the moniker in question. Our hero, Baap Can, is
called Taang-Dâm-Tlaang (*tlaang* meaning sparrow hawk), which gives
rise to:

> *"Taang-Master-of-the-Sparrow-Hawk*
> *flies over the wives of other men;*
> *seeks out Yôong-the-Mad . . .*
> *and has by her a son, Bbaang. . . ."*

This unlocks a flood of heartfelt protestations from the interested party.
For Yôong-the-Mad is the "little mother" of Baap Can's wife; therefore, a
very strong sexual prohibition, an extremely serious taboo, exists between
her and him. On the other hand, Yôong-the-Mad did indeed have a "love
child" (a Mnong expression) some years after her husband's death; later, I
was given to understand that the putative father of little Bbaang was
Bbôong-the-Deputy. To attribute paternity to Baap Can is rather mon-
strous, but jokes that consist in accusing someone of having violated the
taboo of the mother-in-law or of the elder sister-in-law are the ones the
Gar most relish.

Around ten o'clock, while we were joking and carousing on the veranda, some of the young men began to carve up the buffaloes. Nor is
Ndêh's house the only place in Ndut where people are celebrating; several other households have opened jars. Kroong-Biing's brother-in-law is
toasting visitors—relatives of his wife, who came originally from Nyôong
Brah. In the same visitors' room, my *jôok* is entertaining the two women
in the party, Aang-Sieng and Jôong-Sieng. This nets me an enumeration
of the fifteen buffalo sacrifices Kroong-the-Short has performed in the
course of his life.

The victims having now been dismembered, Ndêh personally directs the

Baap Can receives "the exchange of food" from the hands of his jôok, *Ndêh*

distribution of his gifts of meat. Every choice portion is offered to one or another guest. The gift is identical to one previously received from that person, or it serves to initiate an exchange of reciprocal gifts. Two portions are held in reserve and presented as honorariums: by right, a shoulder is allotted to Ndêh's *jôok*—i.e., Baap Can—and an entire tenderloin is awarded to Lôong-Rau, his go-between.

At two-thirty in the afternoon, a small neckless jar of *rnööm* is brought out onto the big roofed veranda. This jar is destined for the final "exchange of nourishment" in this first phase of the *Tâm Bôh*. However, either everyone is weary after a sleepless night or the drink is weak, for the rites that follow take place in an atmosphere of absolute torpor. Next, as tradition requires, the gifts Ndêh is offering are brought out. Called the *tâm triu*, the ensemble of presents is a true sampling of the clothing, adornments, tools, and even the crockery that a Mnong possesses. Compared to equivalent objects in daily use—although ultimately these will be put to such use—each item has been made with particular care and some are even artistically worked. Wickerwork objects are embellished with black designs against their natural-colored background; some utensils are decorated with colored threads. The collection also includes items of a more specially ritual nature: one such is the small loincloth embroidered with black and white motifs and bordered by two all-red bands, which the mistress of the house placed on the dead buffaloes and then tied to one of the sacrificial posts. This *suu troany ding door* is always of very fine workmanship and is woven only for Exchanges of Sacrifices.

Now the beautiful horn filled with rice beer is fetched. Baap Can, Ndêh, and Ndêh's elder brother, Ngee-Ddôong, hold above its mouth a few morsels of buffalo heart, some grains of cooked rice, and little cubes cut from the tuber of the magic plant of the Paddy belonging to Ndêh's clan. The three men recite numerous prayers:

> ". . . May the Buffaloes return on the right,
>   may the Paddy return on the left,
> may there be children whom one can cradle against one's breast.
>   May the Souls not be routed
>   and thereby be enslaved,
>   and thereby be lost to hearing.
>   Souls of the Buffaloes on the crest of the Rlaa,
>   Soul of the Paddy on the crest of the Grain,
> Ntô' Jars, Ntaang Jars aligned the length of the house . . ."

The two brothers open their hands, and the small ritual offerings fall. They peer inside the horn to see what is happening: everything has sunk as it should. In turn, Baap Can releases his handful, and again the auspices are favorable: heart, rice, and magic plant have sunk to the bottom of the horn. The two brothers lift it to Baap Can's lips and, with the shouts of the assembled guests reinforcing their own howls, they make him drink the entire contents of this enormous ciborium in a single draught. Not only must Baap Can swallow two to three liters of rice beer; he also must eat the grains of rice and the bits of heart and magic plant that were dropped into the horn. This feat accomplished, the two *jôok* offer each other glutinous rice and some meat from the buffaloes sacrificed this morning. Lôong-Rau arrives meanwhile with a thong of buffalo hide. He slips it around Baap Can's neck, pretends to strangle him, and, laughing the while, shouts all manner of threats at the *jôok* were he to perjure himself. Bellows and cheers from the other *kuang*.

Finally, the moment of departure comes. People set out in small groups, everyone slightly the worse for drink. The male *rnôom* is so loaded down with the gifts offered his master that he has had to entrust his own long, fire-worked tube filled with rice beer to a friend. Mang-Master-of-the-Ivory totters along the track, coming now and then for a few sips. Baap Can's departure has been saluted with a drum fanfare by his friend's people; Aang-the-Long is carrying little Dür and clutching a white chicken. In small, jolly groups we walk tranquilly along the track home. We are utterly oblivious of the tiger's existence.

It is around five-thirty when we arrive in Sar Luk. Some young men had returned earlier, and they are busy preparing the tall pole mast— stuffing it, that is, with various ingredients. The actual decoration of the *rlaa* is finished. A carved bird has been attached to the very top; three quarters of the way up the trunk are affixed a pair of wooden horns and two broad palm branches arched like immense wings, each extended by a construction of thread and small wooden platelets. These act like a sort of musical mobile; the slightest breeze sets them to tinkling gently.

Each internode of the giant bamboo has been pierced near the base, and it is into these holes that the young men are pouring some horrid concoction they mix in two mortars. *Pae troo (Alocasia?)* and the bark of the *mang blier* liana are ground together; this makes an extremely viscous paste, which they dilute with water. To this the men add a big tubeful of putrid pig's blood; it contributes a nauseating smell. They then rub the entire length of the giant bamboo with pork fat, and quickly pass a flaming torch over it so that the pole mast becomes not only shiny but very slippery. The final touch: one young man has prepared a goodly quantity of wild-pepper juice. He pours some into each hole and over the horns and upper section of the pole, rubbing it in with pepper-plant leaves. When a man tries to scale the pole, they tell me, he naturally sweats and this "unguent" penetrates the skin and causes a frightful itching.

A strip of *mang blier*, securely knotted, seals off the hole in each internode; the lower holes are plugged with pieces of rattan, the outer end of which is rolled into a ring.

With a bamboo borer, Troo-Jôong is digging the pit into which the *rlaa* will be sunk, once it is entirely ready. Bbôong-Mang had chosen a spot directly opposite the small veranda. Baap Can was beside himself: "It's forbidden to dig in this spot!" He indicated another, halfway between the two verandas and at the same level as Kröng-Jôong's big pole, raised a month ago. Nearby, two young men have slaughtered a small porker with one knife stroke, disemboweled it, and now are roasting it on a spit.

Under the roof of the main veranda, assorted objects have been set out: a pot of *rnöom* taken from a small neckless jar, a serving basket of glutinous rice, a pot of pork tripes, a freshly killed chicken together with the piglet, bits of the magic plant of Coolness, the liter of Vietnamese brandy given by Ndêh, three drinking tubes, and the Mnong bowl of wort impregnated with the blood of the slaughtered chicken and porker. A small cone-shaped harvest basket has been filled with glutinous rice, eggs, three bananas, and pork tripes; this *khiu* is then attached to the horns of the pole mast. Baap Can's guests and the men of Sar Luk gather on the ritual veranda around these victuals. Bbôong-Mang is dead drunk and quite unable to come alive; he is replaced as go-between by Kröng-Jôong, who has donned the ritual loincloth he received from his friend Choong-Yôong at the time of their Exchange of Sacrifices a month ago.

Baap Can begins by offering the Vietnamese brandy, first to me, then Kröng-Jôong, then Truu. Someone shouts to the young men, calling for music, and immediately, inside the house of the master of ceremonies, the drum and the orchestra of flat gongs resound. Baap Can next offers us some *rnöom*, and, in accord with the rites, he recites a few wishes. He begins with Kröng-Jôong, he being the substitute go-between, and also gives him the anointing bowl. He then has the other holy man, Bbaang-the-Pregnant-Man, drink. Truu politely cedes his turn to me, and then come two guests who are still able to stand, and Bbaang-the-Stag. Each man returns Baap Can's offering, observing the same ceremony.

A huge bonfire lights the yard. The immense pole mast is lying aslant a series of forked supports of graduated height. It is so long that the flames illumine only the horns and the great palm wings; the crest and the bird atop it remain in shadow. The *cing* file out of the house and line up beside the pole. The *kuang* rise, each having taken a pinch of the blood-drenched wort, and go to squat along the same side of the *rlaa,* which they anoint as they pray:

> ". . . Do not speak to me in anger.
> do not crush me with your wrath.
> We serve you,
> O chief Tree, O chief Bamboo.

The jôok *would be strangled were he to commit perjury*

> *We do as did our Ancestors before us;*
> *as did our female Forebears in the past;*
> *as did our male Forebears in the past. . . ."*

While the *kuang* pray aloud, the six *cing* players move along the row of crouching celebrants, covering the resonant murmur of their prayers with the sound of music. The players turn around the base of the mast and march the length of the bole but do not circle the hole in which the *rlaa* will be set.

When the *kuang* have completed their prayer, they rise to their feet, which is a signal for the other men to rush in a group toward the *rlaa*. They strain to raise it; those near the foot simply push with both hands, while the others use bamboos lashed together in the form of a St. Andrew's cross for leverage. To reinforce and coordinate their efforts, each push is accompanied by tremendous shouts that drown out the music of the flat gongs. Troo-Jôong has stationed himself on the far side of the hole. He steadies a tilted plank against which the base of the pole mast rests, so that he can guide the giant bamboo as it slips into the hole. Throughout this collective maneuver, the flat gongs never stop playing; their deep-throated song resounds in the intervals between the men's "heave-ho's." In the darkness, the torches splash light on the trunk and trembling arms of the pole mast as it jerks upward. Once vertical, it seems to hesitate for a moment, then suddenly plunges into its hole, setting off a tremendous ovation. Four men strain to hold it upright, while others tamp the earth around the base. Then the musicians circle around the mast, towering and quivering in the darkness of night.

Baap Can and the two other holy men move through the dimly lighted yard toward the sacrificial posts, for which holes have been prepared also during the afternoon. The master of the house throws in each some glutinous rice, pork tripes, and bits of the magic plant of Coolness, as he recites:

> *". . . To plant the Bombax,*
> *to hold the thread.*
> *To sink deep in welcoming it,*
> *to sink deep the Ancestor, the Forebear,*
> *to sink deep the bony Bombax. . . ."*

He amplifies this with couplets asking that all accidents may be averted.

The *rnôom* wraps a large sheet of bark around each spiny trunk in order to carry it more easily to where it will be planted. The hole is ringed by a halter.* Krông-Jôong anoints each sacrificial post with blood-drenched

---

* The halter has two main parts: a large ring, which is slipped around the sacrificial post, and the halter proper, made of two arms that encircle the withers. The terminal loops are laced together over the animal's neck. Halter and ring are firmly bound together by a tough

wort and Bbaang-the-Pregnant-Man does the same to the barrier, each man reciting the prayer Baap Can has just offered.

All this while, the *cing* have been circling the tall pole mast. They march around it eight times, then perform another series of circuits, always counterclockwise, around the sacrificial posts and barrier. They then make one turn around the veranda on which the *kuang* have regrouped, and they enter the house through the main door. On the roofed veranda, Baap Can offers his brother-in-law a handful of glutinous rice topped by pork tripes and the two claws of the sacrificed chicken, reciting the same prayer as before. He then performs the ritual exchange of nourishment with all the *kuang* present. People eat and drink, but everyone is weary, and very soon they disperse to get some rest.

October 28

The young men are busy with the final preparations for the celebration. Quantities of water are poured around the pole mast; the earth, having been loosened last night, now turns to mud. The area is enlarged with a hoe, and to make it still more noisome they throw on it all the jar dregs they can find. The piles of sour *coot* help them achieve a nauseating mud (for Kröng-Jôong's *Tâm Bôh*, they went so far as to add buffalo dung). Old Krah sinks several sturdy pickets around the base of each bombax, so that the harness ring can be firmly attached.

At seven o'clock, Baap Can distributes glutinous rice and bananas to his guests and all heads of household in Sar Luk—in a word, to everyone who will be receiving a partner from Ndut Lieng Krak. (For the exchanges of nourishment, the individual hosts will have to supply only the jar of rice beer.) Then Baap Can cuts up the piglet killed last evening and divides it: one shoulder to the canton chief and the deputy, the other to Bbaang-Jieng and Can; one thigh to Bbaang-the-Stag, and so on. . . . Jôong-Kröng, to whom he had given a fine piece, returns it in something of a huff and takes a smaller portion. It seems that their Ndut partner, the *jôok's* own brother, had given her husband a rather meager slice of pig, and "if those people don't know how to do things right, one doesn't have to be overgenerous toward them. And what's more," she adds starchily, "one must give only what one has received, neither more nor less."

Each man brings his jar of *rnööm* to Baap Can's house—his sole contribution to what is a notably expensive festivity. The guests from other villages buy their jars from the people of Sar Luk for five or ten piasters, depending on the size. People dicker about where they will place their

_____
rope that is then slipped through the ritual barrier. This halter-rope-ring combination constitutes a single unit. It is made of heavy rattan twisted around with liana bark, and it securely tethers the buffalo to the sacrificial post, which is protected by the ritual barrier.

jars—in general, everyone tries to be near either a friend or a bon vivant renowned for his songs and repartee.

Finally, at ten past nine, the two buffaloes offered by the former canton chief arrive. Master Bbae and Master Mok are led by a group of young men from Ndut, headed by Ndêh's *rnôom,* a young man from our own village by the name of Nyaang.

Once they have delivered their charges, the young men launch an attack on the pole mast under a shower of gibes from the people of Sar Luk. A long stick has been prepared for their use, and with it they pry loose the rattan rings plugging the holes that had been bored in the internodes. A viscous, nauseating liquid flows out. The liana strips sealing off the upper holes are harder to undo; the young men of Ndut have to strap a saber to their stick, slip it between trunk and loop, and saw through the liana. All this effort is expended in order to contemplate yet another stream of stinking lava flow down the whole length of the pole, to the accompaniment of gross banter from the spectators. With fistfuls of leaves, the visitors swat away, in an attempt to wipe the trunk clean. They fashion a sort of crown of leaves and, with the help of their long stick, scrub the upper part of the mast. Finally, a boy throws himself into the assault. He clasps the greasy pole with arms and thighs, but the bamboo trunk is still terribly slippery; he climbs less than a meter before he drops down into the mud. Jeers from the audience. Another of the men from Ndut presents himself. He rubs the trunk vigorously with sand, and charges; he makes only slight progress and is generously booed. A third has a go at it, then the first youth returns to the attack. . . . You sense that, for all the hoots and banter, the crowd is following these acrobatics with lively interest.

Meanwhile, the *rnôom,* old Krah, and two or three young men have slipped a halter over the head of each buffalo. Next, Krah attaches to the "little man" carved at the top of each bombax one end of a cord woven of red and white thread; using a piece of bamboo as a shuttle, he passes the other end of the cord through the thatch of the roof and fastens it to a lateral crossbar of the granary. This cord is stretched thus so that the Spirit of the Paddy may use it as a path and be present at the sacrifice and the ensuing feast. Once Krah has tied the cord off securely, the drum resounds to attract the attention of the Spirits and bring them hurrying to the scene. Soon the music of the flat gongs also fills the house and spreads in waves beyond its walls.

Out in the yard, the young men from Ndut take turns in essaying the ascent of the greased pole. Some assault it with exceptional fierceness, although the skin on their arms and thighs is rubbed raw by the highly seasoned, peppery ingredients that have been spread over the giant bamboo. They progress very slowly, and the spectators become so enthralled that their raillery gradually subsides. Finally, at half past ten, Taang, who is the youngest of Srae-Jaang's fellow students in Ban Me Thuot, reaches the *khiu* suspended from the "horn" of the pole mast. To applause from below, he hoists himself up to a sitting position on the horns, and placidly munches on the banana and egg he takes from the little harvest basket. Then he unties the *khiu* and slithers down. On the ground, he distributes the rest of the food it contains to his companions. He attaches the *khiu* to the pole mast, but at the end of the festivities, he will bear it off to his own village as a trophy. The young men from Ndut troop down to the river to bathe. There they meet the young men of Sar Luk who, as soon as they saw Taang achieve his goal, had shouldered jerricans and immense bamboo tubes and brought them down to the watering place to fill them; this water will be used to top off the jars already set out in the houses of Baap Can and Kröng-Jôong.

They have in all twenty-seven *rnöóm* jars to fill, and almost as many empty jars and large pots that will hold water in reserve. When all are ready, each proprietor goes to his own jar to siphon off one or two bottles of rice beer for the welcoming ceremony.

At one-fifteen, the flat-gong orchestra moves out along the track leading to the foreign village. It is a false alert, however, and the musicians come back. Furthermore, the vast quantity of food will not be ready and placed on the roofed veranda for another forty-five minutes. In the center stands the offering of Baap Can: a small neckless jar filled with *rnöóm* decanted from a big jar and, notably, a wide winnowing basket chock full of victuals—the head and one thigh of the porklet sacrificed last evening, a large serving basket of glutinous rice, two pieces of manioc split in two, a dozen bananas, a bottle of Vietnamese brandy, glasses, and drinking straws. Each invited guest or local householder has before him a wicker serving basket containing what Baap Can gave him this morning; glutinous rice, bananas, and pork meat, to which he has added one or two bottles of rice beer siphoned from the jar he himself has brought. Everyone is dressed with care, although no one has gone to such pains as when we went to Ndut two days ago. Baap Can, however, looks quite elegant. Over the white shirt his *jôok* gave him yesterday he is wearing the khaki shirt I gave him this morning against the promise of a small *Tâm Bôh* loincloth. He had found no better pretext to extort my shirt, which he had been coveting for some time, than to confide in me his consternation at having received such a beautiful gift from his *jôok* when he, poor fellow, had nothing to give in return—"although the shirt I asked you for the other day would do very well." Since I myself yearned to have a *suu troany ding door*, I proposed a trade; Baap Can accepted and promised that his wife would weave me one.* However, my shirt—vestige of an earlier stint as seaman second class, without specialization—never did join Ndêh's sartorial collection. Baap Can, having tried it on instantly, found the drape of two shirttails over his beautiful loincloth irresistibly becoming, and he kept it for himself. To his friend he gave a mere black *cai ao* (a Vietnamese tunic), which he had bought in Dalat precisely with this reciprocal exchange in mind.

Finally, at two-thirty, the mingled music of two flat-gong orchestras reaches us from the track, and soon the people from Ndut appear in single file, led by the go-between Lôong-Rau. As they come abreast of us, to my great disappointment the visiting *kuang* do not go through the motions of attack or utter the buffalo cry. They simply break ranks and spread out on the veranda, each guided to his place by his partner. The Ndut orchestra moves toward the greased pole that young Taang had conquered this morning, and the women and children coalesce in a mass a few steps from the veranda. Our orchestra, which brought up the rear, enters Baap Can's house directly by the main door and continues playing inside. The Ndut musicians circle the giant bamboo seven times, make two turns around the buffaloes, which are protected from the sun by two mats, and around their sacrificial posts. Then they also go in Baap Can's house, entering by the private door, however, and the two orchestras continue their concert within.

Outside, a vast hum: each pair of partners is busy with the ritual exchange of food. Taking turns, they lift tubes or glasses of rice beer and handfuls of food to each other's mouths while reciting wishes. As soon as these ritual acts are completed, the atmosphere becomes animated, and the men swap jokes and challenges as they drink and eat. This lasts scarcely a half hour, at the end of which time Baap Can takes his *jôok* by the hand and conducts him inside the house. The whole crowd follows. Every foreigner who enters is sprinkled with water. Srae has stationed himself near the door, armed with a *rkôong* branch; he plunges it into the horn in which, three days ago, Bbôong-the-Deputy had placed bits of the magic plant of Coolness and which had been filled with water this morning. As a foreigner comes in, he receives a mere sprinkling of holy water if he is old; if he is young, he gets a real shower, which obviously elicits oaths, laughter, and scuffling every time.

The two go-betweens take their position opposite the door to consecrate the rice beer of a *yang dâm* and cleave the beak of a chicken in order to "anoint with blood the foot" of each foreigner present. Although now the situations are reversed, it is again Bbôong-the-Deputy who officiates.

---

* Actually, two days later, he gave me the loincloth he had received from his friend Ndêh. It is now in the Musée de l'Homme, in Paris, registered under the number 51-3-324.

The gong players circle around the now upright mast

The rites are carried out one after another, without haste or adverse incident. At three-fifteen, the two friends and their go-betweens anoint the leavened pastry and "the weighed rice." Kroong-the-Short and his nephew Taang, who is acting for his father, seize this moment to present Baap Can with their own "weighed rice," in response to his invitation. Lastly, each recipient and his partner open their jar, after which the crowd files by all the jars. Two hours of happy carousing ensue before Bbôong-the-Deputy, brandishing saber and chicken, rises to make the *praang baal* address. His colleague from Ndut refuses to accompany him, and it is Mang-Master-of-the-Ivory who circulates with the horn of *rnööm*. The chicken is wrenched from the *jôok*'s saber by his son-in-law and consumed by the members of the group from Ndut.

A section of the roof thatch has been raised to let in some light. The sun rays that can thus enter must pass through a thick layer of smoke before falling in patches over clusters of two or three heads. The visitors' room of Baap Can and his brother-in-law and the area beneath both their granaries are jammed. Not only are drinkers crowded around the jars suspended from Baap Can's low platform and especially along the long, unbroken line of jars that runs from the last post of Kröng-Jôong's granary to the farthest post of Baap Can's; there are also those who have yet to take their place— or those who have already relinquished theirs—before one or another of the pots that gladden the heart of man. Tubes of fire-worked bamboo or glasses of tinted plastic circulate in their direction. Everybody is chattering, joking, singing, laughing—doing his part to create a hubbub that lasts for hours.

It is well past nightfall when Bbôong-the-Deputy decides to summon the Spirits. He takes a small decorated wicker box containing saffroned rice and a small Mnong bowl filled with blood-drenched wort, and climbs up onto the ritual stall which stands between the covered veranda and the sacrificial posts. All of a sudden, a fierce scuffle breaks out between Can, the son of the master of the house, and his partner, Maang-Ddôong, the *jôok*'s son-in-law. I would never have believed Can such a stalwart. No doubt his strength is multiplied by the *rnööm* he has imbibed. Dduu-Phaang, one of the holy men in Ndut, tries to protect Maang, who has fallen, but Can sends the older man sprawling. The same fate is meted out to Dduu-Phaang's son, Taang-the-Schoolboy. All this is taking place near the veranda. The howls of Can and his opponents bring people outside and a numerous crowd soon surrounds the combatants. Aang-of-the-Drooping-Eyelid begins to bawl over the scene her brother is creating, and she collapses on the ground. Aang-the-Long (mistress of the house, one must remember) smacks her sharply on the nose several times, shouting, *"Beng nyiim! Beng nyiim!"* ("Crying is taboo!") Old Jôong-Kröng and other women from his father's clan seize Can bodily to restrain him, and they do manage to calm him down. Maang-Ddôong goes over to him and says, "We were joking, we were only joking." But Can has been dealt some heavy punches, and lo and behold, he bursts into noisy sobs. Immediately several voices are raised around him: "Crying is taboo! Crying is taboo!" Baap Can is so furious that he is shaking with rage. He dresses his son down, calling him by every unflattering name that comes into his head. A dense crowd encircles the recent battlefield, yet it accounts for only a small percentage of the guests. Most of our guests have not let themselves be distracted by the shouts and vociferations and have stuck steadfastly by their posts. Things quiet down, finally, and the gapers return indoors, where the revelry is going on as usual.

Bbôong-the-Deputy witnessed the whole scene from atop his perch. Now, at last, he can proceed with his ritual. He throws handfuls of saffroned rice in three directions—over the roof, over the buffaloes, and behind him. He places a pinch of wort on one of the plumes of bamboo that cap each post of his elevated platform, and he intones:

> *"O Spirit of the Earth,*
> *O Spirit of the Soil . . ."*

He has no sooner finished his long prayer than a fresh uproar breaks out, this time inside the house. The assumption was that Can had quieted down, but when he goes back into the house and approaches his jar, he promptly hurls himself on his invited guest and in the battle that ensues he knocks over his jar—a fearsome disgrace—and it shatters.

Exasperated, Bbôong says to me, "Can will have to expiate this. First thing tomorrow, he must sacrifice one jar and one chicken. He's the son of the master of the celebration, no less, and if one wants to immolate buffaloes ever again, he must offer a sacrifice. I made the solemn address of the *praang baal*. Mang-Master-of-the-Ivory circulated with the horn of rice beer, and Can drank from it. I, Bbôong-the-Deputy, brandished the saber and the chicken, but Can did not obey my admonitions." It is a great disgrace, but fortunately everything settles down quickly. Can replaces the broken jar, the revelry resumes, and it lasts throughout the night. The mishap provides a good subject of conversation for some, and it gives Baap Can the chance to win admiration for his knowledge of songs of lamentation. However, people have so many things to tell each other and, above all, so much *rnööm* to drink, that presently no one gives the incident further thought.

October 29

All night long, people chattered and drank. The tremendous noise that arose from the house during the evening began to diminish around mid-

night but it never entirely stopped; a good fifteen or so vigorous drinkers
held the torch high until dawn. At five o'clock, a double roll of the drum
shattered the torpor that had finally overcome most of the guests. By six,
the *kuang* are reunited and begin drinking again from a tube or glass,
dipping the *rnööm* from a *yang dâm*. The rice beer has been siphoned
from a large and very valuable jar attached to the base of the last granary
post—the one that stands opposite the private door. Bbôong-the-Deputy
cuts the neck of a chicken above a Mnong bowl in which he has placed
some wort taken from the same old jar. Carrying this bowl, he goes outside to anoint the forehead of each buffalo, praying the while.

Then old Krah advances toward the two great male buffaloes and, with
remarkable skill and dispatch, kills them in a matter of minutes. One
buffalo has lowed, and the female *rnôom* hurries up with a gourd and
pours water over its nostrils. A young man packs the wound of each
animal with leaves cut from their head ornaments in order to stanch the
flow of blood. Blood from each victim is then drawn into a Mnong bowl
for the prayer.

Kröng-Jôong, the holy man in the village, standing before the last
granary post, intones the long "summoning of the Spirits in the belly of
the Paddy." In one hand, he holds the Mnong bowl, and with the other
he anoints a spot on the granary.

His wife, Jôong-the-Healer, is called so that she may verify whether the
Spirit in the Paddy has left a token of alliance. She finds neither the tiny
ovoid pebble (*rtee*) nor the tuber of the magic plant of the Paddy. She
calls another renowned *njau*, Jôong-Sieng, of Nyôong Brah, to the rescue,
but in vain. The two women declare that it is too late: the victims are already cold.

As a funerary offering, Baap Can lays one saber and one *yang dâm* on
the buffalo that lowed, and twirls the handle of the spinning wheel above
its head. Over the other animal he places a blanket.

Several young men disembowel the buffaloes and carry the entrails
down to the river to wash and cut them up. They toss them into a large
metal pot into which they have already poured the contents of the tripes
together with some water. This mixture they set to cook over a wood fire
built out in the yard.

It is raining. The men are crowded together under the roof that shelters
the main veranda; *rnööm* is drunk and the tongues of the victims, seasoned with hot sauce, are consumed without ceremony. Then the female
sacrifice servant and Jaang-Srae fetch glutinous rice, the tripes, and rice
beer for the ritual exchange of food. Baap Can offers rice and tripes first to
Ndêh, then to Kröng-Jôong, to the elder brother of his friend, and to the
male and female *rnôom*. When his son's turn comes, Baap Can sings a
song of lamentation; he lifts food to Can's lips (the young man is very ill at

ease) and prays, but he does not look at him. When Baap Can has presented a gift of food to someone, Bbaang-the-Stag, seated beside the master of the celebration, offers that same person a drink.

The quartering of the two buffaloes commences at seven forty-five. On the veranda, conversation turns almost exclusively around last evening's scandal, to the point of boredom. Aang-of-the-Drooping-Eyelid exhibits a shamed face and sullen air this morning. Taang-the-Schoolboy confides to me that he is worried; he believes Baap Can is going to impose a fine on everyone who got into the fight last night, even the man who was defending his father and his "little father," Maang. He also thinks young Can will have to pay for the broken jar.

In the Rjee house, four jars have been opened. Mhoo offers one to Sieng-Aang, of Nyôong Brah. Truu also presents one to Sieng and his wife, and another to Kroong-Ngee, the headman of Ndut. The fourth jar has been purchased from the canton chief by his *jôok*—Wan, of Paang Pê' Nâm—to honor Bbaang-Mang, of Ndut Sar.

Baap Can presides over the apportioning of the buffalo meat. To his friend Ndêh he gives the shoulder, the same portion he received from Ndêh the day before yesterday. In line with tradition, he pays for the services of his go-between, Bbôong-the-Deputy, with a whole filet. He settles old debts—for example, giving a shoulder to Wan-Yôong—or he builds up credit with people who will soon be sacrificing buffaloes; hence, the gift of one thigh to Kroong-the-Short. A rather brisk discussion ensues between the master of the house and his brother, Truu. Baap Can had had the latter brought half of a buffalo neck (the other half had gone to Krông-Jôong, from whom he had received a like gift in September). The canton chief has had his share of drink; he orders the portion returned and goes to help himself. He takes a breast, declaring that half a neck is too big a piece for him,* that he does not want to run into debt, that—being a poor man—he dares risk no more than a breast. But Baap Can hurries over to him, insists that he accept the gift, and explodes when he sees Truu tranquilly walk off with a breast. He snatches it from his brother's hands and orders the male *rnôom* to carry the neck portion to Truu's house. Half put out, half laughing, the canton chief staggers home.

At this juncture, Bbôong-the-Deputy heaves into sight. His step is distinctly unsteady, his eyes are bloodshot, and he is braying in a thick voice. He is carrying a small neckless jar, which he sets down near Baap Can's door. He shouts to no one in particular, "Here is the rice beer of a *yang dâm*. I call you together in connection with the jar that was broken last night. People quarreled, they fought, and I know nothing about it. I—the go-between—know nothing about it. I was absent. I was out on the ritual

---

* The whole neck measures seven spans, or about one meter fifty, in circumference.

stall, summoning the Spirits. A jar was broken, and I know nothing about it. Today, I take rice beer from a *yang dâm,* and I call all the guests together. Let everyone gather together. The faces of those that fought—I do not know them. If they were drunk, I do not know that. What I do know is that some people flouted the rice beer of the horn and the chicken tied to the saber. Some people listened neither to Mang of Bboon Jaa nor to Bbôong-the-Deputy. I want to know what happened."

From the veranda where he is squatting, Kroong-the-Short, our great jurist, offers a succinct version of events for the benefit of Bbôong, who stands with his back to him. At the dizzying pace characteristic of procedural discussions, Kroong rattles off an account studded with a thousand and one juridical couplets. He concludes that "there is no case." People are in the process of making an Exchange of Sacrifices; it is young men who are involved; it is even the very son of the master of the festivities who has broken the jar. . . . Bbôong calms down and acknowledges his ignorance.

The gifts of exchange *(tâm triu)* are set out on the main veranda. They include: a pipe, tobacco, a tobacco pouch made of dog's hide that contains a "lighter" (a stone, wick, and iron blade); in a word, "what every smoker needs." Also, a whetstone, hoe, bush hook, crossbow and quiver, saber, decorated winnowing basket, small ventral pannier, likewise decorated and containing hulled rice; one large harvest pannier, one soup and one water gourd, one long-nosed gourd; a bamboo stick for stirring, a serving basket for rice; a metal bowl, one large and one small Vietnamese bowl; a fire-worked bamboo tube; some thongs and a piece of buffalo hide; a tuber of the magic plant of the Paddy placed in a buffalo horn; another horn, decorated with multicolored threads and red pompons and fitted with a rattan handle; a black Vietnamese tunic, a turban of georgette crepe; a pair of ivory floats; one antique necklace and one green necklace; a tin ring; a large hairpin for a chignon.

While everyone is examining these objects, Bbôong once again explodes, and abruptly, with long, uncertain steps, he strikes out for his house, from which his hardly civil vociferations are audible to all. The *kuang* are scandalized. Kroong-the-Short smokes his pipe, but you can tell by his eyes and twitching nostrils that he is furious.

Baap Can offers a ritual drink to his *jôok,* then to Kroong-the-Short. Bbôong returns, armed with a rattan switch. His speech is slurred; bawling something or other, he enters Baap Can's house, strikes the front platform, comes out again to where we are on the veranda. He twice clutches the arm of Kroong-the-Short, who controls himself. Baap Can rises to his feet, beside himself with rage, and orders his go-between to clear out. Bbôong wheels about and takes off again, bellowing the whole way home. His words are barely distinguishable, but one can make out some uncomplimentary remarks directed against "those foreigners" from Ndut Lieng Krak. To a man, the *kuang* are indignant, but Baap Can and Kroong-the-Short hasten to tell me that "there is no case."

The ceremonies resume. Baap Can picks up the copper bowl in which he has placed various objects of mystical value (a piece of quartz, a tiny ovoid pebble, a buffalo molar, a bead from an old necklace). He fills the bowl with rice beer, adds a little blood from a buffalo heart, and throws in also a few pieces of magic plant.

For my benefit, Truu, who has just rejoined us, offers this commentary:

> "*Magic Plant of Pride, as far as the jars;*
> *Magic Plant of the Powerful Ones, as far as the low pots;*
> *Magic Plant with the strong flavor, Magic Plant of the Ancestors,*
> *penetrate as far as the ears.*"

I talk to him about his deputy's behavior, while Baap Can has each of the *kuang* drink a bit of his rousing brew.

Bbôong reappears once more, still drunk but, it seems, subdued by Truu's presence. He senses perfectly well that the latter hardly appreciates his behavior. He asks Truu's opinion of last night's incident. Looking at him with a closed, glacial expression, the canton chief answers in an overcareful voice, "*Esoo geh dôih!*" ("There is no case!") To which Bboong responds, "*Khiep!*" ("It doesn't matter!") In token of agreement, he extends his index finger to Truu, who pulls it. The atmosphere relaxes, and Baap Can carries out the last rites with great verve.

The master of the house takes a little coagulated blood from a buffalo heart and places it on the tongues of his friend and the other *kuang*. Then he rises and, seizing a thong of still fresh buffalo hide, he knots it around the neck of his ally and laughingly threatens him: "Henceforth you cannot perjure yourself. There can be no Fire and no Water—no case—between us. We have killed buffaloes in your honor. This thong of hide we have knotted around your throat. We have nourished you with ripe bananas, we have nourished you with glutinous rice, we have nourished you with pork meat. Henceforth you cannot perjure yourself." Numerous guests repeat Baap Can's gesture with their own partners.

Our host then places on his *jôok*'s head the turban he is presenting as a gift of exchange, and helps Ndêh slip on the *cai ao* he is offering him. Taking an arrow from the quiver, he sticks it in Ndêh's hair. Lastly, he waves before his *jôok*'s face a rope, one end of which is smoldering. (The male *rnôom* has just braided it and Can set it afire, quickly quenching the flame so that the rope merely smokes.) Baap Can accompanies his gestures with words no less menacing but they are said laughingly:

> "*Forest fire, fire of lalang grass;*
> *let the fire, the forest fire be lighted.*

If he denies our Fire, our Water, our Cases, Phit yaa!
  Later we will fight him with all our might and main.
If he denies our Fire, our Water, our Cases, O Spirit,
  thou seest us; make him die for it.
Our magic plant was good, as was our glutinous rice, as
  was the beer from our jars. If he perjures himself,
  we shall be able to fight him. . . ."

There follows a free enumeration of the objects given, punctuated with the same threats.

At last, the two *rnôom* and Ndêh's wife arrange the various *tâm triu* items in baskets, in which they will be carried home. For his part, Baap Can gathers together in a copper bowl his mystical possessions (quartz, ovoid pebble, and others), and places it in a pouch that in turn will be placed in a covered basket. The Ndut people have already begun to leave for home in small groups. Can brings Maang-Ddôong, his partner—and last night, his adversary—a white chicken. "It's just a gift," he says to me.

When Ndêh and his family are about to depart, Aang-the-Long rubs soot from the bottom of a pan on all their foreheads to protect them against the Spirits of the track and woods.

The former canton chief and his family take their leave at last, saluted by the deep, full music of the flat-gong orchestra and the double rolling of Baap Can's suspended drum.

These last few days, the prestige of Baap Can has been magnified. Henceforth, he possesses one more sworn friend, a quasi-relative whose alliance with him has been sealed by a double sacrifice of two buffaloes and by the exchange of identical gifts. The celebration held on this occasion, the enormous quantities of food distributed to members of the two villages as well as to numerous other invited guests, have made the new alliance a matter of public record. The munificence of the two men who have carried out the sacrifice will be attested to in the eyes of all by the pole mast and especially by the sacrificial posts. This fresh series of festivities establishes the privileged position of Baap Can among the major *kuang* of the plain. His status and his renown have been increased by the brilliance of this new *Tâm Bôh*.

·🌷·🌷·🌷·🌷·🌷·🌷·🌷·

3
The Incest and Suicide of Handsome Young Tieng

November 26, 1948

IT is a quarter to six: I have just been called to attend the great annual
sacrifice, "the Blood Anointment of the Paddy" (*Mhaam Baa*), which is
being held at Krŏng-Jôong's house. This holy man in the village scrupu-
lously observes and performs the rituals. Yesterday was entirely given
over to a preliminary rite, "the taking of the Straw" (*sok Rhei*), and like all
other agrarian rites, it ended in a great drinking bout. The carousing will
continue and even increase today and in the days to come, for this is the
biggest festival of the agricultural cycle, crowning the end of the year in
brilliant style—"the Blood Anointment of the Paddy."

When I arrive, Krŏng is preparing a paste made with a rice-flour base.
He will use it to brush geometric designs, first on the columns and beams
of his granary, then on all his household furnishings. He has got as far as
his jars when Kroong-Big-Navel bursts in, shouting, "Aang-the-Widow
has fornicated with her brother Tieng!" Baap Can, who is smoking near
the fire, stares at him and seems not to understand. Kroong repeats the
ill-omened news, whereupon Baap Can turns to me. "A serious *beng*
[taboo]," he says. "To put a knife in a pot, *beng*. To fornicate between
brother and sister, *beng*." Then he adds, "The lightning strikes!" and with
his hand he makes a gesture of splitting his head in two. Kroong describes
how he surprised the guilty pair. He goes outside with Kraang-the-Bladder to relieve himself after a prodigious absorption of rice beer, and they
pass behind the house of Chaar-Rieng. There they come upon a couple in
a characteristic position. They recognize Tieng instantly by his tin comb,
which shines. They shout at him, "Dirty dog, you are making love with
your sister!" The man runs off, and in his flight drops his chignon pin,

81

which the other two pick up as evidence. Aang is dead drunk; stretched out on the ground, she does not stir.

"So who was making love to you just now?"

"I don't know. I'm drunk."

"It was Tieng, it was your own brother."

"I don't know who it was."

Tieng hid in the bush, while other drinkers came out to join Kroong and Kraang in questioning Aang and to comment on the scandal. Nothing more was seen of Tieng that night. He waited for all the curious to go to bed before he slipped stealthily into the house of Chaar-Rieng, his *kôony* (maternal uncle),* with whom he lives.

Aang-the-Widow cannot be said to be beautiful. Her figure is poor; she is flat-chested and dark-complexioned; however, she has a humorous face and—rare in a Gar girl—glowing eyes. She lives in the house of her brother, Tôong-Biing, who is a good, steady boy and an accomplished weaver, but extremely poor. The eldest of the family, Sieng, who is also widowed, lives in Little Sar Luk, a hamlet of a single house located three kilometers from the village.

Tieng, on the other hand, is one of the handsomest young men in Sar Luk. And at whatever hour of the day you meet him, he is always impeccably turned out: hair well pulled back and wound in a chignon ornamented with a heavy comb and a tin-plated pin, "necklaces around the throat, bracelets on the arms," his loincloth gathered closely around his waist. After the death of his wife, a year ago, Tieng followed his uncle to Sar Luk, for Chaar-Rieng had gone to get him and his five-year-old daughter in Phii Srôony, the birthplace of their family, where an older brother, Taang, still lives.

I had already noticed that Aang would often linger around Chaar-Rieng's house, especially when his nephew was there.† I had a vague hunch that there was an affair going on, although Gar lovers are always very discreet. What I had forgotten was that these two belong to the same clan: Aang and Tieng are both of the Cil *mpôol*.

Kroong-Big-Navel, as fine a speaker as he is physically ugly, now had a splendid subject to hand, and because he had not altogether sobered up,

---

* More exactly, his mother's younger brother.

† Much later (September 26, 1949), I was told that when the village had been abandoned, in May 1948, after an epidemic, and all Sar Luk was living in small huts set up on the edge of the *miir*, Aang stayed with Chaar-Rieng and slept beside Tieng, who was separated from his uncle and aunt by their son, Ngee. At the time, Jôong-Krông had stressed the danger of such an arrangement to Rieng, who had replied, "There's nothing to fear. They're brother and sister. If there were anything amiss, I'd know about it."

he began to embroider generously on his discovery. One would have thought he had come upon Tieng and found the young man dragging his sister off by the hair, and then raping her. . . . Consensual rape, at most. Only a few days earlier, I had been at my desk when I heard shouts from Tôong-Biing's house. I rushed out on my little veranda and asked another curious listener what was going on.

"Tôong-Biing is beating his sister," he replied.

"What for?"

Silence was my only answer.

Today I am given the reason: Biing-Tôong had scolded Aang for flirting with her brother Tieng. Aang not only told her sister-in-law off but, when Biing persisted, Aang slapped her. When Biing's husband came home, she told him what had happened. Tôong was furious, and punished his sister severely. So people were not unaware of the incestuous relationship between Aang and Tieng, but until then no one had caught them in the act.*

Once Baap Can has recovered from his astonishment, he is gripped by the liveliest indignation, and with reason. "Lightning strikes," he says, "when sexual intercourse takes place between brother and sister. But it does not strike the guilty ones. It strikes the people who are responsible in the forest and the village.

> "The dragon flays . . .
> the tiger devours . . .
> the elephant impales

the holy men in the forest and village. It is a very serious matter. The guilty must eat pig shit, dog shit . . . chicken . . . duck . . . human. . . ."

"Really eat it?" I ask.

"No, just lick it with the tip of the tongue. Then the rain will stop falling. It is *beng* for brother and sister to sleep together. When it's a question of different clans, there is no *beng*."

This is the leitmotif that will recur continually in conversation over the next days. Baap Can is convinced, as are the others, that once the sacrifices of expiation are carried out, it is impossible that this incestuous relationship should be followed by a birth.†

Incest leads to the violent death of all the powerful people. That is to say, not only the traditional *kuang* but also Truu, the canton chief, who lives in Sar Luk, as well as his deputy, and even I, who am intimately connected with life in the village, will be exposed to it. Incest upsets the

---

* Baap Can was to tell me later that there would have been no "case" had they not been caught. Actually, this is an essential tenet of Mnong Gar law.

† And yet, in July 1949, Aang will give birth to a son. See pp. 159–160.

order of nature: rain will wash out gullies, it will cause landslides, water will gush from the earth. . . .

The fact that this affair has become public knowledge will not interrupt the progress of the *Mhaam Baa*. But it will supply a subject for heated conversation around every hearth, and will give Baap Can an opportunity to display his knowledge by chanting "lays of justice" (*noo ngöi dôih*) that censure the guilty pair for persisting in their wrongdoing and underscore the horror and disgust their behavior arouses:

> *"One shakes the blanket, the children run away;*
> *one shakes the body, the children flee;*
> *one stinks, belly and ass, and the children flee far away."*

Toward ten o'clock, Krae, the headman of Bboon Rcae, turns up in the village. He is thoroughly drunk; his eyes are bloodshot, and he is gesticulating and bawling at the top of his lungs. Krae belongs to the Cil *mpôol*, and when he heard what happened in his clan, he—alcohol aiding and abetting—became furious. Now he charges into Chaar-Rieng's house, where he keeps shouting, "They must be lashed together! They must be brought to trial at once!" He runs—staggers—to the canton deputy's house, howling the same thing. Baap Can appears and tries to calm him. Declaring that one can neither lash them together nor judge them on the spot, he improvises:

> *"Drink well, eat well,*
> *tomorrow the matter will be judged.*
> *Drunk from drinking, our body drunk,*
> *Yoo would not make allowance for that. . . .*
> *Tomorrow we will all question them.*
> *Aang has made love with Tieng. . . ."*

With this song, Baap Can is saying, in effect, that today people are taken up with the *Mhaam Baa;* they must drink and make merry; there will still be time tomorrow to settle the matter. Don't cross your bridges before you come to them, we would say.

But Krae will not give up his idea. If people don't want to listen to him, he'll tie the guilty pair together himself, and in his capacity as a village headman and a Cil, drag them to Poste du Lac. I try in turn to make him see reason, but he also stands up to me. Finally, someone hits on the solution and sets him down in front of a jar. When he has drunk his fill, he falls into a sound sleep.

During the morning, the sky has grown overcast and toward five in the afternoon the storm breaks. For four days, it will not stop raining—a tor-

rential downpour interspersed with drizzle; four dark days, without one
ray of sunlight falling on a landscape of mud and water. Obviously, the
refrain returns to mind like a throbbing pain: "Rain, a terrible *beng* for
brother and sister to fornicate, rain . . ."

November 27

The sacrifices for the *Mhaam Baa* continue.

In the house of Tôong-Mang, this venerable man speaks of the long,
hard rain that fell yesterday, of the still heavy weather, the drizzle.
Beyond doubt, it presages an eventual devastating flood, the consequence
of the incest. When he was a child, Tôong-Mang relates, he often heard
the old people speak of an incest that had defiled the neighboring village
of Paang Pê' Nâm.* Daang and Mang, both of the Nduu *mpôol*, had slept
together, had made love. . . . Heavy downpours, then drizzle—a month
of rain without letup, the water rising from the drenched earth. . . . People began to look for the culprits; brother and sister were caught, chained,
and beaten; they were forced to look for a pig and jar beer; then the rain
stopped; they were made to "eat shit" (*saa ê'*) and driven out of the
village.

The richest Cil in Sar Luk is Taang-Jieng-the-Stooped, and Chaar-
Rieng is at his house now with Taang, the elder brother of the guilty man,
who has just arrived from Phii Srôony. The two men seem weary, crushed
by the enormity of Tieng's transgression. Nonetheless, Chaar competes
with Baap Can in reciting the genealogies of the Cil clan, for the latter's
father also was a Cil. Discreetly squatting in a corner, Sieng-the-Widower
and Tôong-Biing, the latter too poor to perform a suitable *Mhaam Baa*,
are utterly devastated.

This evening, it is the turn of Truu, the canton chief, to carry out his
Mhaam Baa. I am not a little surprised to find Aang there. The guilty
woman is busy serving drinks. Her bosom bare, she is wearing no jewelry
as she moves about carrying tubes of *rnööm* to various guests. Her skin
looks rather darker than usual: the effect of shame or of too much rice
beer tonight? When she tries to mix with other people, she is awkward,
but she does not appear to be in the slightest cast down; one would say
that she is rather surprised by the uproar over her adventure. For that
matter, people talk about it in front of her as if she were not there, and
everyone casts his stone at the Cil *mpôol*. Truu, whose father belonged to
that clan, spits on the ground in a sign of deep disgust.

Quite late in the evening, Tieng appears. He has not been seen since

---

* The old man actually comes from Paang Pê' Daak Rgüng, and has been living in Sar
Luk, the village of Mang, his third wife, only since his last remarriage.

the other night but has come now to invite us to drink at the house of his uncle, whose turn it is to perform the sacrifice. The handsome Tieng, usually so elegant, is completely undone. He is wearing no jewelry, his hair is disheveled, his face is lined; his eyes are desperate and he avoids looking people in the face. When he extends the invitation, he does not dare speak above a whisper.

November 28

The holy men are dividing the gifts—chicken thighs and measures of *rnööm*—they have received from each household as remuneration for their ritual intervention in the sacrifices offered these last two days. All the men of the village are on hand, for they are about to discuss the distribution of plots in the future *miir*. Inevitably, they get around to talking about the Aang-Tieng affair, and speculating about how Aang will obtain the sacrificial pig since her brothers own none. The brothers have decided to go work on a plantation; with their modest wages, they will be able to round out the sum they are setting aside to buy a piglet. In addition, Tôong-Biing, who is a good craftsman, will weave me some panniers and winnowing baskets for the Musée de l'Homme.

Bbaang-Dlaang, the sector chief, is briefly in Sar Luk, having come to pick up Truu and several young men of the village. He stops by to see us and repeats to the elders what he told them yesterday: the guilty pair must, of course, carry out the sacrifices of expiation, but they will not have to pay a fine. For normally a case of incest is settled thus: when the culprits are rich, together they must offer in sacrifice a buffalo of one cubit * and five jars of *rnööm;* in addition, each must pay out for three large old jars. Altogether, this amounts to a very heavy expenditure. If the couple is poor, the fine is reduced: for each, one pig of five spans around the neck, one jar of rice beer, and two large jars. The jars are divided among the holy men and other *kuang,* for they are the powerful ones who have the most to fear from the consequences of an incest.

Finally, toward noon, Kroong-the-Short arrives, dressed in a splendid coat of European cut, with long black fur. He is the "brother" (first cousin, we would say) of Baap Can and Truu, and his father also was a Cil. Kroong is a judge of high repute, a man of "great knowledge," and he has been asked to come take part in the trial.

It has been decided, given the absence of Truu and the young men accompanying him, to proceed only to "the settlement of the Tieng case"

---

* The size of a buffalo, on the basis of which its value is established as money, is measured by the length of its horns or, less often, by the girth of its neck.

and to defer the sacrifice Aang must make until the canton chief and his companions have returned. In reality, the matter has already been settled in the course of discussions around the jars; now it is merely a question of having the juridical statement of the offense made public and the sentence—the sacrifice—carried out.

In fact, when we arrive at Chaar-Rieng's house, two medium-size jars are already attached to a post. One of the men present explains to me that the two *rnööm* belong to Tieng, who had taken two *yang drôh* (medium-size jars) because he did not have a large one. Actually, one of the jars is Aang's.* The pig, its back feet tied and securely fastened to a post, is struggling and squealing. A man pulls a long straw from the roof and, with the help of a second, measures the girth of the pig under its front legs: it comes to two spans and two finger widths.

The guilty couple is ordered to convoke the entire village. Aang is embarrassed, and for a moment she hesitates. Tieng scolds her to give himself courage; he, too, seems afraid to cross the threshold. Little by little, the house fills. The women, most of them carrying infants in blankets on their backs, slip under the granary and squat down there. The men take their places on the low platform, which runs the full length of the back of the house, or else they sit on their heels by the door. New arrivals find room wherever they can and push the first-comers toward the back. The last to arrive is Bbaang-Jieng-the-Pregnant-Man, holy man and guardian of the ritual Fire Sticks used in burning off the slashed forest. He is thoroughly drunk, and he shouts and bellows. The theme of his tirade is, obviously, "for brother and sister to fornicate together." He is not alone in his condition. For the last two days, there has been no letup in sucking on the drinking straws. Aang-of-the-Drooping-Eyelid comes to belch in my face the superfluous intelligence that she is tipsy (she will not sober up for two days); Bbaang-the-Stag totters on the heels of Bbaang-the-Pregnant-Man, trying to jerk himself upright. Since there are as many pipes as there are mouths, and since the fires have been rekindled, and since the rain is blocking the smoke inside the house—not to mention the smell expectable from a crowd of inebriates who had been drenched as they walked through a downpour to pile in here—the air quickly becomes unbreathable.

The guilty couple returns before all the village is assembled at Chaar-Rieng's. They finish off what is left in the jars. No one pays any attention to them; the less befuddled are listening as Kroong-the-Short reels off the genealogy of the Cil. He begins with Ting-Mang, who had four daughters—Loong, Jieng (ancestor of Choong, the ex-canton chief of Yön

---

* Tieng is supplying the pig, the duck, and one *rnööm*. Aang contributes to today's sacrifice by fetching the chicken and the second *rnööm*.

Dlei), Dloong (ancestor of Aang-the-Widow), and Bo' (grandmother of Tieng):

> ". . . *Dloong married Bbaang, carried* Grieng,*
> *Grieng married Kroong, carried Nguu, carried Ngaa, car-*
> *ried Sraang, carried Laang.*
> *Laang . . ."*

When he comes down to Sieng, Tôong, and Aang (the guilty woman and her brothers), he goes back in time to Ngaa and recites the genealogy of his father until he concludes with himself, Kroong-Biing.

He has recited this dual genealogy with astonishing speed and brio. Tradition has transformed such enumerations of ancestors into long poems. The first word of each verse is the same as the last word in the preceding verse; also, each verse is punctuated by the words *sae* and *ba'*. †

In his turn, Taang of Phii Srôony, Tieng's brother (born of the same mother and father), recites their genealogy, which is also that of Chaar-Rieng, their maternal uncle, in whose house this scene is taking place.

To find an ancestor common to the guilty pair, it has been necessary to go back fifteen generations. Actually, I am the only person to indulge in this calculation, for these recitations of genealogies have only one purpose, which is by a formal demonstration to buttress the certitude of all: the guilty two have "come from the same belly," they are "sister and brother," ‡ and they have slept together.

Now the order of sacrifice is discussed. Those two drunks Bbaang-the-Stag and Bbaang-the-Pregnant-Man demonstrate the greatest aptitude in this. They are the only ones to think of a major point: gifts the lover has given his sister must be reclaimed. "Necklaces, bracelets, rings, little bells—everything must be brought down to the watering place," Bbaang-Jieng bawls, and he laughs uproariously over his inspired idea. But Tieng is not rich. The only present he has given Aang is one of the small rectangular metal boxes containing a mirror that are called *khôop* in Mnong. To this will be added the hairpin Tieng let fall when he was caught by surprise.

Sieng-the-Widower, Aang's elder brother, hands an internode of scooped-out giant bamboo to several young men, and asks them to gather up some assorted human and animal excrement. They all recoil and re-

---

* *Ba'* (the Gar word actually used here) means literally "to carry or bear on the back in a blanket"; by extension, to rear a child.

† *Sae* signifies both the noun "husband" and the verb "to marry" (here in the past tense).

‡ From our Western point of view, we would consider them related in the thirtieth degree—but would we then venture to call them relatives? And who among us, except for some aristocratic families whose genealogies are made a matter of written record, could claim he was able to thus "recount his ancestors"?

fuse, and the more spirited among them shout at him, "*Beng* to pick up shit!"

One of them explains to me, "It's fear of contagion. You're afraid that lightning will strike you or make you fall sick."

And another adds, "Picking up the shit of a pig . . . a dog . . . a man . . . a buffalo . . . a chicken . . . that is forbidden [*weer*]. You are afraid of contaminating your hands."

So I say to him, "But you collect it to use as fertilizer between your rows of vegetables."

"Between rows of vegetables it's not forbidden. But normally it's forbidden."

Since all the young men categorically refuse, Sieng-the-Widower decides he will get a stick and collect a sampling of excrement himself. "A very little of each," Kroong-the-Short tells me.

For lack of a buffalo horn, the guilty pair fills two bottles with rice beer. Tieng passes his to Tôong-Biing, Aang's second brother, who will also take along some wort and charcoal in a gourd bottom.

When the moment comes to set out, Aang bridles in protest: "I was completely drunk, I didn't know what I was doing. . . . I had no idea what was happening to me. . . . I didn't know who was mounting me."

Her face darkens and becomes even more stubborn. Tieng is a limp rag. In an effort to give himself countenance, he makes a feeble show of urging his "sister" and accomplice to do the right thing.

At one-fifteen in the afternoon, in a drizzle, the entire village slithers through the mud down to the watering place (*daak mpaa*), on the heels of Tieng, who is carrying the little pig. At the confluence of the Daak Mei and the river, Tôong-Biing cuts a bamboo into three sections. He takes two and frays one end of each in small pompons; the other ends he whittles to a point; then he notches both in the middle and sticks them in the ground by the side of the path above the river. He frays both ends of the third piece and lays it in the notches of the two verticals. Thus he has made an altar in the form of an "H," its tips and transverse ends plumed.

Meanwhile, some young men immolate the victims. Slitting the pig's throat, they gather the blood in a large Vietnamese bowl and pour a portion of it over the wort and charcoal in the gourd bottom Tôong-Biing is holding. Above this same receptacle, they cut the throat of the duck, and hold it so that its blood drips over the watering place. Lastly, down by the edge of the watering place they slit the chicken's neck. They brush wort over the wound so as to impregnate it with blood, and deposit this *coot* also in the gourd bottom. This receptacle now holds, in addition to the charcoal, elements of each offering—wort moistened with the blood of all three victims.

Tôong-Biing sets the gourd bottom at the foot of the right-hand altar stick, and intones the prayer. He invokes all the Spirits—those of the Earth, and the Dragon (Spirit of the Water) . . . all except *Yaang Baa*, the Spirit of the Paddy:

> ". . . *In the trees, in the bamboos, the Crow Spirit;*
>   *in the water, in the waves, the Dragon Spirit;*
>   *in the earth, in the soil, the Dragonet Spirit.*
>   *Dragon of one cubit, stay with me;*
>   *Dragonet one finger wide, stay with me;*
>   *Little Lizard of one span, stay with me;*
>   *do not speak to me in anger,*
>   *do not crush me with your wrath*
>   *because I have slept with my sister here,*
>   *because I have slept with my mother here.*
>
> *With this pig I have purified;*
>   *with this jar of alcohol I have purified;*
>   *with this chicken I have purified;*
>   *with this duck I have purified.*
>   *Let the rain cease;*
>   *let the drizzle cease.*
>
> *Do not scold, O mortar;*
>   *do not deny yourself, O pestle;*
>   *do not tread upon the adulterer;*
>   *do not crush us under your feet;*
>   *do not trample upon us and reduce us to dust.* . . ."

The guilty man and woman come forward. With the index finger and thumb of the right hand, each takes some of the pig's blood collected in the large Vietnamese bowl, then some duck and chicken blood, and each brushes both fingers over the gaping wounds of the two victims. Together, Aang and Tieng step into the water and recite an invocation, at the end of which they dip their blood-stained fingers in the water and rub them together.

Tôong-Biing is still crouching in prayer:

> "*One may not fornicate with one's sister;*
>   *consider it not, O Spirit.*
> *One may not make the Exchange of Sacrifices with one's ancestor;*
>   *consider it not, O Spirit.*
> *One may not marry between maternal uncle and niece;*
>   *consider it not, O Spirit.*
> *One may not fight between father and son, between termite and termites'*
>   *nest;*
>   *consider it not, O Spirit.* . . ."

After he has anointed the frayed end (*nsôom*) on the right, he anoints the ground. From time to time, Baap Can or another old man, without moving from his place, recites aloud some verses with Tôong-Biing.

Sieng has placed the gifts* in the bamboo ladle that contains the assorted excrements. He pours beer over all, then lays two feathers—one duck, one chicken—on the front lip of the ladle. Now they proceed to the *siam ê' sür, siam ê' sau* ("giving to eat of the pig, of the dog excrement"). The guilty couple moves out into the middle of the current. Tieng bullies Aang (wrongly) into walking ahead of him. Kröng-Jôong, the holy man in the village, enters the water, followed by Sieng carrying the ladle. Kröng stands in front of the offenders, equidistant from each. He dips a feather in the nasty mixture and brushes it over Tieng's chin, counting "One"; then over Aang's chin, "One." Back to Tieng, "Two," and to Aang, "Two," and so on, eight times, after which he offers a long invocation addressed principally to the Dragon Spirit (the Spirit of the Water). From the outset of this ceremony, the two guilty ones stand with their backs to the audience. Each time the feather touches Tieng's chin, he is shaken by such violent retching that he doubles up. Aang does not flinch once.

At the close of his prayer, Kröng throws the feather into the water; Sieng empties the contents of the ladle, then throws the ladle away also. The guilty man and woman wash their chins, legs, and arms. Kröng is about to walk out of the water without purifying himself. Two or three of the watchers shout to remind him, and he goes back to the middle of the current and washes his arms and legs.

Tôong-Biing has not stopped praying. Finally, he pours rice beer over the gourd bottom containing the wort impregnated with the blood of the three victims. He goes down to the river with this receptacle and the bottle of *rnôöm*. He places the gourd on the water, pours some *rnôöm* into it, praying the while, then lets the gourd float with the current, asking the charcoal to carry the presents to *Yaang Rmeh* (the Dragon Spirit). In conclusion, he empties the remaining contents of the bottle into the water and returns to the bank.

Everyone climbs back up to the village.

Throughout the ceremony, it never stopped drizzling, and at its end the drizzle turned into a violent rainstorm.

Rain notwithstanding, the carcasses of the sacrificed animals will be roasted out of doors, because in such a sacrifice it is forbidden to cook them inside the house, as is customarily done with small animals.

The crowd has reassembled at Chaar-Rieng's. Jars are about to be con-

---

* Actually, only one gift—a pipe (Aang has mislaid the *khôop*)—and the proof of guilt, Tieng's hairpin.

In the rain precipitated by the recently discovered incest, Tôong-Biing
squats in prayer before the little altar built by the watering place . . .

. . . while, standing in the stream, the guilty pair are fed "excrement of
pig and dog"

secrated, this office falling to "those who have rendered justice." The first jar is for the ethnologist and his *jôok*, Kroong-the-Short.* The second goes to Kröng, the holy man in the village, and to Bbaang-the-Pregnant-Man, the holy man of the *Rnut.* We insert our drinking straws to the accompaniment of many invocations mentioning the triple sacrifice that has just been performed. Then the ethnologist by the first jar and Kröng by the second begin to drink.

Bbaang-the-Pregnant-Man takes a Mnong bowl containing wort steeped in the three bloods and, accompanied by the guilty couple, goes to his house to anoint with blood the ritual Fire Sticks used in setting fire to the forest. The sacred sticks have been placed in a basket wedged between a rafter and the thatched roof. It is impossible to dislodge the basket, so Bbaang merely anoints it and the portions of *Rnut* that extrude. In this ceremony, the only actors are the holy man and the guilty pair. The anointment is accompanied by prayers.

When we return from anointing the ritual Fire Sticks, Kroong-the-Short is still drinking from the first jar, where he replaced me. He says to Tieng, "From now on, you will not be able to live here any longer. You will have to go away, you will have to marry somewhere else. . . . I am your *kôony.*† Come live with me. You will look for vegetables in the forest, you will carry firewood. . . ."

Taang of Phii Srôony seconds this, telling his brother, "Go with Kroong-Biing. Aang will look for another husband here. . . ." But Tieng makes no answer either to his older brother or to his "uncle."

Kroong-Biing would like to have Tieng marry pretty Grieng, who as a result of unpaid debts is his slave. A free man does not become a slave by marrying a woman who is one, but his children share their mother's status, and it takes a truly hard-working man to manage to free both wife and children. Tieng is no such man. But this does not seem to be what preoccupies him or dictates his attitude.

Kroong-Biing "of the swift speech" waxes more and more persuasive. He expatiates upon his wealth and his good name, and the agreeable life Tieng will lead with him in Ndut. Taang again supports the *kuang*'s proposals, emphasizing that the guilty pair must separate, that his brother is being offered a really fine chance to live in the household of such a highly esteemed man. For Taang, the proposed solution is already a fact. He

---

* *Jôok* (sworn friend), it will be recalled, is the title by which two individuals address each other who are bound by a double buffalo sacrifice. For professional reasons, I went only as far as the preliminary exchange of gifts with Kroong-Biing.

† The son of the *kôony* (younger brother of the mother) becomes *kôony* himself upon the death of his father. It will be remembered that the father of Kroong-Biing, like Tieng, belonged to the Cil clan.

goes so far as to recommend to Kroong-Biing that he make Tieng work hard; no recommendation could be more superfluous.

Throughout these long palavers that concern his own future, Tieng has not said a word. Squatting in the middle of the group of men, he immures himself in absolute silence: refusal.

After a half hour, Kroong-the-Short elects to change the subject. He sings and dictates some ancient chants to me, and in this connection boasts of his love affairs. The chants soon degenerate into drinking songs, even obscene songs. Laughter explodes on all sides, and the atmosphere is transformed.

Before he returns to Ndut at nightfall and in the rain, accompanied by two young bodyguards, Kroong-Biing comes to find me, for I had gone home to dinner. He asks me if he may lay claim—as has always been done since the days of the ancestors—to a small *yang dâm,* and thereby be cleansed of the taboo. He takes pains to make clear to me that it is not a payment but a purification that is due him.

Thanks to Kroong-the-Short and the rice beer, the company is completely relaxed; even the guilty two are won over by the new mood. Tieng, who has replaced Aang in measuring out the water for the jars, starts to talk. He announces to Chaar-Rieng that this very evening he will make a sacrifice in Chaar's behalf to lift the taboo that, through his fault, weighs on Chaar and his family. And when Aang comes around at about eight o'clock to invite me to attend this sacrifice, she pushes her audacity to the point of entering my house unaccompanied and, being alone with me, of asking me for a cigarette. This is something no woman in the village had ever dared do before.

All the residents in the long house have gathered at Chaar-Rieng's, but except for them, the curious—or the thirsty—are few. The day's events have filled the cup of the first group to overflowing, and the others have little to hope for. Only one tiny neckless jar (*yang ke' it*) has been prepared and placed on the ground near the low platform. Beside it are one chicken, with its feet bound, and one empty *yang dâm.*

Chaar-Rieng brings out the leather pouch that holds his magic quartz. He removes the stones and places them in a Vietnamese bowl at the foot of the small jar of beer. He is seen to rummage anxiously in his small sacred bag: he finds only five stones, of normal size, but cannot put his hand on the sixth, a minute *naar* "like a grain of hulled rice," which appeared one day to his wife on top of the little heap of rice she was winnowing. "It has fled," he deduces mournfully. "Our body is unwholesome, we are being chastised. It has fled. It is going to seal a *tâm nta'* alliance with someone else, and he will become *kuang.*" Happily, when he takes out the ovoid *rtee* remaining in the pouch, he finds his grain-of-rice quartz stuck in a corner. He places the two magic pieces in the bowl with the others.

Now Tieng slits the throat of the chicken above the bowl containing the magic stones. Chaar rejoins his wife and son and little Jôong (Tieng's daughter) seated near the granary. Tieng lets an abundance of blood flow into the bowl. He rises and goes to anoint the foreheads of the four other residents of the house with the bloody wound of the victim. He then takes the *yang dâm* in both hands and revolves it eight times above the heads of the seated group and asks:

> ". . . May the small beams of the granary hold firm,
> may the posts of the granary lengthen,
> may the rice in the heavy pot simmer. . . .
> The wild beasts follow the night,
> the kuang follow the word,
> the thunder follows immediately. . . .
> In the days to come, may one search for the buffalo every day,
> may one search for jars every month,
> may one have rice, hulled and unhulled, every day. . . ."

He sets the small neckless jar down behind them, but they have him place it before them, and each in turn touches it. Then Tieng spits in his hand, touches the *yang dâm* and the breastbone of Rieng; he repeats the gesture with the three other members of the household.

Tieng leaves the family group of his maternal uncle and goes over to the group composed of his brother Taang and his wife and baby, all three of whom are sitting on the low platform. Because they come from the forest, "they may not receive the 'revolving of the jar above the head' " at the same time as "those of the village." Tieng repeats the ceremony for them, starting with the "revolving" (*rwec bôok*), and he concludes by giving one piaster to his brother and another to his brother's wife. Meanwhile, Chaar has lined up his magic stones, which have been anointed with blood.

Finally, assisted by his brother and uncle, Tieng consecrates the tiny *yang ke' it* by the low platform. The three men cough slightly, flick their fingers over the surface of the water so that a few drops fall on the ground. The guilty man takes the *gut* into which he has sucked some beer and, tamping the upper end with his index finger, he sprinkles a few drops of *rnööm* "on the head of the door and on the heads of the hearths," repeating the same prayer as before. He returns to his two companions, gives the drinking straw to his brother, and picks up the Vietnamese bowl. He goes again to anoint with blood the top of the door, the tops of the hearth stones, and the jars. Taang, meanwhile, has inserted the *gut* in the *yang ke' it* and recites wishes in unison with Chaar.

Now everything is in order. Tieng has cleansed the community of the contamination his incest caused, and he has purified the hearth of his uncle and the household of his brother of the evil he brought upon them. His misdeed is erased. During the execution of the rite, he was tense; now his face relaxes. During the late afternoon, it had been apparent that he was only pretending to be at ease but now it is a liberated being who stands before us. Tieng speaks almost joyously. There is no *kuang* in the house to intimidate him, only the family of Bbaang-the-One-Eyed and of his sister, Aang-Kröng, and one foreigner, who happens to be their elder brother, from Sar Lang. Like Bbaang, Kroong-Poong is blind in one eye (the right instead of the left), and he has come to Sar Luk to work out his stint as a *tram* coolie. Bbaang-the-One-Eyed is habitually mute, but this evening he exhibits an astonishing loquacity. He has drunk a great deal, and in a face enlivened by *rnööm*, his one eye has an unwonted sparkle. He tells us the story of how, after a carouse, his father, who was drunk, snatched up a bush hook, and, jumping over jars, pursued his son in a wild chase. He wanted to kill Bbaang, but happily never could catch up with him.

I must leave the joyous little group, for I have been urged to go to the house of Tôong-Jieng. His wife's maternal uncle, Krae-Drüm, has until now lived in Paang Döng, but is coming to live in Sar Luk with Tôong-Jieng, and this move requires an "anointment with blood." It is a sacrifice analogous to the one for adoption. When Aang-the-Widow came to invite me, I was returning from Drüm-Kraang's, who had just fainted. Her mother-in-law, Jôong-the-Healer, had managed to bring her to by dint of heavy, revivifying fumigations with "resin from the Sky." An eventful day, indeed, in Sar Luk!

November 29

As if by enchantment, the rain stopped this morning, and now the sky is cloudless. However, during the night the river rose by almost a meter and the bank by the watering place gave way, carrying with it the little altar, which has vanished with the current. "The Dragon came to carry off the altar," Baap Can tells me.

Aang has disappeared, having followed her brother Sieng to Little Sar Luk. Her other brother, Tôong-Biing, left early for the plantation to earn the wherewithal to purchase the pig she will have to sacrifice.

Taking advantage of the fine weather, we decided to make a collective garden and to sow seeds I brought from France and others offered by the colonial administration. All the men go down with me to the terrace across the river from the village. We had just sown the first few packets when, around ten o'clock, a young man calls me: "Yoo! Tieng is dead! He's hanged himself from a rafter."

We all run to Chaar-Rieng's house. With his *suu troany,* Tieng had tied himself to the double bamboo purlin in the granary and jumped into the void. Out of modesty, he had first replaced his loincloth with a length of material that he passed between his thighs, fastening the two ends with a leather belt. Choong-the-Soldier and Bbaang-the-Stag lay him down on the low platform; his body is still warm. I check to see if he is still alive, but no breath escapes from his mouth or nostrils.

Old Rieng had been sent for, and she arrives breathless, carrying a basket with a few bamboo sprouts. According to her, this is what happened:

When he woke up this morning, Chaar decided to go with Taang to Nyôong Hat to try to barter a jar for a blanket. Tieng asked if he might go with them, but his uncle refused, dressed him down sharply, and ordered him to stay in the village and work with the other men in the garden. Tieng began to sulk and said not a word more, "although last evening he had become himself again," Rieng tells us. "He even ate well. He ate a big bowl of rice." She goes to look for the bowl, to show it to us. She quickly adds that at no point did she scold him.

After his uncle and brother had left, Tieng recovered his spirits, and he set out for Paang Döng. He intended to ask his (clan) uncle, Ngee-Daang, if he might come live with him because, the old woman comments, "he was too ashamed to stay on in our village." But Ngee-Daang refused. The rebuff had a terrible effect on Tieng. When he got back from Paang Döng, he looked utterly crushed.

He tells the old woman to go into the forest and cut him some bamboo shoots; he feels like eating some bamboo shoots. The old woman goes out. At home there remain only Taang's wife and baby, and little Jôong, Tieng's own daughter. Tieng gives his fine necklace to his daughter and tells his sister-in-law to go draw some water from the river, and to take the children with her. When she returned, she found him hanging from the granary purlin.

During old Rieng's recital, the corpse lies stretched out, almost naked, on the low platform. Several checks have been made to be sure that no breath is coming from Tieng's nostrils, for his body has remained warm a rather long time. But he has not been covered; indeed, Tieng does not own a blanket. When she finishes her tale, old Rieng, who has not shed a tear or uttered a ritual lament—people who die a violent death (*ndrieng*) have no right to either—covers Tieng's head with an old rag that was lying in a corner of the squalid hut. This is the only ministration he has received since he was laid on the platform.

Actually, no one dares touch the suicide. The brother of Bbaang-the-One-Eyed and of Aang-Kröng, who occupy the other half of the house, is a young coxcomb by the name of Nyaang. When asked, he refuses to straighten the dead man's legs and stretch his arms along his sides. They point out to Nyaang that because he lives under the same roof as the deceased he would be running no risk. It serves no purpose. He is afraid of violent death, for its taint brings illness in its wake. A moment earlier, someone had gone so far as to claim that a *ndrieng* not only has no right to a coffin or to lamentation but has no right even to have his limbs straightened.

The taboo against weeping and funeral chants is absolute. When the dead man's daughter comes into the room and sees her father's body still and lifeless on the platform, and all these men clustered around him, staring at him dully, animal fear seizes her and she begins to howl with terror. Instantly, everyone shouts at her, *"Beng nyiim! Beng nyiim!"* ("Crying is taboo!") But the little girl wails even more loudly, until she is calmed and persuaded to rejoin the other children. She will play the rest of the day as if nothing had happened—yet somehow giving the impression that she was aware of the interest she aroused.

Conversation turns to sinister topics but hardly touches on the dead man. It is recalled that a *ndrieng* has no right to normal interment and must be buried in a special cemetery for the victims of violent death. That said, no further attention is paid to the corpse. People do grieve, however, for the living, because heavy expenses will devolve on them; they pity the unfortunate Chaar-Rieng, who will have to offer still further sacrifices. "He'll have to look for a pig, a goat, a dog, and a duck," one man enumerates. Bbaang-the-One-Eyed, co-dweller in the house, is in despair. Over and over, he keeps saying that he will be forced to abandon this house and go somewhere else to build another. His one good eye keeps blinking in a face that looks like that of an overwhelmed, mournful Sioux. The idea that perhaps the entire village will have to relocate itself seems to console him. Then: "Chaar-Rieng will have to give up everything that's made of wood and lalang grass—thatch roof, uprights, granary posts. . . . He will have to rebuild with new materials. If Tieng had hanged himself in the forest, it wouldn't have caused all this trouble." A fat insect with red antennae is walking on the ground near the one-eyed man. I ask what the bug is called. He doesn't know, he says; nor do the others. Tranquilly, One-Eye crushes the nameless insect.

Rieng-Chaar comes back to the subject of her husband's nephew, whom she is staring at as he lies on her platform, the cause of all her present woes. "His mother before him slept around in her own clan. Her name was Rieng. Yes, his mother before him slept with a man of her own clan in Rddôong, in Tôong's canton. The very same business. They 'ate' buffaloes and jars, and that was that. They only had to pay a fine, which the family paid out of what they had." Then, after a pause: "If only one had noticed right away, and taken a dog and killed it—well, Tieng would be alive now!" The leitmotif on which the old woman and the men dwell constantly is that Tieng killed himself because he had "shame in his ears."

Suddenly, someone remembers the absent Truu and the young men accompanying him. They must be called back promptly: the members of a village may not remain "abroad in foreign parts" when there has been a violent death at home. I am charged with writing a note; the sector chief has gone to school, and he will read it to Truu.

For some time, people have been talking not inside Chaar-Rieng's house but outside, in the yard before his door. Baap Can materializes, much excited and upset. He rushes up to me: ". . . *Esoo geh dôih!* [There is no case!] He killed himself, Yoo, he died by his own hand. No one insulted or struck him. He didn't die after any exchange of blows. . . . He killed himself!" His words tumble out louder and louder, until he is almost shouting. I reassure him: he has nothing to fear. I was there, I can attest to the manner of Tieng's death and that indeed he took his own life, that he had been neither insulted nor struck; that he had been driven to suicide by despair. The large crowd before Chaar-Rieng's house is an ideal public for Baap Can, who now gives rein to his indignation with the smiling scorn of the righteous man: "Let him be cast away since he has killed himself. Once upon a time, an incest case like his would have cost him a buffalo. He was asked only for a pig of five spans. And in the bargain, they could have offered it together. Even so, he managed to give only a pig of two spans and two finger widths. . . . And then he goes and hangs himself. . . . Let him be cast out." Suddenly, Baap Can bethinks himself: Has anyone wept? When his mind is set at rest on this score, he retires.

Around four-thirty in the afternoon, Chaar-Rieng and his nephew Taang, the *ndrieng*'s blood brother, finally arrive. They had been reached just as they were on the point of selling the jar. The first thing Chaar asks is whether anyone wept for the dead man. He is immediately reassured. The crowd, which had dispersed after Baap Can's speech, re-forms around the new arrivals. The old man has hardly unslung his pannier before he begins to inveigh against Aang-the-Widow. She provoked his death, so "there is a case against her." The argument is repeated over and over, punctuated by the same conclusion, which is becoming a refrain: "There is a case against her." Already, I note, Baap Can has come round and is now entirely of Chaar's opinion. The consequences are easy to foresee. There will be a discussion around a jar, Chaar will rehash his views to the point of satiety, reciting legal maxims over and over, and the *kuang dôih* will simply ratify his arguments. For there will be no one to defend Aang-the-Widow: her two brothers are terribly poor and, for the moment, one is even absent. In the end, Aang will become old Chaar's slave, and Baap Can will receive a jar as his judicial fee.

Especially when one has the "luck" to be present at some unusual oc-
currence, it may be Olympian to allow things to run their normal course
and be satisfied imperturbably to note the march of events. But an ethnologist is not a mere recording machine, and to my way of thinking the
benefit to be had from such observations would have been dearly paid for
by the enslavement of a woman who was, furthermore, in my view in-
nocent. So I now intervene. First, I restate what everyone has been saying over and over since this morning: Tieng killed himself because he
could no longer bear his disgrace. Then I attempt to set forth my point of
view for them. It is not shame that has pushed Tieng to this act of supreme despair but the thought of having to leave Aang forever. His uncle's outburst this morning cruelly reminded him that he had been re-
jected, banned from Sar Luk. His only way to avoid a definitive
separation from Aang would have been for him to live in Paang Döng.
The village is only about a kilometer away from Sar Luk, travel back and
forth between the two villages is frequent, and opportunities to meet
Aang often would not be lacking. But Ngee-Daang, of whom Tieng was
asking refuge, brutally showed him the door. He had, then, no choice
other than to leave for a distant village, which would mean that he could
see Aang only very rarely. He preferred to take his own life.

I have the impression that my interpretation seems to them muddled
but that they have grasped my main point. In the end, the old men con-
cede that there is no case against Aang-the-Widow. Even Chaar assents,
but feels he must exculpate himself: he has never insulted his nephew, he
has never even argued with him. He harps endlessly on these self-jus-
tifications. (Indeed, I have often been told that if, for example, a wife
poisons herself after a scene with her husband, it is deemed an extremely
grave "case.")

Chaar-Rieng's arrival seems to dissipate the depression that had struck
the village. At last, people were going to be able to do something to divert
the dangerous and unforeseeable effects of this violent death. The entire
machinery of a purification exorcism is set in motion.

First, the neighbors living on the same "floor" as the *ndrieng* isolate
themselves with a curtain of magic protection. Nyaang divides the common room (*wah*) that the two granaries share by planting leaves of *tloot*
(*Gnetum latifolium*) and *rhôong* (Graminaceae) above the main door; then
at the foot, the midway point, and the top of the two *wah* columns, the
median line of the pallet being between them; and in the rear wall and on
the roof, in the extension of this imaginary line. A veritable magic frontier
is thus established between the two households. Lastly, Nyaang places
the remaining protective leaves by the main door, on the side of the
"granary" to be protected. While creating his mystical barrier, he has
prayed constantly, repeating the same formulas several times:

> ". . . *May we sleep with a cool body,*
> *may we snore mightily.*
> *Prevent blood from spilling,*
> *the body from being hot,*
> *the horn from breaking.*
> *We, we on this side form only one house;*
> *we, we on this side form only one granary;*
> *we, we on this side have only one soup;*
> *we, we on this side have only one cooked rice. . . ."*

The dead man's relatives, meanwhile, are preparing for his burial. They have unrolled over his feet and abdomen a tattered old blanket, much too short to cover him completely, and on his chest they have placed the *suu troany*, still knotted, with which he hanged himself. Rieng sets a large Vietnamese bowl near the suicide, in homage to his soul.

Since the old couple do not own a *ngkook* (a mat of stitched screw-pine leaves) large enough to wrap the body in, Chaar's wife brings him an ordinary mat, which he cuts in two. He places the two halves end to end over the body. Then, with his son's help, he cuts off the portion of the matting (*nier*) * on which Tieng is lying; together they bend the edges up along the full length of the body before they lower it from the platform to the beaten earth of the floor. Additional thin layers of flattened bamboo are laid over the body and, in order to rope this rigid shroud together more easily, they slip a stick of firewood under it. Before the old man ties top and bottom mat together, he removes the Vietnamese bowl from the packing and substitutes a piaster. And Taang slips inside the improvised *ngkook*, near the arm, the two piasters his unfortunate brother gave him last evening.

Taang tells me that the last few days in Phii Srôony he has dreamed of firewood being cut crosswise; this always presages a serious "case." And last night he had a particularly frightful nightmare, in which he saw flames consume Tieng's *suu troany*. In the dream, he got up and stamped on the fire to smother it. This was a fearsome portent: to see flames devour someone's loincloth announces the death of that person. This morning, Taang could not perform the exorcism such a premonitory dream requires because he had no chicken to kill. He adds that "the *nêet nêet* sorcerer [a nocturnal bird with a sinister call] came to search for its dead man."

Nyaang, Chaar-Rieng's son Ngee, and Maang-the-Thin have tied their funereal package at three different places. The joined feet, which are also enclosed in the envelope of screw-pine matting and flattened bamboo, they bind more tightly. The corpse, thus loosely pinioned in its rigid

---

* A sort of mattress made of flattened bamboo, which is laid directly on the low platform.

shroud, is borne out through the private door and set down near the threshold. They must now attach the long portage pole, which extends about a meter beyond either end. Someone reminds the men not to step over the corpse, for this is severely proscribed.

Old Rieng brings over a pannier and sets it down near the body. In it she places a pot, one large and one small Vietnamese bowl, the very small neckless jar whose contents were drunk last night, a small hoe, a gourd of water and another of soup, a hatchet, what is left of the roll of rattan used to tie the shroud, and also the stick of firewood that had been placed beneath the corpse in order to rope the shroud more easily.

With the help of the pole to which the shrouded corpse is lashed, Nyaang and Maang-the-Thin carry their burden on their shoulders. It seems to be quite heavy. Ngee follows, carrying the basket (eventually he will relieve one of the young bearers), and after him Chaar-Rieng, armed with a bush hook.* Kroong-Big-Navel and Bbieng-Dlaang accompany me. Except that Bbieng will cut a few branches to put on the grave, the two men will do no more than recite a single prayer. Similarly, when I ask Bbaang-the-Stag if he is coming, he replies hastily, "There is an absolute taboo that forbids me and Kraang-Drüm to go to the cemetery. Violent death could seize us and make us sick, for we have a *Tâm Bôh* to make."

As we walk, Kroong-Big-Navel says to me, "He killed himself out of shame. If he had waited just two days, he would have been cured of his shame." Chaar-Rieng adds sadly, "He did not want to eat any more meat here below."

We leave the French-built track to follow the buffalo path, which plunges in a northerly direction into a stand of mixed bamboo. Shortly after we ford the Daak Tloong Kar, we veer northwest, leaving behind us on our left the cemetery for stillborn infants. Twenty meters beyond it, we come to the plot for *ndrieng*, which lies between the big cemetery and the former field of Taang-the-Stooped, a landmark that Baap Can and Kroong-Mae had several times pointed out to us before we left.

As we arrive, three buffaloes appear. Choong-the-Soldier, accompanied by a child, is leading them back to the village.

The three young men joke as they take turns digging the grave. Their tool is a long stick with a chamfered point, which they fashioned on the spot. I am given to understand that Tieng had told some children he intended to marry Aang, which leads me to set forth my view of the matter once again. The banter continues. But Kroong-Big-Navel urges the diggers to hurry: a heavy black cloud is threatening on the horizon. The rec-

---

* It will be remembered that Nyaang is the neighbor of Chaar-Rieng and, therefore, of the dead man. Ngee is Chaar's son, and Chaar himself is Tieng's *kôony*. Maang-the-Thin is the brother of Mang, the wife of old Tôong, who is Tieng's "little father."

tangular grave has been dug on a north-south axis (it is forbidden to make
it parallel to the path of the sun) and close by the grave of the most recent
ndrieng. That was Ndoong, the son of Laang-the-Widow, of the Cil clan,
who drowned two years ago at the age of about twelve. The vegetation has
grown up thickly over his tomb.

When the young men finish digging, the grave is less than knee deep.
Chaar-Rieng steps down into it and levels the bottom with the little hoe
brought among the gifts offered the dead man. He takes a stalk of lalang
grass, bestrides the hole, leans over, and as he steps back he tightens the
knot he has made with the grass and recites:

> *"Souls, vital breaths, do not remain in earth;*
> *return here below. . . ."*

Then he throws the grass away.

The men place the corpse in the grave, with the two tips of the portage
pole resting on either end so that the body, positioned with its head to the
south, does not touch the bottom. With a weeding hoe, Nyaang cuts the
rattan fastenings, taking care not to lean over the open grave. They snap
the pole; Chaar says not to throw it into the hole but to leave it "here
below."

Branches are cut from several tree stumps that have put out new
leaves, and the body is covered with these. Chaar slips a few leaves under
the rattan fastening around the head:

> *"I fear the earth may cover your eyes,*
> *I fear there may be earth in your nose, in your eyes. . . ."*

The men push the dirt back into the grave and over the body with its
protective cover of branches. All pray:

> *"I do not strike you, nor do I belabor you,*
> *I do not trample on you, nor do I crush you underfoot.*
> *It is the Divine Ones who have struck you,*
> *the Spirits who have struck you,*
> *the sorcerers who have struck you.*
> *You are dead, you will eat of the earth;*
> *we who live on, we eat soup and rice,*
> *we remain here below, at peace with others. . . ."*

More branches are spread over the grave, and Chaar sets the jar and
other offerings by its head. From that position, he throws some cooked
rice over and beyond the foot of the grave:

> *"I give cooked rice to the Spirits and to the inhabitants of the Underworld.*
> *I give you soup,*
> *I give you cooked rice to appease your hunger."*

The suicide is borne in his shroud toward the cemetery

He sets the large Vietnamese bowl down and makes a fresh pile of the funerary gifts, this time to the left of the head:

> *"I give you this pot, do not seek the soup of another,*
>   *do not seek the cooked rice of another.*
> *I give you this pot for cooking the vegetables,*
>   *for cooking the rice that you eat.*
> *I give you these Vietnamese bowls into which you may*
>   *pour your vegetables at mealtime. . . ."*

Lastly, the four men break up a few twigs and place them on the grave, declaring to the dead man:

> *"I give you firewood. Do not ask for the soup or*
>   *cooked rice or firewood of another."*

And with this, they hurry to leave. Chaar, who is bringing up the rear, stops a moment to cut off some spiny branches, which he throws across the path:

> *"O violent death, I am returning from there below,*
>   *flee you this way. . . ."*

The trip home is made with all haste. They discuss where the sacrifice must be performed. Everyone is in agreement about the rule requiring that one "eat the dog" in the water if the fatal accident took place in the water, and in the village if it occurred in the village or in the forest. Chaar and the young men cut an armful of *tloot* and *rhôong* stalks. When we reach the big track, we do not return directly to Sar Luk but strike off downstream; at the crossroads, Chaar unloads the bulk of his ritual leaves. We press on toward the site of the purifying bath. Kroong-Big-Navel, always of a facetious turn of mind, makes us laugh by tugging on the back knot of the *suu troany* of Nyaang, who is walking in front of him, and, so to speak, unbreeches him. The spot chosen for the bath is below the former village site, which was abandoned during the most recent epidemic. When one returns from a normal interment, habitually one bathes at the village currently inhabited. However, when death is caused by violence, the danger is too great and the men who have conveyed the *ndrieng* to his grave must purify themselves well downstream from their watering place.

The men bathe and launder all their clothes, including, for those who are wearing them, berets and turbans. They also plunge their *wiah* in the current and scrub them. As each man comes out of the water and dons his loincloth, he takes a leaf of *tloot* and one of *rhôong* from the small package Chaar has brought and fans the air around his body (*prah sak*), reciting:

> *"By the* rhôong *grass and the* sraa *palm,*
> *by the* r'aa *grass and the* gaat *grass,*
> *flee down there, downstream from the water,*
>   *downstream from the firewood,*
>   *downstream from the tall forest,*
>   *downstream from deep night.*
> *Let one offer the small rattan,*
> *let one offer the big rattan,*
> *the rock down there is yours,*
> *let my body be cool. . . ."*

And he throws the leaves into the water.

Of the four men who worked at the grave, only Ngee has not washed his *suu troany*. He goes back into the river and wets the end of his loincloth while praying:

> *"O violent death, flee downstream from the water,*
>   *downstream from the firewood . . ."*

and he comes out again to purify himself with the leaves.

Now we hurry back to the village, for it is cold. At the crossroads, Chaar retrieves the packet of leaves he had left there. We see some people from Paang Döng approaching. They are carrying rice harvested in the *miir* of Taang-the-Widower, who settled in this neighboring village after his wife's death. Among the group are some residents of Sar Luk who originally came from Phii Ko'—Aang-of-the-Mincing-Step (wife of Bbaang-the-Stag) and Yôong-the-Mad.

Near her private door, Rieng-Chaar has placed a pot of boiling water. Everyone washes his feet and hands, and those who have them, their *wiah*. We go inside to dry out and get warm around the fire in the visitors' room.

Taang, the dead man's brother, tells us that last evening Tieng wanted to share in the Great Festival of the Soil, to hunt for a buffalo, and to eat meat. Chaar relates once again how he went to Phii Srôony to fetch Tieng after his wife's death. Then he sets straight the story of the incest Rieng-Chaar had told us about. It was not Rieng (of the Cil clan) but her daughter Aang who had slept with her "brother" Mbün. The affair had been settled by a fine reduced to one neckless jar and the sacrifice of one chicken and a *rnööm*. No pig had been killed; the guilty couple were very poor and did not own one. This event occurred ten years ago, in Bboon Rddôong. Rieng was a sister—"from the same belly"—of Mang, the mother of Taang and Tieng. After the trial, Mbün had enlisted, and Aang had married another young man.

Chaar confides that, in return for a small-size ordinary jar, he hopes to buy the dog and *rnööm* he wants to sacrifice so as to divert his nephew's soul from the celestial domains toward the Underworld. He asks Kroong-Big-Navel, who is sitting beside him, to propose the deal to Nyaang. Without stirring, Kroong speaks up and asks Bbaang-the-One-Eyed instead. The latter refuses.

Rieng offers food to the people who have gone to the cemetery, but my companions on the mission—Kroong-Big-Navel and Bbieng-Dlaang—decline.

Taang relates how, last evening after "the revolving of the jar above the head," his brother told him to go to Koon Ier and look for a Djiring jar belonging to him, adding that he would offer it to Taang as "a gift between brothers." So now Taang deems that he has nothing to offer the little orphaned daughter.

Chaar explains to me that when a man dies a violent death, the Brieng Spirit eats "his buffalo-soul, his spider-soul." A dog is killed, and the soul leaves the Sky (the residence of Brieng) to rejoin the other souls in the Underworld.

Bbieng relates another instance of a violent death. Two years ago, at the festival of the Blood Anointment of the Paddy in Bboon Jaa, a young man died from a cudgel blow received directly on the nose during a fight among some drunken men. That was a very serious matter.

Chaar finally comes back from Tôong-Mang's with a stoppered jar. He has purchased its contents as well as a cat and a dog in exchange for one Djiring jar.* He plans to make this double sacrifice as soon as Truu returns, and to postpone the one with the duck and the goat. This evening, he will kill only one chicken and offer one *rnööm*. But he has no jar prepared other than the one supplied by old Tôong-Mang. So Chaar empties the little *yang ke'* in which he keeps his salt, scrapes the inside, and hands it to his son, who puts in some wort taken from the borrowed jar. Ngee continues his preparation, stuffing the tiny neckless jar with lalang grass, exactly as if he were dealing with a jar of normal size.

Taang wants to know if his brother has been properly buried.† Kroong-Big-Navel reassures him, declaring that the hole reached the groin. (In fact, it was not even knee deep.)

The young men are urging Chaar to carry out the rites before it is totally dark. So our host slits the chicken's throat above the packet of *tloot* and *rhôong* leaves that he had set down just inside the threshold on arriving home. He takes care that some blood drops on each leaf. He seizes a few and ritually brushes (*prah*) his jars, his suspended drum, the low plat-

---

* Ten days later, he will claim that he did not pay for them but merely gave the old man a token piaster. If true, this would be very surprising.

† Since Taang was from another village, he was not allowed to participate in such a serious ritual. —*Trans.*

form (indicating Tieng's place, he says, "There is where he slept"), the inside surface of the roof, and the entire circumference of the granary. His
possessions having been ritually brushed, he does the same to individuals:
Jôong (the dead man's daughter), Rieng, Taang and his wife and son, then
all the men who went to the cemetery. He continues with his exorcism by
sweeping with his bunch of blood-soaked leaves the threshold of the
private entrance and, outside, "the tail of the lalang grass" (that is, the un-
derpart of the edge of the roof), and the route along which the corpse had
passed; when he has traversed the track, he throws his leaves into the
thickets. He accompanies his *prah* with a ritual formula repeated for each
category of objects he names:

> ". . . I fear that mud may reach the joints,
> that violent death may reach the arms
> and cause suffering and illness. . . .
> Now, flee there below, O violent death."

Ngee has brought the little jar out into the yard a few meters from the
house. Nearby, he has built a fire over which he is roasting the sacrificed
chicken. Chaar has everyone touch the short, straight drinking straw,
which he inserts in the beer, repeating the same prayer, with Taang assisting in his orison. He draws a little rice beer into the *gut* and plugs the
upper end with his index finger; offering the same prayer, he takes a few
steps in the direction of the cemetery as he allows the beer to dribble
from the jar onto the ground. Again he dips it in the jar, and each man
comes up to drink a mouthful. The *tram* coolies who are stationed in the
village now also press forward to drink. "People coming from the forests
[i.e., from "foreign parts"] fear the violent death that has struck our village," someone comments for my benefit.

The rice beer is truly bad. The water Ngee poured in the jar has dis-
solved the salt which had impregnated the inside. Everybody, once he
has been purified by sucking up one mouthful, goes home.

November 30

The moment you awaken, you sense that a heavy menace hangs over Sar
Luk. Usually, the pestles are heard from every part of the village; today
the muffled sound of their pounding comes from the most remote outskirts. When there has been a violent death, one may not pound the
pestles in the village, for that would attract the ferocious cohorts of the
Brieng Spirits.

Very early this morning, old Tôong-Mang, the ranking elder of the
Rjee, is at Chaar-Rieng's for a discussion with him and Taang, the dead
man's brother. When I arrive, our host is repeating for the nth time how

he brought Tieng from Phii Srôony. And as always, he adds, "There was no exchange of insults or blows between us. There was no case." The family has slept in its usual place, he says, and there have been no dreams.

Chaar tells me they will not move away but will go on living in this house. In the past, the entire community would have moved, for a violent death in the village would not have been tolerated: "The spring would have refused to yield water." But today such a move is impossible, for the villagers are weary of rebuilding their homes. So Chaar will offer the sacrifice of a goat and a pig, which is necessary if one is to be able to drink water taken from the watering place. The complete list of sacrificial animals, in addition to these two, includes a chicken, duck, dog, and cat. The duck and pig have already been sacrificed in the water, and the chicken was killed yesterday; still to be immolated are the dog, cat, and goat.

Taang explains to me that after a normal death the sorcerers of the cemetery devour the body of the deceased. His soul then departs for the Underworld to rejoin the souls of "his mothers and fathers down there, under the ground." But in the case of a violent death, the Brieng Spirit eats the body, bears the soul up to its celestial domain, and forces the soul to marry one of its daughters. It is because the soul of a man marries a Brieng daughter that he dies and his soul in turn becomes Brieng. Therefore, Taang says, one immolates dog, pig, and cat, and then the soul returns to the Underworld beneath the earth. Because the souls of the sacrificed animals go looking for the Brieng daughter, now the wife of the dead man's soul, and they persuade her to allow her husband to return to the Underworld, where the soul of the *ndrieng* becomes a human soul once again.

First, Brieng eats the soul; then, a day later, the man dies. For that matter, this much is the same in the case of normal death. The buffalo-soul is eaten by the Spirits, and death occurs only the next day.

Taang adds, "The evening Tieng performed the revolving of the jar over the head for us, I saw that Brieng had already eaten him. It was a Rainbow-Brieng poised on the horizon that ate his soul. I saw a fiery glow as big as this," and he raises his arms perpendicularly to the height of his shoulders.

Village life moves slowly today. The men have gone back to work in the garden, and the women have left to gather wild vegetables. Everyone is waiting for the violent-death sacrifices Chaar plans to perform this afternoon, for Truu and the young men have returned.

Sar Luk is taboo to foreigners for seven days. Inversely, its inhabitants may not go to another territory during the same period of time. One must not contaminate others with the stain caused by the violent death. No bamboo or rattan is placed at the entrance to the village in token of the interdiction because, they tell me, the news has quickly spread. Nonetheless, two young men originally from Sar Luk do arrive from Nyôong Brah—the runner Bbür-Aang, son of Jôong-the-Healer, and Bbaang-Jrae-the-Soldier, son of old Troo. Bbür tells me he is only passing through, and this is not forbidden. "But it used to be in the old days." Before they return to Nyôong Brah, they will bathe and fan their bodies with *rhôong* and *tloot* leaves, asking the violent death to flee.

Baap Can is much concerned. He is afraid that this suicide may cause difficulties for the village with the government authorities; he is afraid the Commissioner will blame the *kuang*. He wants to go to Poste du Lac to set forth the facts and plead the village's case. I dissuade him, explaining that according to our law a suicide does not entail a lawsuit; there will be no "case."

At three in the afternoon, all inhabitants of the village are called together by Chaar. They gather before his house for "the trampling of the blood of pig and the blood of dog" *(joot mhaam sür, mhaam sau)*. Actually, a dog and a cat are sacrificed. Despite the hour, it is very dark; the clearing this morning lasted only a few hours and dark clouds have again invaded the sky. The crowd of men, women, and children—some adults are carrying infants in blankets on their backs—is massed in a great semi-circle in front of Chaar-Rieng's main door, where he has placed a pile of *rhôong* leaves. The sacrificer has finally laid hands on a black dog. He holds it up on its hind legs. Krah clubs the victim to death with blows to the head; he must strike several times before blood spurts forth. Chaar lifts the dead animal and brushes its bleeding head over the ritual leaves. He then lays the body on the ground and balances the head on a gourd saucer to catch the blood flowing from it. One has to watch out, for other dogs have been attracted by the smell, and must be chased off.

The white cat Chaar holds by the paws and head above the *rhôong*, and Krah slits its throat with a bush hook. Chaar lets the blood drip first on the leaves, then into the gourd. He drops the cat beside the dog.

Immediately, all the villagers rush to the blood-stained leaves and trample on them feverishly. It is an indescribable melee, from which a hubbub of prayers rises, each person imploring the violent death:

> *"Mud of violent death,*
> *violent death ankle,*
> *great star,*
> *betake yourself off. . . ."*

Mothers lean down amid this mob for a bloody leaf with which to anoint the feet of their babies. The lowering sky covered with dark clouds, the gravity with which the crowd performs the bloody rite, and the anguish that grips each person here confronting the unknown make this a deeply dramatic spectacle.

The exorcism of violent death is performed on the roof of the contaminated house . . .

. . . and by the watering place

LEFT: *Under a dark and threatening sky, jar, cat, and dog are offered in sacrifice*

As soon as they have finished trampling the blood and leaves, people move toward the jar of rice beer, which has been attached to a post outside the house near the private door. Each person, standing upright, sips a mouthful or two. Everyone without exception, even very young children, must drink from the jar.

When the crowd has shifted from the site of the blood to the *rnööm*, Rieng and Chaar bring out their spinning wheel, imported bowls, pots—all their household possessions. However, in the case of bulky items like jars or panniers, they carry only one of each outside, it representing all those in its category. The husband brushes all utensils with blood and all household furnishings with *rhôong* leaves. He then carries them back into the house.

Chaar next takes the gourd saucer holding the blood of both victims; a piece of bamboo, one end of which is frayed and will serve as an aspergillum; a long, flexible *dlei* bamboo; and a "winnowing basket" (actually, a remnant of much-used wicker). He climbs up onto the roof of his house. He sits astride the ridgepole "facing the cemetery" (in fact, he faces the end of the house that is in the general direction of the cemetery). He balances his materials in front of him. He spits out a menacing *phit!*, hits his piece of wicker eight times, dips his bamboo aspergillum in the gourd saucer, and sprinkles the space before him, then the space behind him, with blood. Finally, brandishing the long switch of *dlei*, he whips the surrounding air in all directions:

> "*Mud of violent death, flee.*
> *May you become soul once again, breath that follows*
>   *the debt,*
> *you, sparkling star,*
> *do not remain among the Brieng,*
> *dwell in peace in the Underworld.*
> *I strike, I trample only because you speak rudely to*
>   *me, because you insult me.*
> *Sisters, nephews, children, grandchildren, grandfathers,*
>   *ancestors, today I offer you as funerary gift the al-*
>   *cohol of one jar, a dog, and a cat; I summon the soul,*
>   *the breath that follows the debt. . . ."*

Truu supplies this commentary: "The soul has left for the abode of Brieng. One eats a pig, a duck, a cat. The soul of the cat summons it [the soul of the dead man]; the soul of the dog, the soul of the goat summon it. The chicken is like a coolie, the pig like a village headman, the cat like a runner, the goat like a canton chief. Since we have not yet eaten the goat, the soul [of the dead man] is wandering between the tree and the ground. But as soon as it arrives, the goat speaks to Brieng. Brieng lives in the middle of the skies. 'Let his soul descend to the Underworld so that it may sojourn there in peace,' the soul of the goat says to Brieng. If one lets the Spirit of Violent Death have its way, young women and young men cannot rejoice, everything is sadness." Truu laments the fact that today the Gar have no more goats, the tigers having devoured them all. It will be necessary to go buy one from the Rlâm. A kid is bartered for a Djiring jar; two jars bring only a goat with horns no longer than a man's finger joint.

During Chaar's prayer on the roof, Nyaang has chopped off the dog's head and dropped it beside the cat. With Ngee's help, he carries the dog's body into the house, where he will cut off the testicles before he roasts it.

People drink from the jar in the normal way, each person imbibing his two measures. Truu has drunk first, and given his place to me. Chaar and Taang will follow immediately after me, and then all the villagers will take their turn.

Chaar inserts some blood-soaked *rhôong* leaves in the mouth or handle of each of his jars for fear the Brieng Spirits may take refuge in them. Before each receptacle, he asks the Spirits of Violent Death to flee. Then, once more taking up his gourd saucer and aspergillum, he sprinkles (*mprê'*) his jars with blood, and his granary and everything that is in his house, even the corn heaped on sticks laid over the rafters, because Brieng detests the blood of a dog and the blood of a cat.

Lastly, the sacrificer goes outside, for he must exorcise the village site and all its buildings. (The villagers have already purified themselves.) We watch as the tall, stooped, skinny old man, with his sparse chignon and his dirty, threadbare loincloth, trudges through all the yards of the village. He drags behind him, tied together to the end of a rattan rope, the corpse of the white cat and the bloody skull of the black dog; they bounce up and down over the uneven terrain. As Chaar walks, he shakes the sprinkler he carries in his right hand and mutters an interminable orison; it is merely the endless repetition of the same prayer. In this fashion, he comes to the watering place, where he pauses for a moment. After skirting the vegetable garden, he climbs back by way of the outer houses. He has not forgotten, on his way, to bless the mortars lying in the yards. By virtue of this ambulatory rite, Chaar has definitively chased off any Brieng who could be lingering in the village.

At the end of his circuit, he returns to his own door. He gathers up the remaining *rhôong* leaves and with them sweeps the first section of the path that leads to the cemetery; in passing, he sprinkles his wife's mortar. He crosses the road, walks a few meters into the woods, and stops. His son Ngee, who has followed him armed with a *wiah*, cuts two tall forked pickets and a transverse piece, from which Chaar suspends the body of the cat and the head of the dog. He places some bloody leaves on the transverse and the remainder he lays across the path between the two pickets, adding the club used to bludgeon the dog and the gourd saucer of blood.

As he leaves, Chaar recites the same prayer he uttered when hanging the remains of his two victims on the "altar":

> "You, head of the dog,
> you, head of the cat, summon his soul from the home
>   of the Brieng,
> may it return home to eat of soup and cooked rice.
> Dead, in a state of putrefaction,
> leave him there,
> fear nothing, do not flee in all directions.
> May the kite fly,
> may the young sparrow hawk grow powerful. . . ."

When Chaar returns, light suddenly breaks through the dense layer of dark clouds, and a broad ray of sunlight floods the village. Whereupon Truu says to me, "You see, Yoo, we have eaten the pig, we have eaten the dog, and so the light of the sun breaks forth again."

Near Chaar's private door, the men have clustered to gossip around the jar, and the drinkers follow each other without interruption. The women do not have their customary refuge under the granary, where they feel at ease among themselves, and only a few remain with us. Chaar brings me the dead man's tax card, on which he is registered as Sieng, the name given him at birth. He had taken the name of Tieng after a very severe illness, when the shaman decided that he should change names (*rplee nnaan*) to mislead the Spirits and the sorcerers.

The talk touches on various subjects, most of them calculated to advance my Mnong education. Thus I learn that in the event of incest, it would be in the interest of a rich family to procure white animals for sacrifice, they being more efficacious. That in the event of a violent death, "the sacrifices of pig and goat" lift the interdiction against traveling. That one may neither pound rice nor cut wood in the village for three days, because the effect of such a loud noise is to attract Brieng. Tomorrow, because sacrifices have been made, it will again be possible to fell trees or bamboos without risking an accident caused by the anger of the forest Spirits.

One incident excites some concern: a swallow has just flown through the private door into the house of Bbaang-the-One-Eyed, Chaar-Rieng's "floor" neighbor. Nyaang has managed to catch the bird. He plucks its belly but finds neither twigs (a forecast of "cases") nor hair (a presage of death); he finds only a few flies. He walks over to toss the creature into the bush. When one catches a swallow in normal circumstances—that is, out in the open—one may eat it, but the fact that it entered the house makes it taboo. Had unfavorable signs been found on it, an exorcism would have been mandatory. The consensus is that the bird flew inside looking for Tieng, but violent death had already done its work and therefore the swallow could no longer bear any signs.

The old people shout to the children to move on the double from where they are playing. They have chosen the very spot where the corpse was lashed to the portage pole. People have a tremendous fear of the evil Spirits (*Mâp Mang*) that always loiter in unhealthy places and attack children to make them sick.

Ngee arrives with three large Vietnamese bowls of dog meat cooked with salt, red pepper, and wild mint leaves. He sets them down near the jar, and groups form and dissolve around the bowls, which are quickly emptied.

And here comes Baap Can, bending forward with care as he walks. In a blanket on his back, he is carrying little Dür, his youngest daughter, who has a fever. The illness is attributable, no doubt, to the violent death. Chaar fetches out a *yang dâm* and hands Baap Can a pinch of hulled rice. He himself chews a few grains, then spits them on the foreheads of Dür and her father. He revolves the small neckless jar eight times above both their heads. Lastly, he spits in his hand and touches, in turn, the jar and the baby's forehead; spits in his hand a second time, and touches the jar and the forehead of the father. As he does this, he asks for purification from the illness and expresses the wish that

> ". . . *you be strong, like the jar,*
> *you be sturdy, like the bush hook,*
> *you be agile* [?], *like the roedeer.* . . .
> *Today I have performed the revolution of the jar above the head.*"

Baap Can takes the *yang dâm* off with him, telling me he will return it to Chaar tomorrow; about this I am not at all sure. In fact, the jar has to do with paying the fine incurred because of the incest. Chaar is most insistent that Truu accept a leg of the sacrificed pig in settlement of the same matter, but the canton chief firmly refuses: "I cannot accept it. I was absent during the trial."

No one tarries to drink from the violent-death jar, and by nightfall, all the villagers have gone home.

Around eleven that evening, as I am working at my house, I hear the "pep . . . pep" of a tiger on the hunt. It comes close to Sar Luk, runs along the Daak Mei, and then I hear the sound of a splash as it plunges into the watering place; the wild animal is crossing the river. From his house, Baap Can says to me, "Violent death. Intercourse between sister and brother." *

---

* However, early the next morning, I go with two young men to retrieve the stag that the tiger killed on reaching the farther shore. When I ask Baap Can, "Was that the tiger of violent death?" he laughs and answers, "Of course not, since he attacked and killed a stag." Then, after a few moments: "It is only for the *ndrieng* killed by the tiger that the *tiger-ndrieng* comes lurking about."

·❧·❧·❧·❧·❧·❧·❧·

4

Voyages into the Beyond
in Quest of Souls

BEFORE relating the events that follow, it seems to me that a brief account of Mnong beliefs concerning illness and death is indispensable.*

Every individual possesses several "souls" (*hêeng*), each of which has a form and, one might say, a behavior peculiar to it. The quartz-soul dwells directly behind the forehead; the spider-soul escapes from the head during sleep; the buffalo-soul is reared by the Spirits (*Yaang*) in the Sky, where the giant-bamboo-soul, the canoe-soul, and others reside also. A man's life is closely bound to the life of his souls: let an accident befall them, he becomes ill; he dies if they themselves succumb.

To prevent an illness from taking a fatal turn, one has recourse to the talents of the shaman (*njau mhö'*). The shaman sets the quartz-soul up straight again, he contends with the Spirits and the sorcerers (*caak*) for the survival of the buffalo-soul they are preparing to devour; he searches for the spider-soul and makes it return to its proper abode, the body of the patient. These are exploits that the shaman can undertake only during a *mhö'*, a shamanist séance. After a sacrifice has been offered by the master of the house and several treatments have been administered to the ailing person, the healer, in a hypnotic state (symbolically hypnotic, at least) embarks on a voyage into the Beyond. There he investigates the causes of the illness and seeks out the souls; he ministers to them, dis-

---

* See also *L'Exotique est quotidien*, Ch. 35, and my "Some Mnong Gar Religious Concepts: A World of Forms," in N. Matsumoto and T. Mabuchi, eds., *Folk Religion and the Worldview in the Southwestern Pacific* (Tokyo: The Keio Institute of Cultural and Linguistic Studies, 1967), pp. 55–61. Also pertinent are: "Schéma d'un *mhö'*, séance chamanique mnong gar," in "Chamanisme et possession en Asie du Sud-Est et dans le Monde Insulindien," *Asie du Sud-Est et Monde Insulindien, Bulletin du Centre de Documentation et de Recherche*, Vol. IV (1973), Fasc. No. 1, pp. 61–70, and "Postface" to *ibid.*, Vol. IV (1973), No. 3, Fasc. 2.

120   *We Have Eaten the Forest*

cusses the price of their liberation with the Spirits and the sorcerers, and fetches back to earth the patient's "double."

In addition to these psychopomp magicians, the *njau mhö'*, there exists another and lower category, the *njau proproh*, or healer magicians, whose basic work is ministrations (*proproh*) that consist for the most part of massage. The *njau proproh* possess various magic recipes and formulas taught them by the shamans. However, they cannot perform any *mhö'* into which they have not been initiated, for the Spirits have not conferred on them membership in the alliance which would grant them the gift of high magic.

If the Spirits decide to immolate the buffalo-soul, or the sorcerers to destroy the spider-soul or to eat their fill of the corpse—the gamut of possible misdeeds that the *caak* can perpetrate is considerable—the man dies. His double then descends to the first of seven subterranean levels that constitute the Underworld (*Phaan*), where he will lead a second life, a pale reflection of the one he leads on earth.

January 24, 1949

We are in the middle of the land-clearing period (*môih*). Shortly after the harvest, the rains stopped entirely and the dry season is now firmly established. On December 23, 1948, the holy men led all heads of household into the forest of the Stone Spirit Gôo, and assigned them their respective parcels of land. A period of relative rest followed, during which, between social or trading trips, the men readied their bush hooks, reforging the blades and repairing the stitched bamboo handles. Then the families of the village started clearing the trees and brush that covered their future fields.

Several events have interrupted the monotony of this arduous work. The Plantation, to which every able-bodied man used to have to contribute twenty working days a year, has decided to change its system of compulsory recruitment in favor of a sort of voluntary service. Henceforth, each canton will be required to supply a minimum contingent of young men who will sign on to work for an entire year; the recruiting agent has come to Sar Luk twice in connection with this. Also, there has been a tax collection. And lastly, in the course of a heavy drinking bout, Aang-of-the-Drooping-Eyelid has committed adultery with a European. For the Mnong Gar, such a thing is virtually unheard of, although for Aang it is simply one more instance of immoderate behavior; a few years ago, she left Sar Luk to live with a white man for several months. Baap Can had managed to iron out that affair with the offender's mother-in-law (his older sister, Jôong-Krông), and Aang had promised not to be unfaithful again to her husband and first cousin, Kroong-Big-Navel.

When Kroong was confronted with this fresh outrage, he decided to perform the divorce ceremony. It was to have been held last evening, but altogether fortuitous circumstances interfered. It so happened that the teacher at the Frontier School took advantage of his free Sunday to offer two jars of *rnööm* to the canton chief in the afternoon and, in the evening, the sacrifice of one chicken and one jar to the ethnologist. The latter occasion provided an opportunity for us to witness a fresh dispute between Truu and Baap Can. In quite sharp language, Truu accused his older brother of not having informed him of Aang's current misconduct; it was of concern to the entire family, yet Truu had only moments ago learned of it from the lips of a foreigner, his friend Baap No'. Similarly, Truu charged, a few months earlier Baap Can had kept him in the dark about the betrothal of Jaang and Srae. Baap Can reacted violently to these strictures. By the time the two brothers separated to go to their respective homes, it was very late in the evening and the divorce ceremony had to be postponed a day. Accordingly, this morning at seven-thirty Baap Can and Kröng-Jôong's common room was packed with curious people. Aang somehow contrived to make the trial drag on for two hours. The men of the village, who were in a hurry to get back to their clearing chores, slipped out one by one and took off for the forest. So it became necessary to defer the completion of this public rite until evening.

But once again an entirely unexpected development was to save Aang-of-the-Drooping-Eyelid from divorce. Toward noon, when most of the villagers are out in the bush, Aang's most implacable enemy, Jôong-Kröng-the-Healer (her paternal aunt and mother-in-law), is shaken by a severe attack of malaria as she is preparing the midday meal for her son Bbür, who has come down from Nyôong Brah to be present at the divorce proceedings. Jôong is obliged to take to her bed. Her symptoms intensify and worsen. At nightfall, when people are preparing to resume the divorce hearing, Jôong suffers a violent attack: her limbs stiffen, her tongue protrudes from her mouth, and she faints. Someone calls for help, and the women of the family come on the run; people crowd around the sick woman, who has been stretched out on the low platform near the granary. Drüm-Kraang, wife of the village deputy headman and also Jôong's daughter-in-law, in her capacity as healer assumes direction of the ministrations. Supporting her mother-in-law, Drüm takes the first steps to bring her around. Eight times she revolves the pouch of supple wicker containing the quartz and other magic stones above the patient's head. She does the same with an upside-down bowl on the base of which embers have been placed and "resin from the Sky" (*cae trôo'*) scraped over them. Last, she applies a pinch of the resin, taken from the embers, to different areas of the patient's body—chest, back, elbows, and soles of the feet. Drüm-Kraang accompanies each of these gestures with the recitation of formulas:

> *"Double Stone,*
> *Triple Quartz,*
> *Horns of the Spirits,*
> *track down the soul,*
>   *the spirit that follows the debt.*
> *O soul, thou art borne in a blanket;*
>   *thou art fed at the breast;*
>   *return home, we will welcome thee;*
>   *eat the rice soup the spouse has made sticky;*
>   *eat the cooked rice the spouse has chewed.*
> *Do not break the thong of leather,*
>   *do not flee and become lost;*
>   *do not sleep away from home."*

But Jôong continues to lie motionless; her eyes are closed, and her breath comes in short, hoarse gasps. Someone goes to fetch Mang-Master-of-the-Ivory, who at the moment is visiting the school; he, it seems, knows some very effective procedures used by his ethnic group, the Cil Bboon Jaa.

When the foreign *kuang* arrives, he chews some saffron and spits a small amount on the patient's forehead, throat, and temples, and also on the top of her head. Then he starts to whistle as he places his hands on her head. Drüm lifts her mother-in-law and supports her from behind so that Mang can continue the same ministrations on her chest.

After that, Mang glues his lips to the sick woman's forehead—he appears to be biting it—and inhales deeply. They tell me he is trying to break the thong with which the *caak* (sorcerers who devour human souls) have strangled the old woman. After a long, powerful inhalation, Mang spits into his hand whatever he has drawn from the patient's head and orders us all to move back—which everyone hurriedly does—and he throws the aspirated matter into the fire. (For my part, all I see is a gesture, but no real object falling into the flames.) Once more Mang whistles, with both hands presses the skin of his patient's forehead toward the middle, and blows on it. Thus ends the first part of the treatment.

So far Jôong has seemed to be in a coma. Now she raises a hand and, in a barely audible voice, asks that the shaman (*njau mhö'*) be summoned.

A copper bowl three quarters filled with water in which four grains of raw rice are soaking is given to Master-of-the-Ivory. Mang takes a mouthful and, in two expectorations, sprays enough water to dampen the sick woman's face. He looks into the copper bowl and whistles. Then he revolves it eight times above Jôong's head, again examines the bottom of the bowl, still whistling, and pours a little water on the top of her head, precisely where the quartz-soul stands upright. He whistles and listens, pressing his ear to the bowl. He glances in it again, whistles again, and again dampens his patient's face by lightly spraying it with the lustral water from his mouth. Once more he revolves the bowl above her head, examines its contents, and recites a series of prayer couplets.

Seizing Jôong's head firmly in both hands, Mang applies his mouth to the crown and breathes in vigorously, clears his throat, spits into his hand whatever he has drawn from the patient's head, and throws it far from him. He repeats the procedure. Then, raising the bowl to the level of Jôong's head, he gives the contents of the bowl a few flicks of the finger so that the grains of rice may assume a propitious position. Once more he aspirates the top of her head and pours a few drops of water on it, while he begs the soul to return. Then he flings the copper bowl behind him. The receptacle falls as it should; that is, with its mouth turned upward. (Had it fallen with the opening down, he would have had to keep on throwing it until he achieved a satisfactory fall.) Having thus concluded this whole series of treatments on a favorable sign, Mang-Master-of-the-Ivory dries his hands over the fire.

Baap Can arrives and immediately launches into a long harangue, which everyone present listens to in silence. The old man remains standing, his upper body held erect above the squatting people, who separate him from the sick woman. His face and torso feebly lighted by the fire and the small resinous faggots, Baap Can speaks of his own position and of the situation of Jôong, his older sister, and of his younger brother, the canton chief. The *caak* hold a grudge against them, he declares, but the Rjee are ready to contend with them for the elder sister by the sacrifice of a buffalo. The word "contend" recurs several times in Baap Can's speech, which abounds in threats.

Jôong is asked whether she can hear. With difficulty, she half opens her eyes; muttering something, she points to her right breast. Jôong-Wan, the third healer in Sar Luk, rubs the spot indicated, extends her massage to the area of the kidneys, and, from time to time, shakes her fingers to cast away the unwholesome filth she has drawn from the body. Whence the name of this ministration, *proproh uuk* or *proproh kiek*—"the treatment whereby one extracts mud [or sand]"; it is a question, evidently, of mud or sand which has been sent by the *caak* and which is the cause of the illness. Warm water is brought to the healer. She dips her finger in it and massages the patient's back in the same fashion.

Meanwhile, Kroong-Big-Navel has brought out a large jar, opened it, and poured a part of its contents into a *yang dâm.*

The sick woman is helped to a sitting position. Some raw cotton is placed in a Mnong bowl, and embers are laid on it. Drüm-Kraang takes a peacock quill, strips the feathers from it, and throws them on the embers so that the odor arising from them may make the soul reappear here below. Then, as a measure of protection, she hangs the quill around the patient's neck, for Spirits and sorcerers are afraid of peacock feathers.

Aang-of-the-Drooping-Eyelid revolves the little pouch of magic stones eight times above her mother-in-law's head, asking for her prompt cure. She speaks with great feeling. Her father-in-law, Kröng-Jôong, joins his prayers to hers. After Aang has finished her incantations, he continues, and concludes by slipping a brass bracelet on Jôong's wrist in token of the commitment he is making to the Spirits to sacrifice a buffalo to them. He declares, however, that if his wife were to die, he would kill whichever *caak* the ordeal ceremony exposed as responsible for her death.

Can points out to me that his family has decided on its own initiative to offer up a buffalo. If Jôong-Kröng succumbs in spite of the sacrifice, he adds, they will proceed to the trial by boiling water to discover who is guilty. To one of my questions, Can replies that the shaman never decrees this or that sacrifice: "He would not dare. You learn what you must do by listening to the magician's exclamations during his discussions with the Spirits. If they call for the sacrifice of a pig, you kill a pig and the sick person gets well. If they call for the sacrifice of a buffalo, you immolate a buffalo and the sick person gets well. But if the Spirits call for no animal meat, if they demand the body of the sufferer, then they devour his soul and the sick person dies."

Quite a few people have hurried in to help the ailing woman, and are crowded around her. The light is scarce, as always, supplied by a few resinous faggots and the fire, which has just been rekindled; only faces in the first row, the posts of the granary, and the sick woman's pallet emerge from the shadows. So much smoke aggravates the poor ventilation, yet Jôong seems a bit better; her breathing is a little more regular, and Aang-of-the-Drooping-Eyelid takes advantage of this to redo her mother-in-law's chignon. Finally, with great effort, Jôong even tries to speak. In an extremely weak voice, she tells us that she saw a *caak* fly over her head; then her arms were bound by double loops of rope, and five men tried to drag her away. There is terror in her eyes; with both hands, she pushes the horrible apparition from her.

Aang-of-the-Drooping-Eyelid runs out for some *rkôong* leaves, which Jôong-Wan dips in water and Drüm-Kraang brushes over her mother-in-law's eyes. The same healer then massages the sick woman's closed eyelids. She continues her massage, her hands moving down toward the area of the heart.

Since Jôong is still being supported in a sitting position, I advise that she be laid down. At the sound of my voice, she turns and looks at me, and helps the women lay her down. She asks to be carried near the hearth, and adds in a murmur, "Stir up the fire." Immediately, her daughter Mang-of-the-Crooked-Mouth blows on the embers with all the power of her youthful lungs—and at the risk of setting fire to the granary floor. Drüm comes to massage the sick woman's neck, periodically throwing away "the mud of the sorcerers."

Jôong appears to be dozing but suddenly, in a hoarse, fading voice, she breaks into a little song. Her daughter is frightened and calls, "Mama! Mama!" Aang-of-the-Drooping-Eyelid says authoritatively, "Now one must offer the counterpart, the ritual exchange to the Spirit of the Watering Place"—the Spirit that makes one mad—and she goes out. More calmly, Kröng sends someone to look for a chicken, while he selects an old *yang dâm* for the ceremony. Aang returns, accompanied by two young men carrying a large jar. She indicates, with some emotion, that she has bought it herself—paid twenty piasters for it. She adds that she is also going to get a cock, that she wishes to anoint the holy quartz with blood and to have the jar revolved over the sick woman. She urges the young men not to wander off but to fetch lalang grass and water. (As things turn out, Aang's jar will not be opened today, nor will anyone lay eyes on the promised cock.)

Kröng splits the chicken's beak, collects the blood in a Vietnamese bowl, and fills a copper bowl with rice beer siphoned from the *yang dâm.* He places them on the low platform by the back wall, where, at the foot of the row of big jars, he has also laid the small wicker pouch containing Jôong's magic quartz and stones, thinking her sickness may be a manifestation of their anger. His wife rouses and calls for him. Kröng runs to her and gently answers the inaudible questions she puts to him: "You began to sing. . . . I've already killed the chicken. . . ." Kröng returns to the pouch and liquid offerings; he anoints the magic quartz—or, rather, the little bag containing them—and crouches down in prayer. Making wide gestures of salutation with his cupped hands, as if he were gathering up something before him, he intones:

> "O Spirit of the Pouch,
> O Spirit of the Quartz,
> O Spirit of the Earth,
> O Spirit of the Soil . . ."

Prayer couplets follow, asking that misfortune be warded off and that a cure be granted.

Then the jar is opened. I drink first, cede my place to Kröng, then comes Baap Can's turn. While we are drinking, Aang is seized by a crying fit: "I feel all alone, forsaken. I am so unhappy! . . . I offered the sacrifice of anointment, and it was not accepted. . . ."

Kröng returns to anoint the magic stones again, so that they may consent to take care of the sick woman.

Meanwhile, Can, Mhoo-Laang, two of Jôong's sons—Kraang-Drüm and

Tôong-Jieng—and two other young men have set out for Sar Lang to summon Ddöi, of the Rlük clan, the plain's most highly regarded shaman. Around ten o'clock, the *njau* arrives, escorted by the six young men from Sar Luk.

Kröng and the shaman squat before the two jars prepared by Kroong-Big-Navel. They slit the throat of a chicken, and the *njau* inserts a drinking straw in the *yang dâm.* Kröng anoints Ddöi's magic quartz and stones with the blood (also, for the third time, those of his wife). A woman died the day before yesterday in Sar Lang, the shaman's village, and when a consultation takes place within seven days of a death, either in the village of the healer or in that of the sick person, one must anoint the magic stones with blood before beginning the séance.

Kröng's visitors' room had emptied somewhat, but now, with Ddöi's arrival, it is filling up again. The crowd is larger than before. People who had not come to visit the ailing woman now hurry in to be present at the séance—most out of curiosity, some out of concern. Jôong-Wan, for instance, brings her husband, who walks with difficulty; he took to his bed twenty-two days ago, and his recent improvement is attributed to the three séances accompanied by sacrifices (a chicken and two pigs) that Ddöi held for him. The shaman proudly has me note this fresh success that is to be credited to his skill. (I make my contribution to Wan-Jôong's recovery by giving him pills.) Baap Can, who has learned to recognize the efficacy of Western medication, boasts of how he benefited from the injection I had arranged for him to be given by the nurse who had come to Sar Luk with the Commissioner.

The séance opens, as always, with a series of treatments (*proproh*) similar to those administered earlier by the women healers. A quartz moistened now and then in a bowl of water (this bowl being a part of the *njau*'s gear) is passed over the neck of the sick woman, with a simulated snapping of the small cord that was strangling her; then the quartz is passed over her heart. Massage of her head, which, Jôong complains, aches; more passing of the quartz over her throat; a long massage of her chest and back, and a very vigorous massage of the kidney area. As Ddöi works on her, he asks her what it was she sang, but she does not even remember having sung, she was unconscious. Ddöi laughs. Meanwhile, a Vietnamese bowl of hulled rice has been placed near him, in payment of his services.

Next, Ddöi scrubs the sick woman briskly with a handful of *rkôong* leaves that have been warmed in a pot of water. As he brushes the leaves over her body, he blows on the sensitive spot. Close by, Drüm is commenting on the Kroong-Aang affair: "Let them sleep together . . . eat together. . . . Why divorce?" The *njau* concludes by spitting a bit of a magic tuber (a Zingiberacea) on Jôong's heart area, forehead, and again the heart, accompanying his gestures with the recitation of a charm that is not easily to translate:

> *"Be restored!*
> *Be restored from the tip of the open palm.*
> *Obey the tongue, hearken to the hands;*
> *obey the mouth, hearken to the saliva. . . ."*

Finally, they raise the woman to a sitting position. The shaman presses her eyelids shut, then orders her to open her eyes.

By way of a brief respite, Ddöi takes a small flute from his covered basket, but his thoughts are elsewhere and he forgets to play it. Aang-of-the-Drooping-Eyelid is telling the women that she only did it once and she was dead drunk at the time.

Seated apart, Kroong-Big-Navel is splitting a piece of *ngör* bamboo into strands that old Krah will use to braid a miniature goat and buffalo. Tôong-Jieng asks the shaman if he must model a slave. The latter replies in the affirmative, so Tôong fashions one out of moistened earth.

It is eleven o'clock at night when Kröng and Ddöi come to squat before the big jar. The head of the house hands the *njau* the drinking straw, some *ling ong* (unidentified) leaves, and some *tieng kau* reeds (*Arundo madagascariensis* Kunth), which the shaman ties together at the root ends; lastly, a bush hook, which he rests on his shoulder. Kröng slits the neck of a red cock and passes it to his wife's eldest son for him to plunge in hot water and pluck. He then hands some wort mixed with blood to Ddöi. As the shaman inserts the straw in the jar, he informs the Spirits what is being offered them, and recites prayers; his companion prays with him. After laying the bush hook and leaves on the ground, Ddöi anoints the ground, then the pouch of magic stones:

> *"Hasten in pursuit of the body,*
> *quickly, summon the soul;*
> *travel to the abode of the Intelligences,*
> *enter the home of the Spirits,*
> *go see the Taang Mbieng Spirits,*
> *node of the* Ngör *Bamboo,*
> *mouth of the* Dlei *Bamboo,*
> *horn planted in the forehead.*
> *The water in the ditch is contained,*
> *the water in the ravine is dammed back,*
> *execrable words are withheld.*
> *The women chatter in the evening,*
> *the men gossip at night,*
> *the powerful ones discourse as they drink. . . ."*

While Kröng siphons rice beer into a bottle, the *njau* is administering a "mud massage" to Wan-Jôong's belly. I drink first, and give my place to

Ddöi, who is succeeded by Tôong-Wan. While the latter is squatting before the jar, cries and appeals for help come from his quarters nearby.*
It is Bbaang, the son of Lieng-the-Widower, who has suffered an epileptic seizure. (Because his child had had a fever for two days, Lieng, who lives in Sar Lang, had brought him here to be treated by Jôong-Wan.) Ddöi now treats the child's "strangling by the Spirits" in the identical way he had ministered to Jôong-Kröng for the same affliction.

Aang goes out into the yard with Drüm to pound some rice and saffron, which she carries back into the house in a gourd shard. As she hands it to the shaman, she seizes the opportunity to ask him to give her a simple throat massage.

At last, Ddöi proceeds to the fumigation of the patient (*hôol cae trôo'*), the operation preliminary to his taking off for the Beyond. To the saffroned rice, which has been placed in the Mnong bowl, he orders a few embers to be added, over which he shakes some "resin from the Sky." It gives off a thick, acrid smoke. Lifting Jôong into a sitting position, he covers her with a blanket that conceals even her head. He parts the two front folds to slip inside the Mnong bowl with the burning resin, so that the fumes rise to the patient's face. He chants:

> "Jôong, wife of the resin of the mason bee,
> Jaang, wife of the resin of the tloong tree,
> Dloong, wife of the resin of the Sky,
> walk noisily,
> fly in full cry,
> so that the tumult may swell,
> so that word may burst forth and spread
> of the rich gifts offered the Spirits to settle the case.
> The flat gongs we have left in the forest;
> the jar we have abandoned along the road;
> the axe we have thrown on the wood.
>
> O great pràm Lance, do not blunt your tip;
> you, O Broom, sweep up the dung;
> you, O Pinch, anoint the mouth of the jar;
> you, O Flat Gong, seal the mouth of the case.
> If you wish to eat the male buffalo, go to the Rhade;
> if you wish to eat the female buffalo, go to the Rlâm;
> they increase in number, do the Cham who live in the Low Country. †
>
> The women chatter in the evening;
> the men gossip at night;

---

* Tôong-Wan lives with his uncle Mbieng-Grieng. To review the disposition of the long house: Baap Can, Kröng-Jôong, Tôong-Jieng, and Mbieng-Grieng. See *d* XIII, XIV, XV, and XVI, on the map, pp. 8–9.
† Annam.

the powerful ones discourse as they drink.
Eye of the node of the Ngör *Bamboo,*
mouth of the node of the Dlei *Bamboo,*
horn planted in the forehead . . ."

At the conclusion of his prayer, the *njau* pours water over the embers to quench them. He takes a pinch of saffroned rice from the fumigation bowl, anoints the sick woman's head, then the hollow of her throat, her belly, sides, knees, and the palms of her hands. He rises and, with the same pinch of saffroned rice, anoints the foreheads of Aang-of-the-Drooping-Eyelid, Wan-Jôong, and the wife of Tôong-Wan in behalf of her nephew. Tôong has brought a bowl of hulled rice in payment of the ministrations given the child.

On the platform, at the foot of the row of jars and near the granary beneath which the sick woman has been laid, they set a large winnowing basket that contains the offerings destined for the Spirits: an enormous heap of rice, atop which has been placed an egg flanked by two pieces of quartz; between each quartz and the egg, a miniature weapon carved from a blade of bamboo has been stuck in the rice—a saber on one side, a lance on the other; these objects lie within the circumference outlined by a necklace. Behind the mound of rice, there are a tiny buffalo and a goat of plaited bamboo; a hollow stick into which small bits of the meat and viscera of the sacrificed chicken have been stuffed; a Vietnamese bowl containing white rice; and two miniature flat gongs cut from a gourd. Lastly, a second and smaller mound of rice is topped by a pair of tiny flat gongs like those in the bowl. A hoe has been laid beside the winnowing basket, together with a bowl and a bottle, both full of rice beer siphoned from the jar. The *njau* has draped himself in his blanket, taking care to leave his right arm free. He sits down behind these offerings, places his *wiah* over his left shoulder, and lays within reach of his right hand the *ling ong* leaves and the reeds. He stretches his legs out before him.

The interior of a Mnong house, an upside-down ship's hull fashioned of bamboo and thatch, is always dark, even in full daylight. At night, the smoke from the several hearths seems to make the masses of shadow even more opaque, and what light is given off by the pine faggots does not travel very far. Now only the shaman and the display of offerings, both real and symbolic, are illuminated. The sick woman lies on her pallet to one side, beneath the granary and near the hearth. The crowd pressing around the magician–hunter of souls is a compact wall, enclosing the lighted area. The atmosphere is tense: in the eyes of all, this voyage of the *njau* into the Beyond preserves its character of an adventure rife with risks for the practitioner. However, it is not only danger that rivets their attention. People also hope to have word of near relatives who are ailing or dead. The room is relatively still; people comment on the shaman's exclamations, and some of those who have not been lucky enough to get

places in the first row (generally, the women rush to take over these locations) continue to chatter. One cannot deny the profound beauty of these
shamanist séances, the skill with which they are mounted, their richness
in symbolic objects and actions. The incantations are obscure, the verses
replete with words added "just for the rhyme" or words whose meaning is
now forgotten, but they have a powerful and sonorous musicality. The ab-
struse magic charms; the awkward, blind fumbling of the Wanderer of the
Beyond (the shaman performs the entire séance with his eyes shut); the all
too real illness; the actual presence in the room (no one there would
dream of doubting it) of those agents of death, the Spirits and the
sorcerers—all these elements suffuse the séance with an atmosphere of
authentic mystery and tragic grandeur.

Ddöi withdraws a tiny porcelain flagon from his magic-stone pouch, lifts
it to his lips, blows into it, and raises it to the level of his right ear, saying,
"One." He prolongs the sound of the word with a whistle. Again he blows
into his flagon and raises it to his left ear: "Two," and he whistles. . . .
And so on, up to "Eight," at which point he shuts his eyes and sways back
and forth, back and forth, whistling. "He has fallen asleep," people tell
each other. Among the several indistinct words he utters, like a sleeper
disturbed by dreams, one catches: "My sister Jôong . . ." (In fact, Jôong
is a Rjee and he a Rlük, and the two clans are connected.) He shakes the
bundle of leaves he holds in his right hand and "departs"—he pumps his
legs up and down in a piston-like movement. As he "walks," he chants
prayers in which he invites the Spirits of different sites to accompany him
on his search for souls:

> *"Tôong Traang coming from the Spirit of the Canal by*
> *the fig tree, up, come with me,*
> *Father of Yae, Ngkuâr of the forest of violent death,*
> *up, come with me,*
> *Sieng Laa, rock of the white fish, up, come with me. . . ."*

Suddenly, someone notices that the charcoal, the go-between in the
Beyond, has been forgotten. Coals are quickly placed in the basket of offerings. Still journeying on, the *njau* now addresses the soul of the sick
woman. He exhorts it to return speedily to its body:

> *"Walk, and may you with one step traverse the length of*
> *a drying post.*
> *Fling your leg forward, and may you with one step tra-*
> *verse the length of a canoe gaff.*
> *Bound forward, and may you with one step traverse the*
> *length of a lance stock.*
> *Dawdle, and may you with one step traverse the length*
> *of a wicker handle. . . ."*

Then he reverts to his couplets, enumerating the Site Spirits. He whistles and sways back and forth:

"Listen, elder brother, we bay from here;
listen, younger brother, we call from here;
Oh-ay! . . . Oh-ay! . . . younger brother, we call from here below. . . ."

He questions the souls of the charcoal peremptorily, whistles, "halts," speaks in a low voice, then silently takes off again. Suddenly, he bangs on the ground before him, uttering a *"Trii!"* which is followed by a rhymed charm (the many words added for the rhyme make it difficult to translate): Ddöi has just encountered the souls of the sorcerers and he is intimidating them.

From the winnowing basket, he removes the offerings for his interlocutors and places them beside him, announcing in rhymed verses what he is giving: buffalo, goat, and other simulacra. He takes up a handful of white rice, telling the *caak*, "Go find a big pannier, a big, sturdy pannier." He opens his clenched fist and presses it against his left palm, which is extended and flat. Harder and harder he presses, and not one grain of rice falls. He concludes by rubbing his palms together, as if to demonstrate that his hands are empty. "The sorcerers have eaten the rice," a man near me comments. As he was delivering the ransom, Ddöi kept asking the *caak* not to eat the human being, his patient.

Having surrendered these numerous gifts to the *caak*, he parts the blanket over his chest and clacks his tongue several times, as if he were calling a dog; in actuality, he is attracting the soul of the sick woman. When the *njau* draws his blanket together again, Kröng comes from behind to scoop up the air at his back, and goes to pour it on his wife's head: he is "gathering up the soul brought back from the country of the Spirits and sorcerers" (*dôop hêeng böh Yaang böh caak*).

Still "asleep," Ddöi extracts from the big pile of rice the little stick in which minute shreds of chicken meat have been stuffed. He pulls bits of the meat out now and then, and throws them in front of him. Some fall to the ground, others appear to be volatilized: the *caak*, people murmur, have snapped them up. (I have noted that now and then Ddöi only goes through the motions of throwing pieces of meat when, in fact, he has taken nothing up in his hand.) Eight times he spits *"Phit! Phit!"* He resumes his chanting, whistles, and presents the Spirits—invisible to us— with the Vietnamese bowl of rice beer: "This meat of chicken, be the first to eat it; this *rnööm*, be the first to drink it. I will drink only after you." He encounters the soul of Bbaang, Lieng's ailing son, and gathers it up in his blanket; since the child is still at Tôong-Wan's, the latter's wife pours the soul over herself. Next, Ddöi meets the soul of little Wan, the son of Kraang-Drüm.

After these two soul collections, he says *"Phit!"* eight times, and resumes his "walk."

> *"I go, like the Ancestress Biing, wending my way;*
> *I go, like the Ancestress Biing, who carried her pannier by a strap;*
> *I go, like the Ancestress Biing, she of the shaggy head;*
> *I go, like the Ancestress Biing, who roared with laughter. . . ."*

Suddenly, he brandishes his bush hook and pretends to sever an invisible rope. He replaces the *wiah* over his shoulder, and with his fingernails he cracks something we cannot see, but his mouth is contorted from the effort he is making. ("He has cut the lead line with which the sorcerers had tied the sick woman's buffalo-soul.")

"Phit! . . ." eight times, and he sets out again. A fresh halt: he extracts from his precious pouch the magic plants *Elêt* and "the ginger for awaking," munches on them, and spits them out in front of him eight times. He halts, chants again, and extends his hand toward the hoe; it is passed to him. With it, "he digs the weeds by the foot of the *rlaa*-soul" (the giant-bamboo-soul):

> *"I heap the earth around the foot of the* Rlaa;
> *I hoe the weeds around the foot of the* Rlaa;
> *may the chickens, scratching in the dirt, throw no*
>   *earth on the eggplant;*
> *may the chickens, scratching in the dirt, throw no*
>   *earth on the solanaceous* prêen."

He lays the hoe down and takes off again, now singing "the canoe-soul":

> *"Attach the wood firmly to the canoe. . . .*
> *Canoe, wound round with thread,*
> *Canoe, adorned with necklaces,*
> *Canoe, reinforced with bamboo spikes . . ."*

Once again, he gathers up the soul:

> *"O Jôong, return to your village. . . .*
> *Do not remain in the forest, do not roam the tracks."*

And behold, he now meets one of Krae-Drüm's two children who died this year. From the conversation he has with the soul, clearly it is asking for soup and rice, it is hungry. Next, he gathers up the soul of Aang-of-the-Drooping-Eyelid, who suffers from an incipient goiter. He then throws some soup over his shoulder toward the back of the house and in front of him. Three times he tosses a few grains of rice in the air:

> *"The sorcerers stand, covetous, on the left;*
> *the water in the ditch is contained;*
> *the water in the ravine is dammed back;*
> *execrable mouths are silenced."*

He throws more rice. It does not fall to the ground.

I was about to knock my pipe against the edge of the platform, to empty it, but someone stops me. This act is taboo: my pipe becomes the *rtleh* bird and places the shaman in great danger.

Ddöi holds out his hands sidewise, thereby indicating that he wants some water; it is poured for him. He brushes his dampened hands over his face and now is able to open his eyes; he comes out of his hypnotic state. From where he sits, he waves his hands and sprinkles the sick woman with water. He stands up and arranges necklace and magic quartz in the pouch. He offers me the egg, and lets the women empty all the rice from his *khiu*. Then he walks over to Jôong. Placing himself face to face with her, he presses a magic quartz between her eyes and slips it up over her brow to the top of her head, where he "digs" it in, chanting the while.

He administers the same treatment to the other invalids and even to Kröng and Mang-of-the-Crooked-Mouth since they, being Jôong's husband and daughter, share her household. He returns to his former place, throws the *rnööm* in the bowl toward the back wall of the house (the same spot where he threw soup and rice offerings), but the bottle of rice beer he keeps.

All the simulacra intended for the Spirits have been reassembled in the winnowing basket: buffalo and goat of wicker, slave of mud, and the flat gongs made of gourds. Also left in it are a few grains of rice and the remains of the gourd shards that contained the saffroned rice, a part of which was used in the fumigation. The shaman presents the filled basket to the sick woman, has her spit on it eight times—he counting aloud the while—then he spits on it once, and recites:

> "May the freshwater leech, having sucked, be filled;
> may the terrestrial leech, having sucked, fall;
> may the ringworm, having sucked, let go.
> Betake yourself to the others, there below;
> strong young men are they, those others there below;
> children in full growth are they, those others there below. . . ."

He revolves the winnowing basket eight times above Jôong's head, then sweeps the sick woman with the leaves he used on his voyage into the Beyond.

The *njau* leaves the house by the private door, accompanied by a woman member of the family. When he reaches the village's outermost building, beyond Jôong-Kröng's pigsty, he lays the offerings to the Spirits on the ground—buffalo, goat, slave, and so forth—near a cluster of tall grasses. The last item is the charcoal, on which he spits, and before placing the coals on the ground, he recites:

> "I bring the rhiing *slave*,
>   the rheeng *flat gongs*,

> *the ivory canine of the ancestor.*
> *I offer them with both hands,*
> *I set them down with care,*
> *I speak in a grave voice.*
> *Consent that she be cured, from the tip of the open palm."*

He rises and scatters saffroned rice in the air in several directions, but particularly over the tall grasses. Then he slips the basket under them, shakes them violently, and exhorts:

> *"Appear, appear . . . return to your home;*
> *we will welcome you beneath the granary;*
> *children, husband await you. . . ."*

We all three peer into the basket: a minute spider has fallen into it.* With the back of his empty hand, the *njau* taps the basket, which makes the minute creature jump. Ddöi flicks it into the wicker box the young woman holds out to him, and she swiftly closes the lid. When he has collected several small spiders in this fashion, we return to the house; as we are moving off, the *njau* tears a leaf from the grass he has shaken. Before crossing the threshold of the private door, Ddöi asks in a loud voice, "Is she cured?" From within, they answer, "She is cured."

He approaches the sick woman, opens the wicker box above her head, and taps on it. The area where this scene is taking place is very dark, and one does not see whether or not the spider-souls have regained their home, but this is the assumption:

> *"O soul, spirit that follows the debt, return. . . ."*

He moistens the leaf he has brought back with him, and brushes it over the breast, back, and limbs of the sick woman, reciting:

> *"Be cool like water,*
> *bloom like the taro,*
> *at night, sleep deep. . . ."*

With no further prayer, he slips the leaf into the thatch above the private door. And with this final act, at one-thirty in the morning, the séance ends.

January 25

Around eleven o'clock, Kröng-Jôong receives a visit from his *jôok*, the headman of Sar Lang. Choong-Yôong has come to see Jôong, whose illness he learned of yesterday. As he enters the house, he chews a few

---

* Whence the name of this last phase of the *mhö'*, by which the entire séance is frequently designated: *tau bung*, or "to shake [the leaves] [to gather up] the spider [soul]."

grains of rice and spits them out eight times on top of the ailing woman's head, declaring:

> *"The rice brings them running*
> *to see the sickness,*
> *makes the powerful ones come to visit. . . ."*

He picks up a broom, brushes it eight times over the invalid's body, reciting a series of wishes. He lays the broom across the doorway, a short distance inside the threshold.

The house fills little by little, for the village has been alerted that a pig is to be sacrificed to retrieve Jôong's soul. The victim is killed around noon. A pinch of wort is soaked in a small amount of the blood, and is placed not in a Mnong bowl but on the little heap of wort laid on the jar stopper. Then the jar is consecrated. Kröng hands the drinking straw and a pinch of blood-soaked wort to each of the three men who have joined him to squat before Jôong: Ddöi-the-Shaman; Bbôong-the-Deputy, who has agreed to be the go-between in the sacrifice and, in token of this function, carries a saber over his shoulder; and Choong, the sworn friend of the master of the house. The four men ask, in several varied couplets, that Jôong be restored to health. After this recitation, Bbôong-Mang takes the jar stopper, covered with the blood-drenched wort, and places it by the inner side of the threshold of the main door. All the men present run to take a pinch of the wort, crouch down, and anoint the threshold while they recite numerous prayer couplets. The deputy, his saber resting on his left shoulder, stands near the door and anoints the top, calling on the Spirits:

> *"The sickness makes me groan, and I implore thee, O Spirit;*
> *the pain makes me moan, and I implore thee, O Spirit;*
> *howling with misery, I implore thee, O Spirit.*
> *The rope is snapped; I beg thee to retie it;*
> *the fence is broken; I beg thee to repair it;*
> *one, two, I beg thee to keep watch. . . ."*

Kröng, who has remained alone by the jar, continues to recite wishes. Then, still praying, he goes to anoint the head of the pig.

While young men prepare the sacrificial meat, people drink and chatter. A bowl of salted liver and tripes is passed around first. On the low platform, Kröng, assisted by Ndür-the-Lame, works up a white paste with a rice-flour base to model offerings intended for the Spirits: five seated slaves, each supported by a snake; some pythons, a centipede, a pair of elephant tusks, two rhinoceros horns, a basket of pork meat, and two bowls containing two eggs. They set their finished models on a small bamboo wattle over which they have laid two pieces of banana leaf. Then Kröng moistens a bamboo twig in blood and stains the top of each object with a drop or two. Lastly, he adds the ball of leftover paste to the tray of offerings, which he balances on the mouth of a jar that has been placed where the shaman will officiate. The sacrificed pig's heart has been attached with a wisp of rattan to one of the small handles, or "ears," of a large jar among those aligned at the back of the house. At the foot of this same jar have been set two bowls containing chopped meat and a few pieces of charcoal; also, one bowl and one jar of rice beer. Slightly to the fore of these offerings they place the jar supporting the wattle tray with the rice-paste models and the winnowing basket containing the white rice and the same offerings as yesterday.

By one-thirty in the afternoon, everything is ready. The *njau* takes his place on the low platform, facing the offerings. He has neither *wiah* nor leaves this time, for he is to perform a *grôong* séance. "*Grôong*" denotes a sort of resonant harness of necklaces, bracelets, and little bells strung on a thin cord, which is attached by a brass bracelet to a *yang dâm* support.

As in the earlier *mhö'*, the shaman begins by falling asleep with the aid of his magic flagon. He "leaves" by making his *grôong* jingle like a horse's harness. From time to time, he pulls it brusquely to the right, as if his mount had shied to the left. Chants and actions are the same as before, except for the offering of the gifts. This time, he places them on his head before setting them down on the platform; in this fashion, he offers first the wattle, then a large bowl of meat, then the contents of the winnowing basket.

After he "wakes up," he pours a little rice beer and throws some bits of meat on the floor between the two jars at the back of the house. He then places a quartz on the top of the sick woman's head. He has Jôong spit on all the offerings in the basket before he revolves it eight times above her head, then hands it over to Krōng. In this type of *mhö'* there is no search for the spider-soul. The husband of the sick woman, accompanied by Tôong-Jieng, who is armed with a bush hook, simply places the offerings down on the outskirts of the village. The two men leave and return by the private door.

The meat in the two large bowls that is being offered the Spirits is sampled, after which the daughter of the house serves a real meal to the *njau* and to Krōng's friend Choong and the latter's son.

In a bamboo scoop (ordinarily used as a dustpan), the go-between assembles the pig's jaw, the uncooked rice, a tube of blood, and some charcoal. The dustpan thus garnished he revolves eight times above Jôong's head. He repeats the action, using a broom stalk to which he has fastened a tuft of cotton. He places the stalk in the scoop and leaves the house with Krōng. They walk together to the edge of the woods, where Bbôong sets his gifts of exorcism down by the side of the road. He proceeds to the divination, using the tube of blood (*pool ding mhaam*). First, he rakes the ground to clear a space; then, splitting the tube of blood in two, he lets both pieces fall to the ground as he recites:

> *"Heads for the Spirits,*
> *tails for us.*
> *Recover by virtue of this meat;*
> *recover by virtue of this alcohol.*
> *One pig*
> *and the alcohol of one jar . . ."*

But the two pieces fall in the wrong positions. He starts afresh, and continues the operation until they fall suitably—that is, until the piece near him falls cleft side up (*rblaang*) and the other ("the one that is on the side of the Spirits") presents the round outer side (*rtlup*).

Still squatting, and measuring the while, he inches his way toward the village until he has traversed seven spans; at the eighth, he stands, gathers up a pinch of earth, and cuts a leaf from a nearby plant. Re-entering the house, he applies the pinch of earth to Jôong's head, then brushes the broom, which he has moistened in water from a gourd, over her body. Next, he sweeps the space between the sick woman and the door by which he has entered, and he throws the broom across the threshold. All the while, he has been reciting:

> *"Be cool like water,*
> *bloom like the taro;*
> *at night, sleep deep. . . ."*

Everything is completed by four o'clock in the afternoon. People drink and talk. His task finished, Bbôong-Mang must go, for he has left behind at his home, alone before a jar, Mang-Master-of-the-Ivory, who has come to sell an antique jar. Bbaang-the-Stag, who used to act as go-between for the Cil Bboon Jaa, has managed to whet the deputy's interest in it. However, Bbôong would like to acquire this valuable property without dealing face to face with the visiting foreigner. By dint of running all over the village, he has contrived to put together the sixteen hundred piasters Mang is asking.

People leave us little by little. By sundown, everyone has gone off to Kröng-Aang's. His house is being exorcised by the sacrifice of one dog and a jar of rice beer, because a swallow flew into the house the day Tieng killed himself.

January 26

The villagers went out early today to work in the fields.* For Baap Can, this is an important day, because it is his family's turn to be assisted by

---

* See G. Condominas, "L'Entr'aide agricole chez les Mnong Gar (Proto-Indochinois du Viêt-Nam central)," *Etudes Rurales*, Nos. 53–56 (1974), pp. 407–20.

the team of which his youngest daughter is a member. When they return from the fields in the late afternoon, they find Kröng-the-Stutterer, come to claim the big jar he had been promised in payment of his services as *rnôom* during the September Exchange of Sacrifices.

Jôong's condition remains unchanged. Ddöi has spent the day at the school, where the teacher had summoned him to treat his son, who cries continually.

January 27

Early this morning, Baap Can toured the village to announce to Truu and all other inhabitants that a buffalo would be immolated to recover Jôong's soul; accordingly, no one should go out to work on clearing the *miir*. So everyone, Baap Can included, simply went into the forest to cut firewood and gather wild vegetables. The only people to leave us are Truu, his deputy, and the two runners; they go off to attend the party the Plantation is offering. However, Bbaang-the-Stag and Can will be coming back in the early afternoon.

Jôong is as gravely ill as ever. Sabers and lances the length of a man's hand have been cut from dried pandanus leaves and hung above her mat beneath the granary; they ward off sorcerers. Jôong is not strong enough to walk alone, and must be supported when she goes outside the house to relieve herself. But she is no longer the only one seriously ill. Last evening, her younger sister, Grieng-Mbieng, came down with a high fever. Her adopted son and his wife, Tôong and Wan, have left for Paang Döng to look for the shaman, who is known to have gone there to recover a debt. Around ten-thirty, they are back, and he with them. Tôong is carrying a green jar, which is Ddöi's payment for five séances he held.

Fifteen minutes later, Jôong's son Bbür arrives with wife, children, and parents-in-law, as well as Bbaang-Jrae-the-Soldier and his family. (It will be remembered that Bbaang-Jrae is a Rjee; he is the son of old Troo, of Sar Luk.) Each couple has brought a Vietnamese bowl of hulled rice and a bracelet. The moment Bbür arrives, he chews a few grains of rice and spits them out on the top of his mother's head, declaring:

> *"I have come to pay a visit. May you others, you Spirits, pay a visit.*
> *I have come to pay a visit. May you others, you Divinities, pay a visit.*
> *May her body be cool, may she sleep soundly.*
> *Remain among us until you grow old,*
> *eat until you are aged,*
> *converse until you become* kuang. . . ."

He slips the bracelet on his mother's wrist, asking again that she may enjoy good health. (The bracelet is a threat to the *caak*, who understand that a commitment has been made: in the event that the sick woman died, there would be a case; the guilty one would be discovered through the trial of boiling water, and would be put to death.) In turn, the other visitors repeat Bbür's actions. The Nyôong Brah folk are not the first to have come; Choong, the *jôok* from Sar Lang, arrived an hour earlier.

At eleven-thirty, the sacrifice of a pig at Grieng's; it is the holy man old Bbaang-Jieng-the-Pregnant-Man who summons the Spirits. Almost no one attends the ceremony.

Around one-thirty in the afternoon, Krah, Tôong-Jieng, and the latter's friend Troo-Jôong bring back from the forest a trunk and two straight limbs of *rmuan* (*Spondias mang.?*). Troo steadies the base of the trunk, while old Krah, with heavy blows of his axe, sculptures the other end into a "hornbill beak" (*mbuung kriing*). This motif, which is actually a highly stylized representation of the bird's neck and head, is carved on the top of a post only when one immolates a buffalo in behalf of a person who is ill or dead. People say that in ancient times the sorcerers indicated that they required this sign.

A hole is dug near the edge of the roof, and the post with the hornbill beak is placed upright in it. The two limbs that had been stripped of their branches and also brought back from the forest are stuck into the earth in a slanting position, so that they cross underneath the sculptured motif; a third is placed horizontally and tied to the base of the first two. At the point where they cross, the two oblique branches are firmly fastened to the upright trunk with ropes of heavy rattan. Then, with a *wiah*, the two upper branches are trimmed, the whole forming, in effect, a St. Andrew's cross.

The installation takes a few moments, and at Mbieng-Grieng's, the first *mhö'* for his wife's illness is commencing. The shaman "leaves" for the Beyond, armed with a *wiah* and a whisk of leaves. Since the ceremony is identical to the first one Ddöi performed for Jôong, let me simply note that en route to the Beyond the *njau* has a very sharp altercation with a sorcerer in regard to Jôong: "I do not fear you," Ddöi says. And, threatening the *caak* with his *wiah:* "You have devoured a pig, and now they give you, in addition, a buffalo. So be quiet." A little later, he meets the soul of Tieng, the suicide. Lastly, he searches for Grieng's spider-soul, as he had in behalf of Jôong.

Kroong-Big-Navel and Maang-the-Thin arrive at four, leading the young buffalo that is to be sacrificed. They are famished, having eaten nothing since they set out this morning. They had gone first to Nyôong Brah to borrow Bbür's buffalo, but before they reached the village the roedeer belled, so they could not take a buffalo from there. Nonetheless, Kroong took advantage of being there to alert his brothers, Bbür and Bbaang-Jrae, that the sacrifice was to be offered. Next, he and his companion went on to Sar Lang to get the animal of Mhoo-Laang (maternal nephew of Kröng-Jôong), which was grazing there.

The animal is led to a salina near the village to wait until the big male buffalo is brought in and tethered for the night.

The jars to be drunk are brought into Kröng-Jôong's visitors' room. It has not been swept since the first séance, for one may not clean a room in which a *mhö'* has been held until some days after the ceremony. Seven jars of *rnööm* must be offered when one immolates a buffalo.* Some of those brought in now are empty, and wort taken from a *yang dâm* is thrown into them.

Indeed, the quota of seven jars is surpassed, for they manage to line up eleven. First, there is the jar Kröng offers for the *mhö'*; then come the jars of Baap Can (brother of the sick woman), Tôong-Jieng (her son), Bbaang-Jieng (sworn friend of her younger brother and father-in-law of her eldest son), Kraang-Drüm (her eldest son), Kroong-Troo (her husband's "brother"), and Nyaang of Nyôong Brah (father-in-law of Bbür, the youngest of her sons), Mhoo-Laang (maternal nephew of her husband, and married to a "sister"), Troo-Jôong (the *jôok*—via the pig—of her second son, Tôong-Jieng), Kroong-Mae ("distant brother"), Wan-Jôong (who hopes to perform a *Tâm Bôh* with Jôong's brother-in-law, Mbieng-Grieng), and Bbaang-the-Stag (future *jôok* of her eldest son).

Once all the jars are in place, Baap Can orders everyone to be convoked. From each jar, a small amount of wort is removed and placed on one of its ears; Kröng puts additional wort from each jar on the stopper of the first; then all are stuffed with leaves and filled with water. Only when all jars are properly prepared is the buffalo tied to the sacrificial post.

Little by little, the room is filling up. One of the first to arrive is old Tôong-Mang, the senior Rjee and oldest man in the village. He walks over to spit some rice on Jôong's head; since he has no bracelet to offer with the rice, he has brought a Vietnamese bowl.

The buffalo is killed by the usual method: the rear hocks are slashed and the right side pierced. But the beast is full of vigor and is not hindered by any immense head decoration or big ritual barrier. It defends itself strenuously and, as it falls, it bellows. People rush up to pour water over its nostrils.

Then Kröng, the shaman, and Bbaang-the-Stag, who has been appointed go-between, crouch and insert the drinking straw in the first jar. Bbaang rises to his feet, holding the stopper of this jar, which contains wort that has been removed from each of the receptacles offered; the stopper has been moistened with the victim's blood. Bbaang places it on the

---

* Eight, actually; a *yang dâm* is also needed as payment to the go-between, "the man who summons the Spirits."

threshold. Standing erect, his saber over his shoulder, he anoints the top of the door and "summons the Spirits," while all the men hurry over to take a pinch of the wort and bless the earth of the threshold, asking for prosperity and health. They then draw back and Bbaang-the-Stag prays alone. When he has finished his long incantation, he returns to the ailing woman and anoints her with wort and blood. Kröng, a feather in his hand, goes back to the jar and, standing beside it, prays.

Next, each man goes to the particular jar he is offering and consecrates it with a prayer as he inserts the drinking straw. The go-between leads the crowd, in single file, to sip from each *rnööm*. Outside, the buffalo is being dismembered. One shoulder is reserved for the shaman, Ddöi, and one portion of the breast for Bbaang-the-Stag in payment for their services.

While the others drink, Bbieng-Dlaang, the son of Bbaang-the-Pregnant-Man, models from rice paste the persons, animals, and objects to be offered the Spirits: six little men, a buffalo, a mounted rider gripping the reins of his horse, three ivory tusks, a bird, a rhinoceros horn, six stools which he places behind the six little men, a pig, a duck, a centipede, a python, a pair of flat gongs, and a mortar and pestle.

At six in the afternoon, the focus of interest in the long house shifts from Jôong-Kröng's to the quarters of her younger sister. Grieng-Mbieng's illness is to be banished by the sacrifice of a dog.

Tloot and *rhôong* leaves have been scattered before the main door. While an assistant grasps the dog around its middle, Tôong-Jieng stuns it with two blows of a club to the head. Tôong finishes the animal off with a heavy blow on the skull. Leaves are scattered over the bleeding victim, which is jerking in its final death throes. Other famished dogs detect the smell of blood; with noses to the ground, they come on the run and must be driven off. With his *wiah*, Tôong chops off the muzzle, then severs the neck. The jaws and the rest of the head, together with the bloodied leaves, are placed in a dustpan; to them are added a tube of blood, wooden miniatures of tusks and rhinoceros horn, and miniature gongs made from gourd shards. Several young men carry off the carcass to dismember and dress it.

The dustpan and its contents are handed to Bbaang-Jieng-the-Pregnant-Man. He prays as he presents it to Grieng and her husband. Then he takes the jaws and simulacra and revolves them eight times above the head of the sick woman, asking for her recovery. He continues to pray as he receives from Mbieng the club used in killing the dog; he spits on it before placing it in the dustpan. Next, with both hands he grasps the dog's head by the ears and what remains of the tongue, spits on it eight times, then revolves it eight times above Grieng's head. He concludes by brushing the patient with bloodied leaves. He gathers up all the exorcism equipment and the club, and he goes out, followed by Mbieng, who is armed with a bush hook. They walk as far as the track, on the outskirts of the village. Bbaang-Jieng lays his burdens down, except for the tube of blood. The dog's jaws he disposes so that they face the outside, foreign world threateningly (upstream, as it happens), and then, after spitting on the charcoal, he pronounces a charm. He splits the tube of blood in two, lengthwise, and reseals the two halves with dust. He prays and drops the tube several times, always in a new spot, until the farther piece presents its rounded back and the nearer its hollow side. Crouching, he turns back, counts eight spans behind him, and, rising, gathers up a pinch of dust and tears a leaf from a nearby bush. When he re-enters the house, he asks, "Is she cured?" "She is cured" is the response. He presses the dust between Grieng's breasts and between her shoulder blades. In conclusion, he brushes her head with the leaf he has brought back.

He returns to the door with a pointy winnowing basket and a gourd of water. He pours some water into the basket, and throws some outside. This he does eight times, counting aloud. He concludes with a *"Phit!"* and closes the door.

After the quasi-sacramental meal of dog meat, the crowd flows back to the house of the older invalid. The setting for the shamanist séance—made up mainly of offerings—has been completed. To the rear of the house, on the jar in the row which will be opposite the *njau,* the buffalo heart has been suspended from an ear of the jar by a length of rattan. A bottle and a bowl of rice beer have been placed in the space between this jar and its neighbor, and, a little to the fore, the Mnong bowl of "resin from the Sky," the small tray bearing the human and animal figures and the other objects modeled in rice paste, a bowl of cooked rice topped by a hard-boiled egg, and a large Vietnamese bowl of raw buffalo meat. Also to the rear, the big winnowing basket, in the center of which rises a heap of white rice topped by a raw egg. The egg is encircled by tiny weapons (lance, saber, bush hook) carved from a thin strip of bamboo, and the whole is girdled by a necklace. Encircling the bottom of the mound of rice are some charcoal, miniature figures of a buffalo (a rope run through the nose), a goat (rope around the neck), *cing,* a slave, a copper bowl containing a magic-plant tuber, a stick for stirring rice, a loincloth, a double pompon for a man's chignon (the soul of the giant Ancestor Jjöt). Behind the winnowing basket, and therefore nearer the *njau's* right hand, three pouches with magic stones and quartz (they belong to Ddöi, Jôong, and her daughter-in-law Drüm), a gourd shard containing saffroned rice and a hoe. Lastly, the buffalo's head is placed at the base of the low platform, with its muzzle resting on the edge; a cord strung through the nostrils extends to where the shaman will be seated. To the right of the buffalo head, a *yang dâm* surmounted by a large Vietnamese bowl; these two items are the major part of the shaman's fee. Small morsels of the victim's

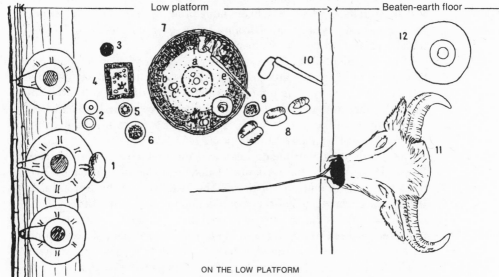

ON THE LOW PLATFORM

1 – The buffalo heart suspended by a rattan cord from an ear of the large jar, opposite which the shaman (*njau*) will take his place   2 – Bottle and Vietnamese bowl filled with rice beer   3 – Mnong bowl with "resin from the Sky"   4 – Small tray bearing the figures and objects modeled in rice paste   5 – Vietnamese bowl with cooked rice topped by a hard-boiled egg   6 – Large Vietnamese bowl with raw buffalo meat   7 – Large winnowing basket with offerings: a heap of white rice (a) on top of which has been placed a raw egg surrounded by tiny weapons (lance, saber, bush hook) carved from a thin strip of bamboo, and by three magic quartzes (placed by the shaman), the ensemble encircled by a necklace; (b) several pieces of charcoal; (c) a miniature buffalo and goat of wicker, a pair of flat gongs (*cing*) carved from a gourd, and the figure of a slave modeled in mud; (c¹) a second pair of *cing* made from a gourd; (d) copper bowl containing a magic-plant tuber (and in which a bracelet will be laid and water poured); (e) stick for stirring rice; (f) loincloth (*suu troany*) and double pompon for a man's chignon wound together   8 – Three pouches of magic quartz and stones belonging, respectively, to the shaman, Jôong-the-Healer, and Drüm-Krang   9 – Gourd shard containing saffroned rice   10 – Hoe

ON THE FLOOR

11 – Head of the buffalo, with the rope slipped through its nostrils, lying on the spot where the shaman will sit   12 – Small neckless jar (*yang dâm*) surmounted by a large Vietnamese bowl   13 – Musical harness (*grôong*)

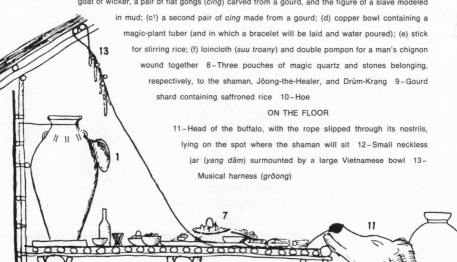

liver, lungs, spleen, and large and small intestines have been stuffed into a stalk of rattan, which has been hung from a *yang dâm*. A musical harness (*grôong*) is suspended from a rafter over the platform, its cord trailing down to where the shaman will sit.

All of a sudden, Baap Can explodes: the *caak* have it in for him! Are they not simultaneously attacking his two sisters, the fruit of the same womb? But he will not be done in. If the women die, he will order the trial by boiling water, and whoever withdraws a red, scalded hand from it—that man will be put to death. The whole canton will submit to the test; no one will be allowed to escape it.

Then, indicating the buffalo head and the vast quantity of offerings, Baap Can makes his final recommendations to Ddöi, as the shaman prepares to climb up onto the platform. The Wanderer of the Beyond is to tell the *caak* what mischief they have done; he must remind them that a buffalo sacrifice is being offered them, that an entire buffalo is being provided for them to eat. But if they do not do their part, if they do not set his sisters' souls free, then he, Baap Can, will bring suit against them. It will be the trial by boiling water, and no mercy will be shown.

Ddöi takes three magic quartzes from his pouch. He dips them in the bowl of rice beer and embeds them around the raw egg atop the heap of rice. He moistens his pouch of magic stones with rice beer, praying the while, and then anoints it with blood from the buffalo heart hanging from the jar.

As a preliminary step to the séance proper, the shaman fumigates the sick woman with "resin from the Sky." She is sitting enveloped in her blanket; he douses the live embers he has thrown on the resin, takes a pinch, and applies it to Jôong-Krông's head, chest, and joints. (The fumigation is not repeated; to do it once leads to a cure, but not twice.) Lastly, he examines his quartz attentively: if it is very transparent, there are chances for recovery; if it is opaque, there are none.

The séance is of the "Bboon Jaa rider" type. The shaman has no bush hook; he unfolds his blanket and wears it over his head, rather than over his shoulders like a toga. With his left hand, he grasps the lead rein slipped through the buffalo's nostrils; in his right hand, he holds the cord with the small bells (*grôong*). Eight times he breathes into his magic flagon, and each time lifts it to his right ear, then to his left. He yawns, he falls asleep, and, singing, "he rides off on horseback." Around him, the spectators are talking noisily, which makes the horse leap violently; silence is enjoined on all present. The *njau* pauses to get a firm grip on his rein, then takes off at a gallop, singing still. He halts and places his hand over his face, which is concealed by the blanket. With hands joined, he greets and, in a low voice, palavers with his interlocutors, who remain invisible to us. He wags a threatening finger: "Abandon her, you hear?

Leave her truly at rest." Again he bows to a void and makes a gesture of kissing hands. He sings a lament, offers the miniature goat, buffalo, flat gongs, and slave; then, from the winnowing basket, some meat and the stirring stick. To his interlocutors he says, "The rice beer you have already drunk. As for the buffalo you demanded, you have already eaten its meat." And, menacingly, "Your face I see, your countenance I am familiar with. No one suspects you, no one envies you. Go away." He lowers his voice, so that we barely make out the words ". . . trial by boiling water . . . trial by resin . . . She is a Rjee, I am a Rlük; leave her in peace. . . ." He terminates his discussion by reciting a charm. As he starts to leave, he makes the hand-kissing gesture.

Suddenly, he pretends to snatch up a warning bell. Jôong is brought to him. He presses his fist against the sick woman's head, and breathes on it. Grasping in his right fist the cord attached to the little bells, the *njau* taps the top of Jôong's head with it, singing:

"Oh, abandon . . . Oh, abandon . . ."

and at the end of his chant he again blows on his fist, which still rests on the sick woman's head.

Next, he picks up the bowl of cooked rice topped by a hard-boiled egg, and as he describes the offering, he places it on her head, then sets it down before him on the platform. He does the same with the large bowl of meat, the tray holding the tiny paste figures, and the bottle of rice beer. He begs his adversary, "You will leave her in peace, will you not?" Again, as he takes off, he sings.

He takes up the warning bell a second time, and breathes on it. Wan-Tôong comes to receive the breath on behalf of Grieng, who is still abed at home.

The shaman resumes his ride. He stops, spits eight times before him, and argues: "They are six in all, there will be no one to cook for them. Do not take the soup, do not take the cooked rice. There is Kroong, a man; there is Kröng, a man . . . to go searching for wild vegetables, to fetch firewood. . . ." In a word, he is insisting with the *caak* that the sick woman is indispensable to her family, that she must remain with them to keep the household going. "Do not allow your heart to swell with anger, do not become enraged." He ends by offering his "partner" a finger, so that it may be pulled in token of agreement: "She will bathe in three days, is that not so?"

He sets out again, halts, spits in front of him, and argues too low for us to catch every word: ". . . fish . . . even water . . . clear flow of water . . ." He gropes for something in the copper bowl. . . . "There is no bracelet." Quickly, a bracelet is placed in the bowl and water is poured over it. Ddöi lifts the copper bowl and places it on his head. Then, abruptly, he causes it to fall behind him as he recites, "May the young sparrow hawk grow into a large male." The bowl has fallen in an ill-omened position. It is returned to the shaman, and he repeats the operation from the beginning. This time it succeeds. Kröng takes the bowl and places it on his wife's head, and brushes the bracelet over her forehead.

The shaman claps his hands. Water is poured into them; he scrubs his face and sprinkles the sick woman's with it. Now returned among us mortals, he removes the miniature weapons stuck into the top of the rice pile, gathers up the air above the three quartzes embedded in it, and pours this air over Jôong's head. He quickly packs up his equipment and puts the rice in the winnowing basket.

Now Ddöi places the quartzes on Jôong's head. He is "putting her soul back in place." He does the same to Wan-Tôong, on behalf of Grieng, and to Bbür, for his ailing wife and children.

The shaman scrapes Jôong's forehead with the bracelet before slipping it on her wrist, and he throws the copper bowl under the platform. Finally, the *njau* assembles all the offerings in the winnowing basket, which he revolves eight times above the head of the sick woman. He leaves the house and goes to throw it over the cliff, after having spat on the bits of charcoal, which he asks to act as good guides.

Because Jôong has complained of a pain in her side, Ddöi "extracts the little sticks" (*tok möng*)—arrows sent by the sorcerers, which are the cause of her pain. With all his might, he aspirates the sore spot. He straightens up and removes from his mouth a splinter the size of a match, which he places in a small bamboo tube. He chews on one end of a magic tuber, spits the softened fiber on the sick woman's head, and breathes on it; he repeats this operation on the patient's chest. One piaster and a bowl of hulled rice have been set beside him in payment for these last ministrations.

Finally, after a fresh jar of rice beer has been consecrated by Kröng, Bbür, and Bbaang-the-Stag, the latter exorcises the sick woman. First, he dusts her off with a broom straw tipped with a bit of cotton. Then, eight times he revolves above her head a dustpan in which he has placed the lower jaw of the buffalo and some charcoal. The three men go outside to dispose of these objects, which are now contaminated by the exorcism, and to consult the tube of blood. The go-between brings back a pinch of earth (forgetting this time, however, to measure eight spans). Lastly, Kröng pays Bbaang-the-Stag—a bowl of hulled rice (both receptacle and contents)—and hands him the drinking straw at the foot of a *yang dâm* of rice beer. As in every such payment, it is Kröng who drinks first. By the time the ceremony is over, it is almost eleven in the evening. A few moments later, by dint of gently insisting, the shaman gets the sick woman to swallow a portion of cooked liver and some rice soup. He recites several verses of wishes for his patient's prompt recovery. It is now eleven o'clock.

People drink all night long. Shortly before dawn, the *njau* was supposed again to extract sorcerers' arrows from Jôong's body, but for all Bbür's efforts, it was impossible to rouse him; he was dead drunk.

January 28

Jôong continues to waste away. However, on her the effects of illness are less striking—she already looked like an old woman—than on her younger sister. Grieng had not been exactly fat, but she was generously proportioned and had been the picture of health. Three days of illness have reduced her to a gaunt old woman.

This morning, at nine-thirty, a pig "of four and a half spans" (actually, three spans and four finger widths) is sacrificed in her behalf. Kraang-Drüm is the go-between today, for one may not have the same man "summon the Spirits" twice in a row.

While we are at Mbieng-Grieng's, Mang-Master-of-the-Ivory comes to Kröng-Jôong's door. He wants to borrow the latter's four-span pig, but is warned in the nick of time that he may not enter the house. Had Kröng agreed to supplement the pig with a dozen pannierfuls of rice, Mang was prepared to give him a young buffalo he had not yet trained to the lead rein. He would have liked to take the pig today, for he plans to immolate one for the great sacrifice of the Blood Anointment of the Paddy, which his village must soon perform. However, for eight days after a *mhö'* séance, it is taboo to receive foreigners and to make any commercial transactions. Kröng is unable to accept the proposal, although the deal seems to suit him perfectly.

At twelve-fifteen, a fumigation of the invalid is followed by a shamanist séance of the *grôong* type (harness with bells and bracelets). The ceremony proceeds without incident, except for their having to silence a barking dog. (One must not let dogs bark at such a time, else the shaman's quartz-soul may be frightened by its yelping and run off to the underground regions, thus causing the *njau*'s death.)

After the séance, Ddöi treats Jôong with a massage. Kröng lays by his side a bowl of hulled rice and a single one-piaster note.

Bbür's in-laws return to Nyôong Brah. Before they leave, the forehead of each is marked with a sooty fingerprint, the soot having been rubbed off the bottom of a large pot.

Toward four o'clock, the exorcism that utilizes the pig's jaw is performed. After ministering to Grieng, the shaman is able to get her to take a little food.

Finally, after these several consecutive days during which he has demonstrated his unparalleled powers, Ddöi prepares to return to Sar Lang. When he arrived five days ago, his baggage was extremely light—one small pannier with a lid containing all his magic equipment. On his return home, five men must accompany him to carry all he has garnered in fees: jars, hulled rice, and meat. Of every animal sacrificed he has received one thigh (for himself, as *njau*), the heart (intended for the Spirit of the magic quartz), and additional meat (for himself, as a clan brother; his clients, being Rjee, are "brothers" to him, a Rlük).

Shortly after the *njau*'s departure, Kröng disassembles the "hornbill beak" tripod, and carries the two slanting supports and the transverse to the edge of the village; he throws them away, asking "the execrable mouths" to return to their own village.

January 29

All Sar Luk is out clearing land, except for members of households who have been struck by illness and who must remain behind.

Kröng-Jôong and Kroong-Big-Navel set out around nine to "cast out the Spirits of the abandoned fields" (*waih mpôh*). The sick woman's husband carries a large serving basket that contains saffroned rice, a miniature slave and pair of flat gongs, and some charcoal. The son bears on his back a small decorated wicker box, wrapped in a blanket like an infant.

They soon reach the fields which were abandoned after the last harvest. Only a few months ago, the vast expanse was covered by an undulating carpet of paddy; today, it is a desolate sight. Irregular, low brush has invaded it everywhere; broad patches of lalang grass are interspersed by more vigorous growth of bushes or young bamboo; charred trunks and the shambles of former field huts rear above this brush and the long branches half eaten by fire that once fenced the field. The whole scene reminds one that this scrub is caused by man, who has slashed and burned an area of forest to grow food for his own survival.

When they come to Kröng's old field, he "casts out" one of the posts that marked the borders of his plot. He lifts the post and tosses it into what used to be the field of a neighbor, asking the border between their land not to become angry. Then he takes a pinch of soil from the border area, which, on his return home, he will apply to his wife's head. The two men walk toward the middle of the field, along a narrow embankment; near it stands a *nier* (*Irvingia oliveri*). During the season just past, the *nier* was the main support of a now collapsed field hut. Kröng first moves toward a slope rising to one side of the embankment, at the foot of which there is a porcupine's hole. He tears a leaf from a nearby weed and takes a pinch of dust from the entrance to the burrow. (The porcupine is reputed to cause coughs.) Then he walks to the foot of the *nier*; it is one of the few to survive last year's burning, deep traces of which are visible on it. He squats, deposits slave and *cing* simulacra, and spits eight times on the charcoal before begging for the tree's indulgence. He throws several handfuls of saffroned rice over the trunk. Beanstalks are still growing up along the trunk; Kröng shakes their leaves and also some of the old hut thatch over his serving basket to collect spider-souls. Kroong-Big-Navel puts them in the small box he carries in his blanket as carefully as if it were an infant. Before leaving, Kröng pulls up a weed.

As soon as he gets home, Kröng opens the box above his wife's head and taps on the bottom to make all the spiders tumble out. The soil he applies to the sick woman's forehead, chest, back, and joints. Lastly, he sticks the few leaves he has brought back into the thatch directly over the door:

> "*Returned now from the abandoned fields, from the fields of stubble,*
> *I order you to get well.*
> *May your body be cool. . . ."*

Late in the afternoon, Kröng goes out to cut some *tloot* and *rhôong* leaves, which he places above his doorway. He waits to perform the duck exorcism until people have come back from the fields.

At last, around six-thirty, the holy man splits the duck's head above leaves he has laid on the ground before his door. He gives the head, together with some charcoal, hulled rice, and a pair of miniature *cing*, to Troo-Jôong, who has been promoted to go-between. Tôong-Jieng supports his mother so that, with his saber, Kröng can cut off four locks of hair, two from each side of her forehead. These he also hands over to Troo.

Troo-Jôong revolves this handful of objects, except for the duck's head, above the head of the sick woman. He counts aloud as he does so, and then, with Kröng joining in, he recites:

> "*I offer a duck in exchange;*
> *mouths, beaks, tips of tongues,*
> *mouths run dry of saliva,*
> *keep far away from her. . . .*
> *Today I offer a duck in exchange;*
> *I exorcise enemy mouths,*
> *mouths of Nyôong Brah,*
> *mouths of Nyôong Rlaa,*
> *mouths of Nyôong Hat,*
> *foreign mouths from here,*
> *foreign mouths from there,*
> *return to your own homes in foreign parts.*
> *Today I have sought one duck,*
> *one duck I have offered in exchange. . . ."*

He repeats the operation, but this time with the duck's head and the blood-covered ritual leaves, which he holds in his right hand. (The earlier objects were held in his left hand.)

Kröng accompanies Troo-Jôong along the path leading out of the village. The go-between lays the blood-soaked leaves across the path, then adds all the other objects of the exorcism. He squats behind this barrier. Before he lays the charcoals down, he spits on them, and describes aloud what he has done, adding, "I have paid you one pannier of hulled rice, two pigs, one buffalo, and today one duck. . . ."

Eight times he gathers the air toward his chest, and recites again, "Today, I exorcise with one duck." Kröng stands, silent, beside him.

Preparing to leave, Troo takes up a pinch of earth, tears off a leaf, and whistles. "O Jôong my mother, come back. O Jôong my mother, come back." (Jôong-Kröng, it will be recalled, is the mother of his friend Tôong-Jieng.)

Before Troo re-enters the house, he asks, "Is she cured?" And the reply comes: "She is cured." He walks over to the sick woman, rubs the earth between her breasts, then on her forehead; the leaf he sticks into the thatch roof above the door.

The exorcism with duck is not accompanied by a jar of rice beer.

An hour later, Aang-of-the-Drooping-Eyelid stops by every house in the village to invite people to come drink at "the revolving above the head" she is offering her in-laws. The women in particular come on the run. The reason given for the ceremony is that a few days ago Kroong-Big-Navel had a nightmare. In his sleep, he saw his "brother" Kraang-Aang, who died last year. Kroong saw the former deputy headman of the village flying in an airplane and landing in Sar Luk. Such a dream, in which one sees the soul of a dead man return and, what's more, in which the sky is the background—such a dream is among the most baleful of signs: "The Sky is about to strike." It is a threat of death, of epidemic, even. Accordingly, Aang-of-the-Drooping-Eyelid offered to erase this dire warning with the sacrifice of two chickens and a jar of *rnööm*, plus the revolving above the head of a large jar. Kroong accepted her offer; in other words, he has consented to forgive her.

Aang is making feverish preparations. Her "sister" Mang and her "brother" Maang-the-Thin (both are her first cousins) are assisting her, as is Kraang-the-Dogtooth, Maang's closest friend. Baap Can is overseeing the entire operation. He hands the two chickens to Kraang-the-Dogtooth, who slits their throats. Aang-of-the-Drooping-Eyelid, standing behind the already prepared jar, hands the drinking straw to her husband, who squats on the other side. The pouch of magic stones belonging to Jôong-

Kröng is fetched and laid at the foot of the jar. Baap Can gives his daughter some advice:

> *"May you go to draw water without being surly;*
> *may you go to look for wood without being surly."*

Aang anoints the pouch with blood, while Kroong-Big-Navel, reciting rhymed wishes, inserts the straw in the jar.

Aang dips her finger in the water of the *rnööm* and brushes it over the large adjacent jar, then over her mother-in-law's forehead. She begins again, this time brushing the foreheads and chests of her husband, her father-in-law, and her sister-in-law, Maang-of-the-Crooked-Mouth. Baap Can drinks first. To brush one's finger over a jar is an acceptable substitution for revolving it above the head when the receptacle in question is too heavy.

Thus, Aang-of-the-Drooping-Eyelid has washed away her husband's bad dream, to which Jôong's bad health could conceivably be attributed. At the same time, Aang has washed away the very grave wrong she committed, which could also be the cause of the family's current misfortunes.

Baap Can drinks first with Kraang-Drüm, then Kroong-Big-Navel with Kröng; next come Can, Bbaang-the-Stag, old Tôong-Mang, Ngee-Truu, and Aang-the-Long. While we drink, Drüm-Kraang treats her mother-in-law by "extracting the little sticks"—the arrows sent by the sorcerers. Jôong-Wan follows, with a massage and the application of a magic quartz.

Conversation reverts constantly to the two sick women. Baap Can says to me over and over that the trial by boiling water must be held; the person it indicates is guilty must be struck dead with a *wiah*. I try fruitlessly to persuade him to have the accused person referred to the government court in Poste du Lac. Baap Can sticks to his own plan.

January 30

Today is the third day of the buffalo sacrifice, and one may not work in the fields.

To hasten an improvement in the condition of the two invalids, which is judged too slow, it has been decided to build them each a sick hut. All the men in the village have been asked to help out. They work in two teams. Eight men under the direction of Kroong-Big-Navel build Jôong's little hut opposite where Bbaang-Jieng-the-Pregnant-Man lives—that is, opposite the extension of the most southerly long house in Sar Luk, which belongs to Troo-Jôong and Wan-Jôong. Within two hours, from eight-thirty to ten-thirty, they have sunk the pickets, attached the walls (two sacrificial platforms placed end to end), laid the two sections of roof, com-

pleted the rounded ends of the hut, and set up the low platform, which
occupies half of the back. A wood fire replaces the usual hearth. For
Grieng, the work has been simplified: the stilts of an outdoor granary
standing behind the extension of her house have been enclosed in a *cai-
phen*. Inside this shelter, a low platform has been installed and a fire laid.

At two-thirty in the afternoon, Kröng is going to make an "offering of
reciprocity to the Bear" (*sal Muu*). To this end, he has fashioned a *wiah*
with a wooden blade and a *kaa piet*—a press for smoking fish, made of a
double tray of bamboo layers on which the fish (*kaa*) are represented by
shavings of firewood. On the press he has laid a pipe-cleaner stick into
which he has stuffed a very ripe pepper. He has his wife spit eight times
on the pieces of charcoal, spits on them himself, then revolves them
above her head, asking that she be cured, that she "have once more a
body cool as water." Then he revolves the *kaa piet* above Jôong's head
and goes out.

As he comes to the place where bear tracks have been noted, Kröng
espies a trunk with a hole in it, and he stops. He plants his *wiah* handle
upright in the ground, and inserts the pipe-cleaner stick with the pepper
into the bark of the tree. He squats at the foot, spits on the pieces of charcoal, and lays them down, begging the Bear not to be angry and to grant a
cure. As he leaves, he cuts off a bit of bark from the edge of the hole and
takes it with him; nearer the village, he tears off a leaf.

Back home, he massages his wife between her breasts, praying the
while. Then he sets fire to both ends of the bark, allowing the wood to
burn a moment; he extinguishes the flames by pouring water over them.
He applies a bit of the charred bark first to his wife's forehead, then to her
chest, asking for her recovery.

Kröng has judged it indispensable to perform this rite, speculating that
his wife's illness could have been precipitated by negligence on the part of
some member of the family. Perhaps someone inadvertently walked or
spat on the tracks or dung of a bear and thus unleashed its anger; the bear
is reputed to inflict colds, coughs, and asthma in reprisal for such an
affront.

It is not until late afternoon that the sick women are carried to their
isolation quarters. The move is full of both promise and risk, so obviously
it requires a sacrament: tradition calls for the sacrifice of a dog. The
animal is killed and beheaded in front of the hut, before the invalid's arrival. All the men of the village are on hand. They dip ritual leaves of *tloot*
and *rhôong* in the blood that flows from the dog's neck. When the sick
woman, supported by two of her sons, arrives at the door of her new shelter, she is literally bedaubed with blood by the crowd of men, while they
call loudly and in unison for her recovery. Still praying, they wheel about

and go to throw their leaves over the edge of the cliff. They return, and again brush the invalid with leaves, but this time the leaves are some found on the roof of her hut and they do not have blood on them. These the men take also to the edge of the cliff and throw away.

The ailing Jôong is installed in her new quarters, and a new exorcism is begun. Kröng prays, as he hands Tôong-Biing, the current go-between, portions of buffalo and goat meat that have been tied together, charcoal, white rice, the head of the freshly sacrificed dog, and the club with which it was killed. The sick woman ritually spits eight times; the ritual leaves, the exorcism gifts, and the dog's head are revolved, in succession, above her head. Lastly, bearing the leaves and gifts, Tôong-Biing departs, followed by Kröng. They strike out along the path, but before they come to the track, the go-between sets the club down across the path and places the other objects behind it. Before depositing the dog's head, he inserts an upright piece of wood between its jaws to keep them open and menacing "so that the Divinities and the Spirits will become frightened and go back home." Deposition of the coals and the accompanying prayers completed, Tôong takes a pinch of earth and tears a leaf from a weed, after which the two men return to the invalid's hut. Before entering, the traditional question: "Is she cured?" followed by the usual response: "She is cured." Tôong-Biing applies the pinch of earth to Jôong's chest, and inserts his leaf in the thatch above the door.

An identical ceremony is held to inaugurate the hut to which Grieng will withdraw: the sacrifice of a dog, with all the men but no women participating; then the exorcism, using the victim's head. By six-fifteen, everything has been completed. Outside the shelters, the men drink the beer of exorcism and eat the dog meat.

January 31

Although the day is taboo (because a pig was sacrificed three days ago), Can and Bbaang-the-Stag lead some coolies, who are paid workers, out to Truu's field. "His body is strong," they tell me, by way of explanation. "Also, he doesn't know about the prohibition because he's away." The other villagers observe the ritually imposed day of rest, however, and people go looking for wild vegetables and firewood.

This morning, two of Jôong's sons, Kroong-Big-Navel and Kraang-Drüm, went to get Ddöi-the-Shaman. They lead him to the shelter where their mother is in quarantine. The older son and the *njau* squat before a jar of rice beer; Kraang-Drüm hands Ddöi the drinking straw, some ritual leaves, and a young chicken. The shaman slits the little creature's neck over the pouch of magic quartzes, imploring their aid. Then he inserts the straw, calling for a complete recovery. A bottle is filled before people start to drink. Bbaang-the-Pregnant-Man leads off, with Kroong-Big-Navel. Then Ddöi and Kraang-Drüm drink.

After a fumigation with "resin from the Sky" and a revolving of the magic quartzes, the *njau* takes his place on the low platform by the ailing woman's side. He is about to perform an "extraction of the little sticks" (*mhö' tok möng*). Wrapped in his blanket but with his right arm free, he is equipped with a bush hook balanced on his left shoulder, and with leaves, which he holds in his right hand. He breathes into the magic flagon, staggers . . . and "takes off," waving his leaves and singing. He argues with his interlocutor in the Beyond. He bites off a piece of magic tuber, chews it, and spits it out eight times in front of him, then on the bared belly of the sick woman at his side. He massages her abdomen by pinching it. He leans over and takes a fold of flesh between his lips, inhales vigorously, straightens up, and removes from his mouth a long splinter, which he inserts in a tube. He repeats this operation several times, withdrawing sticks of diminishing size until he has filled the tube. Ddöi bites off more magic plant and spits it out, his mouth almost touching the woman's belly. He then appears to force something into it by pressing with both hands. He "takes off" once again, and gathers up the soul in his blanket.

Now he stretches out full length. He has descended into the Underworld. His hands seem to be poised to catch something. Suddenly, they dart out and seize an invisible being, which they press close to his body. He has captured the frog-soul. At this point, a member of the watching group throws salt on the fire, which makes it crackle. This is to drive off the souls of the dead, who would like to follow the soul of the sick woman and detain it in their subterranean village. However, they are afraid of salt, for its flaming up could kill them a second time and hurl them down to the second level of the infernal world. The *njau* turns for a moment and, still prostrate, draws a flute from his little box; he plays an air "to touch the souls of the dead." At last, still outstretched, he extends both hands to one side, and water is poured over them to awaken him.

He is unable to right himself alone, and must be helped to a sitting position. He brushes his dampened hands over his face and shakes them in the direction of the sick woman. The operation is concluded with a search for the spider-soul, the setting out of symbolic gifts, and pouring of the spider-souls over Jôong's head. . . .

A medium-size jar worth forty piasters is given the *njau* in payment for "the extracting the sticks" taboo; it is feared that otherwise the quartz might become angry and punitive.

At one o'clock in the afternoon, Ddöi treats Jôong with *sii ddiing* (Rutaceae) and *sii pêt ier* (not identified) stalks. First, he lays them in the fire, then presses the charred ends against her throat to cure her cold and thus restore her appetite. He repeats the gesture, this time applying the ends to her head. He moistens his fingers in a bowl of water containing a magic quartz; he brushes his fingers over his patient's throat, then rubs the quartz itself over her neck. Finally, he lays the little branches in the fire again and, in the same fashion, treats the sick woman's belly.

A young girl comes in to have an ulcerous wound seen to.

Jôong is given some rice soup, to which powdered *plee rko'* (not identified) has been added.

By two-thirty, the *njau* is ready to return home. Before crossing the threshold, he licks a finger and rubs it several times over the sick woman's forehead, asking that she recover. When the moment to depart comes, Ddöi himself carries his finely worked little lidded pannier containing all his shaman's gear. Kroong-Mae swings over his shoulders the big pannier of hulled rice topped by the medium-size jar, both honorariums. Kroong-Big-Navel starts to follow, carrying his saber, but when he sees that he is doubling with Krah as bodyguard, he turns back. Tôong-Jieng carries two large branches of trimmed *ndroong;* the bark is used in plaiting strong ropes.

In the evening, people drink at Bbaang-the-Stag's. He is entertaining two Bboon Jaa men who have come to bring him the rice of invitation for their big sacrifice of the Blood Anointment of the Paddy. In fact, the Bboon Jaa are "eating" the forest of Phii Ko', and they still need Bbaang-the-Stag and Baap Can to continue to play their role as holy men on this terrain, which was sold to them—that is, to foreigners.

February 1

Despite the duck taboo (this is the third day since one was sacrificed), Mhoo-Laang and the Rjee women go out to clear land.

The condition of one of the two ailing women has at last definitely improved. Grieng is still very weak and short of breath, but with the help of a stick she is able to walk. Accordingly, her husband has led her down to the watering place for her first bath—the bath for the lifting of a sickness. Grieng steps into the river and holds herself upright while her husband sweeps her eight times with leaves of *rkôong, siep sür (Scleria laevis* Retz), and *mat dlei* leaves. As he does this, he recites:

> "One, two, three . . . *eight repayments of the debt.*
> *Be now as cool as water. . . .*
> *Downstream from the water, downstream from the water's*
>   *deep course,*
> *downstream from the tall forest, downstream from the*
>   *deep night,*
> *flee, return to your homes.*
> *Begone, for now all has lost its savor;*
> *may the body draw itself erect, stand straight, restored."*

It is fiercely hot today. The bamboo shingles on my house crackle from the heat.

This morning, Jôong was able to eat half a bowl of soup. It was hoped that she would regain strength quickly. But this afternoon she was seized by fits of breathlessness again. Ddöi was sent for, but he refused to come. Around four-thirty, Baap Can is about to leave with his family for Bboon Jaa; he asks that he be alerted if the sick woman's condition takes a sudden turn for the worse.

At six o'clock, Kröng decides to carry his wife back to her own house. In his opinion, she cannot be left alone in quarantine. He now fears the worst and does not want death to overtake his wife in the hut. The ceremony is like the one performed when she was conducted there: a dog is sacrificed, and all the men—and the men only—sweep the woman with *tloot* and *rhôong* leaves that have been dipped in the victim's blood. However, the exorcism is performed only with the animal's jaws, not its entire head.

The chief of the neighboring canton, Bbieng-Dlaang, and his wife, the daughter of old Troo, arrive shortly after the ceremony. They have come to visit Jôong. Truu follows soon afterward. Immediately upon entering the house, he goes to his sister and spits rice on her head, then gives her five piasters on behalf of the teacher and five more from himself "so that she may start to eat." Suddenly Truu erupts: people have it in for him; people envy his and his family's power. "I am going to gather all the villagers together, and we will hold the trial by boiling water. . . ." Then, with great energy, he forces his sister to drink some rice soup.

Truu is in top form, bolstered by the various jars he has been offered along his way home. He passes from the condition of his older sister to the splendors of the feast the planters provided. Kroong-Mae, who is go-between in the imminent exorcism, brings a chick and some charcoal. He spits on the pieces of charcoal and passes them eight times above the sick woman's head; then he spits on the chick's claws, brushes them over Jôong's forehead, and goes out.

In the common room, Kröng is consecrating the jar, which he offers to Bbieng-Dlaang and to Bbür. Truu asks Jôong, "Where do you hurt?" "I have trouble breathing." "It's the Bear that has struck you down. Has the Bear been driven off?" All the women chorus, "It has been done."

Truu dusts Jôong's skull with a broom, after dampening the fibers. Then he sweeps the path leading from her to the door, and throws the broom across the threshold.

Kroong-Mae returns to anoint Jôong with dust gathered outside the house.

Kröng passes over his wife's forehead and chest a tin bracelet, which he then slips onto a cord he has been holding in his hand and now stretches across the house. Furnished with a tin bracelet, the cord is a sign of taboo, particularly serious in this instance because it signifies that, in the event of the sick woman's death, one will proceed to search out and put to death the sorcerer responsible for her demise. Lastly, Kröng presents a drinking straw to Kroong-Mae, so that he may initiate the jar offered him as go-between in the exorcism.

In reply to Truu's questions, Kröng says that he has done everything. Truu is furious: here is proof that people have it in for him. He goes away, and his family is attacked. The trial must be held. He explains to me how it is carried out: "A big metal pot is filled with water and placed on the fire. Into this you put a bracelet, an egg, a ring, and some dark *môong* stones. All these things are placed at the very bottom of the pot. Someone works the bellows. There are only seven pieces of firewood, as big as this. [He shows me his thumb.] The water's boiling. Everyone comes in turn to plunge his hand in to get the egg—one time for each man. A *caak* man cannot get hold of the egg—the water boils up and 'grabs' his hand. All the clans will go through the trial, even the Rjee."

The talk turns back to the Plantation feast. Truu speaks highly of the largesse the planters showed the government officials. They were all transported by truck; each canton chief was presented with a Cambodian blanket; each deputy chief and village headman was given an armful of black or plaid calico. At meals, each guest received two bowls of beans, two of fish, two of salt, and as much rice as he wanted. Each wife received a necklace or a comb. Two buffaloes were killed; unfortunately, one was white, wherefore he, Truu, could have none of it because of his adopted daughter's clan taboo against eating the meat of a white buffalo.

Laang-Mhoo, wishing to follow her sister (Dlaang-Bbieng, the wife of the neighboring canton chief) to Sar Luk, rubbed her baby's forehead with soot from the bottom of a pot.

All of a sudden, Kröng sees the light! At the close of the harvest, Baap Can had had only one pannier of glutinous rice to store. So he had asked him—Kröng—to pour it into his big rattan silo, where he keeps this variety of rice. Without thinking, Kröng had agreed. But now, now he remembers that it is strictly forbidden to pour the rice of a brother and sister into the same silo. That is the cause of Jôong's cough!

The contents of the silo are swiftly removed and thrown outside. Kröng has taken a few grains, which he lays on his wife's chest, asking for her recovery. In the middle of the night, two young men go down to the river to wash the big rattan receptacle.

Conversation reverts to the feast and the Plantation. A Rhade overseer was present, and he is a real *caak*. "The bald-headed Frenchman"—the European recruiter of Plantation labor—forbids the Rhade to strike the coolies, and orders him to guide the men in their work, or to criticize, but without physical abuse. However, no sooner has the Frenchman turned his back than the Rhade strikes and curses the workers. Bbür went to work on the Plantation once, and Sieng-the-Little—the Rhade overseer—wished a cough on him. It took a buffalo sacrifice, finally, to cure him. But, on the other hand, Mia', who has only one leg, gets along there very well.

February 2

This morning, they cut Jôong's hair. Then it is decided "to repay the Spirits in kind" (*sal Yaang*). Tôong-Biing is named go-between. He has the sick woman spit on a basket containing a pinch of saffron, white rice, saffroned rice, charcoal, and a collection of wooden or rattan miniatures: buffalo, goat, elephant tusks, rhinoceros horn, and flat gongs. Revolving the basket above Jôong's head, he enumerates what he is offering:

"Today, I give in ritual counterpart one slave, one buffalo . . ." He leaves with the basket and its contents, as well as a little bamboo crossbow thirty centimeters long, which he fashioned this morning. Kröng follows him, carrying on his back a decorated rattan box wrapped in a blanket.

When they reach the grove, the two men pause before the tallest tree. Tôong-Biing places the little crossbow behind him, and lays at the foot of the tree all the offerings except the saffroned rice and the arrow tipped with a bit of saffron. He spits on the charcoal, and as he lays it on the ground, lists his offerings. Then he scatters handfuls of the saffroned rice on the nearby foliage, calling, "O Jôong, come back. . . . O Jôong, come back. . . ." He shakes several leaves over the basket to catch little spiders; Kröng gathers them up and places them in the small box he has brought and which now, rewrapped in the blanket, he replaces on his back. This done, Tôong-Biing rails against the Spirit of the tree. As he hurls threats at it, he seizes the crossbow and shoots the tree with the saffron-tipped arrow. Quickly, he drops the crossbow at the foot of his victim (the tree) and snatches up its "child"—that is, he chops off a hanging root and takes it with him. He also takes a leaf, which he will stick in the roof above the door on his return.

Before crossing the threshold, he asks, "Is she cured?" . . . "She is cured." The spider-souls are poured over the sick woman's head. The root end Tôong has brought back he lays directly under the shove net placed against a granary post. He is "imprisoning the ankle of the Spirit's child," so that the Divinity will give back the soul she is detaining:

"I imprison your child, O Spirit. If you do not restore the soul of Jôong to me, I will kill your child. Give me back the soul of Jôong, and I will give you back your child."

After the capture of the hostage, Kröng pays Tôong-Biing one bowl of hulled rice and one piaster, a settling of accounts that the two men accompany with a prayer calling for the sick woman's recovery.

A number of women went out for firewood today. Can and his "brother" Maang-the-Thin accompanied them. Suddenly the two men came upon a tiger lying in wait. Maang stood guard while Can yelled at the top of his lungs. The animal moved off.

People are drinking at Mhoo-Laang's in honor of Bbieng-Dlaang. Kröng is cleaning the jars that were emptied last evening. All unexpectedly, an old friend of his, Kroong-Dloong, known as Baap Caang Siing, arrives from Nyôong Brah to pay a visit to the sick woman. So Kröng opens a fresh jar.

Aang-Who-Stinks, the daughter of Yôong-the-Mad, comes to give Jôong a treatment. She simply dips her fingers in a long-nosed gourd containing a few grains of rice, and brushes them over her own throat, then over the invalid's throat, which she also breathes on. She counts "One," repeats the gesture, "Two," continuing up to eight, asking the while that the sufferer may have a cool body and that she may recover. This procedure is the *sam gun*, a simple anointment with the magic plant. Earlier, Aang suffered severely with her throat, and since her recovery she is considered to have within her medication against a cough.* She receives for her pains a bowl of hulled rice and an old silver coin. Then Dloong-Kroong—the wife of the visitor from Nyôong Brah—feeds the sick woman some rice soup fortified with *plee rko'*. Presently, Bbaang-the-Stag and Baap Can, back from Bboon Jaa, come in to swell the group of drinkers and share the news of the visitors' village.

February 3

Today, the taboo of the seventh day after the killing of the buffalo: one may not go out into the fields. Tôong-Biing takes advantage of the enforced leisure to perform "the blood anointment of the Fire Sticks" (*mhaam Rnut*). His sister, Aang-the-Widow, owes the sacrifice because of her incestuous relationship with her "brother" Tieng. The animals immolated earlier, at the time of the trial, had been supplied by Tieng-the-Widower, because Aang and her "brothers of the same belly" owned no pig at the time. Now they have finally succeeded in obtaining the needed victims.

Aang has made few appearances in the village since the trial. She has been living in Little Sar Luk with her other brother, Sieng, who has remarried meanwhile; his new wife is a very pretty girl called Öot. The scandal of incest is not Aang's only reason for being discreet. Her condi-

---

* See footnote on p. 344.

tion is becoming quite obvious: she "is carrying a love child"—the child of an incestuous love, to boot.

At Tôong-Biing's house, the holy man and guardian of the *Rnut*, Bbaang-Jieng-the-Pregnant-Man, has unrolled a mat on the low platform. On it he has placed the dusty winnowing basket that contains the Fire Sticks of Sar Luk, together with the accessories—the basket of Fire Sticks of Phii Ko' and an old, battered Bénédictine bottle filled with "water of the master." To this collection Kröng adds his wife's pouch of magic quartz; Truu and Bbôong-Mang bring their official canton-chief badges; the latter even contributes a decoration, the Dragon of Annam, which he bought for forty piasters from a former soldier from Paang Tiing.

Tôong-Biing slits the throat of a brown cock and a pig over a Mnong bowl filled with wort. The guilty woman and the two holy men present, Kröng and Bbaang-the-Pregnant-Man, take some wort and with it anoint each object laid out on the platform, reciting:

> "*O Fire Sticks,*
> *do not speak to us in anger,*
> *do not crush us with your wrath,*
> *O* Rnoh *Spirit,*
> *O* Rnut *Spirit. . . .*
>
> *The fire of the Rnut, we spit it;*
> *the fire of the* Rnoh, *we light it;*
> *the young child of the sorcerers, we strike him.*
> *Thus we do as did the Ancestor of Bygone Days;*
> *thus we do as did the Mother of the Past;*
> *thus we do as did the Forebear of Ancient Times.*"

Aang passes a drinking straw to the canton chief and another to the holy man of the Fire Sticks. Truu inserts his in the big jar, and Bbaang-the-Pregnant-Man his in the *yang dâm*. All three ask again for the indulgence of the *Rnut* and for everyone's good health.

Then they drink. Bbaang-the-Stag arrives only after the anointing; the holy man of Phii Ko' performs no rite but he drinks with us. The atmosphere is not at all festive, despite there being *rnööm* to sip and food to eat. Truu continues to elaborate on all he saw at the Plantation feast. If only yesterday he could not say enough in praise of the establishment, today he dwells on the fact that the Rhade served themselves the lion's share, while the Gar people got ridiculous portions. At the feast in Poste du Lac, he added, the Rlâm had behaved in the same way, but on that occasion the Commissioner had dressed them down severely for it.

At one-thirty in the afternoon, an immense surprise: the son of the pastor in Ban Me Thuot, a white boy of perhaps sixteen, arrives at my house accompanied by the Rhade evangelist and two other Protestants belonging to that tribe. The boy has taken advantage of the dry season to risk coming this far by bicycle, and plans to try to reach Dalat on foot via Mount Mbür. Killing two birds with one stone, his father included in his escort the mission's best preacher to bring "the good word" to this still ignorant valley.

The young American does not seem to be particularly interested in the life of the village, so we remain in my house. However, Truu is again in top form and is repaying his debts today. He has just given Tôong-Mang-the-Cook two new Djiring jars, one large and one small, in payment for the pig he had borrowed to offer a sacrifice for the Commissioner. On this occasion, he has offered Tôong-Mang *rnööm* from a *yang dâm*. Truu is in high spirits after drinking, and he offers me the sacrifice of a white cock accompanied by a round of rice beer from a big jar; this is by way of thanking me for the earlier gift of a raincoat (an old pea jacket I had had waterproofed). Lastly, he opens a third jar in honor of the visitors. However, none of them, neither the white boy nor the Rhade, is willing to taste the jar of *rnööm*. I explain to Truu that it is a taboo imposed on them by their *Yaang*. He accepts this but is nonetheless cast down. Now he pays the coolies who came to clear his field: three piasters each, plus ten piasters to Bbaang-the-Stag and an equal amount to Can for having accompanied them and supervised their work.

This evening, we witness the first performance of its kind that Sar Luk has ever seen—a sermon. The pastor's son is tired after his trip and goes to bed, but his companions betake themselves to Truu's house. I miss the beginning of this séance and when, my guest safely abed, I arrive at the canton chief's, I enter a house that is jammed—crawling—with people. Not one resident of Sar Luk is absent, and the proceedings are extraordinary. The preacher has taken his place on a mat spread on the low platform, where he is flanked by the two other Rhade. In front of them, Truu is seated on a stool placed on the earthen floor. A solid mass of listeners surrounds this group. The scene is—for once—well lighted by an abundance of resinous pine torches. The preacher delivers his remarks in Rhade. Broadly speaking, he tells the Gar, "You are still obeying Spirits who are evil creatures. They are fierce and greedy, they are always demanding sacrifices. I have come to talk to you today of a kind God, who insists on no sacrifices whatever. . . . He looks on us all! On Frenchmen, Englishmen, Vietnamese, Laotians, Cham . . . All believe in Him. This God is *Aê Diê*. He created the world and all that is therein." Then he undertakes to give an account—abridged—of Biblical history, from Genesis to the New Testament, illustrating each episode with vivid St. Sulpician lithos, which he exhibits for the admiration of all.*

---

* The St. Sulpicians produced lithographs of a notably inferior quality. —*Trans.*

The revelation of this vast mythic ensemble to people who until then knew nothing whatever about it is in itself fairly spectacular, but the event is further enhanced by Truu's being in such exceptional form. His remarkable translation clothes the narration in a splendid garb that heightens the sensational character of the evening considerably. Since early afternoon, Truu has drunk from three jars—the three *rnööm* he himself offered Tôong-the-Cook, the ethnologist, and the Protestant team—to which must be added the two *rnööm* that accompanied the morning sacrifice. He has drunk generously from each and, while he is never conspicuously modest, the alcohol has released his need to show off with a display of his talents. The sermon offers him a means to enhance his prestige: by acting as interpreter, he demonstrates his profound knowledge of a foreign language unfamiliar to most of the women. What's more, the peripeteias of the story are unknown to everyone in Sar Luk. And this *noo pröö*, this epic, includes the Creation of the World, the Flood, the man swallowed and then spat out by a monster, a sea engulfing an entire army, a Son of the Spirit offering a whole multitude a feast with only a few loaves. . . . As he translates, Truu conveys the impression that he himself is relating these ancient myths, that he knows all about these astonishing stories. The Gar much appreciate a well-told tale, and the person who is capable of relating a sacred story properly—even one everybody knows—is held in high esteem. What, then, when the story is one nobody has ever heard of! Truu is more than a little tipsy, and as happens with many *kuang*, alcohol releases all his oratorical gifts. This evening, the audience is large and attentive as never before, the tales are unknown and astonishing, and Truu shines—it is his finest hour. In his mouth, the Bible is no mere narration; it is an epic harangue. Marvelously quickened by rice beer, his eloquence deploys a splendid background for the exploits of Heroes who are proposed as models by a religion that, insofar as the sect appearing here today is concerned, forbids indulgence in any kind of alcoholic beverage.

Such was the first contact of the community of Sar Luk with the religion of the white man.

Jôong slowly returned to health. She received various ministrations from the other two healers of Sar Luk, her daughter-in-law Drüm-Kraang and fat Jôong-Wan. On February 7, leaning on a stick, she was finally able to go outside her house and even, seated on the small veranda, to give herself a complete bath. Ddöi, the psychopomp magician, was no longer asked to travel into the Beyond to bargain for her soul with the Spirits and the sorcerers and to lead it back to earth.

However, on February 16, the *njau* was summoned to Sar Luk by the ailing Truu, and this visit provided the opportunity to ask Ddöi, in Jôong's behalf, to "send the Spirits away and order them to eat vegetables" (*nhaat sôor saa pae*). This is a rite performed at the end of a long illness.

Rice was cooked, also manioc and a dish of mixed wild vegetables—rattan hearts (*gool*) and *Gnetum gnemon* (*pae sei*). One bowl of each of these three foods was placed at the foot of the jar the shaman consecrates by inserting a drinking straw Kröng hands him. After prayers in which the two men adjure the illness to return permanently to its home, Jôong takes her place by the jar and drinks. The shaman rises and dips the blade of his saber in the receptacle, then places it against the drinker's forehead and repeats his prayer. Then he himself "feeds" his patient a part of the contents of each bowl: he places in her mouth a small ball of rice, a mouthful of wild vegetables, then a piece of cultivated tuber. Lastly, he vigorously anoints the erstwhile invalid's body from top to bottom with a pinch of the vegetables, and he prays:

> "I nourish with wild vegetables; I nourish with chicken;
> I nourish with sugarcane; I nourish with meat;
> I nourish with fish; I nourish with tuber. . . .
>> May it not strike again;
>> may no trace of it remain.
>> Return to your home,
>> with your feet and your hands,
>> to your forest and your village,
>> to your infants and your children,
>> Phöt Puu.
>> Ddoong sorcerers, flee from both banks;
>> Divinities, Spirits, flee from all parts;
>> Spirits of Violent Death, flee from all sides.
>> May her body be cool;
>> may she sleep deep.
>> Eating pork, do not chatter about it;
>> eating dog meat, do not inflict pain,
>> Civet Cat Sorcerer,
>> Cat Sorcerer, do not show your claws."

5

The Wedding of Jaang,
Baap Can's Second Daughter

February 21, 1949

No one went out to do any clearing today. Rain last night and this morning placed field work under an interdiction. You would incur the risk of meeting one of the animals that are taboo at this season—civet cat, rabbit, tarsier—and of thereby being forced to let a section of future cropland revert to brush.

Even yesterday no one went to the *miir*. An order from Poste du Lac mobilized all the men to gather rattan needed for some government building project. The order included a summons for Bbôong-the-Deputy, Kraang-Drüm (the village deputy headman), and Taang-Jieng, of Paang Döng (brother of the headman of Bboon Rcae) to present themselves in Poste du Lac.

Baap Can betook himself to Phii Ko' territory to check into whether the Bboon Jaa had indeed come to fish collectively on the right riverbank. Accompanied by old Krah, his two older daughters, Aang-of-the-Drooping-Eyelid and Jaang, the fiancée of Srae, went to Ndut Lieng Krak to gather wild vegetables.

This morning, nine men from Sar Luk and ten from Paang Döng went out to work on the road. The men left behind do odd jobs; the women weave or pick vegetables. Truu is suffering from a pain in the small of his back, and has Kroong-Mae exorcise his ailment. To this end, Kroong attacks a *rchah* tree and kidnaps its child—a piece of bark—which he keeps as hostage. As for me, I went to do some research in Little Sar Luk.

This evening, the doyen of the Rjee, old Tôong-Mang,* whom Truu

---

* Not to be confused with Tôong-Mang, the son of Taang-Jieng-the-Stooped, who belongs to the Daak Cat clan and works as cook at the Frontier School. The old *kôony*'s wife, Mang, belongs to the Bboon Jraang clan, like Can and Aang-of-the-Drooping-Eyelid; in our terminology, she is their first cousin.

and Baap Can call *kôony* (maternal uncle, their mother's younger brother), receives some clan brothers who have arrived from Jaa Yuk. The travelers are en route to Kudduu territory, where they will be selling some blankets.

The crowd around the jar of hospitality is quite large. The talk is burbling on when, quite late, a joyous song is heard outside. Everyone recognizes the voice of my friend Kroong-Biing, called Kroong-the-Short because of his small stature. When he comes in, jolly as always, he cracks some joke that makes the assembly laugh. Rarely have I seen him dressed with such care: he is got up entirely in Western clothes—shirt, vest, trousers, socks, and shoes.

As soon as this *kuang* of Ndut Lieng Krak has taken his place, he launches into a song competition with the Jaa Yuk visitors, who are his clan brothers. Soon thereafter, his son Srae appears, dressed in the magnificent black fur-lined coat his father has consented to lend him today. Jaang's fiancé is followed by three boys who also attend school in Ban Me Thuot, and by Chaar-Sraang, whose marriage we attended last October in Düng Jrii. Soon Tôong-Mang's house overflows with a high-spirited, lively throng. The new arrivals from Ndut Lieng Krak—the Bboon Jraang and their family—have brought in with them some Sar Luk villagers who had been preparing to go to bed. As usual, Kroong-the-Short turns his talents as singer and wit to good account.

Around nine-thirty, the crowd from Ndut Lieng Krak sweeps on to the house of Mang-of-the-Jutting-Jaw. In her visitors' room, the wife of the deputy has set out a small *yang dâm* of rice beer. Srae has laid a small decorated pannier beside the jar. It contains some thirty bamboo tubes; two of them end in a pair of carved crooks, which extend beyond the side of the basket. These *ding paa* are filled with bamboo-shoot preserve; a piece of buffalo hide is stuffed in the bottom, and another is used as a stopper. Leaning against the tubes are a tin-plated comb, a necklace of glass beads, a brass bracelet, another of tin, and a small bottle. A chicken has been tied by the feet to one of the pannier straps. These are the ritual offerings a young man must present to his future wife. Other gifts—a jar of *rnööm* and a pig—are likewise deposited in Mang's house. The reader will recall that Bbôong-the-Deputy had been chosen as go-between when Srae and Jaang were affianced; now, he being absent in Poste du Lac, his wife assumes this office. The matchmaker from Ndut is still Ndêh, former canton chief and Baap Can's *jôok*.

Ndêh and Kroong-the-Short join Mang-of-the-Jutting-Jaw at the foot of the *yang dâm*. Mang passes them wort, and all three "anoint the tubes"— or, rather, the pannier and its contents:

> "On one side the tubes, on the other the bamboo shoots;
> on one side the jars, on the other the pigs;

on one side the porcelain, on the other the captive chicken;
on one side, the chicken in its little cage, the white fish in the tubes;
on the other, the beads strung with care."

This rite is a repetition of the sacrifice of a chicken accompanied by the drinking of a jar of *rnööm* with which the *paa* tubes had been consecrated by the Bboon Jraang before they left Ndut. Kroong-Biing drinks first, followed by the former canton chief, who cedes his place to Mang-of-the-Jutting-Jaw; in other words, the first to drink from this jar are the father of the groom and the two go-betweens.

Presently, we leave the principals drinking at the deputy's house and move on to Baap Can's. No one is home—everyone is still at Tôong-Mang's—and nothing is ready to receive the foreigners. Finally, but not before eleven, Baap Can, Aang-the-Long, Jaang, and Krah arrive. As soon as our host enters, he circulates among us to give each person a pinch of tobacco. A half hour later, Kroong-the-Short, Biing, Srae, and a few other latecomers join us, bringing with them a small neckless jar and a pig. All the visitors from Ndut are now on hand, and those Sar Luk people stouthearted enough to stay awake so late.

Jaang, the heroine of the evening, is seated by one of the granary uprights. She is a still skinny girl, and her breasts are only now beginning to swell. Stiff and timid, her eyes lowered, she seems terribly embarrassed by the attention concentrated on her. Ndêh presents her with the small basket of ritual gifts. She squirms and averts her head. Her mother and her half sister squat beside her beneath the granary, and alternately scold and encourage her. At last, she brings herself to touch the two longer, carved tubes. Chanting couplets of wishes the while, the go-between places the necklace around her throat, sticks the comb in her hair, and slips the knife in her chignon. Lastly, he slips the two bracelets on her wrists. Aang removes all the tubes from the basket; reclaiming all the adornments the go-between has just given Jaang, she distributes them among the women of the Rjee and Ntöör clans: * the little pannier to old Troo, the chicken to Jaang Bibuu, Truu's adopted daughter; the comb to Grieng-Mbieng; the knife to Aang-Who-Stinks (daughter of Yôong-the-Mad); and the bracelet to Jôong-Kröng.

Srae has watched the ceremony sitting in a corner at a discreet remove. Even though this well-built young man is in school and has therefore moved beyond the frame of village life—and reputedly is more sophisticated than his peers—tonight he is awkward and timid. Now he approaches Baap Can, his future father-in-law. He holds a cock and two bamboo tubes the go-between had removed from the pannier before he presented the gifts to Jaang. Baap Can takes Srae's hand and shows him

---

* It will be recalled that Baap Can is a Rjee, Aang a Ntöör.

the family's pallets, and where his own mat will be located to avoid any infractions of the mother-in-law taboo and the wasting away that results from a failure to observe it (*nôot*). When Baap Can comes to the private door, he has his son-in-law drink eight swallows of soup from a gourd he lifts to the young man's lips. Then, taking a small bottle that contains some magic Paddy tuber, he pours rice soup into it. He lifts this to the height of his son-in-law's left ear, blows on the mouth of the bottle, and counts "One"; he recommences at the level of the right ear—"Two"—and so on, up to eight. He then launches into the recitation of wishes.

The two men climb up to the granary, the old man still leading his son-in-law. Baap Can has Srae "caress the Paddy" (*rbii Baa*). They descend from the granary, at which point Srae hands his father-in-law the live cock and the two *paa* tubes he had been carrying throughout this rite.

Inside the house, they slit the neck of the pig Kroong-Biing has brought from Ndut. Assisted by his witness, Kroong has Baap Can consecrate the little jar he has also brought. The former canton chief drinks first, then the father of Chaar-Sraang, then Baap Can, Kröng-Jôong, Mang-of-the-Jutting-Jaw, Bbaang-the-Schoolboy (a Bboon Jraang, and Srae's *kôony*). . . . Ndêh rises and anoints the head of the sacrificed pig with beer wort from the jar.

Baap Can has placed a *yang dâm* near the granary and at its base set a Mnong bowl filled with white rice and covered by an upturned Vietnamese bowl. He gives this rice and *cai bat* to the young man. The small neckless jar is consecrated, and Baap Can sits before it; he will be the first to drink. He has Bbaang-the-Stag (the bride's *kôony*) and Can, his oldest son, taste the *rnööm*, then he relinquishes his place to his son-in-law. Srae drinks the two measures prescribed, returns the straw to his father-in-law, who drinks his equal share, and immediately returns the straw to Srae. The second couple to crouch before the *yang dâm* are Biing, Srae's mother, and her husband, Kroong-the-Short.

At one o'clock in the morning, a meal is served to two groups: on the low platform, the families of Kroong-Biing and Ndêh; near the granary, Jaang and the little Bboon Jraang girl, who carried the pannier with the gifts from Ndut, as well as two Cil women who have taken refuge with Kroong-the-Short.

In the place of honor in his visitors' room, Baap Can installs an antique jar—a splendid "*taang sôh* with twelve ears," its neck decorated with an antique necklace of large beads. Mang-of-the-Jutting-Jaw attaches a large jar to the same stake; this one will be offered to Ndêh, as go-between. Each of the following has brought a *rnööm*: the Ntöör (relatives of the bride)—Bbaang-the-Stag, her *kôony*, and Yôong-the-Mad, her great-aunt; also all the Rjee (her father's clan)—Kröng-Jôong, Tôong-Jieng, Mbieng-Grieng, Mhoo-Laang, Kroong-Mae; Can, her half brother; and also several sworn friends of some of them—Brôong-the-Widow, Troo-Jôong, and Wan-Jôong. (Truu, her uncle, is still ill and has not come.) Counting the jars offered by the two fathers, fifteen jars in all are aligned in the visitors' room.

At three in the morning, Baap Can's sow is killed. The animal is enormous, its girth measuring nearly six spans; it is almost as wide as it is long.

The two fathers and the two go-betweens inaugurate the large antique jar. Shortly thereafter, the go-between opens the *rnööm* offered by the deputy's wife. Carrying a Vietnamese bowl with wort from all the jars and blood from both victims, Ndêh goes out "to summon the Spirits in the belly of the Paddy."

At three-thirty comes "the leading to the water of the jars" (*lâm daak yang*). Baap Can opens the march, followed single-file by the ethnologist, Ndêh, Kroong-the-Short and Biing, Mang-Ndêh (wife of the former canton chief), Aang-the-Long, Mang-of-the-Jutting-Jaw, Jaang and Srae, Kröng-Jôong. . . .

Twenty minutes later, at the second crowing of the cock, Ndêh anoints the head of the huge sow with blood and beer wort.

Each person from Sar Luk who has offered a jar chooses one or even two from among the Ndut visitors as drinking partners. The two go-betweens, by virtue of their function, must join before the same *rnööm*, but the others group themselves according to personal affinities or relationships. When Kroong-the-Short and Biing have drunk from the great "*taang sôh* with twelve ears," they are succeeded by Jôong-Kröng and her husband (her status being that of elder sister to the father of the bride), then Ndêh and his wife, the second go-between, Mang-of-the-Jutting-Jaw, and lastly, Baap Can and his wife. The revelry lasts until sunup.

February 22

Early this morning, each of the women of the family brings Jaang a small Vietnamese bowl filled with rice and covered by another, larger bowl. (Some forget the second bowl.) These offerings of hulled rice and crockery are intended for distribution to the relatives of the groom.

And now the old *kôony* of the Rjee appears—Tôong-Mang, at whose house we drank last night. He comes to remind Baap Can that he must not forget Tôong's guests in the distribution of gifts to foreigners. "Each of them must be given a Vietnamese bowl," he says, "and a piece of meat." Baap Can is vexed, and answers his uncle tartly: "Do you come to remind me because you think I am 'deaf' or because you think I don't know the proper thing to do?" "I came to tell you," the old man replies, "because they are about to leave."

Baap Can does get together some meat and, having no bowls—or not

wishing to give away any from the quantity just brought to him—he substitutes piasters for them. He holds out his gift to Tôong-Mang, but the
old man expostulates, "After what you have said to me, I would be
ashamed to take that." So Baap Can orders Krah to carry the presents to
the foreigners.

When old Tôong came in, Baap Can had been deep in discussion with
his *jôok*, Ndêh, and his "brother," Kroong-the-Short, the latter tippling
from the large antique jar. The groom's father now has his say. "I'm a
grown man, I know all about these things. Why must you come and tell
us what should be done, as if we were children? You're stepping on the
toes of Kroong, the son of Dür. I won't stand for it." But the old man is
not daunted by this duo of nephews, big *kuang* though they be. Baap Can
tries to cut the argument short, declaring that it gives him a headache to
have to listen to such things. Although Kroong-the-Short is annoyed, he
offers the old *kôony* a drink. With a slight smile, Tôong declines: "You are
drunk. I refuse to taste your water. Your being rich doesn't matter, you
don't impress me." Now all magnanimity, Kroong says, "I give in," and he
sings:

> "*Do not open your eyes at night, not at night;*
> *do not open your eyes at night, not to the nightjar.*
> *Do not open the blanket spread beneath the eye of the sparrow hawk;*
> *do not uncover the lance, the hoe, under the eye of the roedeer.*"

The old *kôony* replies with another song:

> "*I pay no heed to the mouth of empty speech, mouth of the magpie;*
> *I pay no heed to the chops of empty speech, mouth without sense;*
> *I pay no heed to a mouth bearing bombax tusks, bombax tusks;*
> *I pay no heed to chops of deceit, chops of deceit. . . .*"

And with this, he stalks out.

During their exchange, Mbieng-Grieng, near the granary, was cutting
up the pig Kroong-the-Short had brought, the smallest of the victims sacrificed last night. Next, he attacks the carcass of the big sow sacrificed for
Baap Can. When the old *kôony* returns, Kroong-the-Short will offer him a
fine slice of leaf fat.

The *kuang* are not the only ones drinking. Young men and women
have gathered around those jars in which the rice beer is not too much
diluted after last night's revelry. Some are quiet and pensive, like Yaang;
this Cil girl has taken refuge, together with her mother, in Kroong-Biing's
ménage, and now she sits motionless, her head leaning on the shoulder of
Krae-the-Widower, of Ndut. Others, like Aang-of-the-Drooping-Eyelid,
are in high spirits. Aang amuses herself by smearing soot from the bottom
of a pot on Krae-the-Widower and Bbaang-the-Schoolboy. The first time,
Krae simply wipes the soot off; when Aang showers him again, he gets

even by wiping his blackened hands on Kroong-Big-Navel's face. The young bride, Jaang, is in tears because she is being forced to drink *rnööm*, and she bites Krae's hand. The young men begin to talk "the upside-down language of the Underworld"—a sort of "pig" Mnong. The gibberish Krae utters is particularly difficult to decipher. He is not content with inserting an extra syllable in each word; he retains only its first letter, and in addition he voices it when it is a mute consonant. Thus, *tuk mee lööt* ("Where are you going?") becomes *dieng mee laang*.

Can and Bbaang-the-Stag are not of the party. They left us this morning to transmit to Ndut Lieng Krak the government orders concerning the collection of heavy rattan and to see the sector chief, who is supervising the work on the track.

After the eleven-o'clock meal, everyone sleeps on the low platform. At three in the afternoon, people eat again. After this second repast, bowls destined for the foreigners are set on the platform, as is a pot of white rice that has been brought by the women of the family. Preparations begin for the second day of the wedding. Various items are placed in a pointy winnowing basket with a spout: a very old buffalo horn belonging to the Rjee clan; a serving basket of cooked rice; a large bowl of pork; an antique bowl Jaang is giving her mother-in-law; a pot of beer siphoned last night from the ancient jar "with twelve ears" before it was consecrated; also, a young chicken—a pullet, really—that has been caught with a net and roasted.

At last, the two fiancés step up onto the low platform and sit on either side of the ritual winnowing basket. The two go-betweens, Ndêh and Mang-of-the-Jutting-Jaw, take their places on the platform, as does Baap Can. The old *kôony*'s young wife (like Srae, Mang is a Bboon Jraang) stations herself near Baap Can to fill the glasses. Presently, Kroong-the-Short joins the group.

To open the ceremony, Baap Can offers a drink to his *jôok*, Ndêh, who is the principal go-between in his daughter's marriage. Ndêh reciprocates the gesture and recites the same wishes. The ceremony really gets under way at three-thirty, when Baap Can cleaves the pullet's head and lets the two halves fall on the serving basket of cooked rice, the top of which has been leveled off. He succeeds with his first try: "Heads for the Spirits, tails for me." That is, the half nearer Baap Can has so fallen that it rests on its round outer side, and the half farther from him lies on the severed side.

By way of congratulation, Kroong-the-Short lifts a glass of *rnööm* to his "brother's" lips. By way of encouragement, Baap Can returns the courtesy, for now it is Kroong's turn. He "consults the head of the pullet" (*poal bôok ier*), but on his first try fails, then fails again. Baap Can picks up the omens once more. Invoking in sequence the ancestors of the Rjee, Ntöör, and Bboon Jraang clans "together with the Cham, the French, and the Vietnamese," he lets the pieces fall again on the cooked rice: failure. He begins afresh, with loud exhortations, and this time succeeds.

The father of the bride now launches into a long discourse in which he retraces the marriages of his children—Can, Aang-of-the-Drooping-Eyelid, and now Jaang—and he concludes with a eulogy of the ancestors of the three clans concerned.

Ndëh has the horn filled with rice beer, lifts it to Srae's lips, praying the while, and then has the young girl drink. He next offers the horn of *rnööm* to Srae's father, but does not hold it while Kroong drinks.

Mang-Tôong refills the horn with *rnööm*. Into it the *kuang* drop some magic plant of the Paddy, which has been cut into small pieces, and the two halves of the pullet's head. While casting these magic ingredients into the horn, the two fathers and the two go-betweens pray fervently that everything will go as it should: and, indeed, all the pieces sink immediately to the bottom of the horn.

Mang-of-the-Jutting-Jaw lifts a tube of fresh water to Srae's mouth, counting "One," while Ndëh lifts the horn of omen-enriched beer to the lips of Jaang. Then "Two"—that is, *rnööm* to Srae and fresh water to Jaang; and so on, up to eight. Baap Can has his son-in-law eat the chicken's head and all that remains of the *gun Baa* at the bottom of the horn.

The moment has come for one of the most important steps in the ritual—at least, its name serves often to designate the ensemble of marriage ceremonies. Ndëh places himself between the two fiancés, who incline their heads toward each other, forehead almost touching forehead. The go-between takes a lock of hair of each, which he knots together and then unknots while asking that the young couple may enjoy prosperity and wealth. Then, roughly seizing both their heads by the hair, he knocks them together, to the great joy of all present. This is the *tâm bôok*—"the knocking together of heads." While the senior partners remain on the low platform to drink, the young newlyweds rise to their feet, more flushed and awkward than ever. Srae rejoins the young men, and Jaang takes refuge beneath the granary. Her mother reminds her, however, that now she must distribute the gifts to her husband's relatives. Jaang "feeds" each of them; that is, she lifts to the lips of each a handful of cooked rice topped by a few morsels of pig entrails, and she gives each a large Vietnamese bowl. First to be so honored are the two go-betweens—Ndëh, former canton chief and her father's *jôok*; then Mang-of-the-Jutting-Jaw, her "little mother" (her father's "sister"). Then, in succession, she "feeds" and bestows a gift on the wife of Ndëh; on Rau-Lôong, the elder sister of her husband's mother, Biing-Kroong; on Kroong-Biing-the-Short, her father-in-law; Kraang-Jieng, her mother-in-law's brother; Lôong-Rau; and so on, until she has honored not only all the Bboon Jraang and their friends who have come from Ndut but also the old Rjee *kôony*, Tôong-Mang (because he is married to a Bboon Jraang).

Bbaang-the-Stag re-enters the mainstream of events in the afternoon. As *kôony* of the bride, he normally would have played a particularly prominent role, but it is rather hard to be in the forefront when you are competing with a personality like Baap Can. Also, Bbaang-the-Stag has permitted himself to be somewhat excessively served by the jar. I hear him mumble something about his "little mother," Yôong-the-Mad, but cannot make out what he is saying.

However, now Bbaang-the-Stag must participate, for the question of the dowry is about to be settled. In this, only the bride's *kôony* can represent her clan. Bbaang weaves his way up to the platform, where the go-betweens and the two fathers-in-law are seated. His tongue is thick as he enumerates the jars he is demanding as dowry; to represent them, he lays bits of straw before him. Kroong-Biing finds the figure of six *yang dâm* decidedly excessive. After a good twenty minutes of discussion, he nonetheless finally concurs. Two lengths of iron offered by the groom's family are declined on the bride's behalf "because women do not know how to forge."(!) As always when Kroong-the-Short participates in a discussion, it ends with an exchange of songs—this time between the *kuang* of Ndut and the *kuang* of Phii Ko'.

Baap Can is forever intent on strengthening the magic power of associates. Accordingly, he has gone to get his pouch of precious talismans, and from it he takes some grains of hulled rice, two tiny ovoid pebbles (*rtee*), a large antique bead, a buffalo molar, and a minute quartz (*naar*). Before he places them in a copper bowl, he shows us one transparent pebble and tells us proudly that he consecrated it with a duck, a pig, and a goat, all three of them white. He fills the bowl with beer and, to the recitation of many wishes, has Srae drink from it, then his brother-in-law and his daughter's *kôony*, Bbaang-the-Stag. As he is replacing his magic pieces, he cannot find the quartz; the grains of rice he abandons.

Then the gifts for the parents of the groom are presented in a large pannier: one small harvest pannier filled with crockery;* the shoulder of the sacrificed pig, which Jaang's parents are herewith returning to the donors; the head, tripes, and liver of the sow which her parents sacrificed in honor of Kroong and Biing.

At five-thirty, Baap Can offers the two go-betweens, Kroong-the-Short, and Bbaang-the-Stag a pinch of wort dipped in blood. Together, they anoint the head of the pig, asking for prosperity and wealth. The master of the house and his colleagues exchange hand kissings, after which Baap

---

* Three large and three small Vietnamese bowls, and a plate, also imported.

Can offers Ndêh the gift-filled pannier. The pig's head is retained by the bride's father. The Vietnamese bowl containing the wort and the blood of the two victims is given to Ndêh in thanks for his good offices. Baap Can adds to the gift a large bowl for Srae's older sister and a small bowl for Kroong-the-Short's younger sister, who lives with him. The two women have remained in their own village to watch over the house.

Now people drink from glasses. Bbaang-the-Stag is in high spirits thanks to the happy occasion and the *rnööm* he has downed; when Yôong-the-Mad sings, he delivers himself of an endless rhapsody, exalting their clan. This morning, old Tôong-Mang had done the same, praising the Rjee when Kroong-the-Short was singing with the foreigner, who is also a Rjee.

Kroong-the-Short returns to the giver a shoulder of the sow Baap Can sacrificed in his honor. He cuts off a fine slice of leaf fat and offers it to me; he gives some also to his "sister," Grieng, and to his "mother," Troo.

The visitors from Ndut are already starting to leave us. Before Ndêh's wife sets out, she gives a big plug of tobacco to Baap Can; in return, he offers his *jôok's* wife a small pot of blood.

Drüm-Kraang appears with a long-nosed gourd of water, in which a few grains of rice are soaking. She presents it to the departing guests, and each in turn moistens his fingers in it and touches them to his forehead and heart. This is to obtain medicine against drunkenness, for Drüm's daughter, Aang, is lying on the ground at home, dead drunk, having indulged in too many "exchanges of drink" with other young people. Her mother goes through the village making a collection of this sobering remedy, then returns home to splash what has become a medicinal water on Aang's chest, forehead, cheeks, and, lastly, eight times over the area of the heart. Apparently its curative powers are not too great. Pretty Aang merely stirs once or twice and, when finally she is carried up onto the platform, falls sound asleep.

Baap Can distributes the marriage tubes throughout the village. He has his son, little Choong-of-the-Big-Belly, deliver two tubes and a piece of pork to each household.

The young people of both villages are exuberant. Jaang lets herself be borne off by Bbaang-the-Schoolboy, her husband's *kôony*, to eat at the home of the Bboon Jraang. She consents to my treating a rather deep cut on her big toe. After sipping from last evening's jars, people go off to Bbaang-the-Stag's to taste a jar he has just opened. Dloong-the-Black-Girl challenges Yaang, the young Upstream Cil girl who has taken refuge with Kroong-the-Short, to a singing contest. But Dloong understands none of Yaang's songs, so the couplets they exchange have no connection whatever.

February 23

This morning, there is little activity in the village. The young people spent last evening drinking and exchanging songs, but they went to bed rather early, for they had been up throughout the previous night and over the last twenty-four hours had drunk prodigiously. Those from Ndut leave in a group around nine o'clock.

The former canton chief and Kroong-the-Short have slept over in Sar Luk. Ndêh is busy now stripping a branch of *ndroong* (not identified); this tree grows abundantly in Sar Luk, and he wants to take some bark home with him, for it makes excellent rope. Kroong-the-Short, Bbaang-the-Stag, and Baap Can have one last short talk before the visitors leave. On several occasions, I have noticed that whereas Kroong-the-Short often offers something without asking anything in return, Baap Can requests things frequently and in a rather servile manner at that; a case in point was his asking yesterday for salt and tobacco, which he claimed he was too old and poor to procure for himself.

As Kroong-the-Short is finally about to leave, he advises Srae not to dawdle in Sar Luk. His marriage must not prevent his returning to the school in Ban Me Thuot; the school, Kroong reminds his son, is opening the way for him to amount to something later on in life. "You see, I began to work with the Europeans when I was very young, and I have become a *kuang.*" Srae stands staring at the ground. He has not even shown his father the dictionary I gave him at one point during the marriage festivities. In four days, he will return to his parents' house with his wife, for he has already spent three days at the home of his parents-in-law.

He does make one gesture. He brings his mother a puppy he has been given. She wants to leave the jar they brought to drink the evening of their arrival. (Acutally, the jar will be returned four days later.)

Baap Can and Kroong-the-Short take leave of each other with hand kissings and recitations of good wishes.

Someone says to Srae's mother, "Don't become angry, don't quarrel with anyone."

"Why should I?"

"Because you are giving up your child."

After his parents leave, Srae is helped by his "brother," Maang-the-Thin, to empty and clean the party jars. Down by the river, children are fishing with lines and have even built a little dam so as to catch fish with setnets. Presently they play at preaching a sermon. The "congregation" assembles for the show. Mang-the-Dwarf is crouched under the shelter of the forge between Tôong-the-Stutterer and Kroong-the-Tokélo.* All

---

* *Tokélo* is a skin infection found in Oceania and Southeast Asia. —*Trans.*

three, squatting before a small cleared rectangle where they have placed some bits of wood, bawl incomprehensible songs in which now and then one distinguishes the words *"Aê Diê* ["God," in Rhade], *Aê Diê."* When I question them, Mang answers, to the delight of the children's republic, "Why, we're doing like the Christians who came the other day. We're singing psalms. I am the Rhade pastor. Tôong-the-Stutterer is one of the assistants who sang. And Kroong-the-Tokélo is playing the young Frenchman who came with them, the one who wore a towel on his head."

At two o'clock, Truu's crew returns from the *miir*. The canton chief has finished slashing his field today. Toward late afternoon, the other teams of workers come back in turn.

In Baap Can's house, life has resumed its normal course. The family now includes one more member; for all, this increase is only the beginning of future growth for the family and for the clan.

On February 27, Baap Can accompanies the newlyweds to the home of the young man's parents. Contrary to what tradition requires, however, Srae returns—in the old man's company—the next day, for he must go back to Ban Me Thuot at once. He will actually leave the morning of March 2, and the evening before, his father-in-law will not neglect to sacrifice a chicken and a jar to ensure him a safe journey.

· 🌷 · 🌷 · 🌷 · 🌷 · 🌷 · 🌷 · 🌷 ·

6
We Eat the Forest of the
Stone Spirit Gôo

March 14, 1949

THIS afternoon, Sar Luk is deserted. The entire village is off on a group
fishing expedition. For this, the river is dammed (*böt daak*), upstream
from the present village site, at a place called "the arm where one draws
the canoe."

The young men went to the forest this morning to cut poisonous *kroo*
roots (*Milletia pierrei* Gagnepain?), which they peeled on the spot. After a
brief pause in the village, they waded upriver and, some two hundred
meters above Sar Luk, built a dam by the rapids near the left bank. The
dam consists of a broken line of trunks, arranged horizontally; bamboo
stakes are wedged against them, and atop these are placed armfuls of
lalang grass and masses of broad *tlôong* leaves (*Dipterocarpus obtusifolius*). The men consolidate the dam with chunks of sod and clumps
of leaves that lie rotting in the mud by the bank. Thus the current is
diverted from "the arm where one draws the canoe" and rushes into the
narrow channel left open on the right bank. Among the rocks in the
rapids, the water level is now considerably lowered. A few small dikes
block the rivulets of shallow water, and under them the men set their
nets.

Around two o'clock in the afternoon, the women and children are summoned. They enter the river at the watering place and wade up to the
fishing site. Young men are stationed on several rocks near the dam "to
strike the *kroo*"; that is, with a club each man vigorously pounds a mass of
the poisonous root peelings, which now and then he dips in the current so
that the juice thus extracted spreads through the water. Soon, asphyxiated

fish float to the surface. The women do not wait for this, however. The moment they arrive at the site, they enter the shallow channels, stirring up the bottom with their shove nets as they walk against the current. The men throw cast nets into the deepest parts; some, crouching on rocks, use square dip nets. This busy crowd is swarming about in a relatively small area. The roughly semicircular dam is some fifty meters long, and its efficiency is greatly increased by the many rocks that form the rapids here and by a sandbank that extends for almost a hundred meters. As it is past the middle of the dry season, it is extremely hot; the sun is scorching and the glare intense. Children are naked, women wear only threadbare skirts, and men are clad in the scantiest loincloths they own. Only the very small children remain on the rocks or on the exposed sand spits, from which they try to snare tiny fish, shrimp, and crabs. The rest of the village wades about in the current. In the deepest spots, men are moving in water that reaches to their waists or even as high as their necks. They are careful not to submerge their heads too often for fear of irritating their eyes. The women, especially the young ones, are less prudent. They move ahead as quickly as they can, bent over in the water to keep their shove nets close to the bottom, and they straighten up only to remove their catch and drop it in the wicker boxes they carry suspended at the thigh. The first hour of fishing, when the work rhythm is extremely fast, yields the biggest catch. Then fatigue overtakes the old and the very young; also, the fish become more scarce. By the end of the afternoon, when one family strikes out for home, everyone else follows suit. A long line of people wades single-file from the fishing site back to the village. A few—almost exclusively men—are, so to speak, "hooked," and they linger a while longer, but when they have lifted their setnets and partly dismantled the dam, they also call it a day.

Collective fishing expeditions, which mobilize all or most of the village, are made during the dry season, from January to June, when the water level is low. Today's foray has been special, however. It was carried out on orders from Bbaang-the-Pregnant-Man, the holy man of the Fire Sticks, and it has taken place on the eve of burning off the fields.

By March 8, all households had finished chopping down the trees on their individual plots. The dry season being at its peak, any wood left where it was cut has dried rapidly. After verifying the condition of the slashed area the day before yesterday, Bbaang-the-Pregnant-Man passed by every house to announce a general assembly for the next day, when around the outer boundaries of the *miir* a firebreak would be cleared to protect the surrounding forest. Yesterday morning, with no magic protection rite (little did it matter if the roedeer were to bell that day), men, women, and children betook themselves en masse to the Stone Spirit Gôo and cut a border three meters wide all around the *miir*. Men fell the trees, women and children clear the ground, digging up roots and sweeping up fallen leaves.

On their return last evening, the holy man set the time for today's fishing.

Back from the expedition—the catch was abundant—everyone goes about his own affairs. Some women weave; Aang-of-the-Mincing-Step, Bbaang-the-Stag's wife, is weaving a handsome ritual loincloth for the *Tâm Bôh* her husband must soon make with Kraang-Drüm. Krŏng-Jŏong castrates two pigs belonging to Taang-Jieng-the-Stooped. Men sweep the yards before their doorways: the village must be very clean or tomorrow's *miir* fire will not catch well. A group of Mnong Laac carrying panniers of salt approach the village, but people run out to warn them that today Sar Luk is taboo. The foreigners say they intend to stay the night, but are briskly informed that this is impossible. The oldest man knows me; he turns to me and asks my permission for them to camp under my house. I have to explain that there is absolutely nothing I can do for him, that tradition forbids anyone to enter the village the night before and especially the day the cut wood is to be burned. However, the villagers do permit them to exchange their salt for hulled rice.

This evening there is a full moon. All heads of household gather at Bbaang-the-Pregnant-Man's, and each brings with him a small packet of "tree leaves." *

The master of the house has brought out a *yang dâm* of beer, at the foot of which he has placed the winnowing basket that holds the *Rnut*—the ritual Fire Sticks. He puts the packets of leaves the men have brought in it, and arranges the lengths of sacred wood side by side. The room is soon full, and the two other holy men, Baap Can and Krŏng-Jŏong, are on hand. Bbaang-the-Pregnant-Man slits the neck of a very young chicken over a Mnong bowl filled with wort, then hands a drinking straw to the first holy man, and the Mnong bowl to the second; he does not kiss their hands, and he prays alone. Finally, Bbaang-the-Stag arrives, and the holy man in Phii Ko' joins his three colleagues around the winnowing basket. Together, the four *croo weer* anoint all the Fire Sticks and all the packets of tree leaves, as they recite:

> "Devour, O Fire, down to the log,
> devour the foliage down to the log. . . .
> I do as did the Ancestor of bygone days,

---

* These "tree leaves" (*nhaa sii*) include leaves of *rkôong* (Euphorbiaceae?), *chaa* (Cupuliferae), *haa baa* (literally, "paddy leaves," or Melastomaceae), and *rboo* (a tree with alternate leaves). The grass that binds the packet is *ül tlaa* (*Carex indica*).

> *I do as did the Mother of yesterday,*
> *I do as did the Forebear of olden times.*
> *The fire of the* Rnut, *they taught me to blow upon it;*
> *thus I blow upon it.*
> *The fire of the* Rnoh, *they taught me to light it;*
> *thus I light it.*
> Gruu, *child of the Sorcerer, they taught me to strike him;*
> *thus I strike him.*
> *I cut down the child of the Plain, doing as did the Ancestors;*
> *I fell the child of the Tree, doing as did the Ancestors;*
> *I clear the forest and the bush, doing as did the Ancestors. . . ."*

Baap Can has passed the drinking straw to Bbaang-the Stag, who inserts the *gut* in the small neckless jar, but no one interrupts his long invocation. Finally, the four men rise, and Bbaang-the-Pregnant-Man goes to sit before the jar and drink first. Baap Can embarks on a long speech. He commences by asking the villagers not to quarrel among themselves, not to insult or fight with each other; he declares that after the ceremony of burning the forest *(chuu ntôih)*, the flat-gong orchestra will circulate, and that then they will all go "abroad" to buy buffaloes in order to celebrate the Festival of the Soil. His brother-in-law, Kröng-Jôong, briefly seconds his speech, then elaborates on the same theme—the purchase of buffaloes for the *Nyiit Döng*—while Baap Can succeeds Bbaang-Jieng at the jar. But even while he drinks, the old man continues to talk. He cedes his place to Kröng-Jôong, who, when he has drunk, passes the *gut* to me. So as to drink less, I want as usual to invite a member of the group to come sip from the jar in my place, but I am told, *"Beng!* Taboo!" I learn that this evening one may offer neither the drinking straw nor a glass to anyone, no matter whom; one must drink alone. Otherwise, stags, wild boar, and elephants will eat the paddy in the future field. Tomorrow the same will be true, but in addition one will be forbidden to drink standing; one will have to squat or sit. Tomorrow, likewise, the taboo against foreigners must be rigorously observed. Ropes will be stretched around the village. Furthermore, no one shall bathe; this ritual prohibition, which goes into effect as of today for the master of the Fire Sticks, will include the three other holy men in the village and in the forest and obtain until the morning of the day after tomorrow.

After me, Bbaang-the-Stag comes to drink. One by one, all the heads of household in Sar Luk follow.

The sacrificed chicken, little more than a pullet, is shared among the four holy men. Conversation is rather dull and aimless. People do not linger, for there is only one jar to drink—a small one at that—and what's more, tomorrow will be an exceptionally important day, on which the future of the crops depends. So the evening ends very early.

March 15

In good time this morning, Bbôong-the-Deputy went with two other men to set out along the "French" track the signposts brought back from Poste du Lac yesterday. By seven forty-five, all Sar Luk was en route to the slashed fields. Midway between the village and the future *miir*, one corner of a bamboo grove was chosen as a ceremonial encampment. The men quickly cleared a small area ten by twenty meters, and here people took their places. Two young men have brought along a drum, suspended from a bamboo pole. Now a support is fashioned for it, a transverse pole resting on two vertical posts; the ends of both pole and posts have been tufted. Drüm-Kraang, the daughter of Bbaang-the-Pregnant-Man, has brought her sheller; she sets it down by the winnowing basket to which the master of the *Rnut* has transferred the holy Fire Sticks. Rising above this basket is a long *dlei* bamboo stake, from the top of which has been hung one of the fish from yesterday's catch. Bbaang-the-Pregnant-Man adds more ritual items to the Fire Sticks: a tufted wick, some bamboo fibers, a leaf of corn containing beer wort, and the dried spongy heart of a *buuny baa (Luffa cylindrica)*, which he has just peeled. Each household has brought either a giant gourd or a *yang ke'*—a neckless jar even smaller than a *yang dâm*—filled with rice beer.

During the initial rites, several young men top all these receptacles with water, and siphon off into a pot some rice beer taken only from the gourds.

At nine o'clock, Bbaang-the-Pregnant-Man slits the throat of a young chicken—again, scarcely larger than a chick—above the wort in the leaf of corn, and places the chicken in the winnowing basket. The three holy men, aided by Mhoo-Laang (recruited as assistant after the death of Kraang, his wife's brother), anoint the contents of the basket. In anticipation of their consulting the bamboos (*pool dlei*), stalks of *dlei* bamboo, each about a meter long, have been split in two lengthwise, and these are anointed together with the rest. Baap Can picks up the two halves of one *dlei*, prays for the success of the ceremony, and drops them over the basket. They fall in an unpropitious position. He repeats the gesture several times; to reinforce his invocation, he enumerates the names of those who are absent—notably Truu, the canton chief, who left the day before yesterday for Ryôong. He finally casts the *dlei* successfully. He places the piece that fell with its "tail" or cut side down (*rtlup*) on the *Rnut*, and sets aside the half that fell on the outer curve of the stalk (*rblaang*).

He consults another bamboo fragment. Since these two pieces fall in an inauspicious position, he promises a Festival of the Soil. The two "tail" halves, two unsplit *dlei*, the Fire Sticks of Sar Luk and those of Phii Ko', still in their pannier, and the packets of "tree leaves" remain in the basket.

At nine-thirty, Baap Can offers drink to Bbaang-Jieng, who is holding

Baap Can consults the halves of the dlei *bamboo*

OVERLEAF: *The ceremonial encampment in the bamboo grove*

the two bamboo "heads" and the leaf of corn with wort. Bbaang-the-Pregnant-Man returns his courtesy, then invites Kröng-Jôong to drink and hands him the ritual objects he has been holding. Thus, the two bamboo halves and the beer wort pass from Kröng to Mhoo-Laang, from Mhoo to Bbaang-the-Stag, and end up in the hands of Kraang-Drüm. Each receives a drink from the man handing him the ritual objects.

Then all the men insert drinking straws in the gourds, which have been arranged in one row to the rear of the ritual encampment. The men pair off. Baap Can inserts his *gut* in the gourd of Bbaang-the-Pregnant-Man, and Bbaang dips his straw in Baap Can's gourd; Kröng-Jôong does the same with his nephew Mhoo-Laang, and Bbaang-the-Stag with his *jôok*, Kraang-Drüm, etc. A child keeps the receptacles filled to the brim with water, which he pours from a sacred gourd (it may not be washed), which was among the items in the Fire Sticks pannier. Then comes "the leading to the water of the jars"—everyone present passes single-file to sip from the straws in all the gourds and *yang ke'*, led by Kröng-Jôong, Baap Can, Bbaang-the-Pregnant-Man, and Mhoo-Laang, behind whom come Jôong-Kröng, old Troo, Jieng-Bbaang, and so forth.

Near the winnowing basket and the *dlei* stake, old Krah and Tôong-Wan are splitting bamboo into thin thongs that will be used in "sawing" the Fire Sticks. Each owner of a plot in the *miir* brings a *kriet*—a wicker seed box—containing cucumber, squash, bean, and other vegetable seeds.

At ten o'clock, the master of the Fire Sticks gives Kröng-Jôong a *Rnut* and some flexible bamboo thongs. Kröng passes them to Baap Can, who hands them back to Bbaang-the-Pregnant-Man. One villager presents himself and receives from Bbaang a piece of Fire Stick and one thong. Baap Can offers him a drink, lifting a tube of rice beer to the man's lips. The cleft in the head of the *Rnut* is stuffed with a bit of tufted wick. The man places the thong in one of the lateral gashes in the *Rnut*, and places its head against the tufted tip of bamboo which rests on the loofah (*buuny baa*). With both hands, he seizes the two loops at either end of the thong. Squatting on either side of the operator, Baap Can and Bbaang-the-Pregnant-Man hold the Fire Stick firmly, while the man pulls the bamboo thong from right to left, faster and faster, until the friction makes a spark. The two holy men invoke the protection of the Spirits; the third *croo weer*, Kröng-Jôong, anoints the stake to which the fish is tied and "summons the Spirits." It is impossible to make out what they are saying, for Drüm-Kraang has squatted by her sheller and is turning the handle, which makes a grating sound, like a huge rattle. Also two men have crouched by either side of the hanging drum and are striking it with all their might, while beside them others are blowing on the deep-throated horns.

When the first man tires of sawing, another replaces him, and so on. Baap Can offers each a drink before he is allowed to saw the Fire Stick.

A resounding cheer greets the birth of the fire. Not only the wadding but also the wood of the *Rnut* must catch, although very slightly. Meanwhile, wood for a fire has been laid, and the ignited wick is carried to it. Bbaang-the-Pregnant-Man and Mhoo-Laang, both armed with two Fire Sticks from the sacred winnowing basket and pannier, strike opposite ends of the drum. Baap Can is able to get the wood fire to catch with the wick that has been ritually set aflame. The ceremony has been successful; the other holy men and their assistant come, each in turn, to offer a glass of *rnööm* to their colleague, who likewise honors them.

At ten twenty-five, the *croo weer* anoint the seeds for the first sowing, which all households have brought in little hampers.

Then each man offers food to his partner and to the holy men, lifting to their lips this day's ritual nourishment: cooked rice and fish (caught yesterday), wrapped in a *tloong* leaf. Chaar-Rieng offers Baap Can a chicken thigh instead of fish. The leaf that is used as bowl or plate must be fresh; if it is old and shriveled, the fire will not "eat" the fallen wood.

Then Baap Can approaches the fire, grasping a second young chicken, which is still alive. The children station themselves around the fire site to form a compact fence. The holy man binds the chicken's feet and tosses it onto the fire, but it manages to escape. Baap Can catches it and throws it on the embers again; he does this several times, until the victim perishes in the flames. Meanwhile, people have been coming up to throw their packets of "tree leaves" onto the fire.

When this rite is completed—it is now eleven-thirty—young men snatch flaming brands from the ritual fire and each runs to a different spot in the forty hectares of felled trees. Presently, dense, black smoke rises to the northeast. A lively argument breaks out about the direction of the wind. For the moment, the smoke is rising vertically, but some people believe that the breeze is blowing upstream—that is, east. This could be dangerous, for no firebreak has been cut on what happens to be Choong-Kôong-the-Soldier's plot because it was thought that in this vicinity the swamp would offer sufficient protection. However, at the moment this otherwise muddy area is dry and covered with fairly high grass, which could quickly ignite.

When we arrive on the scene, Kraang-Dlaang, whose plot lies to the north of Choong-Kôong's, has taken advantage of a breeze blowing downstream and has set fire to the grass. Luckily so, for the wind soon reverses and his new firebreak serves its purpose well.

The burning of the forest is a spectacular sight. The day is very hot, the sun blazing down with all its might. The vast slashed area is littered with large trunks recumbent amid a profusion of smaller brush. Yellow and red predominate—the colors of the now dead leaves and branches of all this felled vegetation. Completely surrounding the parti-colored expanse of the future *miir,* the forest raises a wall of green; like thick carpeting, it mantles the hills rising to the north. At this hour, however, colors are much attenuated, as if bleached by the sun. The intense crackling sound reaches us even before we glimpse the first column of smoke forming to the northeast. At this season, the blue arc overhead is paled by the sunlight, and the sky seems unusually high and remote. The smoke climbs slowly upward and does not spread toward the left until it has attained considerable altitude. Other spots begin to snap and crackle, other columns of smoke begin to rise skyward. Soon the whole area is a deafening inferno; it is like an aerial bombing attack punctuated by brisk machine-gun fire. The rapid explosions are caused by the many bamboos among the cut wood which are bursting. Along the borders of the future fields, the heat becomes unbearable; even shade offers no relief. Forty hectares of erstwhile forest are now one huge brazier burning with unimaginable fierceness. Columns of smoke are coalescing, and their enormous mass climbs slowly into the sky, where, at a certain height, it spreads in an immense plume. "Flowers of the fire"—leaves reduced to ash—are borne on the wind like black birds that hesitantly alight far away.

All around the flaming clearing, people bustle about anxiously. A sudden tongue of fire could reach the forest and, from there, expand toward the village, which would be leveled in an instant. No such worry can dissipate the joyous atmosphere, however, for people know that the danger is also rich in promise, that the power of the fire is a force generating good things for them. Some whistle to the wind to flow downstream; others pray: "O Divinities and Spirits, be merciful and devour." At noon, Baap Can and Bbaang-the-Pregnant-Man inspect the periphery of the *miir.* We are not the only people to be burning off land today. Some five kilometers to the east and fifteen to the south, two huge black columns streak the limpid sky: Paang Döng and Paang Tiing-on-the-Plain have also given over their fields to be eaten by the flames.

From a distance, our fire must appear also as an enormous mass of black smoke rising vertically before, way up in the sky, it diffuses into the shape of a giant, grayish black mushroom. Nearer at hand, a few dozen meters from the burning wood, as you move through a thick gray cloud two or three men will suddenly emerge from it; they patrol the spread of the fire and are armed with branches to beat it back, if necessary. Elsewhere, a group of women carrying the little *kriet* of blessed seeds advance to the boundary of their future field. When one walks by the stream, one sees bundles of manioc stalks soaking; they are only partially covered because the bed is nearly dry.

When we return to the encampment, the two sacrificed chickens—one

The sacrifice of the young chicken, tossed alive into the fire that will spark the burning off of the land

At the edge of the burning forest, Kraang-Dlaang lights a firebreak

killed with a knife, the other thrown alive onto the fire—have been hung from the ritual stake that also bears the fish (*kaa sak*). This is to prevent the women's stepping over them and thereby violating a taboo; the punishment would be the invasion of the future fields by stags, wild boars, and other forest denizens. Aang-of-the-Drooping-Eyelid is lying on the ground, somewhat the worse for drink; several young men have amused themselves by covering her with leaves. Aang-the-Long is munching on a big-rattan heart. Her son, little Choong-of-the-Big-Belly, has drunk more than a six-year-old can carry; he is blowing into the straws left in the jars, which sets the contents a-bubble. It is pointless for his mother now and then to shout at him, "Don't do that! It's taboo!" The little boy is not impressed and goes his merry way. Suddenly, Baap Can notices that his son has disappeared, and hurries to look for him.

By three o'clock, the machine-gun fire has greatly diminished. The cloud of smoke that envelops us has somewhat lightened and the blaze is subsiding, but the "flowers of the fire" float through the air still, or here and there alight. Where a fine forest once stood, you see only a thick layer of ashes covering the ground, and a tangle of half-burned trunks, some of them glowing still. Here and there, wisps of smoke rise from the trunks or clusters of twigs erupt like tiny geysers.

The smoke-laden air is still suffocating. Yet by three-thirty, from every household a woman goes out into the *miir* to make the first ritual sowing of vegetables. I follow Aang-of-the-Drooping-Eyelid to the field of Kröng-Jôong. She goes toward the *nier* (*Irvingia oliveri*); it had not been cut down, but flames have devoured its crest. The future field hut will be built against this tree, and at its base an earth terrace will be left clear of any planting. Aang first plants some cuttings of manioc about fifteen centimeters long. With her hoe, she digs a short T-shaped trench, and sets two slips in the middle, one perpendicular to the other. She plants several pairs thus, in parallel rows. Then, at the foot of the *nier*, she plants some black beans (*Vigna sinensis*), and steps back beyond the manioc to sow her corn, which she hulls on the spot "so that there will be no more foreigner taboo, so that the roedeer will not enter the field, so that the stag will not go into the field." She digs holes with one stroke of her hoe, and drops a few seeds into each.

I move on to visit Baap Can's plot. The embers are dying down, and Jaang-Srae is stirring them so that as many branches as possible will be consumed; this will make for less work later. Her mother, Aang-the-Long, is planting her manioc in the shape of a cross on a patch of land that has caved in near the stream; then some paddy (she does not cover it), then some wax squash. Her *kriet* also contains cotton and yam seeds, but these she will not plant today; she removed them only to anoint them. Choong-of-the-Big-Belly tags along at the heels of his mother and sister, still making a nuisance of himself. He nibbles on the squash seeds, and although his mother shouts at him that this is taboo, he persists. He imitates the hoarse cry of the crow; she tells him that this also is taboo, that "lightning will strike," but he keeps right on.

On the way back to the village, I am walking with Krŏng-Jôong when we meet Yôong-the-Mad. In a very loud voice, the holy man tells me that she is going to offer a jar of rice beer and a chicken, to thank the Spirits because the fire ate her plot so clean. Yôong starts with surprise and says to me, "He's lying, he's lying!" Half laughing, half serious, she asks Krŏng, "Why do you say such things?"

Around seven o'clock, Bbôong-the-Deputy and his nephew Choong-the-Soldier go out to burn off a small area they have cleared on the outskirts of the village, by the riverbank just this side of the forest. The fire catches well, and tall flames light the oncoming dark of evening. They will make a garden and plant bananas there. Tonight we should perform "the blood anointment of the Fire Sticks," but for this we will have to await the canton chief's return.

March 16

This morning, three families took off to cut lalang grass needed to repair the roofs of their houses. A group of women went to gather up wood that yesterday's burning had not consumed. Poong-the-Widow and old Troo stayed behind to throw some pottery, each woman working by herself.

At twelve-thirty, a good part of the village sets out in a group. We leave the path to the *miir* on the right and plunge into the bush, heading for the broad bend of the Daak Mei, which pours into the Daak Kroong at the watering place. The villagers are embarked on a collective fishing expedition, called *paang daak*. This is very different in kind from the one two days ago. At other times of the year, the Daak Mei is wide and fairly deep, but now it can be forded; upstream from the bend it is about three meters wide, downstream five. The bend is closed off by two unbroken rows of setnets, their open ends turned toward the pond thus enclosed. Each net is firmly attached to two bamboo stakes, as are those on either side, and its narrow end is secured on the river bottom by a third stake, to which it is fastened by two crossed bamboo wedges. The setnets placed downstream are heavier and, in addition, are consolidated by a length of bamboo spanning the current. Both barriers are reinforced with branches. Krŏng digs the sand away from in front of his net—so that the water will be deeper, he tells me.

Yôong-the-Mad is searching for iguana eggs in the sand by the river's edge.

When everything is ready, some forty people rush into this fish pond,

the longer sides of which measure six and thirteen meters. Excitement
runs high. People bump into each other, shout, laugh, and shriek with admiration at a fine catch. Most are equipped with shove nets, with which
they rake the riverbed, but several men wield two cast nets and two square
dip nets. The sun, breaking through the canopy of branches beneath
which the water flows, casts flickering patches of light on the surface of
the current near the banks; midstream, these enlarge and become shining
discs floating on the long, sinuous band carved from the dense forest. In
this half shade, half light, the fisherfolk splash about in every direction.
Since the area is small, they are forever colliding, challenging each other,
and laughing heartily. The catch is abundant, but this time the fish have
not been drugged and are correspondingly harder to get. Some fine speci-
mens are seen to leap from the water. Active fishing lasts for perhaps
twenty minutes, after which the nets are pulled up. Those downstream
are reset, but in the opposite direction—that is, their opening turned
toward the lower river. The nets forming the upstream line are now
moved and strung in a row twenty meters below the other, their openings facing toward the current. The river is wider here and too few nets
have been brought, so they reach only two thirds of the way across. The
branches used to cover them before are thrown into the bend of the Daak
Mei, to attract fish for some future expedition; heavy branches hanging
over the water are also cut, and old Tôong-Mang lays them in the stream-
bed.

At two-thirty, the men pull up their nets, empty and reset them, while
the women light fires. Each person cooks a few fish from his catch. Seasoned with ground pepper brought along in a leaf envelope, they are consumed on the spot, accompanied by rice soup drunk straight from the
spout of a gourd. People eat with gusto, for no one had stopped for the
midday meal.

Fifteen minutes later, they go back into the water thirty or so meters
below the second line of nets. Slowly, in serried ranks, the fishermen
walk against the current, dragging the bottom with shove nets; a few work
with cast nets. When they reach the short line, owners of these nets haul
them up. The rest continue upstream as far as the barrier of heavier nets;
these are hauled up shortly after three. The fishing is over. People walk
single-file back to the village, weary and wet; many are chilled to the
bone. Each person carries his own fishing gear and also his catch in a *kriet*
or, if it is very large, strung on a slender thong of bamboo.

Truu and his wife have returned from Ryôong-in-the-Mountains, and
Wan-Jôong, of the Mok clan, is back from Paang Pê' Döng. In the course
of the recent rites, Truu was represented by his adopted son, Kraang-the-
Dogtooth, and Wan by his youngest son, Kraang-Dlaang. Now that the
canton chief is back, one can perform "the blood anointment of the Fire

Sticks." While waiting, Truu plays with Baap Can's two youngest children. He grasps Choong-of-the-Big-Belly by the arm, and in a childish treble, says to Dür, "Give him a hard-on, give him a hard-on"—encouraging his niece, who is three, to catch hold of her brother's little penis. The boy struggles furiously but helplessly, and the chief roars with laughter. This hard, ambitious man was disappointed, it seems, to have married a sterile woman and in time his affection centered on his wife's niece, whom they adopted. By now Jaang Bibbu is in her teens, and Truu's longing for small children has led him to take up Dür as his favorite, for all that she is the daughter of his elder brother, with whom he often quarrels violently. Of an evening, the steely-eyed canton chief is often to be seen relaxing and playing the fool with his little niece.

Sieng-Aang, of Nyôong Brah, has come with rice of invitation. The day after tomorrow, in the morning, he is immolating a buffalo for a "Blood Anointment of the Paddy," the rice having been harvested some months ago. This evening, he stops over with old Troo, who offers him a jar. Her son-in-law lets the guest drink alone, however, for like all the inhabitants of Sar Luk, Mhoo-Laang must go to Bbaang-the-Pregnant-Man's, where this evening one will anoint the Fire Sticks with blood. For the *mhaam Rnut,* each man brings a large gourd prepared like a *rnööm* jar, a chicken, and a fragment of wood charred by yesterday's fire in the *miir* and taken from the individual's own plot of land. The canton chief has had his flat gongs brought over. By six-thirty, everything is ready in the house of the holy man. The Fire Sticks and Truu's flat gongs have been placed on the low platform; the gourds of rice beer have been lined up on the ground in the visitors' room.

After he has inserted the drinking straw, Baap Can slits the neck of a young chicken offered by the master of the house. He brushes the bleeding wound over the fistful of charcoal Bbaang-the-Pregnant-Man holds, and over the canton chief's *cing,* the drum, and the *Rnut:*

> "Spirits of the Burial Grounds by the hundreds,
> Spirits of Violent Death by entire clans,
> do not strike us,
> do not insult us,
> do not speak to us in anger,
> do not crush us with your wrath.
> We will make the Day in the forest and in the village,
> we will circulate our flat gongs;
> so that when searching for buffaloes we may obtain them,
> so that when searching for jars we may obtain them,
> so that when searching for goods of value we may obtain them."

Bbaang-the-Pregnant-Man follows Baap Can and revolves his fistful of charcoal above the flat gongs, the drum, and the Fire Sticks. Then he goes out alone to throw the coals on the road to the cemetery. He spits on the coals and asks:

> "Phit! *August Ancestors,*
> *O black Coals,*
> *announce to my Uncle, younger brother of my Mother, there below,*
> *announce to my Uncle, elder brother of my Mother, there below,*
> *announce to my Mother,*
> *announce to my Father,*
> *announce to my Forebear.*
> *I exorcise the days of the small rattan by the hundreds,*
> *the days of the big rattan by the thousands,*
> *the festival days by flocks.*
> *Do not become angry, O Spirit of the Underworlds,*
> *do not hurl insults, O Spirit of the Underworlds,*
> *I use flat gongs, do not break them;*
> *I use pots, do not shatter them;*
> *leading younger brothers,*
> *leading elder brothers,*
> *spare them from being taken sick,*
> *spare them from returning home ill. . . ."*

Again he spits on the coals and sets them down on the path, looking as he does so in the direction of the cemetery; then he returns. The purpose of this rite is to announce to the ancestors dwelling in the Underworld that one has performed the ceremony, so that they will not become angry.

Indoors once again—it is now seven-thirty—Bbaang-the-Pregnant-Man slits the neck of a chicken Baap Can holds over a Mnong bowl containing wort. He brushes the wound over the pieces of charred wood and the *Rnut,* then lets the blood drip into a Vietnamese bowl. He does the same with all the chickens all heads of household have brought, each man immediately taking back the victim he has offered. The color of the fowl does not much matter; it is enough if the chicken is not tail-less, for that breed may be sacrificed only in the event of illness or for a funeral service.

Then the gourds of beer are consecrated in the same fashion as yesterday in the forest: the men form couples, each drinking first from his partner's gourd. When the *rnööm* has been consecrated thus, Baap Can takes the Mnong bowl containing wort and blood from all the victims and goes "to summon the Spirits."

People drink and chat. The news is extremely bad—epidemics, which break out every year toward the end of the dry season, have just struck two upstream villages hard. Traang-in-the-Mountains numbers twenty dead. Ndut Trêe Pül, only seven kilometers away, has been spared the scourge for a long time but now counts three dead already, and the inhabitants have decided to quit their homes to go "live in the forest."

At nine-thirty, there is the ritual round of the flat gongs (rok cing). Six musicians striking their instruments walk in single file through all the houses in Sar Luk, entering by the private door at one end and leaving by the door at the other end. If a house has a drum, two musicians step out of the group to strike it. The firm decision to offer the great Sacrifice of the Soil in the near future is being reaffirmed to the Spirits. This tour of the cing lasts a good half hour.

Truu tells us that he went to Ryôong-in-the-Mountains to find his wife's kôony and persuade the old man to come live here with him. The old man agreed and has begun to divide his possessions between his son and his niece, Truu's wife. He has decided to arrive here within five or six days.* The canton chief then describes his trip to Ban Me Thuot. He and his party were put up with noncommissioned officers of the Garde Montagnarde. Truu is surprised that they were not permitted to sleep in town, and surmises that it was because the authorities were afraid they would run off. Speaking more directly to me, he reports the promotion of Blieng, the former chief set up by the Viet Minh, to "general" in the Ban Me Thuot election. He itemizes for us all his purchases from a French tradesman.

During the canton chief's account, I observe a group of young people: Kraang-the-Bladder is brandishing the hairpin he has just taken from pretty Jôong-the-Hernia. Two of his close friends have confided in me that he is wildly in love with the girl. But he invests no delicacy in his sport now, and appears to be in his cups. Dloong-the-Black-Girl notices me watching the scene, and she snaps, "They're future man and wife."

The drinking and singing lasts until very late. As I am going back to my house, I overhear Truu dressing down the tram coolies: it was Paang Döng's turn to furnish them today, but the men assigned to this forced labor, thinking that all the houses in Sar Luk were still taboo, had not showed up; Kraang-the-Bladder and several other young men had to be dispatched to look for them in the middle of the night.

March 17

A few dalliers are still drinking from last night's gourds. Each head of household brings one thigh of the chicken he sacrificed; all the offerings are immediately slipped, en brochette, on a strip of rattan.

At nine-thirty, in the house of the canton chief, a jar of rnööm is opened in response to the rice of invitation Sieng-Aang brought from Nyôong Brah. Truu, whose vanity swells in proportion to the amount of beer he

---

* Actually, we will not see him in Sar Luk until April 22, when, accompanied by his son, he comes only for a visit.

imbibes, is playing the big chief, and he orders his "brother-in-law" to carry out this ceremony. So Mhoo-Laang pours the proffered rice into a plate, which he places at the foot of a large jar, and hands the drinking straw to Sieng. Sieng drinks first. At the Bboon Jraang's, Kroong-Poong-the-One-Eyed has arrived from Sar Lang; he has brought a bowl of rice to his "brother-in-law," the bearded Kroong-Mae, not to invite him but to borrow (*caan*) his white buffalo.

A dispute erupts between Baap Can and Truu, but I am unable to discover the cause.

Finally, at eleven-thirty, a new assembly at Bbaang-the-Pregnant-Man's "for an exchange of wishes and the instruction of others" (*tâm rec ntii nae*).

A winnowing basket has been placed beside the *Rnut;* it contains, in addition to the thighs people have brought and the chicken immolated by the holy men, a low pot filled with rice beer and the Mnong prayer bowl.

Bbang-the-Pregnant-Man lifts a glass of *rnööm* to the lips of Baap Can. Someone orders the flat gongs and the drum to be sounded. Near the door, Bbaang-the-Stag seizes a *cing* and begins to play, but no one follows him and he stops. Our host makes a lengthy speech in which he tells everyone to look for buffaloes; after the *löh ruih* (the burning of partially consumed branches), everyone must engage his *rnôom*. Baap Can interrupts: "Not after the *ruih!* As of today!" Bbaang-the-Pregnant-Man ends his harangue with a recitation of wishes; then, in the same ceremonial fashion as before, he offers a drink to the other holy man, Kröng-Jôong. Having warned the canton chief and his deputy, "I am about to make a speech," Kröng embarks on a long discourse: "We do as our ancestors did. What we do our parents taught us, and we teach our children." Then he begins to enumerate all the sacrifices that have been taught them. Unhappily, his fine speech is scarcely attended to, except by his two colleagues and his son-in-law, Kraang-Drüm, and by Kraang-Dlaang, the son of Wan-Jôong. The others chatter among themselves and make no pretense of listening to what he is saying.

Then Bbaang-the-Pregnant-Man offers a drink to young Kraang-Dlaang, who does not say a word. Then a drink to Bbaang's own son-in-law, who immediately returns the compliment. A second ago, Kraang-Drüm had collared Bbaang-the-Stag, with whom he must soon make a *Tâm Bôh*. He reproached his *jôok* for delaying to invite Lôong-Grieng, of Bboon Jaa, to a meal. Lôong is not only a famous shaman but also a sorcerer and is preventing Bbaang-the-Stag from eating buffalo; if Bbaang were to invite the *caak,* he would surely lift his curse.

Bbaang-the-Pregnant-Man offers a drink to Bbaang-the-Stag, accompanying it with many wishes, and receives a tube of rice beer in return. Then a drink to Mhoo-Laang. . . . Meanwhile, Baap Can is exhorting (he is almost shouting) those present to set about getting buffaloes immediately. Kröng-Jôong seconds his brother-in-law, and berates all and sundry. Thus, to Troo-Jôong he says, "Go out and sell your fine white jar! Then you'll be able to get a buffalo." The other man protests, but the holy man is already speaking to Kroong-Mae: "Give your white buffalo to Kroong-the-One-Eyed. You hoped to make a *Tâm Bôh* with Taang-Brôong but, alas, your friend is dead. . . ." Kroong-Mae loses his temper, but it all ends with a grasping of the index finger extended in token of agreement.

Finally, at half past twelve, Kröng divides the thighs: half for the *croo weer*, half for "the Vietnamese" (the canton chief and his deputy), although normally all the thighs should be given to the holy men. After this, everyone goes home.

Around five in the afternoon, I leave the village with Sieng-Aang and his other invited guests. We are going to attend three buffalo sacrifices that will be held tomorrow at dawn, in Nyôong Brah, in honor of the Spirit of the Rice.

When the land has been slashed and burned off (*chuu ntôih*), a new phase of agricultural labor begins, which is called *löh* ("to make")—or *sreh* ("to cut")—*ruih*. The fire has burned principally small branches and brush. It has not entirely consumed heavy branches or trunks, particularly those in damp or poorly cleared areas. So, after the fire, the ash-covered ground is still littered with half-burned trunks and limbs that, especially in neglected areas, are piled in a dangerous confusion. The *ruih* period is devoted to cutting up the partly burned logs, if they are not too thick, and stacking them. Generally, the morning is given over to this. Then, after the midday meal, which is eaten out in the field, the women and girls set fire to the piles, and the men and boys spread the ashes with a sort of scraper they fashion on the spot—a thirty- to forty-centimeter crosspiece fastened to a handle about two meters long. It need scarcely be said that spreading the ashes is hard work. We are still in the dry season, and the temperature is torrid; the many fires set on ground that has been hardened by drought and the previous burning generate still more heat—in a word, the air is suffocating. Floating ash makes it even more unbreathable. To refresh themselves, the workers go hourly to bathe in the nearest stream, when they are lucky enough to have one nearby. Many suffer from eye irritation. However, this phase of the agricultural work lasts only a month and a half, and even if the fire has left a great deal of debris, the cultivators are not obliged to go out into the fields every day.

Indeed, this period of arduous and disagreeable labor allows the villagers some leisure time, and they take advantage of it to perform their buffalo sacrifices or to go on trading trips. Thus, from March 31 to April 2, in Sar Luk the *Tâm Bôh* of Kraang-Drüm and Bbaang-the-Stag was held; a week earlier, Bbôong-the-Deputy had bought a set of *cing* from some people who had come on from Bboon Dduung; and Truu had purchased a huge flat gong (*chaar*) from a group of Rhade. A number of Sar Luk residents "went abroad" during the *ruih:* we were invited not only to the Blood Anointment of the Paddy in Nyôong Brah but also to an Exchange of Sacrifices in Bboon Dlei Daak Rhiu. However, indubitably the most spectacular ceremonies to which we were bid were two Festivals of the Soil (*Nyiit Döng*). The first, and the more elaborate, in the course of which thirty-three buffaloes and one ox were immolated, took place from April 3 to April 9 in Nyôong Rlaa, and the second, from April 14 to April 16 in Bboon Sar.

Unfortunately, at this time of year—the end of the dry season—big epidemics tend to break out. After Traang-in-the-Mountains and Ndut Trêe Pül, Paang Döng is in its turn ravaged by "blows from the Sky." (Paang Döng, only two kilometers from Sar Luk, forms, together with the latter, the administrative village of Bboon Rcae.)

May 5

Finally, the *sreh ruih* is finished: limbs and branches have been burned, and the ashes spread over the fields. The rainy season is very near. Today, the villagers proceed to the ceremony that opens the sowing season, the ritual planting of the magic plant of the Paddy (*tâm gun Baa*). Two mornings ago, under the direction of Bbaang-the-Pregnant-Man, the men cleared the track that leads from the *miir* to the village. They made it twenty meters wide, which will allow the villagers to move back and forth safely, without risk of being surprised by a tiger. For the same reason, yesterday Bbaang-the-Pregnant-Man supervised the task of clearing away underbrush on the outskirts of the village. These labors took only a few hours each morning. Even people who have not completely finished their burning did not go out to their fields, for these were two days of rest: May 3 because of the death of Choong-Kôong-the-Soldier's infant, which had occurred three days before; and May 4 because of the death of Mbieng-Grieng's big sow, which had been killed May 1 by a tiger—in broad daylight and inside its sty. The single outstanding event: the day before yesterday, offering one big jar and a *rnööm*, Truu ritually repaid the sacrifice of a pig that his "brother-in-law," Mhoo-Laang, had offered him April 31 last to purify him from the tiger's attack the night before.

As early as five-thirty this morning, the men set out either alone or in groups of two or three for bamboo groves near the village to choose the *dlei* each must erect as a ritual post in the center of his *miir* plot. And those who were unable to do so yesterday must press on as far as the abandoned fields to root up the magic plant of the Paddy.

Kröng, whom I accompany, hesitates between two or three *dlei* speci-
mens, and finally decides not on the tallest but on the one that has the
finest crest falling in an elegant curve.

He chops the bamboo down with his bush hook, which he uses also to
strip it of its leaves and trim it. Back home, he plants the *dlei* upright in
the ground close by his door. He goes inside for some "head rice" (the
grain skimmed from the surface of the first pot of rice cooked that day)
and comes out again to anoint his *dlei dôong:*

> "Soup, head of the rock,
> Rice, head of the pot,
> Rice Beer, strong before drinking. . . .
> May it become dark as indigo,
> ripe as the reed,
> robust as the night star."

At eight o'clock, Kröng slits the neck of a chicken over a Mnong bowl
filled with wort; he holds the carcass high for a moment so that the blood
may flow plentifully. The bowl is set in a winnowing basket in which a few
magic plant of the Paddy roots have also been placed. Kröng dug these up
yesterday in his old field, without ceremony or recitation of any sort; he
merely took the precaution, as he was leaving the village, to blow on a
rkôong leaf to ask that the roedeer not bell.

Also in the winnowing basket is a *kriet* containing mixed seeds of
paddy, waxy squash, cucumbers, corn, beans, and gourds. He calls Baap
Can, his neighbor; together, the two brothers-in-law anoint the magic
plant of the Paddy and the *kriet,* while the mistress of the house, Jôong-
the-Healer, brushes the bleeding wound of the victim over jars and pots.
All three recite the verses for today—in so doing, we imitate the ancestors, and we honor the Paddy.

Kröng puts the bowl of wort and blood in the granary, after placing a
dab of the mixture on a *gun Baa* leaf, which he places in the small basket
of seeds. He arranges the *kriet* and magic plant in a pannier and crosses
the common room to assist his brother-in-law, Baap Can, in carrying out
the same rite.

Then Kröng slips the straps of his pannier over his shoulders, picks up
his bush hook and, on the way out, the long *dlei* bamboo, which he carries over his shoulder. Accompanied by his daughter, Mang-of-the-
Crooked-Mouth, and his daughter-in-law, Aang-of-the-Drooping-Eyelid,
he sets out for his future field.

When Kröng reaches his plot, he deposits his burdens near the *nier*
that will mark its center. His first concern is to search among branches set
apart at the time of the *ruih* for a pair of straight, solid pieces from two to
two and a half meters long. He sharpens one end of each and hardens the

tips in a fire; these are his two *rmuul* (digging sticks), with which he will make holes in the soil for seed.

He transfers all his equipment some steps from the *nier* to a well-cleared area where the ashes have been properly spread. With a hoe, he digs several closely spaced pockets in which he will plant his magic tuber; he prays when he drops in the largest root of *gun Baa,* but otherwise he is silent. Then, armed with a *rmuul* in each hand, he circles the *gun Baa,* striking the earth at regular intervals. He has thus marked out, with evenly spaced holes, an area of about nine square meters in the middle of which are the magic plants. Picking up his *kriet,* he removes the seed—mixed, but chiefly paddy—and with his thumb carefully flicks two or three seeds in each hole. He prays as he sows, and with his foot pushes soil over each. Lastly, he plants his *dôong dlei,* the long sacred bamboo stalk, in the middle of the magic plants, and anoints stalk, plants, and earth with blood. A long prayer at this point, a few couplets of which he has recited earlier:

> "*I anoint the Spirit of the* Dlei *with blood. . . .*
> *I plant straight in the lalang grass,*
> *I sow sideways in the bush,*
> *I give way before the impediment of the charred trunks.*
> *I put paddy in the earth,*
> *I sow paddy in the hole,*
> *I ejaculate the child in the belly.*
> *May it become dark, like the indigo,*
> *may it become ripe, like the reed,*
> *robust like the night star. . . .*"

While his daughter and daughter-in-law continue sowing corn, Kröng plants the ginger roots he dug up yesterday together with his *gun Baa.*

Jôong-Wan, the "sister" of Kröng (she belongs to the Jaa clan), is seriously ill. A young pig has just been sacrificed at her house, and the shaman is performing a séance. But almost no one is present; the planting rites win out over curiosity.

It is past nine o'clock when the holy men gather at Bbaang-the-Pregnant-Man's. In the large common room, two jars have been brought out for consecration; one is set down on the *croo weer*'s side of the long house, the other on the side belonging to his son-in-law and neighbor, Kraang-Drüm. Kraang is ready before his father-in-law. Between the two jars near the back wall, he places a Vietnamese bowl filled with *rnööm,* announces to the Spirits what he is offering them, and tells them that he acts in accord with the indications of the Ancestors. Returning to the middle of the common room, he hands Kröng-Jôong a drinking straw and the Mnong bowl with blood-steeped wort. The two men recite prayer couplets as the holy man inserts the *gut* in the jar. The holy man then rises to his feet and goes "to summon the Spirits in the belly of the Paddy," while Baap Can drinks from the jar. Bbaang-Jieng does not wait for the rites at his daughter's house to be completed before he himself goes to bear his offerings to the Spirits at "the head of the bed." When his mother's husband has finished his prayer, Kraang-Drüm takes the Mnong bowl and anoints all his jars with wort and blood, as well as the tiny ovoid pebble (*rtee*) that is kept in the oil lamp his wife holds out to him. The woman climbs up into the granary to anoint "the head of the paddy" and to deposit there the lamp with the *rtee*. (This pebble was found on the horn of the buffalo sacrificed during the recent *Tâm Bôh* made jointly with Bbaang-the-Stag.)

At Bbaang-the-Pregnant-Man's, Baap Can has finished summoning the Spirits. By way of thanks, the head of the house lifts a tube of *rnööm* to his lips. He himself goes to anoint his jars, after which he relinquishes the Mnong bowl of wort and blood to his wife, who climbs up into the granary to bless the paddy.

In both households, some people are drinking, but the crowd is not yet very large, for most are still busy preparing for their own rites. Less than a half hour after the ceremonies here have been completed, Bbôong-the-Deputy is already calling to the three holy men to come to his house. His nephew, Choong-Kôong-the-Soldier, is also urging them to move on, so the *croo weer* leave the house of the master of the Fire Sticks. Following the passage that runs beside the granary of Kraang-Drüm, then that of Bbôong-Mang, they enter Bbôong's quarters. The same ritual unfolds here, except that it is the deputy and not his wife who climbs up into the granary to anoint the paddy. The identical séance follows at Choong-Kôong's. In this fashion, the holy men visit all households one after another, in a sequence determined by proximity. They are permitted to drink and talk for a while after they have performed the rites, but then the head of the adjacent house rises and says to them, "Let's go, now come to my house!" He is obliged to repeat his invitation, for as time passes, the holy men become increasingly cheerful and relaxed, and their step increasingly unsteady. (The consensus is that not only must they sip from each jar but they must also drink first, when the alcohol is most potent.) From each household they receive, collectively, two chicken thighs, spitted on a length of rattan the more easily to be carried, and a tube—or, if the jar is large, a bottle—of rice beer, which is poured into a *yang dâm* that accompanies them on their rounds.

At one o'clock, just after I have gone home for lunch, a storm breaks; it is the first of the season, and of unbelievable violence. Winds of hurricane force bend the trees and sacrificial poles, and send roof thatch flying. Rain beats down on the village in a veritable cloudburst and turns the yards to mud. The tall pole mast with its wings of palms that Baap Can erected for his *Tâm Bôh* is brutally assaulted by the wind, until the immense bamboo trunk rising so majestically beside Kröng-Jôong's pole crashes, snapped off at ground level. Its neighbor bent low but straightened again, as did the masts of Bbaang-the-Stag and Kraang-Drüm. The accident will turn up in conversation this evening at Kröng's. His wife, Jôong-the-Healer, tells me that her brother had a bad dream but did not describe it to anyone, so obviously no one came forward to offer the sacrifice in his behalf that would have cleansed him of the nightmare. Had this been done, she says, his pole mast would not have broken. She is speaking to me from a distance, so her brother can hear what she is saying. Baap Can does not turn a hair. But he is affected by what has happened: the fall of the pole mast entails a taboo that must be exorcised.

Another afternoon event occurs as we are drinking at Mbieng-Grieng's. Mbieng has sacrificed only one chicken and one jar, although his nephew Tôong-Wan, who lives with him, cultivates a separate plot. Suddenly, a jeep heaves into sight bringing the former Resident Commissioner, his successor, and two other Europeans. They have come for a quick look at this, the most remote area of the province.

In the evening, it rains again. The last hearth to have the rites performed is Baap Can's, but by now the holy men are, so to speak, at the end of their rope, and everyone goes home early.

May 6

The round of rites resumed at seven this morning. About nine-thirty, we are all gathered at the canton chief's house. Kröng-Jôong consecrates the jar and Bbaang-the-Pregnant-Man goes out to summon the Spirits. When he returns, carrying the Mnong bowl of anointment, Truu says to him, "Why are you bringing it back?"

"So that you can put it away."

"You can set it on the edge of the granary"—this said in a rather dry tone of voice.

But good-natured Bbaang-the-Pregnant-Man, even as he walks toward the granary, asks, "Where should I put it?"

"On the roof of Bbaang-the-One-Eyed's pigsty!"

Roars of laughter on all sides. But Bbaang-Jieng, good fellow, is nonetheless vexed. "What a way to talk between *kuang* who are sworn friends," he grumbles. (Truu and he have made a *Tâm Bôh* of two buffaloes each.) And when the canton chief presents him with the glass of thanks, he declines it: "That was no way for you to speak to me." But then, immediately, he bursts out laughing.

Truu makes no offering of beer to the Spirits nor does he anoint his jars and paddy. Indeed, these days Truu inclines more and more to play the big wheel. He is growing arrogant and imperious, and he talks down to everybody. His progressive rise toward the highest administrative ranks open to a Mnong Gar and the Commissioner's evident confidence in him have intoxicated Truu. Very recently (in early March), he, together with Kroong-the-Short and the sector chief Bbaang-Dlaang, was elected to the newly established District Council, and these fresh honors have quite turned his head. Wishing to impose his authority by fear and base his prestige on force, he has recruited two soldiers (*kahan*) who follow him everywhere as his personal bodyguard. They are two of the most solidly built young men in the village, Kraang-the-Bladder and Maang-the-Thin. Elevation to this new status has altered Kraang's character; the excellent youth tries to put on soldierly airs, he sports military boots and talks like a tough old trooper. Maang-the-Thin now sleeps in Truu's house every night.

Children attend today's ceremonies, and some ask to drink while their father or mother is at the jar. Even if they are quite small, they are given *rnööm*. Wan, the little son of Kraang-Drüm, has stuck by his grandfather's side all morning long, and now he is as drunk as a small owl. He is weeping, which touches Bbaang-the-Pregnant-Man to the quick. To console his grandson, Bbaang lies down beside him, but then his turn to drink comes and he gets up, whereupon the tot starts to bawl again at the top of his lungs. To tease him, people shout at Bbaang-Jieng to hurry with his drink and come back and shut the child up. Caught between grandson and jar, the old man calls his son-in-law to the rescue and asks him to carry the boy away; then, not too certain on his own feet, he totters over to squat by Mhoo-Laang's *rnööm*.

By noon, we have progressed only as far as the house of Bbaang-the-Stag. After the rites here, Baap Can drinks first. Young Rieng, Wan's wife, pours the water into the jaw. (Wan-Rieng, son of Kröng-Aang's first marriage, does not reside with his father but with Bbaang-the-Stag, husband of his paternal aunt, Aang-of-the-Mincing-Step. Wan signed up for a year's work on the Plantation, and his wife is living here alone.) Like his colleagues, Baap Can has drunk an enormous quantity of rice beer; he starts to poke fun at Rieng-Wan, suggesting that she is the future (second) wife of Bbaang-the-Stag. In confusion, the young woman keeps saying. "He's joking, he's joking."

But now Baap Can is maintaining that Rieng let herself be fondled by a Cil Bboon Jaa who had come to Bbaang-the-Stag's house. She cries vehemently, "The sun sees what I do!"

Baap Can persists: "He knows what he's about."

"I refuse to argue with you."

At first, the old man seemed to be joking—he was even laughing. But perhaps the alcohol is dampening his spirits, for suddenly here he is, speaking gravely and affirming with apparent conviction that Rieng is pregnant by the Bboon Jaa. Baap Can is now well launched into a speech, and no one can stop him. As the young woman pours the measures of water into the jar, she tries to refute the drunken old man's malicious allegations. When she cannot stem the stream of calumnies, she begins to cry quietly.

We move on to the other occupants of the long house: Brôong-the-Widow and her brother Taang-Jieng-the-Stooped. At Taang's, the jars of Wan-Jôong (brother of Jieng-Taang) and of Kroong-Troo (Wan's brother-in-law) are consecrated, for although yesterday morning the *njau* came to conduct a séance for Jôong-Wan, the sick woman's condition has not yet improved.

Can wants to offer the sacrifice of a pig in his father's behalf, to cleanse him of the bad dream that made the sacrificial pole mast fall down. Still foul-mouthed, Baap Can refuses. He goes so far as to claim that Can is attempting to fleece him. (The relative who receives a sacrifice must, in return, make a substantial gift to the son or younger brother who has so honored him.) Poor Can is at a loss; there are tears in his eyes. Everybody sides with him, yet Baap Can temporizes: today one may not; today is taboo; one may perform an anointment with blood only on a normal day, not on a day like today. But Can's feelings have been hurt, and he protests vigorously: "I am ashamed to hear my father speak of me in this way. I propose to offer a sacrifice in his behalf and he answers me by claiming that I want to fleece him. . . ."

Kraang-Drüm seconds the young man: "Baap Can has said, 'All my sisters and mothers have anointed me with blood, and only Can-Groo and Kroong-Aang have not yet done so.'"

Kroong-Aang (that is, Kroong-Big-Navel) remarks to me that only last evening Baap Can asked to be anointed with blood, and that today he is making a scene because he is afraid of a ricochet (that is, he doesn't want to have to make a gift in return).

As we leave Taang-the-Stooped's to go to the house of Chaar-Rieng, I walk by the home of the Rjee women, Truu's "sisters and mother." Here I see one of them, Brôong-the-Widow (not to be confused with the Brôong we have just left, who is a Cil), squatting outside her door. In front of her threshold, she has piled an old bush-hook handle minus the blade, a thick bamboo tube that has served as a pot, a torn pandanus net, a tattered pouch, and some white rice and ashes. All these objects have been assembled to threaten her daughter Sraang-Kroong with a curse. This morning, pretty Sraang came back from her fishing with only a small catch, including a single *kaa laang*. She set the *kaa laang* apart for her daughter, Poong, although the infant does not yet walk and is still feeding at the breast. But Brôong-the-Widow cooked the *kaa laang* with the other fish in a highly seasoned sauce. When Sraang returned again from the watering place, she discovered what her mother had done, flew into a rage, and began a most intemperate quarrel. "That fish was for Poong! I've nothing to give her to eat! You're snatching food from my daughter's mouth," and other even less agreeable remarks. Under this avalanche of insults, Brôong grew angry in turn. She was sufficiently carried away to shout, "May you drop dead! May you never become a *kuang*," et cetera, et cetera, ending up with "Get out of my sight!" Instead of leaving, her daughter took to her bed. Whereupon, to panic her, Brôong hauled out all the paraphernalia for curses; however, peace will be restored and Brôong will not have to carry through with her threats.

Despite his father's rebuffs, Can, firmly supported by Kraang-Drüm, had resolved to offer Baap Can the sacrifice of a pig this very evening. However, less than a half hour after we have left the house of Bbaang-the-One-Eyed, who was the last in the village to celebrate the rites of the planting of the *gun Baa*, we are called to attend the sacrifice of a buffalo at the house of Jôong-Wan. Her condition had worsened in the course of the day. The sick woman was afraid she would not live, and asked that a buffalo be immolated. While some men were erecting the tripod post— the special "hornbill beak" post for illnesses—others set out for Sar Lang to summon the shaman Ddöi and Nyaang, Jôong-Wan's son, who is married and lives there. The village headman, Choong-Yôong, "runs to the bedside of his own sister," as he puts it. (The sick woman became his "sister" through the *Tâm Bôh* he exchanged with Krông-Jôong.)

All the households of Sar Luk, carrying bowls of hulled rice, file by the ailing woman to spit a few grains on her forehead. The house is full and bursting at the seams. The buffalo is executed at nine o'clock in the evening, in total darkness. It is Bbôong-the-Deputy who, armed with a saber, "summons the Spirits" from above the main door, while below men are anointing the threshold. Baap Can had been asked to act as go-between but had declined the offer: he has noticed that as go-between in cases of illness he has not been enjoying success, whereas his prayers to the belly of the Paddy are always granted.

There are only five *rnööm*, for the family is not very large. In addition to the jar the head of the house himself offers, there are those of Krông-Jôong, "brother" of the sick woman, of her two sons, Mhoo-Laang and Nyaang-Jôong (who had brought his with him from Sar Lang) and the *yang dâm* of Tôong-the-Cook, whose *kôony* is Wan-Jôong. Four jars are consecrated, and people drink.

Truu arrives from Taang-the-Stooped's house, followed by his two pouter-pigeon *kahan*. Truu's eyes are vague; he gives me a stiff military salute, a show of courtesy he does not make when he is sober.

People drink and chat. The foreigners report on the latest news from Sar Lang. Currently, Lieng-the-Widower gets top billing for his amorous exploits. At any cost, he must sleep with young Jaang (young in comparison to him), who is Kröng-Yôong's slave. He promises Jaang that he will buy her freedom by paying her master one *chaar* (giant flat gong) if she will consent to his nocturnal visits. The young woman agrees, but soon realizes that her elderly swain has been lying, although Lieng—who, for that matter, has nothing to his name—continues to brag: "Husband of a slave? What does that matter! Baap Can has told me he will supply a *chaar* for our marriage." Jaang has confided in Choong's wife, who now tells us the whole story. Baap Can does not possess a giant flat gong, and when he hears this tale at the same time we do, he is dumbfounded by his clan brother's cheek. (Like him, Lieng is a Rjee.)

Then the *njau* performs his séance. After the fumigation of the sick woman, he installs himself on the low platform, which is covered with offerings. He holds his reins decorated with small bells, bracelets, and necklaces; the lead rope which pulls the head of the buffalo is placed behind him. His voyage into the Beyond is concluded a half hour past midnight, after which the go-between proceeds to the exorcism, using the buffalo jaw; then Kröng-Jôong's jar is opened.

This sacrifice has been performed in some haste, not so much because Jôong's condition is so grave but because last night she had a nightmare. She dreamed that her soul was transported to the dwelling of her first husband in the Underworld. There, her former spouse offered her a double sacrifice—a pig and a large jar of rice beer—to welcome her to his abode. (This first husband was the brother of the deputy's wife, Mang-of-the-Jutting-Jaw.) He now lives in the Underworld with Choong-Bbô', their son, who had died together with all his family in an epidemic, as well as with Dlaang, the daughter of Bbôong-Mang. (On earth, Choong, the husband of the maternal niece of the deputy, used to live under the deputy's roof.) Upon Jôong-Wan's arrival in the village of the dead, the entire household welcomed her, saying, "Come with us! Rejoice with us!"

"She is sick, her eyes are turning inward," Bbôong-the-Deputy says to me when he tells me about this dream. "She can see, but the rest of us, having normal bodies, cannot see." Then he relates a personal experience. "Ten years go, Truu was coming back from the Festival of the Soil held in Daa' Mroong. I was very sick at the time, so he had me carried to his house. He was village headman then.

"I was lying on a mat on the ground. Spread out in a winnowing basket was the meat Truu had brought from the foreign village. I was wide awake, you understand, I was not dreaming. Suddenly, I see the *caak* throw themselves on the meat and carry it off. I am terrified and I hide my face. The sorcerers are afraid they will be recognized and killed, so they had their eyes turned up, the pupils of their eyes rolled up.

"Truu made me a sickness sacrifice with a pig of three spans and two jars of rice beer. It was the shamaness Ddôong-Bbaang, from Paang Tiing, who performed the séance. They paid her one jar, and I was cured."

May 7

This morning, early, people continue to drink. Wan-Jôong directs the sharing of the buffalo, which was carved up last night. Two pieces are held in reserve: one shoulder for the shaman, and one filet for the go-between. The other shoulder is given to Baap Can and Kröng-Jôong, who must divide it, and the other filet to Choong, the headman of Sar Lang. A thigh goes to Mhoo-Laang, the sick woman's eldest son, and to Kroong-Troo, her brother. Nyaang, the second married son of Jôong-Wan, and Taang-the-Stooped, Wan-Jôong's brother-in-law, receive the other thigh. The canton chief is offered a breast, Bbaang-the-Pregnant-Man receives one rump, and his son-in-law Kraang-Drüm, the other. The rest of the animal is distributed to the village: everyone receives a rib.

At eight-thirty, the holy men and "those who work with the gentlemen" gather at the house of Bbaang-the-One-Eyed; last evening, the brochette of chicken feet and the *yang dâm* were left here, the collection having been made throughout the village. The holy men remit to Truu half of the thighs, which he then divides with meticulous impartiality among all those who have a governmental function: himself, his deputy, his two runners, the village deputy headman, and not forgetting his friend the teacher. The ethnologist finds himself favored with two feet offered by the public servants and with two more conferred by the *croo weer*. Furthermore, the holy men give a foot to every curious caller who drops by the house. People drink from glasses.

Around eleven o'clock, a group of women set out for Ndut Sar to gather wild pepper (*mre' gâk*).

Late in the afternoon, Kraang-Drüm makes the rounds of the village carrying a Vietnamese bowl of hulled rice topped by an egg. He asks everyone he meets whether he has seen his bush hook; he cannot find it anywhere. But no one else has found it, and Kraang returns home with his reward intact.

In the evening, the Rjee and Bboon Jraang gather at Baap Can's house, for his son is going to anoint him with the blood of a pig (*mhaam sür*). The victim has been brought by Wan-the-Rabbit and Tôong-Wan (a Bboon Jraang, and the husband of a Rjee) and killed by old Krah. Can has asked Bbôong-Mang to be go-between; people often have recourse to the dep-

uty either for the *Tâm Bôh* or for equivalent sacrifices performed for
parents or elders—in this instance, the *bôh sür baap in*.

At seven-thirty, Can gives Bbôong-the-Deputy the drinking straw and
the Vietnamese bowl of wort and blood. Bbôong passes both, one at a
time, to Baap Can. An exchange of hand kissing between the offerer and
the go-between, between the go-between and the father, and, lastly, between father and son. . . . Then Baap Can inserts the straw in the jar,
reciting together with his son couplets of wishes, while the deputy takes
his place on the other side of the jar.

Can, clearly in a state of nerves, goes to find the various instruments
needed to perform the ceremony. He is apparently not too well informed
about what he should be doing, and instead of assembling all the objects
at once, he keeps making unnecessary trips back and forth. He unrolls a
pandanus mat on the ground one cubit away from the jar, places a *yang
dâm* near the jar, and an axe blade in front of the mat, on which his father
has taken his place. Baap Can lays his right foot on the axe blade. Lastly,
Can hangs a brass bracelet on the ear of the jar of *rnööm*.

Aang-the-Long must be coaxed into bringing her children and coming
to sit on the mat with her husband. Finally, she drags Choong-of-the-Big-
Belly and little Dür over, and Jaang-Srae, blushing, follows. Aang-of-the-
Drooping-Eyelid remains on the sidelines, a simple spectator.

Bbôong-the-Deputy has picked up the bowl of *coot* mixed with blood.
He takes from it a pinch, with which he anoints the top of the jar post,
and announces to the Spirits what is offered (Baap Can enumerating with
him). Then, still blessing the top of the carved post, he chants a long appeal to the Spirits, while Baap Can holds the drinking straw in his right
hand (he has not yet lifted it to his lips). Bbôong concludes with a couplet
of wishes, rises, and goes to Baap Can's side. He withdraws the blade on
which Baap Can has been resting his right foot; pouring a little blood and
beer on it, the go-between touches the blade eight times to the forehead
of the receiver, his wife, and each of their three children. He does the
same with the bracelet (which he merely dips in *rnööm*) and slips it
around Baap Can's wrist. He then lifts the *yang dâm* and revolves it eight
times above the heads of the group; grasping the mouth of the jar in one
hand, he spits on two fingers of his other hand, brushes them over the
body of the receptacle and over Baap Can's chest; he repeats this gesture
for each member of the family. In his perturbation, Can has forgotten the
magic plant of Coolness, which normally should be used in the course of
this rite.

Finally, Bbôong-the-Deputy goes to anoint the pig with blood and *coot:*

> "Let us eat of pork without eating to excess,
> let us eat of the buffalo without eating for no reason,
> let us kill the chicken without killing for no reason."

Truu inaugurates the jar, Baap Can drinks after him, then comes the deputy—in his capacity as go-between—and then the Rjee, the Bboon Jraang, the Ntöör (Aang-the-Long's clan), or the spouses of persons belonging to these clans. Lastly, the drinking straw passes to the other people present.

Baap Can is in fine fettle. He tells us the story of the prodigious feats of Kêel Kok, son of Aang and the hero of his son's *mpôol*, the Bboon Jraang. "One day, Kêel Kok had the idea of diving into the water while smoking with the horn of a male buffalo, so that the smoke rose up from the water. Kêel was afraid of nothing. Once when there was no rain and everything was sizzling in a torrid drought, he had meat cooked with fruit, but this did not bring on the rains. He stuck a bamboo shoot into the hole of a *wül* [this huge black velvety spider lives in a hole it hollows in the earth], but again the Sky did not respond. He 'sported' with his sister, and still nothing. So he takes a leech, a dab of earth, plasters the dirt against the backside of the leech, places a frog on top, and puts the whole thing on a *rmoong* leaf [*Panicum*]. Out of this leaf he makes a canoe and sets it to float with the current. Then the rain begins to fall. And the lightning flashes. It tries to strike him, but he hides under a *chaa* [Cupuliferae]. The lightning blasts the *chaa*, so he hides under a *ti'*. It falls on the *ti'* and turns into a sow. He kills it, and the lightning is dead, and he tears out a molar.

"One day, he is angling with rod and line. He catches a fish, a *jöt*, which he leaves in his canoe. The tiny fish rots, and an ant eats it—oh, a very little bit of it—and then she grows and grows until she becomes a dragon as big as this! The dragon wants to jump into the water, but it catches a dewclaw on the side of the canoe. Kêel crushes the claw and carries it back to the village, where he preserves it like a treasure. Only the claw was broken on the side of the canoe; the rest of the body escaped into the water. Back in the village, Kêel looked for a chicken and a jar of beer to anoint the dragon's claw with blood. The claw exists still, it is preserved by his descendants, and now it is Yaang-Drüm—his wife belongs to the Nduu clan—who is keeping it. When Yaang dies, the claw will go not to his children but to his maternal nephews, to some Bboon Jraang."

7

The Birth of Baap Can's Third Son

TWO days after "the singeing of the pig offered to his father" by Can, word of an extremely serious incident spread like wildfire: the massacre of the sorcerers in Phii Dih.* Its repercussions were to shake the Gar world to its foundations. A complaint lodged by some Sruk of Bboon Juu with the authorities in Ban Me Thuot brought to light the fact that eight months earlier a ritual carnage had occurred in Phii Dih, a village located eleven kilometers downstream from Sar Luk. An epidemic had previously ravaged this village, which led its former headman, Maang-the-Mud, to form an alliance with the Sruk of Rsaal, Bboon Juu, and other villages "in the mountains" to slaughter members of the Sruk clan living in Phii Dih and Phii Ko', whom the headman accused of witchcraft. All the Gar were convoked to share in this ritual massacre, in the course of which nine persons were killed and eight others sold into slavery. In spite of the number of people present at the rite, the French authorities were unaware of it. They would have remained so had not a quarrel broken out between the Sruk "in the mountains" and the inhabitants of Phii Dih over the division of booty taken from the *caak.*

Furthermore, to this ritual execution had been added what was quite simply a foul crime that had no pretext whatever of being religious in nature. The Cil of Paang Döng (whom Chaar-Rieng had joined), led by Krae-the-Widower, their village headman, had savagely murdered Sieng-Dee, the school cook, for no motive other than envy and fear. Since Sieng was only the husband of a Sruk, he should not even have been reduced to slavery.

---

* For details of this affair, see *L'Exotique est quotidien*, Ch. 35 (pp. 388–426), entitled "Massacre de sorciers à Phii Dih."

The repercussions of this affair in Sar Luk were as follows: Chaar-Rieng, as one of the murderers of Sieng-Dee, was imprisoned in Poste du Lac. Truu, then at the peak of his power, was likewise arrested, as was his deputy, Bbôong-Mang, and charged with having failed to notify the authorities of what had taken place in Phii Ko'. Considering the status of these two men in the community, their imprisonment understandably had a profound effect on the village. A sort of despondency, an ambience of fear pervaded Sar Luk, and was aggravated by frequent summonses for Baap Can, Bbaang-the-Stag, and Taang-the-Stooped to report to Poste du Lac for interrogation. On the other hand, there was some slight comfort in the fact that every second day two young men went up to Poste du Lac to take rice to the jailed leaders and to relieve their cooks.

One happy event did occur shortly after the Phii Dih affair exploded. In late May, a nurse was appointed to manage the Public Health Station built by the Frontier School.

None of these developments affected the course of the agricultural work, which the village is obliged to follow with absolute scrupulosity. The rites have been performed in accordance with the rules, so the sowing (*tuuc*) may now begin. It calls for a strict division of labor by sex. In front, the men advance abreast in a line, striking the ground with the point of their *rmuul,* which they hold in both hands. The women follow, their *kriet* of seed tied with a string around their waists. Bending forward, they drop two or three seeds in each hole. The sowing calls for a large, fast-working labor force, which is why, on this occasion, you can see not only the young men but heads of families team together to get the job done. Two days—one per team—suffice for them to sow a large field like Kröng-Jôong's.

As soon as the sowing is completed, steps must be taken to protect the crops against the intrusion of forest animals. Proprietors of plots located near the edge of the forest employ young men from their first team to construct a fence that must completely enclose the vast *miir.* Lookout huts are erected—generally on tall stilts—in the middle of each field; this, too, is a specifically masculine task and is entrusted simultaneously to the younger men of the teams. Building the fence and *miir* huts takes very little time, actually, from the weeding (*jiik*), which must be done during most of the rainy season, from the end of May to mid-September. This, although it is the lengthiest of the Gar's agricultural chores, is also the least strenuous and the gayest. Weeds do not grow so fast that you must combat them constantly, and no taboo says you may not have a good time and sing in the fields, so the teams of young men and women can work more freely. They indulge in individual song contests, and make the vast open expanse of the *miir* resound with the crystalline, cascading music of the *tling tlör,* a xylophone with wooden pendants. Nobody works much, except when the teams are weeding in your own field, and there is time to travel. For some people this is actually a necessity; last year's crop yield was meager, and they must go to neighboring villages to borrow rice.

The long weeding period is interrupted midway by "the ceremony of the Pincers" (*nyiit Keep*). In this rite, the fields are ritually fanned with a bamboo stalk (*plaa*), into the forked end of which various ingredients have been inserted that are intended to make the plants strong and resistant during this period of rapid growth. The *nyiit Keep* crowns the first cultivation phase, during which one clears away "the hardy weeds." The second phase of the *jiik*, "hoeing the tender weeds," is known also as "the season of the corn" (*dööm mbuu*), for this is the time when corn is harvested. Despite the new supply of food, people travel about to borrow rice; corn is looked upon as a second-rate grain, whereas rice is the main staple, the only real food. In this transitional period, people rely heavily also on wild vegetables, especially bamboo shoots, which are now to be found in abundance.

As the corn ripens and the rice develops, weeding is gradually reduced and more time is given to guarding the fields against marauding wild animals. Most *miir* huts are occupied every night, but for all the watchers' precautions, wild boar, deer, roedeer, and bears manage to elude their vigilance. On two occasions, there have even been unwelcome visits from a herd of elephants that hitherto had been content to ravage the Ndut Lieng Krak and Daa' Mroong areas. During the day, clouds of predatory birds swoop down on the young grain and must be driven off; the sharp crackle of the scarecrows and the shouts of the watchers blend with the clear-toned music of the *tling tlör*.

September 11, 1949

Aang-the-Long has been in labor since last evening. She has not had much sleep, nor has Baap Can, who has watched over her through the night. When his wife first began to groan, he spread a mat near the hearth beneath their granary,* at the foot of the low platform on which they habitually sleep. Aang stretched out on this rather uncomfortable pallet, under a blanket, her head resting on a little pillow of rags. Baap Can tied both ends of a long stout cord to two of the bamboos forming the floor of the granary. When the contractions become sharper, Aang drags herself to the bottom of her mat and, squatting on her heels, grasps this rope support.

Toward eight-thirty this morning, a new wave of more severe pains shakes Aang. Baap Can immediately tries to relieve her. He seizes a

---

* Whence the term *gô uiny* ("to remain [near the] fire"), which denotes childbirth.

handful of shavings from around the stack of firewood and a few pieces of charcoal from the ashes in the hearth. Passing them over his wife's belly, he utters this incantation:

> *"Blow your nose by the river,*
> *spit on the road,*
> *split wood on the track.*
> *Enemy mouths and beaks,*
> *tips of enemy tongues,*
> > *return whence you came. . . ."*

He goes outside to cast away the debris, which is now charged with the pains visited on Aang by unknown enemies and guided to her by the go-betweens, the charcoal.

He returns to her side and smokes his pipe. Baap Can's face is a calm mask, but his nervousness and anxiety are nonetheless apparent. Here a woman in labor is always in danger of dying. To relax, he goes down to the river to fill a jar with water for his wife's bath.

An hour later, Aang groans under the onslaught of fresh and more violent pains. Baap Can rushes to perform a second exorcism. As the contractions become more frequent, he calls his sister, Jôong-Kröng-the-Healer, to his wife's aid. The old woman stands in front of her sister-in-law and administers a vigorous treatment. Using both hands, she seizes the skin of Aang's lower abdomen between thumb and fingers, and the folds of flesh thus formed she twists with a reverse motion. In this fashion, she massages the lower belly from the top of the right groin to the bottom of the left; then she strokes the entire abdominal area. She dips her hands in water and begins the operation anew, this time with wet hands. Aang complains of a stabbing pain in the tip of her shoulder. Jôong massages the painful spot, ritually rubbing on it some smoked spider web taken from the bottom of the granary above the hearth. This particular pain, they tell me, is caused by the *tei* bird, and this is the treatment prescribed for it since ancestral times.

Baap Can asks his daughter-in-law, Groo-Can, to fetch a bowl of white rice to pay for his sister's good offices. Jôong protests: "Whatever for?" All the same, when she goes home she takes the bowl of rice with her.

Baap Can observes, "She is slow to give birth because the child is putting off coming down, coming forth into the world of men." He confides that the night before he had had an excellent dream. He witnessed the birth of a young buffalo. This means that a "buffalo-soul" is being born into the world of the Spirits and, in the world of men, a child who corresponds to that buffalo-soul. "The future of a child born the day after such a dream is heralded by good auspices. He will have buffaloes, gongs, and jars in abundance. He will grow up to be powerful," Baap Can explains to me.

Since this morning, the house has seen a lively traffic as women come by for news. Some stay, so as to be on call for whatever eventuality. Beneath the granary, Aang's "little mother," Yôong-the-Mad, and the skillful midwife Poong-the-Widow sit near the patient. In the visitors' room, on the low platform where I am sitting with Baap Can, we are joined by his daughter-in-law, Groo-Can, and his niece, Sraang-Kroong, and two other young women. Poong-the-Widow disappears for a moment and comes back with some busy work—a small pannier of corn to be husked; Groo goes for a walk; the other women return home. We are not long alone. Troo (Baap Can's "little mother"), accompanied by her daughter Laang-Mhoo and her son-in-law, comes in for word of Aang; they speak briefly to her and Baap Can, and leave. A niece by marriage drops in for a moment; neighbors come by, etc. . . .

After treating Aang, Jôong-Kröng also leaves. She goes home for some gourds and, with her husband in tow, walks down to the watering place to fill them. When they return, they pour the water into a big jar in which Jôong is preparing her indigo dye. Baap Can calls to his brother-in-law, who after these exertions is resting on his platform and smoking his pipe. Aware of Kröng-Jôong's skill, Baap Can asks him "to consult the lance" (*pool taak*). Groo-Can brings her husband's uncle the necessary materials: a small Vietnamese bowl, containing a very small amount of water; another bowl filled with rice; a lance; and a sliver of bamboo. Kröng takes the bowl of water, throws in a few grains of rice, places the blade of bamboo across the bowl, and carefully inserts the tip of the lance into the piece of bamboo. To the Spirits he announces what he is about to do, and asks the child if he is soon to be born. He chews a few grains of rice and spits them over all—bowl, bamboo sliver, lance tip—then very gently lets go of the lance. It seems to hesitate for a moment, then starts to topple over. Kröng quickly catches it. He places it more firmly in position, spits more rice, and asks, "Are you waiting for your older sister who is there below? Are you waiting for Jaang-Srae, who is there below?" Again he releases the lance, which remains upright. Speaking of the unborn infant, Baap Can remarks, "He is tired from walking along the long track [which descends to the world of men]. It is obvious that he will not arrive until this afternoon."

Baap Can suddenly remembers that recently he buttressed the stones of his doorstep with some sticks of wood. That was a dangerous thing to have done—to sink blunted objects into the ground: it prevents the child from "coming out" and makes the mother suffer. An exorcism must be performed forthwith. From each stick Baap Can takes a pinch of dust and brushes the dust over his wife's belly, chanting an incantation against enemy tongues. It is now Kröng-Jôong's turn to be inspired: he advises his brother-in-law to loosen the roof thatch. Accordingly, Baap Can climbs up onto the ridgepole and separates the lalang grass by a span (about twenty-two centimeters); that is, he unties the rattan knot that binds it—a malefic reminder of the umbilical cord that by mischance may become entwined around the neck of the fetus. As he pulls the thatch apart, a shaft of light strikes the floor. Before he comes down, Baap Can pulls out a stalk of lalang grass and with it exorcises the upper part of his wife's abdomen.

It has been a good half hour that Aang has not lain down; the pains are constant now, and keep her on her knees, clinging to the suspended cord. Poong-the-Widow squats in front of her, watches closely, and encourages her, waiting for the moment when she must intervene. Suddenly, toward noon, the contractions seem to quicken. Poong orders Baap Can's younger sister, who is crouching beside her, to station herself behind the laboring woman and support her while the midwife massages her belly with a downward, sweeping motion. Grieng-Mbieng diffidently obeys. Poong shouts to the men "to summon the Spirits." They dash outside, Baap Can snatching up a pestle on the way. Grouped near the edge of the roof, they bawl a confused miscellany of prayers: one man invokes the Spirits of the Mountains and Waters; another, the Ancestors who first practiced childbirth; this man asks that mother and father be spared all suffering; another promises the infant the most splendid raiment if only he will consent to be born. . . . The hullabaloo lasts but a few minutes, for Grieng has scarcely seized Aang from behind when a wail is heard: in a pool of blood, the child is lying on the ground surrounded by the placenta.

The midwife "strangles" the umbilical cord, which is trailing from the infant's neck. She ties if off with a black thread, which she knots about one span from the navel; then she snips it off just behind the knot, using a very keen-edged bamboo knife cut and honed for this occasion. She carries the newborn baby near the front wall of the house and washes him in cold water, which Yôong-the-Mad pours from a gourd. When the child is thoroughly bathed, Poong does not dry him but wraps him in a blanket and lays him down near the hearth beside Aang, who is stretched out on her mat, pale but smiling. Lastly, Poong places near the baby's head a small decorated wickerwork box containing white rice "to make him strong, so that later he will not fall when he can walk alone and sit down without help." Little Dür, who has witnessed the entire scene, comes forward slowly. The sight of the intruder pressed warmly against her mother, whose every moment until now has been for her alone, overwhelms her. Sniffles threaten to turn into sobs, but the women manage to console her.

Meanwhile, all the young mothers present bring their babies to the afterbirth and, with some difficulty, try to make them tread the blood trickling from it "to avoid their fighting with the newborn baby as they grow up." With a small hoe, Yôong-the-Mad gathers up the placenta, umbilical cord, and stained earth in a bag of ordinary wicker. She carries it outside to the rear of the house, where Baap Can has just dug a hole close by the wall. (For a girl child, this hole would have been dug near the front wall.) Yôong-the-Mad deposits her package, and Baap Can covers the hole over with a big stone and earth. He encircles this mound with small sticks, which he inclines inward to join the upper ends and form a sort of cone. He protects this construction with interlaced spiny stems and, as he does so, loudly asks the *caak* to go far away. Were the sorcerers ever able to slip into the hole, they would devour the placenta and the child would fall ill, perhaps die.

At the exact spot where the baby was washed, Yôong-the-Mad scrapes a big hole in the earth, which she connects with the outside by a narrow trench passing under the front house wall. She places several logs over this basin of sorts, on top of which she unrolls the crushed-bamboo mat that ordinarily serves Baap Can and his wife as their pallet. On this, Groo-Can sets the enormous pot of water which she had heated on her own hearth as soon as her mother-in-law gave birth. Yôong pours cold water into the pot until she estimates that its contents are no longer scalding. She throws in a pinch of paddy chaff, asking:

> *"May the pain no longer increase,*
> *for I have already thrown;*
> *may the pain cease,*
> *flattened like the chaff of the paddy. . . ."*

Then she adds a few bits of a magic plant called *gun Baa lêh* ("magic plant of the Paddy to prevent the fresh recurrence of pain"; a cultivated Zingiberaceae):

> *"O Gun Baa Lêh,*
> *ward off all fresh outbreaks of pain,*
> *when again one will eat vegetables;*
> *ward off all fresh outbreaks of pain,*
> *when again one will eat bamboo shoots;*
> *when again foreigners will come for the festival,*
> *ward off all fresh outbreaks of pain.*
> *I throw the Gun Baa Lêh."*

The women have set up two wattle screens between the front wall of the house and the granary posts, thus closing off an area where the young mother can wash herself with copious amounts of water while sheltered from indiscreet eyes. Aang retires behind the screens, takes her bath, and returns to lie down, all unaided.

Meanwhile, Baap Can has taken down a jar from the back wall and set it in the center of the visitors' room, where the women who were present at the birth are chattering, some seated on the low platform, others squatting on the floor. It is twenty past twelve when the drink is ready. Baap Can slits the neck of a chick above a terra-cotta bowl containing beer wort he has taken from the jar. He presents the drinking straw to Poong-the-Widow; the midwife politely declines it, declaring that the honor of inaugurating the rite properly belongs to Jôong-Kröng-the-Healer. A flurry of civilities between the two practitioners ensues; finally, it is Poong who inserts the straw first.

Previously, Baap Can had anointed the palm of Poong's right hand with blood-impregnated wort. While he circulates to anoint the hands of the other women, the midwife rises and blesses the child with an anointment similar to the one that has just cleansed her of the defilement of the delivery.

After purifying all the women who helped Aang-the-Long, Baap Can repays everyone who came to assist him in the ordeal. To this end, he has set down by the foot of the jar some large-size Vietnamese bowls and a handful of piaster notes. The first and largest bowl he offers to Poong-the-Widow and distributes the rest to the other women. All the men, including the ethnologist, receive a one-piaster note. Sraang is given one also, although our host's niece had come only to see if she could sell a necklace on behalf of some foreigners who were staying with Mhoo-Laang.

The drinking begins. Kröng-Jôong drinks first; Poong-the-Widow and Jôong-Kröng follow him. The children enthusiastically take on the task of replenishing the jar with water, for they have been promised cucumbers in payment. The conversation turns to this and that. Kraang-Drüm makes everyone laugh by relating how yesterday he told Dür that she had married Srae, her elder sister's husband. The little girl, who can scarcely yet talk, retorted, *"Dôok braak!"* ("Monkey-peacock!")—a distinctly impolite term and, when addressed to an individual, an insult. (The expression is comparable to a scatological four-letter English word.) I try to steer the conversation around to beliefs and practices connected with birth. The women confirm what Baap Can had said: when a human child is born here below, a "buffalo-soul" is born in the Sky. Also, I am told that a son may never bear the name of his father, but no reason is given.

Suddenly, a shocking thing happens: a dog steps over the newborn baby. People shout, and several leap up to chase the animal away. Outraged, Baap Can bellows, *"Tlaa kap!"* ("May the Tiger devour you!") The unfortunate dog has violated a prohibition, for which he will have to pay with his life this very night.

Once the agitation aroused by this crime has subsided, conversation resumes, turning to the visit of the Cil Koon Ddôo' who have come to sell jars and a necklace, and also to demand that Tôong-the-Cook settle an outstanding debt. They are staying with Mhoo-Laang, who offered them food and agreed to serve as their go-between in the village. He describes the endless palavers he had to endure before the foreigners were satisfied with a partial payment of the cook's debt. Kröng-Jôong is much interested in the jars, and leaves with his nephew to have a look at them.

Jaang and Srae do not get back from Ndut Lieng Krak until around four in the afternoon. Despite the lance's prediction, the baby had not waited for them to make his appearance in this world. Because they spent the night "abroad" and were still absent when the birth took place, the maternal house is taboo to them. It is protected by a long rope Baap Can has strung from his private door to the common-room door (shared by Baap Can and his brother-in-law, Kröng-Jôong), which closes off both entrances. Two tall stakes support the rope a few meters in front of the façade, thus marking off the area forbidden to all foreigners. The young newlyweds will have to spend the rest of the day and tonight in their uncle's part of the long house, from where they will be perfectly able to see everything going on in their own home. Even the fruit they have brought may not be taken across the imaginary boundary that separates the two hearths. Because Kröng-Jôong also shares the common-room door with Baap Can, it, too, is taboo for today, so Jaang and Srae must enter their uncle's quarters by his private door. This door is also used by Mhoo-Laang when he comes to bring the foreigners' jars Kröng is thinking of buying.

The evening is enlivened briefly by the sacrifice of the offending dog, which is killed, dressed, cooked in a jiffy, and eaten on the spot by all present. People talk about the wild elephants that visited the *miir* a day or so ago, the buffalo "borrowed" by a Sar Lang friend, and so on. Aang-of-the-Drooping-Eyelid captures everyone's attention for a moment by wistfully evoking memories of days gone by—how gay work in the fields was when love and laughter were richly mixed.

Laang-Mhoo, who is still nursing her infant daughter, has taken the newborn baby in her arms. He is crying, so she offers him her breast, which he refuses. She admires his size and weight—"He looks as if he were already a month old"—and the other women warmly endorse this judgment. The chatter continues. Yôong-the-Mad says she had a visit today from Sieng-Ôot and his wife. (He is the brother of Tôong-Biing and of Aang-the-Widow, and the latter has been living in his house since the incest verdict.) They came so that Yôong might bless their baby, who is none other than the reincarnation of Ngkoi, one of the Sruk massacred in Phii Dih. In fact, Ngkoi had appeared to Ôot in a dream even before she was pregnant. He had said to her, "I want to see my aunt Yôong-the-Mad once more." (One must remember that Yôong is the widow of a Sruk.) After reporting on what her visitors said, Yôong adds, "They had not dared tell me this before, and when the baby was born, they named it Kraang. But the child never stopped crying—he was refusing the name. So they called him Ngkoi, and that name the child accepted."

September 12

It is about nine o'clock in the morning. Aang has already taken her first bath and drunk her first bowl of rice soup for the day. Yesterday, she had three baths and three meals in all—a small bowl of rice soup with each bath.

Baap Can consults the magic plant of Coolness (*pool gun Ik*) "so that the child may soon begin to nurse"; actually, the purpose of his consultation is to give his son a name. The ceremony is called "drawing the name of an ancestor by lot" (*tok yoo*). Clearly, a child who cries continually and who refuses the breast is expressing by this behavior his desire to have a name or, if he already has one, his wish that it be changed.

The old man settles himself beneath the granary on his wife's mat; she sits with legs outstretched, holding her baby on her thighs. Baap Can squats facing Aang, at the height of the newborn child. With one hand closed over the other, he holds the two halves of a cylindrical piece of magic tuber (*gun Ik*), split lengthwise. He shakes them, calling out "Njaang"—not the name of an ancestor—and quickly separates his hands. The two pieces fall to the ground in no meaningful pattern; ergo, a veto. He begins again, asking for Srae (the younger maternal uncle of his wife). A second veto. Then Kroong (Aang's father), then Bbaang (a direct forebear of Aang's). Still nothing.

While his father is drawing a name for his little brother, Choong-of-the-Big-Belly plays with the baby; humming softly, he blows on his tiny arms. He tires of getting no response, and abandons him to play outside with children his own age.

Baap Can continues to "draw ancestors." Mang . . . Chung . . . Par . . . Repeated refusals. He invokes only his wife's forebears, for of the three earlier children Aang has borne him, two—Choong and Jaang—are named after his ancestors. However, since his wife's ancestors persist in refusing to appear, he now invokes his own. With the very first name— Ddoong—the two halves of magic plant fall in an absolutely favorable position.

I assume that that's that: the infant will be called Ddoong. Nothing of the sort. Baap Can takes up his magic dice again and casts them twice more for Ddoong, both times with negative results. The old man says to me, "The *gun Ik* did indicate that name on the first throw, but they have refused it on the last two." Within the limits of my knowledge of Gar divination, this cannot be considered valid reasoning. To my amazement,

Baap Can again proposes the name of his wife's father, Kroong. For my benefit (and somewhat for the benefit of the Spirits), he comments, "He has Kroong's nose, Kroong's eyes." (If this day-old baby resembles his grandfather so much, I guarantee that the latter must have been very homely.) Addressing himself to this forebear, Baap Can assures him that the dog that had stepped over the newborn child had, in accordance with the rules, been sacrificed the same evening with blood anointment and libation. Vain precautions: Kroong does not wish to appear. Back to Ddoong, but again with no results; then Kroong once more, and still nothing. In annoyance, Baap Can throws the magic plants away and is obliged to ratify their one favorable indication: Ddoong. He fetches a necklace made of cotton thread from which a piece of *gun Ik* has been hung. He spits ritually on it, slips it around his son's neck, and announces, "I name you Ddoong." He asks for the child "coolness of body and deep sleep."

The baby now possesses a name, but other extremely important precautions must be taken to protect him against the sorcerers, who are ever on the prowl. One of the infant's souls may attach itself to his father and follow him to the watering place or out into the forest, and thus risk falling prey to the numerous *caak* who haunt these areas. It is necessary, therefore, magically to isolate the father and chase the sorcerers from these unhealthy places. Baap Can promptly sets about doing so.

He intertwines four threads of different colors (yellow, red, white, and black) by rolling them between his palm and thigh. This multicolored strand he cuts in two and twists the longer piece around the tip of the batten of a loom—a sort of long knife of fine wood polished by use. He then attaches two clinkers ("iron excrements," or *ê' loeh*) to the end of the thread he has left dangling. The remaining bit he also divides in two, attaches three clinkers to one half, and fastens it around his left ankle. As he is doing this, he declaims:

>"Phit! *Dragon of one cubit,*
>> *Dragonet one finger broad,*
>> *Little Lizard of one span,*
>> *flee, return to your homes,*
>> *do not remain on the wide track,*
>>> *on the path I take to go draw water,*
>>> *on the path I take to go bathe.*
>> *Flee, return yonder whence you come!*
>> *Flee downstream from the water,*
>>> *downstream from the firewood,*
>>> *downstream from the tall grove,*
>>> *downstream from the deep night, there below.*
>> *Flee, return yonder whence you come!*
>> *Else the iron will strike you!*"

Repeating the same magic formulas, he ties the remaining length of multicolored thread around his right ankle and attaches three clinkers to it also. Then he gathers up all "the iron excrements" he has left in a food tin (from my kitchen), pours some fragments of ground rice obtained from Jôong-Krông's house over it, and places a bit of saffron on top of the lot. Aang has meanwhile dozed off. Before Baap Can goes out, he awakens her so that the *caak* cannot surprise her while she sleeps. In the yard, he spies one of his wife's mortars, in which he grinds the rice bits and saffron, thus obtaining golden-yellow granules.

Armed with his magic equipment and a pannier piled with large gourds, Baap Can goes down to the river. When he reaches the watering place, he casts several handfuls of the saffroned rice and clinkers downstream, then upstream, reciting the same incantation as before. He wades out into the current and repeats his magic sowings in all directions, issuing the same orders to the *caak* and threatening enemy mouths. He keeps repeating these formulas as he comes out of the water and on the riverbank plants the batten decorated with the colored threads and clinkers. Now Baap Can is at peace. He is immune—and with him, the frail "souls" of his son—to all evil influences that can menace the father of a newborn child. All serene, he fills his gourds with water and climbs back home, not forgetting to take the tin with him. (What remains of the saffroned rice and clinkers will be useful in protecting himself in similar fashion against the spiteful Spirits who haunt the forests.) He will no longer be afraid to come to the river to draw water or to bathe: the saffroned rice reinforced with clinkers has driven off the soul-eating sorcerers and the ferocious Dragons. By the bank of the Daak Kroong, the batten rises like a saber, ready to intervene against any evildoing on their part.

I return to Baap Can's house around six in the evening. Yôong-the-Mad is giving suck to the new baby; it is she who has fed him all day, for Aang still has no milk. Such a service is paid for with one Vietnamese bowl. The child has not been bathed today; except for the bath at birth, a newborn infant may be washed only after the umbilical cord has dropped off.

Aang-the-Long does not leave her mat; Baap Can sees to the cooking and housework.

This evening there is a shamanist séance with a pig sacrifice at the house of Wan-Jôong, who has been ailing for several days. Few people are present. Perhaps it is because Ngee-Mang, the pretty *njau* from Ndut Trêe Pül, is rather unskillful, or so she seems to me. I do notice that when the shamaness is traveling into the Beyond, all the pregnant women in the village are on hand. They come in the hope of gleaning some information about the condition of the man-to-be-born they carry in their bellies.

September 13

Baap Can is still dissatisfied with his son's name, and has decided to perform a second drawing of a name from the ancestors as soon as Aang has eaten and had her bath. He is going to change his divination procedure, and this time will "consult the salt tube" (*pool ding boh*). The tube in question is not a receptacle that has actually been used; it is merely a bamboo tube which resembles the ones used for storing salt but which is cut to order for the ceremony. He fills it to the brim with hulled rice, then transfers the contents to a thicker tube. He cites a name and pours the rice back into the "salt" tube through a funnel fashioned from the top of a pierced gourd. He taps the bottom of the tube against the ground, which obviously acts to pack down the contents. At the mention of the first name, the tube remains full almost to the top. He repeats the operation several times. When, finally, he pronounces the much desired name "Kroong," as if by a miracle the rice no longer fills the tube to the top but comes to within a centimeter of it. The ancestors have given their consent!

Now that the child is supplied with a suitable name, he may be anointed with blood and consecrated. Two small neckless jars are brought out. One is empty; the other, which is stoppered, contains rice-beer wort. Both are placed in the middle of the common room. A chopstick is inserted in the empty jar; on it have been slipped five copper bracelets, another and heavier one of cast brass, and two necklaces, one of tin and one of "antique beads." Two blankets, three short men's tunics, and a turban are placed on top of the jar; beside it, a saber. This entire display is to cajole the infant's "souls" into fearing nothing so that they will not run away but, on the contrary—seeing that one wishes them only good things—will consent to remain with his body and with his parents.

Srae-Jaang fills the little *rnööm* jar with water. Baap Can has seized a fine rooster and squats beside the jar to bless the newborn baby, whom Jaang brings to him. He nicks the cock's comb with his knife; holding its body and head firmly, he brushes the bloody crest eight times over the child's forehead. He identifies each anointment by number, and immediately launches into a prayer, asking the soul of the newborn not to flee and to fear nothing. . . . Finally, showing the fowl to the baby, Baap Can says to him, "See this fine cock. He is yours. Later, you will raise other animals far bigger than this one. . . ." Now Baap Can takes the pinch of cooked rice that, with this ceremony in mind, was taken this morning from the first pot set to cook on the hearth. He mashes a few grains on the baby's forehead, again counting each gesture and repeating the same prayer. Once more the same rite, but performed this time with a necklace—a simple cotton thread strung through a piece of the magic plant of Coolness—which is passed eight times across the child's forehead.

Next, Jaang carries her little brother to the jar of rice beer and makes the infant's hand touch the drinking straw Baap Can inserts in the *rnööm* as he announces his offering. Jaang restores the baby to his mother, who has not left her mat beneath the granary. Baap Can brings over all the objects offered to the child's soul. He spits into his right hand, places it on the jar, then on the baby's forehead, and counts "One!" He repeats the gesture, up to a count of eight, whereupon he shows the jar to the child, saying, "Here is your jar. Later, you will put *rnööm* in it to ferment." The same operation is performed with the saber, which eight times is sprinkled with water and applied to the infant's forehead. "Later, you will carry it on your shoulder when you set out along the tracks to feast or to sell buffaloes or jars abroad. . . ." Then the father presents each object— bracelets, tunics, and so on—to the child, telling him with each presentation that the object belongs to him. Aang also comments every time.

When the ceremony is completed, the jar is opened. As the younger brother of Aang-the-Long, Bbaang-the-Stag is the child's *kôony,* and he drinks first. Can, the baby's eldest brother, drinks second; then comes the turn of Srae, little Kroong's brother-in-law.

While we are drinking, Aang leaves the house to do her washing; she places it on a plank near the sacrificial pole masts and treads on it. On the other side of the common-room door, Jôong-Kröng and her daughter are stirring the indigo dye they prepared yesterday in a big jar tied to a stake just beyond the edge of the roof.

September 15

I left the village on the afternoon of the thirteenth to accompany people from Sar Lang who had come to invite me to the preliminary rites for their Great Festival of the Soil. I returned to Sar Luk only yesterday, around four in the afternoon. I found the Commissioner here; he had come to inspect the work of the sector chief and to be present at the election of the new headman and deputy of Bboon Rcae. Choong-Kôong, the former infantryman from our village, and Ndür-Yoon, an erstwhile schoolboy now living in Paang Döng, were elected. Kraang-Drüm is not altogether demoted to the status of coolie; he will help both men in the performance of their duties, and for at least this year will pay no tax.

At eight, the Commissioner sets out on the track for Poste du Lac. Four hours later, however, he reappears in the company of the Big Yoo of Ban Me Thuot (delegate of the High Commissioner), a young civil servant, and his wife (my sister-in-law), all of whom have come to pay me a short visit.

After the Commissioner's departure, village life returns to normal—but not entirely, for it is a feast day of sorts. Numerous households are offering a jar "in response to the hulled rice." People from Sar Lang who will be sacrificing one or two buffaloes on the twenty-ninth came this morning with the rice of invitation for their future guests. (Some entrusted this mission to a son or near relative.) The invited guest responds to this honor by opening a jar of rice beer. Since the same person may be invited by several Sar Lang households, he offers the ritual drink to all their messengers collectively.

Around eleven, it is Baap Can's turn to reply, according to the traditional forms, to three envoys from Sar Lang. Shortly before their arrival, Aang-the-Long bathed her baby under the attentive eye of little Dür. She does not pour the water from a long-nosed gourd directly on the child's body, as is done when children are somewhat older; she pours it first on her own hand and rubs the baby's body—or rather, because her movements are so careful and gentle, she pats it with her damp hand.

She began to give the child his daily bath only yesterday. Kroong's umbilical cord fell off the evening of the thirteenth. Some well-dried *tereh* (small cockroaches?) and spider corpses were gathered from beneath the granary floor and ground together into a fine powder; a pinch of this medication was placed on the infant's navel and tamped in with the index finger. This procedure, I was told, hopefully will prevent infections and umbilical hernias.

It was only two evenings ago that Aang was able to start nursing her baby.

September 16

Today, a private ceremony of great importance is held at Baap Can's— "the coming out of the child" (*njür koon*). For the first time, the newborn infant is carried outside the maternal house. This morning, the jealous isolation in which he has been sheltered ends, and the ban protecting the house against all visits from foreigners is lifted. Since his birth, the baby has lived beneath the granary, either lying on his mother's mat or in her arms when she was sitting up. They tell me that at first she will carry him wrapped in a blanket on her back (*ba'*), in the traditional Montagnard way; actually, she carries him slung over her hip.

This ceremony should take place normally on the seventh day after birth, but Baap Can has already taken more than a few liberties with the "calendar," and a difference of one day more or less does not worry him. Besides, the Festival of the Soil in Sar Lang is to begin this afternoon.

Baap Can has brought out a sampling of everything a boy will possess when he grows up—a hoe, one gourd for water and one for soup, a pipe

The first outdoor appearance of the baby of Baap Can and Aang-the-Long

and tobacco pouch (in this instance, it is a wallet), a pair of ivory plugs, an antique necklace, a tunic, a turban. All these items are crammed into an openwork pannier; in addition, there are a saber, a crossbow, a lance, and a man's setnet.

Carrying the child on her hip, Aang-the-Long comes out and squats before this heap of objects, which has been placed a few steps from the private door. Taking them up one by one, Baap Can shows them to his child, explaining to him how he will use them later on. The ceremony ends with the presentation of the last item. Aang goes back into the house with her baby, followed by Baap Can and Choong-of-the-Big-Belly carrying the various articles, which they will put away indoors.

The newborn child must now pay a visit to all houses in the village. Aang-of-the-Drooping-Eyelid comes for her little brother, and bears him off in a blanket over her hip. In each house, the mistress of the house anoints him with the magic plant of the Paddy, signifying by this ritual gesture that she acknowledges him as a member of the village community. Henceforth, on the threshold of the house that has thus received him taboos leveled in certain circumstances against foreigners no longer apply to him. This is a simple rite. The woman scratches one of the white-paint motifs with which the posts of the granary and the lintels were decorated at the time of the great sacrifice to the Spirit of the Paddy that closes the harvest period. This paint has a base of rice powder moistened with water and contains, among other ingredients, some magic plant of the Paddy. The woman takes a pinch of the white powder and applies it to the forehead and over the heart of the child, as she recites:

> *"Magic Plant of the Paddy,*
> *you who bestow power and wealth,*
> *strike neither the child nor the nephew,*
> *   neither the son nor the grandson.*
> *Number and welcome this child*
> *among your own;*
> *henceforth you know him."*

By this ceremony of his coming out into the world, Kroong is freed of the taboos that have set him apart since birth. The series of anointments by which he has been acknowledged in each household has made Kroong an integral part of Sar Luk; that is to say, of a village, the largest community traditionally recognized by the Men of the Forest.

·🌱·🌱·🌱·🌱·🌱·🌱·🌱·

8

The Great Festival of the Soil
in Sar Lang

September 17, 1949

NYAANG-THE-SOLDIER's leave is up today, and he left for Dalat at noon. Five young people—his four brothers and one niece—went with him; for them, it is a chance to take a long trip and do some shopping at the market. However, this departure does not account for the great bustle pervading the village at the same time. In every household, people have donned their best finery; they are calling back and forth to each other, hurrying, hustling their offspring along, for the children always lag behind. In a word, Sar Luk has assumed a holiday air reminiscent of how the entire community is in a ferment on the occasion of a *Tâm Bôh*. Fifty-four people, in fact—representing sixteen households—are preparing to go as guests to the Great Festival of the Soil in Sar Lang, the neighboring village four kilometers upstream.

Sar Lang counts no more than eighty inhabitants, and since the first of the year has been joined administratively to its neighbor, Ndut Sar, a hamlet of equal size. Sar Lang aligns its four long houses, one of which measures thirty meters, on a narrow embankment of the Daak Kroong, at the foot of Poot Rloo, the small col which constitutes the boundary between the territory of Sar Lang and that of Sar Luk. Frequent intermarriages have established quite a few family relationships uniting the two Sars. This closeness has recently been strengthened by two important ritual alliances: the first was made by Bbôong-Mang-the-Deputy, the *jôok* of Sar Lang's deputy headman, Bbôong-Dlaang; and last September the second allied our holy man Krŏng-Jôong with the headman of Sar Lang, Choong-Yôong. Sar Lang looks poor and rather dirty, yet it enjoys a measure of importance on the "plain" because it is the home of the most famous shaman in the valley, Ddöi-Dloong, of the Rlük clan.

The most recent *Nyiit Döng* held in Sar Lang goes back twelve years. It was Mbieng-Jieng, of the Düng Jrii clan, who conducted the ceremonies then. Upon his death, Yaang-Dlaang, of the same clan, succeeded him as go-between in the Festival of the Soil.

Three years after the great event, a terrible famine struck Sar Lang. Yaang-Dlaang decided to perform "the uprooting of the Rattan" (*dok Reh*). "After the sowing," Yaang tells me, "I called all the people together, the whole village, and I offered a *yang dâm* of beer and I roasted a chicken. Then I ask each man if he will play his part with brio in the next Festival of the Soil. 'Can you look for a buffalo, yes or no?' I ask them. This one says yes, that one commits himself to supply only a pig. . . . Choong-Yôong, our village headman, promised he would sacrifice a buffalo. But then, just a year ago, he sacrificed two for his *Tâm Bôh* with Kröng-Jôong, and he hasn't been able to make good on his promise. While I am still holding a drinking straw and the chicken that's to be sacrificed, I ask each man in turn what he will look for. Then I pass the *gut* to Bbaang-Aang [their holy man of the Fire Sticks], who inserts it in the little neckless jar, and he prays:

> " '*In searching for buffaloes, may we obtain them,*
> *in searching for jars, may we obtain them. . . .*
> *May the buffaloes come toward us;*
> *may the jars come toward us. . . .*'

"The next morning," Yaang concludes, "we went to 'uproot the Rattan.' "

For this particular ceremony, the entire village repairs to the appointed site. In single file, an orchestra of flat gongs heads the march; immediately behind it, also walking in single file, come the go-between, Yaang; the holy man of the *Rnut*, Bbaang-Aang; the other *croo weer;* and, lastly, the villagers. Had there been a second *cing* orchestra, it would have brought up the rear. The powerful voices of the horns blend with the deep-throated music of the gongs. Yaang-Dlaang recalls it for me: "When we come to Poot Rloo, in the midst of the tall sacred grove—you see, the rattan chosen for this ceremony must come from 'the home of the Spirits' because rattan that grows in the woods is used for ordinary building—the palm is uprooted with one good pull, and everyone cheers. It is not cut down, mind you; it is uprooted." It is the go-between and the holy man of the Fire Sticks who pull up the rattan root while reciting the same prayers as before, asking that one may find buffaloes and jars. The crest and root of the rattan are chopped off. Only a section about a meter long is stripped and kept; the rest is discarded.

With great pomp, the length of rattan is borne home; a young girl carries it on her back, wrapped in a blanket, like an infant. She lays it in the big winnowing basket of ritual Fire Sticks that has been placed on Bbaang-Aang's low platform. The holy man of the *Rnut* opens a large jar of rice beer and sacrifices a pig; then he offers a drinking straw to the go-between and to the other two holy men. Once the jar has been consecrated, the four *kuang* anoint the rattan and the *Rnut* with blood and wort, and they drink from the jar. Then, preceded by the flat-gong orchestra, the go-between carries the winnowing basket with rattan and ritual Fire Sticks to the adjacent house; here the master of the house offers the sacrifice of a chicken and a small neckless jar of *rnööm*. The ceremony is followed by a libation, after which everyone moves on to the next house, and so on until all the granaries in the village have been visited. "In following years, one man will offer a goat, another a duck, each in turn. . . ." Nevertheless, I could vouch for the fact that these particular sacrifices were carried out last year at the rite of the Paddy posts (*nyiit ndah*), to which the Sar Lang villagers had invited me on November 5, 1948. The final ceremony of this rite was most appealing. After one last sacrifice of a chicken and a jar of beer, the holy men, led by the go-between, open the march, followed by the *cing* orchestra, which precedes the rest of the villagers, who now and then break into resounding shouts. Night is falling as the procession moves toward "the hut of the Spirit Nduu" (*tum Nduu*), which stands a few steps back from the edge of the cliff by the river. The Spirit Nduu's hut is a ritual construction, a miniature hut on stilts; it resembles the high-perched shelters built as lookouts in the *miir*. The four stilts—bamboo stalks—are enclosed by a rectangular fence of sticks a few centimeters high. This tiny temporary temple is built in honor of the most important Spirit of the Mnong Gar pantheon, which represents both the soul of the Rice and the mythic Hero, or prime mover, who has initiated mankind into many things. The holy men halt before the *tum Nduu* to deposit a tube of rice beer, cooked rice, and chicken feathers. Then they squat to offer each other a ritual drink, while the *cing* orchestra marches without interruption in a counterclockwise direction around the little temple and the crouching men. The crowd stands apart, in a circle. Holding a bottle filled with *rnööm*, the go-between stands near Nduu's hut and, now and then pouring a few drops of rice beer on the tiny temple, he intones a long, deeply resonant chant, a couplet from a sacred song called "the sayings of the gongs" (*noo goong*). The master of the Fire Sticks has risen to his feet and stands facing the singer on the other side of the Spirit's hut; when the master of the Fire Sticks has finished his hymn, Bbaang-Aang intones another "saying of the gongs" in response to the couplet sung by his partner. As he finishes his song, the holy man sets on the threshold of the miniature hut the two bottles of *rnööm* he has been holding, and from which he has poured several drops as he sang. The go-between responds with another couplet and concludes this exchange of sacred songs by also placing his bottle on the threshold of the *tum Nduu*. This ritual miniature temple and "the sayings of the gongs" (which we will encounter later) together with the length of rattan constitute the intrinsic elements of the Great Festival of the Soil and the agrarian rites of the years that prepare for it.

Since the go-between and the *croo weer* had decided to immolate the buffaloes at the conclusion of the second weeding period, some people took steps to engage their male and female sacrifice attendants (*rnôom*) after the corn harvest. Others feared they would not have enough to feed the *rnôom* over a long period, and elected to recruit them only at the last moment and to fabricate their ritual decorations themselves.

Only the three holy men—Bbaang-Aang, Mang-Dlaang, and Choong-the-Widower (he playing this role only temporarily)—went on September 5 to cut down and carry back ceremonially a giant *rlaa* bamboo for each. As a *croo weer*, Kroong-the-One-Eyed also had the right to erect a sacrificial pole mast, but he lacked the means and did not accompany them. By September 12, most of the sacrificers have instructed their *rnôom* to perform "the blood anointment" of the ritual apparatus and objects required for the consummation of the sacrifice. (Actually, only wort is used; a *yang dâm* is opened without even the sacrifice of a chicken.) The male servant anoints the pile of firewood, ritual verandas, low platform, and so forth, while the female servant consecrates the hulled rice that will feed the guests.

On September 13, Bbôong-Dlaang, the deputy headman of Sar Lang, came to invite me to attend "the raising of the giant-bamboo pole masts" (*ntöng ndah rlaa*) and "the blood anointment of the Fire Sticks and the Rattan rope" (*mhaam Rnut rsei Reh*).

This series of rites begins in the house of Bbaang-Aang, the holy man of the Fire Sticks. Our host, his fellow *croo weer*, their assistant Sieng-Dloong, the go-between, and the ethnologist squat at the foot of a medium jar fastened to the central picket of the ritual barrier that has been set up in the middle of the common room. The master of the house hands a drinking straw and a black cock to me, a drinking straw and a young brown hen to Kroong-the-One-Eyed, and a drinking straw to Sieng-Dloong, who is only assisting the holy men and is too poor to offer a sacrifice himself. Let me point out parenthetically that two fowl add up to four feet and are equivalent to one pig. We give cock and chicken to Mang-Dlaang, who slits their throats over a Vietnamese bowl. Bbaang-Aang gives each of us a pinch of blood-soaked wort and performs the hand-kissing gesture. We insert our drinking straws in the jar and bless the earth with *coot* and blood, asking in rhymed prayers for prosperity and success. The feathers of the cock are stuck in the roof thatch. I inaugurate the jar, and surrender my place to the village headman; this will be the pattern followed subsequently in each household; after Choong-Yôong has drunk, the usual practice is resumed, in which a holy man, the head of household, the other *croo weer*, and the go-between drink in no fixed order.

People have not finished drinking at Bbaang-Aang's before it is time to cross the common room and carry out the same ceremony in the quarters of his immediate neighbor. Choong-the-Widower lives here with his daughter, Dloong, the wife of Ddöi-the-Shaman. The rite is identical, except that our host sacrifices only one chicken. (Bbaang-Aang had insisted with me that offering only "two claws" is forbidden.)

While we are drinking from two jars, Nyaang-Jôong (the son of Jôong-Wan, of Sar Luk, who is married to the eldest daughter of Bbaang-Aang and lives in his father-in-law's house) places the offerings on the small altar (*ndrööng yaang*) suspended from a purlin at the back of the house. They consist of one cooked egg placed on top of a bowl of glutinous rice and another in a bowl of beer siphoned from the jar before its consecration:

> "*I lead the family*
> *I lead the village,*
> *I lead the young women,*
> *I lead the young men.*
> *I give the day in back,*
> *I plant the day in front,*
> *I undo the tin from the ears,*
> > *like Möt-Dlöng,*
> > *like Möt-Dlaang.*
> *The Ancestor Jjöt gave a feast, imitating them,*
> *like Jjôot, like Jjuu,*
> *like Nduu, like Ndoong.*
> *Do not speak to me in anger,*
> *do not crush me with your wrath. . . ."*

An enumeration of Spirits, and sites of Sar Lang, follows. These verses will recur throughout the prayers recited during these festival days. Bbaang-Aang, who has dictated the couplets to me, explains that Möt-Dlöng and Möt-Dlaang are Heroes of ancient times, as are the Ancestor Jjöt and the other beings named in the verses. It is they who offered the first sacrifices, and we today are merely following their example. "Möt-Dlöng and Möt-Dlaang hold a festival, they attach [i.e., they sacrifice] a dog, a crocodile, an iguana. Their prayers are not heard, and they abandon this sort of sacrifice. They attach [immolate] a dog, but their prayers are not heard: the rain and the fine drizzle continue to fall without respite. They remain still for one, two years. Then, in a moment of inspiration, they find the answer by themselves; they look for buffaloes, they recruit *rnôom*, they offer their festival, and their prayers are heard. Today, we merely imitate them. That happened before the Flood."

The young jar attendant is about to plunge the horn used as a measure into water, but an old man stops him: "It is forbidden to plunge the horn into the water. There is the foreigner taboo, the *rnôom* taboo. One would risk precipitating trials, illnesses. Fill the horn with a long-necked gourd." Once the foreigners have left for home, it is again permissible to dip the measuring horn into water.

It is late at night when Bbaang-Aang asks us to follow him outside and find places on his principal ritual veranda. The Mnong bowl of wort soaked in blood, a pot of rice beer, a decorated winnowing basket that contains a serving basket of glutinous rice, a large bowl of chicken meat, and several drinking tubes, had been taken outside earlier. The *rnôom* fills the tubes and hands them one by one to his patron, who in turn offers them to each of his guests, lifting them to their lips without reciting any special formula. Then he performs the hand-kissing gesture with each and recites a series of rhymed wishes. When he has finished, Kroong-the-One-Eyed kisses Bbaang's hand and lifts a tube to his lips, reciting the same formulas; the go-between, then the other holy men do likewise.

The female sacrifice servant brings the male *rnôom* a decorated wicker box containing two bananas, a raw egg, and glutinous rice. The young man fastens it to the giant-bamboo pole mast, beneath the two great palm wings. Then Bbaang-Aang and the sacrifice servants, their way lighted by the servant girls' torches, go to get the *rlaa* bamboo mast, which was set to one side on crossed supports. They carry it to the foot of the veranda, where the hole for it has just been dug. They slip the base of the giant bamboo into the hole and, with their arms or with the help of bamboo forks or crooks, strain to raise it to an upright position. From the very beginning of this operation, two flat-gong orchestras support the efforts of the holy man and his assistants, who are encouraged also by the shouts of all the onlookers. The *rlaa* is only about ten meters long; for sacrifices in honor of the Soil and the Paddy, in which the mast does not serve as a greased pole, as it does in a *Tâm Bôh*, one does not look for an exceptionally tall bamboo. In the darkness, the two great arms of the *rlaa* wave as it slips slowly into its hole and, suddenly taking hold, rights itself, thereby unleashing a tremendous ovation from the crowd. While the *rnôom* tramp down the earth around its base, the holy men and the go-between anoint the pole and the two flat-gong orchestras circulate counterclockwise, without pausing, around the giant mast and the roof that shelters the rear section of the veranda. The other holy men withdraw, and Kroong-the-One-

Eyed holds the Mnong bowl with its ritual ingredients in one hand, and with the other anoints the trunk of the bamboo. Standing on the edge of the veranda, he "summons the Spirits." It is a long chanted invocation. As in all important sacrifices at which it is sung, it first convokes all the Spirits, beginning with those of the Earth and of the Soil; then it tells the Spirits what action is being taken, recalling the archetypes supplied by the mythic Heroes, and it asks for prosperity and health. The flat gongs do not stop playing throughout this prayer, and they continue their round when Yaang-the-Go-Between comes and, relieving Kroong-the-One-Eyed, anoints the big sacrificial pole with "rice and vegetables" (in fact, with a pinch of glutinous rice and small bits of chicken).

After the go-between has "fed" the pole, the master of the house "feeds" in turn the *kuang* assembled on his ritual veranda, offering glutinous rice and chicken meat, first to "him who summoned the Spirits" and the go-between. Near him, his two *rnôom* are regaling those of the other sacrificers—the girl feeding other female servants, the youth feeding the male servants. As always, the person who thus receives food (or drink) ceremonially reciprocates, giving the officiant an equivalent to the offering with which he has been honored. Bbaang-Aang concludes this series of sacramental exchanges with offerings to his male *rnôom* and to his sons-in-law. Then everyone goes back into the house.

At the foot of the row of jars are two winnowing baskets. One is brand-new and decorated; it holds wicker boxes with geometric designs that contain the rice of invitation to be distributed "abroad" to foreigners, starting tomorrow. Each man who will presently be sacrificing a buffalo has brought a box. The second basket is old and full of holes. Like its contents—the Fire Sticks, the ritual Rattan shaped into a hoop, and various ritual utensils—it is covered with a sort of plaster, a black paste made of dust, spider webs, and soot. This wretched, filthy winnowing basket, together with its contents, is the very soul of this festival, the post, which all these rites will restore to life. Bbaang-Aang gives a pinch of blood-soaked *coot* to the go-between and to the holy men and their assistants, who are grouped around the two baskets. The five men anoint the *Rnut*, the ritual Rattan, and other utensils, as well as all the wicker boxes containing rice of invitation. Together, they recite the couplets which recall that they are following the example of the mythic Heroes and ask for prosperity and health.

Then Bbaang-Aang and the go-between lift the basket of *Rnut*. (The "feet" of the wood always point toward the back of the house "so that the fire may eat up all the felled wood.") They transport it to Choong-the-Widower's side of the common room. While carrying the ritual basket, the master of the Fire Sticks sings a "gong saying":

"In the beginning of time, there was only a land of mud,
    the land of Nduu and Ndoh.
In the beginning of time, there was only a land with earthworms;
    seven alone crawled upon it.
In the beginning of time, there was only a land with bamboo shoots;
    a single dlei *clump grew on it.*
In the beginning of time, there was only a land with wild vegetables;
    a single plot of ground they covered."

The assembled people listen in silence to this deeply resonant chant
that retraces the origins of the world. Finally, the two *kuang,* saluted by
an immense ovation, set their precious burden down on the low platform
of Choong-the-Widower. Sieng follows them, bringing the new basket
that holds the rice of invitation.

Then everyone goes outside. People gather on the ritual veranda,
where the two heads of household—Choong-the-Widower and his son-in-
law, Ddöi-Dloong-the-Shaman—offer drink to their guests. As before, the
scene is lighted by minute resinous torches that produce tall flames. We
watch the raising of Choong's sacrificial pole, conducted by Bbaang-Aang.
When the pole mast is upright, the men anoint it with cooked rice, Mang-
Dlaang "summons the Spirits," and the two orchestras of flat gongs play.
Ddöi-the-Shaman comes forward to replace the holy man at the front end
of the veranda, by the foot of the pole mast. Holding a tube of *rnööm,*
from which he now and then shakes a few drops, he chants an ancient
song. His wife stands anxiously behind him, poised to catch him should
the Spirit of the Paddy "strike him down"—that is, make the *njau* lose
consciousness. The glow of the pine torches casts a dim light over the
shaman's face. His eyes widen, his glance becomes fixed and shining, but
nothing out of the ordinary happens, and at the end of his chant, the
shaman comes safely to his senses. We go back inside to anoint the contents of Choong-the-Widower's two winnowing baskets. This rite concluded, the baskets are ceremonially borne to the home of the third holy
man who has set up a sacrificial pole, Mang-Dlaang. The six gong players
lead the procession in single file, followed by Bbaang-Aang carrying the
new winnowing basket (the one with the rice of invitation); Bbaang precedes Yaang-the-Go-Between, who carries the old basket with the Fire
Sticks, although the latter had pointed out that the reverse order seemed
more logical. Then come the other holy men, the shaman and his wife,
and lastly the second *cing* orchestra.

At Mang-Dlaang's, the same combination of rituals unfolds for the third
time today: the sacrifice of two chickens and the consecration of a jar of
rice beer inside the house; outside, the offering of drinks on the ritual veranda; the raising of the big pole (this time, however, the flat-gong players
do not circulate but remain in place, in a semicircle); the anointing with

cooked rice; the summoning of the Spirits by Bbaang-Aang; the chant at the foot of the pole by the shaman, with the mistress of the house standing behind him; and, lastly, "the exchanges of food." When we re-enter Mang-Dlaang's house, he himself sets his offerings of food on the small suspended altar, after he and the other *kuang* have anointed the ritual Fire Sticks and Rattan and the rice of invitation.

The retinue re-forms to transport the two winnowing baskets in procession to the quarters of Kröng-Yôong, who lives at the other end of Mang-Dlaang's long house and who will sacrifice two buffaloes. Here the rites are simplified, for our host, not being a *croo weer*, erects no pole. The anointment of the Fire Sticks and Rattan and rice of invitation takes place after the chicken sacrifice and the consecration of the jar of *rnööm* without any intermediate ceremony. In conclusion, Kröng-Yôong himself, praying the while, sets the raw egg, cooked rice, and bowl of rice beer on his small suspended altar.

While the *kuang* converse around the new jar they have consecrated, in the house they have just left the *rnôom* and other young people have gathered around the jar abandoned by their elders. The musicians join the group, and a boisterous party explodes in the house now unencumbered by the powerful. A concert by the flat gongs, a double roll on the suspended drums, a strident hooting of horns, song competititions, laughter, dares between young men and women in "exchanges of drinking"—the atmosphere could not be more joyous. Only a short distance away, the *kuang* officiate or talk gravely around the jar. Among other serious topics, they tirelessly count off the number of days remaining before the great festival. There is momentary laughter when Kröng-Yôong describes how he is trying to train his newlyweds—his slave, Jaang, and her old beau of a husband, Lieng-the-Widower ("brother" of Baap Can). Only last evening, he says, they quarreled like two young lovers. The slave fled into the fields in the middle of the night, with her old husband in full pursuit. There the discussion begins anew, intermixed with cooings, reproaches, and arguments. The girl flies down the ladder of the high-perched field hut, her graybeard close on her heels; up she clambers again, and he after. . . . The squabble had to do with nothing more than picking corn and the fact that she left him to work alone. But among the mature men or elders in Sar Lang, moments of gaiety are rare. There are no teasers, no wits among them, and if no foreigner is on hand to share in their celebration, it unfolds in doleful gloom.

The rest of the night is spent drinking—and sleeping—at Kröng-Yôong's.

The next day, September 14, the rounds for "the blood anointment of the Fire Sticks and the Rattan" and of the rice of invitation resume as early as seven in the morning. Rites identical to those we witnessed at Kröng-Yôong's unfold in succession at the houses of Kroong-the-One-Eyed; Bbôong-Dlaang, the deputy headman; and Yaang-the-Go-Between. Execution of the rites has become noticeably relaxed because of fatigue—and the quantity of alcohol imbibed. Bbaang-Aang is temporarily out of the running, so Kroong-the-One-Eyed himself must accompany the go-between to find the two baskets. They are transferred to the house of Bbôong-Dlaang without escort. The village headman has no buffalo to sacrifice, but nonetheless counts on inviting a friend from Sar Luk. The Commissioner has been invited to attend the festival, and because of Bbôong's administrative position, it will devolve on him to receive the European official. The go-between and the master of the *Rnut* accordingly come to his house to consecrate a tiny neckless jar and to bless the rice he will send to his one invited guest.

It is past noon when, preceded by six flat-gong players and followed by Sieng-Dloong bearing the basketful of wicker boxes with the rice of invitation, Yaang-the-Go-Between carries the Fire Sticks and the Rattan back to their guardian. All the *kuang* assemble at the house of Bbaang-Aang. Each has brought a few threads of equal length. They start debating about the date for the festival. "In five days," some propose, but others say, "In three." Four days also has its partisans. Everyone talks at once, yet the master of the *Rnut* appears to be guiding the discussion. Indifferent to their vociferous patrons, all the female servants of the sacrifice have gathered near the granary and are drinking beer the male *rnôom* of the house offers them in libation tubes. In the end, Bbaang-Aang's opinion carries the day. The holy man ties four knots in each thread offered him and places it in one of the rice boxes in the new winnowing basket set down before him: the festival will take place in four days. Each man identifies his own box, which he will take home with him; there he will prepare additional threads and distribute his blessed rice among the messengers who will carry his invitations "abroad." But before the group disbands, the master of the Fire Sticks attaches the stem of Rattan to the rope by which his drum is suspended; it will remain there until the end of the festival.

I set out for Sar Luk as soon as the *kuang* left Bbaang-Aang's. The Commissioner arrived before me. He has come to see what stage the construction of Bbaang-Dlaang's official house has reached, in connection with which the sector chief has committed some irregularities. But his primary purpose is to be present at the election of the headman and deputy of Bboon Rcae on the morning of the fifteenth. As we saw in the preceding chapter, the people of Sar Luk spent most of September 15 and 16 "responding to the rice of invitation" by opening jars of rice beer for the Sar Lang messengers. All over the village, people are drinking. Only seven households have not been invited. Among them is Wan-Jôong's (Wan belongs to the Mok clan, and is the husband of the Rtung clan's healer). Of all the people who have been left out, only he is angry. He was so sure of being invited to the festival that this morning he asked his neighbor Troo-Jôong to set him up with a large Djiring jar. The messengers came to the house of his neighbor but not to his. Kroong-the-One-Eyed did not even bother to greet him. "But," Wan says to me, making no effort to hide his resentment, "after the festival, I will go and demand my due— one shoulder given by Jôong's parents to Kraang-Laang [father and mother of Kroong-the-One-Eyed] and another shoulder I myself gave Kraang-Laang."

Late in the afternoon of the sixteenth, I return to Sar Lang to be present, as invited, at the erection of the sacrificial posts. The village is not as lively as two days ago. Quite a few messengers have not yet returned, but I do meet some guests who have arrived early. There are even some foreigners—Upstream Cil—visiting Sieng-the-Widower, who lives in a hut by himself. Sieng has no horned victim to offer come the big day, so foreigners may enter his home; however, no one from outside is permitted even to cross the threshold of a non-sacrificer if he lives in a house where another granary is going to sacrifice a buffalo.

People offering a sacrifice must not only bar foreigners from entering their houses but must also protect their homes against all the disturbances that the arrival of guests en masse might precipitate. This morning, in each such household the *rnôom* has dug an oblong hole the width of the main door and in it buried a pair of pincers, some potsherds, *kiep mêem* shells, "dark pebbles," and *mpat* fruit. He has asked that everything go well and, above all, that "neither the Sky nor the Year strike with illness or suffering"—that is to say, may there be no epidemic. He then placed a stick across the filled-in hole and wedged it firmly with pointed wood chips. Behind this sign, he spread a long piece of banana leaf. However, the *rnôom* have not similarly barred the path that leads into the village by placing a stick across it, as I saw done in Nyôong Rlaa in the same circumstances. A good two hours before nightfall, the sacrifice servants bring their patrons' buffaloes back from the forest. They tether the future victims not to their respective ritual posts but to ordinary stakes. For that matter, the posts are still attached to the ceremonial barriers and have not yet been sunk in their holes.

Around six, while his neighbor is killing a pig, Bbaang-Aang slits the throats of a cock and hen and has the fowl prepared. His fellow holy man Mang-Dlaang comes to borrow a large jar of *rnööm*. As for Bbôong-Dlaang, with whom I am staying, he arrives home quite late and immediately on arrival asks his wife to serve his guests their meal, for they have preceded him during the afternoon. Among them are Mang-of-the-Jutting-Jaw (she is the wife of his *jôok*, the deputy) and Troo-Jôong and his family. The women eat on the low platform to the rear and the men on the ritual platform set up along the front wall, between the private and main doors. As people finish their meal, they drink from a gourd of water at the foot of each platform, and also rinse their hands.

Six *rnôom*, each carrying a flat gong suspended from his left arm, play as they march in single file around the village. They call at every house, and if the house has a drum they beat it.

Bbôong-Dlaang is afraid that by arriving late he will not be ready on time. He accepts the help of Troo-Jôong, from Sar Luk, and entrusts him with the task of slitting the throats of a cock and young hen, and of plucking both.

It is eight o'clock when finally we are asked to come to Bbaang-Aang's ritual veranda. His two *rnôom* and Kaar, his youngest daughter, bring out a large new winnowing basket and several other receptacles—a small serving basket of glutinous rice, a shallow pot of rice beer, two Vietnamese bowls of cooked chicken, a teapot of rice beer, and some other ritual ingredients. The first ceremony of the evening opens with an "exchange of food" offered by the master of the house. He lifts to my lips not the usual handful but—an innovation, this—a Vietnamese bowl of glutinous rice that he topped with pieces of meat and a chicken thigh. He moves on to his *rnôom*, to the one *croo weer* present (Mang-Dlaang), to the village headman, and then to his guests. Each receives cooked rice and chicken. This communal meal is finished off with reciprocal offerings of drink, for which libation tubes are used.

Mang-Dlaang, the holy man, rises to his feet and, slipping behind the sacrificial barrier, squats before the hole in which the post will be planted. He throws a fresh gourd into it, both flesh and seeds, and the ritual ingredients that have been handed to him—a bit of tuber of the magic plant of Coolness, a *kiep mêem* shell, a "dark pebble," and two circular potsherds that represent flat gongs. He prays, asking for coolness and protection.

The holy man withdraws, and the *rnôom* lays the ring to which the buffalo's halter will be attached over the hole; it encircles it rather like a collar. Assisted by other young men, he lifts the sacrificial pole, protecting himself from its spiny trunk with a strip of cork. The *kuang*, meanwhile, address the buffalo: "Rise, Master Duung." (Duung is the name of the victim Bbaang-Aang chose.) The young men strive mightily but to no avail: the hole is too narrow for the post. All the ingredients must be removed and the hole enlarged with a stick, and the entire procedure begun afresh. The orchestra of flat gongs supports the workers with lively music. The scene is lighted, as always, by pine torches.

Once the sacrificial post is firmly fixed in its hole, Bbaang-Aang lays at its base the three grasses used in construction rites: "white horn" (*kei naang; Eleusine indica* L.); "quail bone" (*tiing rgut; Sida carpinifolia* L.F.); and *pae troo* (*Alocasia?*). Beside him, Mang-Dlaang anoints the foot of the bombax with blood-infused wort. The two men ask the trunk not to be annoyed but to sprout anew into a fine tree, and to bring them health and prosperity. All the *kuang* repeat the same formula when they stand to anoint the sacrificial post.

People now assemble on the veranda of Choong-the-Widower to carry out the same rite, this time in his behalf. But since neither he nor his son-in-law, Ddöi-the-Shaman, is there, their male sacrifice servant "feeds" the holy men and guests. Bbôong-Dlaang-the-Deputy, who has a feeling for European proprieties, decides not to allow the servant to offer me the food; he himself lifts the glutinous rice and the pork to my lips. He, too, feeds the *rnôom* when the latter has completed his offerings, although the young man had asked to be "fed" by the son of his patron and not by the deputy, the head of another household. As the guests receive the handful of food or the tube of rice beer, they ask what are the names of the two victims—Master Bbae and Mother Dlaang.

Then the *rnôom* hands the Mnong bowl and the ritual ingredients (double portions) to Bbaang-Aang. He casts some bits of fresh gourd in each hole, and the holy man drops the ritual ingredients in each, praying the while. An ovation salutes the young men when they raise the first pole. This one stands beside the main door and hence is destined for the male buffalo, to whom they say, "Rise, Master Bbae!" A second ovation breaks out when the bombax is firmly implanted. And the same shouts for the raising of the post by the private door. This pole is destined for the female buffalo, and she also is encouraged: "Rise, Mother Dlaang!" Then Bbaang-Aang and Mang-Dlaang together plant the ritual grasses, the former going to the foot of the *blaang* intended for the male victim, the latter to the foot of the bombax intended for the female. They pray in unison, and still in unison anoint the feet of the poles they are consecrating with bloody *coot*.

In front of the long house, three sacrificial posts now occupy their definitive positions. Today their elegant musical trappings are intact, but these will disappear in time, succumbing to storms and the rising of the sap. However, each bombax will put forth vigorous roots and new branches, reminding men in years to come of the spectacular sacrifices offered by Bbaang-Aang, Choong-the-Widower, and Ddöi-the-Shaman. Everyone goes back into the house. Bbaang-Aang's jar is consecrated first. The master of the Fire Sticks hands a drinking straw to his colleague Mang-Dlaang, and another to me. We insert our *gut* and pray, but we do not exhibit as much energy and fervor as our host, who sticks his finger in the *rnööm* and carefully rubs it back up along each *gut*. The drinking commences.

While the village headman is drinking, we cross the common room to bless the jar of Choong-the-Widower. Disconcerted by my presence, the *rnôom* hands me the longest drinking straw, originally intended for Bbaang-Aang, and gives him the one Mang-Dlaang should receive. He hesitates to bring out a third.

The *kuang* take turns at both jars; to drink from both one has only to cross the room. When Bbôong-Dlaang observes that almost all heads of family and guests have drunk, he runs home to prepare, on his ritual veranda, the communal meal and the ceremony of implanting the sacrificial poles. When everything is ready, he comes back to summon us.

The same ceremony is repeated, as it will be thereafter in each household offering a buffalo sacrifice. But the holy men have already drunk a lot in the course of their day "abroad," where they have been offered jars in response to their rice of invitation, and they have accepted the *gut* here with undiminished pleasure. So, when the *rnôom* is unable to arouse them, Yaang-the-Go-Between throws the ritual ingredients into the hole for the post. In the end, the master of the Fire Sticks does manage to plant the sacred grasses but that is all he can manage; he cannot make it to the house of his colleague Mang-Dlaang, so the village deputy headman volunteers to replace him.

All these rites take time, and as the night progresses the officiating group dwindles. As we leave each house, we successively leave behind one or two men sacked out on the platform, sunk in a sleep that nothing could disturb. The young *rnôom* make a great din into the middle of the night, men and women competing in drink and song. But when we set out for the last house, the female sacrifice servants litter the platform, their faces smeared with soot—the final practical joke of their male colleagues.

September 17

At the first crowing of the cock, around four-thirty in the morning, the more courageous servants of the sacrifice run through the village to awaken the other *rnôom*, who are still fast asleep. Fires are rekindled, the pine torches are lighted, and the male *rnôom*, helped by other young men—family members or guests—go outside to prepare the buffaloes and tie each to its post. First, they adjust the lead rein: they slip one end through the small loop of woven rattan in the animal's nostril, and through the barrier the other end is firmly tied to a picket under the eaves behind it. Last evening, with ropes they had already solidly attached to this picket the enormous ring of the halter by which the victim will be tethered to the post; it is through this ring that the *blaang*, the bombax pole,

Water buffaloes bedecked and tethered to their sacrificial posts in Sar Lang

is slipped. The two loops of the halter are joined over the animal's neck, and then its head is adorned in the same way as for the *Tâm Bôh*. The arc of the horns is completed by a large hoop of woven liana bark and barred horizontally by a small board painted with geometric motifs and carved at either end in a crook shape; two large sheaves of long grasses depend from a feathered section of giant bamboo.

By the time daylight floods the village again, it has donned its festive garb. Everything is ready. In each long house, those who are offering sacrifices have extended their doorways with ritual verandas; some—those before main doors—are covered with a pitched roof. Three tall pole masts have risen, new companions to the one that has been standing alone for a year and that commemorates the *Tâm Bôh* of Choong-Yôong and Kröng-Jôong. During the night, the sacrificial posts, which until then had simply been attached to their barriers, were permanently set in position, and to each of them a buffalo with its sumptuous headgear has been tethered. Also finished during the night was the vegetal decor for the eleven buffaloes to be sacrificed by nine of the thirteen granaries that comprise the village.

I take advantage of the morning lull to make a quick trip to Sar Luk and return with the Commissioner. The leading citizens of Sar Lang have followed the example of the Nyôong Rlaa villagers and invited him. Actually, this mountain village had asked us to attend its Festival of the Soil (*Nyiit Döng*) last April; we had an opportunity then to admire the rare virtuosity of Sieng-the-Kuang, who is deputy headman and the most powerful personality in the village. Sieng is a vain man and a great braggart, but he has true style and knows how to entertain his guests. The compliments he received on that occasion only inflated his ego and his eagerness to have others share his sense of his own worth. So, when he heard that the Commissioner was going to attend the *Nyiit Döng* in Sar Lang and, furthermore, that Bbôong-Dlaang had told his nephew Bbür (substituting for Truu while the canton chief is in prison) to come to the festival without the ritual invitation, Sieng could not resist coming down to Sar Luk in hopes of getting himself invited. From the traditional point of view, this is a questionable departure from custom. When I explained to him that I felt I had no right to violate tradition by imposing a friend on the village, Sieng simply waited for the Commissioner to arrive, slipped into the ranks of his escort, and so got to participate in the festival. Such behavior was not at all well received and made for a certain stiffness, but fortunately that dissipated in time.

On our arrival, around four in the afternoon, we find Sar Lang completely transformed. The poor, drab, straggling village is swarming with visitors. Almost two hundred guests—two and a half times the local population—have come from nine different villages or hamlets. People circulate in small groups, moving from house to house, lingering on the ritual verandas or on the earth terraces in front. The crowd is noisy and joyous. A festival of this kind enables people to meet many old friends from places they have had no chance to visit in a long time. Phlegmatic amid this effervescent humanity, the eleven buffaloes, with their monumental vegetal headdresses, stand by their posts and quietly chew their cuds. Above them, the immense articulated arms of the three lofty pole masts undulate in the wind; their palm fronds rustle and their long chains of small wooden platelets make a cheerful clatter, a restrained concert played above the human hullabaloo below.

Toward five o'clock, there are signs of movement toward Bbôong-Dlaang's house. The deputy headman is "anointing the feet [of his guests] with blood." He has set a *yang dâm* at the base of the upright before his main door, and now he slits the neck of a hen. As each guest offers his foot, Bbôong-Dlaang brushes the bloody wound over it. People press forward in indescribable confusion toward where he is officiating. When the rite is completed, Bbôong joins the twenty-three heads of family on the low platform, where they are crowded around a large winnowing basket for "the weighing of the hulled rice" (*weh phei*). He "replies to their rice" by offering a large jar of *rnööm*. This is consecrated by ten drinking straws representing the the ten participating villages. Each of these rites calls for the recitation of wish verses spoken simultaneously by all those officiating. Their voices are lost in the brouhaha of the crowd jammed into the house. The eldest guest initiates the jar. But some guests who have received rice of invitation from Bbaang-Aang are already leaving for the house of the master of the *Rnut*, who repeats the same rites. Others go to Choong-the-Widower's. In other words, several celebrants are performing the same rites at the same time. The tremendous drinking bout also begins at about the same moment in all nine granaries that will be sacrificing buffaloes tomorrow morning.

Around seven in the evening, Bbôong-Dlaang climbs up onto the ritual veranda near his main door "to summon the Spirits" by throwing saffroned rice into the air over roof and buffaloes. He intersperses his prayer with powerful blasts from his deep-toned horn. In some houses, the sacrificer prefers to entrust the performance of this ceremony to a visiting *kuang*; for example, Bbaang-Jieng-the-Pregnant-Man "summons the Spirits" at Yaang-the-Go-Between's, and my friend Kroong-Biing-the-Short officiates for Mang-Dlaang.

A simple "anointment of the feet" is judged inadequate to hail the coming of the Commissioner and to bless him. As a compatriot of the district chief, I may not be left out and so am associated with him in the ceremony. Accordingly, an hour later, we meet at the house of the village headman, who is to immolate a pig in our honor.

Two jars have been placed side by side in the visitors' room. A banana leaf is laid at our feet, and on this are deposited an axe head and a Vietnamese bowl filled with rice beer and blood. The Commissioner and I each sit before a jar, holding the drinking straw inserted in it, and each of us places one foot on the axe head. The master of the Fire Sticks has been called on to preside at this rite. He dips the claws of a hen he holds in both hands into the water of the first jar, counts aloud, "One," and slides the fowl's feet along the length of the straw; he dips them in the second jar and repeats the gesture: "Two." He returns to the first jar: "Three," and so on up to eight, at which point he "summons the Spirits": "O *Yaang!*" The prayer follows, accompanied by the flat gongs. Continuing to pray he revolves the chicken above our heads, slits its throat, and anoints our foreheads and hands with blood.

Squatting now, he prays and dips his finger in the bowl of pig's blood and *rnööm.* He brushes it over our feet, which still rest on the axe head. He recites several wish verses and slips a brass bracelet on our wrists. We start simultaneously to drink from our jars. While all this has been going on, several young men behind us have been carving up the sacrificed pig.

As always when a buffalo sacrifice brings a very large group together and liquor flows freely, one must not delay the *praang baal,* the harangue that reminds people they must drink peacefully and not quarrel or fight. In each house where people are celebrating, one guest brandishes the saber from which a chicken is suspended, and as he delivers the exhortation another makes the rounds with the horn decorated with threads and filled with rice beer. Someone in the assembly gets up and wrests the chicken free, to cook and eat it on the spot with the other guests.

All the rites that inaugurate the drinking or take place as it continues are the same as those we have already seen during the *Tâm Bôh.* They are common to all buffalo sacrifices. However, there is one that is peculiar to the Great Festival of the Soil: the *broo rnôom*—"the general visit of the male and female servants of the sacrifice"—and it takes place late at night, long after the young men have "sung to the buffaloes" to put them to sleep.

Around one o'clock on the morning of the eighteenth, all the *rnôom* gather in the house of the master of the Fire Sticks, who has just set out a large jar of rice beer in his visitors' room. Each female servant brings a small decorated basket of glutinous rice, and the male servants divide among themselves a set of flat gongs; those who have no instruments bring their long fire-worked tubes of giant bamboo, which are filled with rice beer.

The master of the house invites the two other holy men and the go-between, as well as two distinguished guests who have agreed to serve, to follow him onto his low platform. Here he places the winnowing basket with the Fire Sticks and the Rattan, a Mnong bowl of *coot* (not mixed with blood), and a mound of glutinous rice topped by an egg. Bbaang-Aang entrusts to the visiting *kuang* the two emblems of the *praang baal*—the saber adorned with a chicken and the horn decorated with multicolored threads. He distributes four drinking straws.

The six men squat around the *Rnut* basket and anoint its contents with wort from the Mnong bowl. The same couplets that have been recited from the outset of the ceremonies are repeated, interspersed with the same wish verses. The men rise and together consecrate the jar, into which the four who hold drinking straws insert them. The master of the house "leads the water"—he drinks, then gives up his place to the go-between; the two foreign *kuang* drink next (the elder man first), and the two other holy men of Sar Lang follow them.

They do not linger over this jar, for the procession to which the ceremony gives its name—*broo rnôom*—is about to commence. At the head marches the orchestra of six flat gongs now manned by the male *rnôom;* the go-between follows carrying the winnowing basket with the Fire Sticks and Rattan; then the *kuang,* including the two foreigners still bearing the saber and chicken and the libation horn; a third *kuang* carries still another horn. These are not the only guests to join the procession. Everyone who was on hand as it set out—the two Europeans among them—takes part in the parade. Bringing up the rear are the female sacrifice servants, each concealing under a blanket a small decorated pannier of glutinous rice; also three male servants, each furnished with a libation tube of fire-worked giant bamboo. Several marchers brandish pine torches; people laugh and joke in order to seem at ease; the flat gongs play in a slow cadence. The procession stretches out in the courtyard, and as it winds its way through the night, torches illuminate the faces of their bearers; now and then their light flickers over a pair of buffaloes tethered to their sacrificial posts, or strikes the lower part of a tall pole mast or ritual veranda. From a distance, the cortege must resemble a long caterpillar spotted with lights.

The *cing* orchestra enters the house of Bbôong-Dlaang by the private door and is greeted by hearty cheers. The master of the house has readied a big jar of *rnôöm.* The visitors' room is invaded by new arrivals who respond with huzzahs to the welcoming shouts of their hosts. The male servants and the *kuang* carrying the large libation tubes or horns offer the short drinking straws of their receptacles to every person in the room. The female servants give each a handful of glutinous rice. They are careful to keep the decorated panniers containing the rice well concealed under their blankets; at all costs they must prevent any male celebrant from plunging his hand into them, or they risk having "a love child." As the women move about the crowd, the men try to catch them unawares and they tug on the blankets, which obviously gives rise to some salty jokes. Bok, Bbaang-Aang's daughter, has got separated from her companions and has been unable to parry the combined attack of Kroong-Big-Navel and the sector chief, who are applauded by all. The former triumphantly exhibits his trophy—a handful of rice—and makes some erotic comments on his exploit. The girl clucks in anything but dismay and, laughing, hurries back to her companions. The three holy men, the go-between, and the two foreign *kuang* are consecrating the jar with the four drinking straws handed out by Bbôong-Dlaang. They have already anointed the Fire Sticks and Rattan with wort taken from the jar and put in a Mnong bowl.

The drinking begins, with the *kuang* following each other at the drinking straw, but Bbaang-Poong (son-in-law of Yaang-Dlaang-the-Go-Between) is urging people to come drink from his jar. Reluctantly, the holy men rise and the orchestra moves slowly toward the door. The procession re-forms as before, except that some *kuang* desert it, while others who have been drinking at Bbôong-Dlaang's swell our ranks. We set out—the same parade, and at Bbaang-Poong's, the same rites, the same games. They are repeated at the home of everyone who is offering a sacrifice. The host awaits the procession, standing by the large jar of rice beer he will open in its honor. Not at Mang-Dlaang's, however. The holy man has not deigned to offer drink to the members of the procession. His colleague Bbaang-Aang is outraged. "I have sacrificed chickens, ducks, goats, pigs," he says to me, "and today a buffalo. Mang has never been willing to sacrifice anything. Today he's furious because this time he *had* to procure a buffalo. Well, you'll notice he poured two jars for his guests instead of reserving one for the *rnôom* procession." But he does not reproach Mang directly.

The last house to be visited is Choong-the-Widower's, so, to return to our point of departure—Bbaang-Aang's—we have only to cross the common room they share. Bbaang has brought out a small *yang dâm* to salute the return of the *Rnut*. The go-between, Nhee Pöt (one of the foreign *kuang*), and Choong-the-Widower consecrate it together with him, and anoint the Fire Sticks with wort. Then Bbaang-Aang picks up the winnowing basket with the *Rnut* and puts it back in its proper place on the bars above the low platform from which the small neckless jars are hung.

The early-evening clamor, swelled by song and punctuated by laughter, has subsided. Now sonorous snores are embroidered by the murmur of voices from those houses where the stouter trenchermen are holding out; now and then someone breaks into a raucous, hiccupy song.

But dawn is already breaking; the cocks have crowed twice. The houses shake themselves awake to the sound of morning coughs and the crackle of relighted hearths. Soon, from one house after another, the voices of women rise in a long, slow, grave chant with, as its accompaniment, the gurgle of water being poured from one receptacle into another. In all households offering a sacrifice, a woman "sings to the jar" (*tong yang*), just as early last night young men "sang to the buffaloes." Jar and buffalo— these two essential elements of sacrifice, intermediaries between men and Spirits, are honored with profound respect. Before sacrificial victims are immolated, one retells for their benefit the story of the origin of the world; one reminds them that their execution is not a mere matter of killing but is an act of piety that renews the sacred example set by the mythic Heroes.

For the buffalo sacrifice, the oldest and most beautiful jar in the house is always selected. It is attached to the last granary post, facing the private door, from which one "summons the Spirits in the belly of the Paddy." The jar is not filled in the ordinary way, by using large containers—giant bamboos, big pots, or jerricans. Rather, the usages of an ancient rite are observed: seated on a stool facing the jar, a woman dips a small long-nosed gourd into a large vessel (if possible, a metal pot), and then pours the water into the majestic receptacle. As she slowly fills the valuable jar, she chants the resonant, moving verses of old songs that tell of the mystery of the Creation of the World.

Today, in Sar Lang, the jars are filled by sunup, and the sacrifices can begin. The first to be ready is Bbôong-Dlaang. He prays as he lifts a libation tube to the lips of the master of the *Rnut*, to whom he then gives a Mnong bowl of wort and a chicken. After returning homage to the deputy headman, Bbaang-Aang slits the chicken's neck over the *coot*, and together the two men "anoint the heads of the buffaloes with blood." Then, slipping between the edge of the roof and the ritual barrier, the holy man anoints the barrier with blood-soaked wort and "summons the Spirits." He recites a few verses only, then surrenders the field to old Krah, of Sar Luk, who, armed with a saber, moves into position, ready to immolate the victims.

Bbaang-Aang has already returned to his house. He gives a Mnong bowl and hen to Choong-the-Widower, who hands them on to Kroong-the-One-Eyed. Kroong drinks from the libation tube, anoints the head of the buffalo, and "summons the Spirits" to the sacrificial post, to which he applies a pinch of blood-stained *coot*. At the conclusion of his prayers, the victim offered by the master of the *Rnut* is killed. The same rite takes place at the house of the go-between and of the other sacrificers. Actually, the buffaloes are killed quickly; it takes less than a half hour to immolate eleven animals.

The village headman, who was "unable to find a buffalo," offers a pig. The animal is dispatched with a single saber stroke behind the shoulder. Then Choong-Yôong has Kroong-the-One-Eyed insert his drinking straw in the ancient jar attached to his granary pillar; the holy man will now

Anointing the head of the buffalo before . . .

. . . it is immolated

Bbaang-Aang offers drink to the man he has chosen to quarter the
sacrificed buffaloes . . .

. . . then, with his knife, traces on one victim's hide the lines to be followed in cutting it up

"summon the Spirits in the belly of the Paddy." He drinks the rice beer in the tube lifted to his lips in gratitude by the master of the house, then returns to the pig and anoints its head.

Young Caang-Aang hoped to sacrifice a pig also, but was able to procure only a chicken. Yet he is not the person most to be pitied: Sieng-Dloong can offer only five eggs and the rice beer of one small *yang dâm*.

Each sacrificed buffalo is entitled to a "funerary offering," which is presented by the mistress of the house: a blanket, a small neckless jar, and a spinning wheel, which she twirls for a moment before laying it down. Then the holy man the head of the house has retained as his go-between takes wort from the Mnong bowl, with this sops up blood from the gaping wound in the victim's side, and walks to the last granary post to intone the long prayer called "the summoning of the Spirits in the belly of the Paddy."

Bbaang-Aang has had a new decorated winnowing basket placed on the ritual veranda before his private door. It contains a smaller serving basket of glutinous rice, a pot of buffalo tripes cooked in their contents, another pot filled with *rnööm,* and some fire-worked libation tubes. This collation is intended for "the meeting for the wort" (*biet coot*)—food and drink the head of family serves his guests to hearten them as they carve up the animal. The first guest the master of the *Rnut* honors with a tube of beer is a young man named Kroong, whom he puts in charge of quartering the sacrificed buffalo. He hands Kroong the knife as he lifts to his lips a tube of rice beer. In return, Bbaang receives a tube of *rnööm* from the young man. He rises, takes back the knife, and makes deep incisions in the victim's hide. The butchers are to follow these lines in cutting up the buffalo, once they have disemboweled it. Assisted by other youths and even older men like Kraang-Jieng, brother-in-law of Kroong-Biing-the-Short, Kroong falls to, and the work proceeds briskly. In short order, the team has cut the huge carcass into impressive-looking quarters that are stacked on the main veranda and the ritual stall. In every household which has sacrificed a buffalo, the same gestures and the same actions are being repeated at the same time.

Once Bbaang-Aang had traced the main guidelines for dismembering the buffalo, he returned to his veranda "to exchange food and drink" with his guests: bowls of glutinous rice topped by a few morsels of tripe, and libation tubes of *rnööm.* No guest is overlooked, and old Troo, doyenne of the Sar Luk Rjee, receives her portion with proper priority. After the communal giving and receiving of food and drink, the guests go on drinking. Throughout the village, the sacrificers are entertaining their guests on their ritual verandas. Some *kuang* have been invited to more than one house, so they circulate, but otherwise there is not much coming and going. The young men and amateur butchers are busy with the victims, near the verandas where the rest of the population has gathered to tipple and enjoy the minced meat served them in Vietnamese bowls. A few elegant types are eating with chopsticks, in the manner of people in the Lowlands. But mostly one drinks, and the women are not the last to apply themselves. Liquor may glaze the eye, but it also sharpens the memory and emboldens the heart. Pöt-Nhee, for example, the wife of a *kuang* from Düng Jrii, has managed to find a worthy partner; these two tipsy mothers of families compete in singing, to the delight of the children and young girls clustered around them.

When the carving chore is finished, each head of a household divides his beast among his various guests. In general, a man who is being reimbursed for an earlier gift accepts his portion without much urging. However, in the opposite case, knowing that one day he will have to reciprocate in kind, the beneficiary protests that he is being too generously favored and, with a show of false modesty, professes his poverty. Nonetheless, the donor stands firm, for he has given much thought to how his animal should be apportioned. In the end, the receiver carries off the share that had been destined for him—realizing full well that he will be obliged to supply the identical counterpart at some future time.

Some guests return home laden with considerable booty. Those who were invited by several sacrificers leave bearing several pieces of meat, some of which are sizable. Thus, on behalf of his father, Can receives a whole thigh from Bbaang-Poong in repayment of the one Bbaang received from Baap Can on the occasion of the latter's most recent *Tâm Bôh;* also, a rump given by Choong-the-Widower as the counterpart of a gift he received at that same *Tâm Bôh.* Three additional gifts are offered, not to settle debts, but to establish credit with Baap Can, which in time he will have to honor. In this category, a rump from Kroong-the-One-Eyed, a filet from Mang-Dlaang, and three ribs from Bbôong-Dlaang. As for Kröng-Jôong, he has received only one "return" and an insignificant one at that—some ribs from Ddöi-the-Shaman for those Kröng had offered him seven years ago during a buffalo sacrifice in honor of the Paddy. On the other hand, Kröng has received as gifts half a shoulder (to be shared with Kroong-Biing) offered by Mang-Dlaang, a filet from his nephew Nyaang-Jôong (Bbaang-Aang's son-in-law), and a breast from Bbôong-Dlaang.

Once a family has been given its share of meat, the members do not tarry. They stow it away in their pannier and bid farewell to their hosts, who unfailingly offer one last "exchange of drinks" with libation tubes. When small children have made the trip, the wife of the man who has offered the sacrifice rubs her finger on the bottom of a pot and daubs the foreheads of her guests with soot—a protection against the Spirits of the paths and woods. Otherwise, a host merely gives the leader of the depart-

Dismembering the carcass

Two women engage in a singing competition

ing group a pinch of uncooked rice—"to eat on the road"—and the man
ties this symbolic provision in a corner of his blanket. Goodbyes are long-
drawn-out and flowery, and marked by great tenderness—as is always the
case in giving and receiving.

Finally, people take off in little groups, unsteady on their feet but gay.
Not everyone: there are always some sad drinkers, but even they, if they
are *kuang*, never fail to boast about the great quantity of meat they have
received. Thus, with a hiccup, old Troo confides in me, "My children are
furious. . . . Laang-Mhoo, she is furious. . . . They are mad at me, Yoo,
because they got dead tired having to carry all the meat I was
given. . . ."

September 21

Back from Sar Lang, a few villagers began to cut their buffalo-meat gifts
into strips. But most people were worn out and needed a rest. It was only
the next morning that they set about this task. Presently, the fronts of
their houses were bedecked with strips of meat hung on rattan lines they
had strung between stakes and upright pestles.

All these activities notwithstanding, weeding has not been neglected.
Teams of young people set out for the fields that same morning; the next
two days, their ranks were increased by adults who had stayed at home
the first day to dry their meat.

Some young men from Sar Lang come early this afternoon to invite me
to a ceremony called "the deposit of the buffalo skulls" (*yôh bôok rpuh*).
When a private buffalo sacrifice is offered, the head of house simply goes
to the outskirts of the village and deposits the skull shorn of its horns, the
halter, the ritual barrier, and the top of the jar post. But in the case of a
Nyiit Döng, which concerns the whole community, all those who have
sacrificed meet to render final homage to the Spirits—in particular, to the
Spirit Nduu—and thus they conclude an enterprise that will have preoccupied the community for several years. Because this year their Festival
of the Soil has been held when the rice is nearly ripe, the people of Sar
Lang have taken advantage of the fact to celebrate the post of the Paddy
rite and the *yôh bôok rpuh* simultaneously. The pole is fashioned the evening before, and in several cases even two evenings before. It consists of a
long bamboo trunk with a small "Paddy hut" on top. The hut is a square
of wickerwork (generally about fifteen centimeters per side) and a pyrami-
dal roof, also of wicker. The Paddy hut is decorated to suit its maker's
fancy, and it may be positioned higher or lower on the post, as he pleases.
To perform this rite, one must sacrifice a chicken and a jar of rice beer; in
honor of the Spirits, minute bits of the meat and a swig of the beer are
placed in a little bamboo reed that is suspended from the Paddy hut.

However, the *kuang* of Sar Lang have been financially ruined by their great festival, and they deem that the fact of their *Nyiit Döng*'s having taken place so recently sufficed to justify their dispensing with these sacrifices. Accordingly, this morning the master of the *Rnut* anointed the post (left in anticipation near his door) with some "head rice" (skimmed from the top of the pot) and entrusted his son-in-law, Nyaang-Jôong, with the responsibility of planting the Paddy pole in his field's sacred square and of anointing it with *coot* mixed with the blood of the buffalo sacrificed during their Festival of the Soil.

Most of the others who had offered sacrifices did the same: in the village, they anointed the post with rice taken from the surface of the first pot cooked that morning; and in the field, anointed it with wort mixed with three-day-old buffalo blood. Kröng-Yôong did, however, sacrifice a chicken, but he deferred consecrating his jar until I arrived.

After the post of the Paddy ceremony, the master of the *Rnut* and Choong-the-Widower convoked all the servants of the sacrifice. (Those who lived "abroad" had gone home with their relatives after the meat distribution, but they have returned for this occasion.) The two men led them along the *miir* path to a spot some fifty meters behind the village. Here, to the left of the road, they face in the direction of the sun's course, and assemble the remains of the impressive sacrifice. Each great carcass has been reduced to its skull—the frontal bone and the horns, which still form a single piece. These are piled one on another and wedged between three tall stakes on one side and two on the other, making a sort of wall that faces the sun. One may not pile them up at right angles to the sun's path or "squash and cucumbers, salt and rice, would refuse to return. The buffaloes would be furious and would pick a quarrel with us."

The ritual barriers for jars are divided into two lots and placed behind this pile to form two obtuse angles with it. Halters, jaws, and other assorted detritus are tossed into the area between the barriers and the stack of skulls. The bamboo posts, embellished with Spirit huts and decorated with leaves, feathers, and mobiles, have been stuck inside the barriers, which, being painted red and blue, lend a cheerful touch to this heap of funereal trophies. In front and to the left of the horns, the men erect "the Spirit Nduu's hut"—a miniature reproduction, perhaps a meter high, of the graceful huts built on tall stilts in the *miir*. To the right of the skulls and opposite a small ladder leading up to the terrace of the Spirit Nduu's hut, they dig a hole in the ground and set a twelve-centimeter-long piece of giant *rlaa* bamboo in it. The *rlaa* has been cut off just above the membrane of the internode, so that it can serve as a receptacle. This will be the center of the ceremony. The village headman tells me that one is not obliged to present the sacrificial trophies in such perfect order or to include the placing of the giant-bamboo tube in the hole. However, the village suffered so severely from hunger this year that people decided to invest the greatest care in the execution of this rite—and, I might add, to its staging.

When I arrived in Sar Lang, everything was in place. They were waiting for me in order to begin the ceremony, which is very short. Foregathering at the house of Bbaang-Aang, the master of the *Rnut*, those who had offered sacrifices at the *Nyiit Döng* set out along the *miir* path, in single file and in no special order, for the place where the skulls had been stacked. Each man carries a libation tube filled with rice beer in one hand, and in the other a handful of glutinous rice and a little buffalo meat. (Bbôong-Dlaang has strained decorum to the point of putting these ingredients in a Vietnamese bowl.) These offerings come from the small hanging altar on which they placed the glutinous rice the evening the ritual posts were raised; the rice beer and the meat come from the actual day of the sacrifice. When they reach the trophy site, the officiants squat around the sunken *rlaa*-bamboo receptacle. They place their rice and meat in it, then pour in their *rnööm;* the village headman, who killed only a pig, puts in a morsel of meat but no rice beer. The sacrifice of a chicken does not qualify one to participate in this final rite.

> ". . . *May the buffaloes grow,*
> *may the jars grow,*
> *may the Paddy flow,*
> *may the beer flow tomorrow, and the day after tomorrow. . . .*
> *I feed thee, Spirit of the Earth,*
> *Spirit of the Forest, of the Green Trees,*
> *Spirit of the Forest,*
> *Spirit of the Village Sites;*
> *decree that the Paddy grow,*
> *that the Fire devour.*
> *Leading my younger brothers,*
> *leading my elder brothers,*
> *tomorrow, and the day after tomorrow, I will again act*
> *in the same way. . . ."*

We all leave the site in a group, but back in the village each man goes to his own house to put away his libation tube. Then we reunite at Kröng-Yôong's, then at Kroong-the-One-Eyed's. Both men have kept their jars for the ceremony of the Paddy post in reserve for this afternoon. We stay even longer in the house of Mang-Dlaang, who insisted on performing this agrarian rite in its totality after the final ceremony of the *Nyiit Döng;* so did old Sieng-Rau.

The *Nyiit Döng* had been promised to the Spirit of the Soil and to Nduu, the Spirit of the Paddy, nine years ago. In every intervening year, the villagers had discussed it constantly and spoken about it to the *Yaang.*

Ritual stack of buffalo horns, and (right) *the hut of the Spirit Nduu*

Now, finally, the Great Festival of the Soil has been performed, the promise has been kept, the sacrifices have been offered. With this final rite, the villagers have sent the Spirits on their way sated and satisfied. Now it is the Spirits' turn to compensate the village for this tremendous holocaust, which has temporarily ruined the community, but also has given it renewed prestige and beguiles its hunger with the hope of abundant harvests in a more or less near future.

9

The Death and Burial
of Taang-Jieng-the-Stooped

OUR village celebrates the rite of the Paddy posts (*nyiit ndah*) a few days later than Sar Lang. The purpose of this ceremony is to ensure that the Soul of the Rice remains in the *miir*. Our festivities are on a far grander scale than those of our neighbors, for we have not had to meet the exorbitant expense of a *Nyiit Döng*. We spend two whole days—September 25 and 26—consecrating the Paddy posts.

While we are drinking from the final jar, Truu suddenly appears. He was released from prison only this morning, and has made a nonstop trip home. The deputy was also let out, but he is staying over with his sister in Bboon Dlei and will not arrive until tomorrow. More sensational events yet are to come. The next few days are given over to sacrifices that the former prisoners had promised the Spirits. On the twenty-ninth, Truu even immolates a buffalo. The men are busy carving up the animal in his yard when cries of lamentation are heard coming from the far end of the neighboring house: Jôong-Wan, of the Jaa clan, "real sister" of our holy man in the village, Kröng-Jôong, has just died. The village's entire attention is diverted from the house of the demoted canton chief to the bereaved household. For two consecutive days, the funeral rites unfold without interruption. The evening of October 1, by which time the inheritance has been divided, the dead woman's eldest son, Mhoo-Laang, anoints his brothers and sisters with blood, for now he takes them in as members of his household; by the same rite, the dead woman's husband, Wan, is made part of the household of his sister, Jieng, the wife of Taang-the-Stooped. Suddenly, fresh wails of lamentation are heard: Mae-Kroong, of the Bboon Jraang clan, has breathed her last. The next day, October 2, is taken up with the burial of Mae and the related funeral sacrifices. At last, on November 3, after ten days of variously joyous and melancholy rites, life in the village resumes its normal rhythm.

It has been a bad year. Rice has been in short supply, and people have had to scurry about and borrow from neighboring villages. So it is urgent that the early rice be harvested as it ripens. Yet at this season the real work is to stand guard over the fields—during the day to drive off flocks of predatory birds, and at night to keep out wild animals.

But in its own time the "real" rice is ripening, and as early as the evening of November 6, Kröng-Jôong "announces his harvest" (*nhêel kec*) to his fellow holy men and next of kin. At the foot of a large jar of rice beer, he offers each of them a bowl of hulled rice and either a hen or a Vietnamese bowl. Until November 11, each head of household will, in turn, make a similar gift of white rice accompanied by a hen or a bowl to each of the holy men, each of his relatives, and to his *jôok*.

After the living come the dead. On the eleventh, Kröng-Jôong, among others, goes out to his field "to announce the harvest to the people of the Underworld" (*nhêel kec Phaan in*). Around five in the afternoon, I find him under his *miir* hut "weaving a blanket." Actually, the "blanket" is a strip of banana leaf about one span long and four fingers wide. He "weaves" it by slashing the middle section lengthwise in fine, equal strips and slipping a "thread" cut from the same banana leaf through the strands. To keep them separate, he uses a tiny knife carved from a chip of *ngör* bamboo. Jôong-the-Healer tells me that her husband intends the two blankets for his two "sisters" who have recently died, Jôong-Wan and Dlaang-Taang. "Vietnamese bowls"—cup-shaped halves of the fruit of the *chaa* tree—are also offered to her husband's "sisters and mothers." The "chicken"—bits of kindling in a miniature cage—and the "fish"—wood shavings in a small press for smoking fish—are given to her "uncles [her mother's younger and older brothers] and her mothers and fathers." Now Kröng fashions two slender bamboo batons—*paa* tubes symbolizing marriage—for his wife's relatives. He rolls a leaf into a cone, secures it with a bamboo needle, and fills it with earth; he has made "a Mnong bowl full of hulled rice." A larger cone will be "a serving basket of rice." The two receptacles containing rice are each capped by an "imported bowl" and are intended for his own "sisters and mothers."

When everything is ready, Kröng collects his offerings, not forgetting "the jar of *rnööm*"—a gourd filled with bran in which he has stuck two stalks of straw—which his own and his wife's dead relatives will share. He walks toward the field of Can-Groo, and stops this side of the charred tree trunk marking the boundary between his *miir* and that of his neighbor. This is where, for the rite to strengthen the Paddy, he planted a *plaa*, the stick of bamboo containing various ingredients that communicate vigor and stamina to the young grain. He arranges his offerings with care: first, those he intends for his own dead; then, "the jar of beer," propped against the *plaa;* to the left of this, the gifts he is presenting to his wife's dead relatives. Lastly, he spits on the pieces of charcoal in his hand and asks them to announce the harvest to the Underworld. He enumerates what he is offering his "sisters and mothers," then what he is giving to "the younger and older brothers of the mother, to the mothers and fathers" of his wife. He concludes with a long recital of wishes, in which he asks for health and prosperity and begs the Paddy to fear nothing, and not to flee.

Now that he has done his duty by the living and the dead, Kröng-Jôong can begin his "real harvest" tomorrow morning. First, however, he has to take certain precautions with regard to the capricious and fearful Spirit of the Paddy. To keep the Spirit in the *miir*, Kröng must bind it firmly and appease it with a sacrifice. This is the purpose of the rite called "knotting the Paddy" (*muat Baa*), which comes immediately after "the announcement of the harvest to the people of the Underworld."

November 12

Kröng and his wife spent the night in their *miir* hut on its high stilts to guard their crops against incursions by denizens of the forest.

At seven in the morning, the team of Aang-of-the-Drooping-Eyelid arrives, five women in all. They slip off their panniers and have a smoke before Jôong-the-Healer leads the group to the area that will be harvested. Kröng sets out immediately with various ritual herbs, a young hen, and some head rice (*pieng bôok*), skimmed from the surface of the first pot of rice cooked this morning by his wife. He walks toward the sacred square and squats before the ritual post (*dôong*) and the Paddy post. Setting his offering down on the ground, he seizes the tuft of paddy nearest the post and, without uprooting it, ties it around the post, as he launches into a long prayer:

> "*Remain truly close to me,*
> *rest, forever firm, close to me.*
> *I grasp your leg,*
> *I grip the bend of your knee,*
> *I stroke your face,*
> *I pierce the lobe of your ear,*
> *I seize your right hand,*
> *I kiss your left. . . ."*

Reciting still, he knots several more tufts of paddy around the base of the sacred post. Into these knots he slips some leaves of waxy marrow, *krae* (*Memecylon scutellatum* Lour.), "quail bones," and "white horns." He binds the whole firmly together, using a beanstalk as string. Lastly, he places the head rice in the hollow between knot and post.

" . . . *Do not remain on the col,*
do not tarry by the crossroads,
do not venture into foreign villages,
do not return to foreign villages.
Eat this head soup, unctuous soup; here it is;
eat this head rice, savory head rice; here it is;
the alcohol will quench your thirst. . . ."

He slits the hen's neck and, continuing with his prayers, brushes the bleeding wound of his victim over the tufted knot bearing the ripe heads of grain, over the magic plants of the Paddy growing at the foot of the posts; then over the ground, the nearest rice stalks, the base of the Paddy post, and, lastly, over the *rkôong* leaves he has brought with him:

"*I anoint you with blood, O Paddy.*
The caterpillar clings to your leaf, fear nothing;
the caterpillar eats your stalk, fear nothing;
the hornet sucks your flower, fear nothing, O Paddy.
The wind blows hard, do not flee;
the sky makes us flee, fear nothing;
the pig begins to root, fear nothing;
the hen begins to peck, fear nothing;
the younger brothers, the older brothers come to beg,
    do not flee. . . ."

Carrying his *rkôong* leaves and chicken to the spot where the team has set down its panniers, he blesses them by rubbing the bleeding wound of his victim against them. Then, still reciting his long prayer, he fans the air above the panniers with the blood-stained *rkôong* branches:

". . . *Weary of remaining with the* kuang, *dwell henceforth*
    with me who am but a child.
Weary of placing yourself under the protection of the
    kuang, *remain with me who am but a boy.*
Weary of capering with the kuang, *caper with me who am*
    but an orphan.
The others who are kuang,
    the others who are rich, leave them behind.
With me who am a youth,
with me who am an orphan,
flirt and unite in marriage with me.
The others search for a pig, I search only for a fowl;
the others search for a fowl, I search only for an egg;
if they take an egg, I make offerings only in words. . . ."

Krŏng retraces his steps, deposits his chicken under the *miir* hut as he passes by, and strikes out along the path to the boundary that separates his field from Can's. Here he plants his *rkôong* branches to bar the way to another's bad luck.

> "*Fear nothing,*
> *do not flee.*
> *May your soul not be frightened*
> *into becoming a slave,*
> *into becoming hard of hearing.*
> *Return to us who will welcome you. . . ."*

Under the direction of Jôong-the-Healer, the five teen-age girls and young women are filling their *khiu* (ventral panniers) with fine ripe grains, which they empty into big baskets. Kröng, meanwhile, dips the chicken in scalding water, plucks it, and cooks it. He cuts a thin strip of rattan, and on this he threads a little chicken meat and small bits of tuber and leaves from one of the magic plants of the Paddy he gathered on the sacred square. Reciting no prayers, he attaches this necklace of offerings to the upper part of his own pannier, between the two straps. He smokes a pipe, and then, strapping a *khiu* around his loins, joins the six women who are busy harvesting. The team tackles the field of paddy in a single line. Each worker carries a *khiu* in front, secured around the waist with a woven strap. Using both hands, the reaper strips the panicle against the grain and drops the kernels into his little ventral pannier.

This alternating action of the hands enables the reapers to maintain a steady, brisk rhythm. When they have filled their *khiu*, they empty them into one of the large harvest panniers (*sah kec*) lined up nearby. On this, the first day of the harvest, the head of the house has just ritually fanned them.

By ten-thirty, six big panniers are full. Kröng carries his, filled to the brim, to his *miir* hut. From a gourd of rice soup, he pours a few drops on the top of his load of grain:

> "*I pour the rice soup,*
> *head soup, which is unctuous,*
> *head rice, which is savory,*
> *beer, which quenches the thirst.*
> *I gather, I scrape, I amass it,*
> *I strip the straw,*
> *I fill the panniers,*
> *Ritually I fan the* khiu,
> *I girdle the ladder. . . ."*

Slipping the straps of the heavy pannier over his shoulders, he carries it to his *rdae*—his temporary granary built at the exit from his *miir*, beside the path leading to the village. As the only man in the group, his main

Kröng-Jôong "announces the harvest to the people of the Underworld" . . .

. . . and, next day, blesses the harvest panniers with the blood of a hen sacrificed for "the knotting of the Paddy"

work will be to carry and empty the panniers as the women fill them; between trips, he will work for short intervals at the actual harvesting. By the end of the day, among them the seven people will have gathered twenty-one large panniers of rice.

Kröng is not the only one to have "knotted the Paddy" today. Bbaang-the-Pregnant-Man has performed the rite also. Truu has been less fortunate; he had to turn back when the roedeer belled as he was heading for the fields. During the next two days, numerous families will "knot the Paddy" in their turn.

The big harvest season—the *kec*—is open. Until all the crops are brought in, it is forbidden to travel or to drink; all energy is concentrated on the strenuous field labor. One may take time off from harvesting rice to pick cotton, however, for that crop also cannot wait.

Only the death of a member of the community can oblige people to desert their fields briefly and sanction their opening jars.

In the upper part of the village, set beyond Truu's house, stands a straggling building that for many years was the longest in Sar Luk. Taang-Jieng-the-Stooped, of the Cil clan, is its unchallenged head, despite his great reserve and his disinclination to intervene in community discussions. Like all the Cil here, he had no doubt been personally involved in the Phii Dih massacre. Be that as it may, what has been confirmed is that he was supposed to get his share from the sale of little Mang (a Sruk) if such a sale went through. However, Taang-Jieng was not of the same family as the other members of the Cil clan living in Paang Döng and Sar Luk. The relatives of these Cil came, actually, from the predominantly Sruk village of Bboon Juu, whereas Taang had been born in Ryôong-in-the-Mountains. He settled in Paang Döng only after his parents, who had first emigrated to Rcae, moved there. He again changed residence when he married Jieng, of the Daak Cat clan, who was the daughter of his maternal uncle. For many years, the couple lived in the wife's village, Phii Srôony, at the foot of the high chain of mountains to the south. Here their oldest son was born—Tôong-Mang, who became cook at the Frontier School after Sieng-Dee was murdered in 1948 by the Cil from Paang Döng. Taang-Jieng emigrated again, this time to Paang Döng, where Jieng gave birth to fat Aang, since June 1949 the widow of a Sar Luk Rjee by whom she had one daughter, Jieng. Then Taang moved to Phii Ko', where Jieng bore Dloong-of-the-Crooked-Mouth, who is now about fifteen. It was only the year when they "ate" the forest of the Stone of the Tiger Pit (*Mau Trôom Tlaa*)—which is to say, in 1943—that Taang-Jieng-the-Stooped settled for good in Sar Luk.

In this elongated dwelling, Taang-Jieng's granary occupies the central section, bordered on one side by the granaries of his sisters, and on the other side by those of Jieng's brother and the latter's brother-in-law. On one side Cil, on the other Jaa, allied by a Daak Cat. Taang-the-Stooped shares his common room with his younger sister, Brôong-the-Widow. She and her daughter, Jôong-the-Hernia, live with Laang-the-Widow—another Cil, and a distant relative—and Laang's daughter. Adjacent to the widows' granary is the granary of Bbaang-the-Stag (husband of Taang-the-Stooped's younger sister, Aang-of-the-Mincing-Step), which also shelters two households—those of Aang-of-the-Mincing-Step and of Wan-Rieng, who is the eldest son of her brother Kröng-Aang's first marriage. Kröng-Aang himself lives in another house with his brother-in-law, Bbaang-the-One-Eyed. So much for the Cil. On the other side, the granary of Wan-Jôong abuts that of Taang-Jieng; Wan is Jieng's brother, and is married to a Jaa. He shares his common room with his wife's brother, Kroong-Troo. (The reader will recall that the holy man in the village Kröng-Jôong also belongs to the Jaa clan.)

The one truly outstanding personality in this long house has always been Bbaang-the-Stag. Well built, dynamic, jolly, never one to refuse a drink, this brother-in-law of Baap Can (he is, let us not forget, the brother of Aang-the-Long) discharges both a pseudo-governmental function as a canton runner * and a traditional role as the only surviving holy man of Phii Ko'. Also, his Exchange of a Buffalo Sacrifice with Kraang-Drüm has incontestably established him as a *kuang* in the eyes of all.

This long house would have had an uneventful history had not the voracity of the Spirits suddenly struck it and, in the space of a few months, decimated the Jaa clan members living there. During last year's rainy season, Dlaang-Taang, the younger sister of Jôong-Wan and Kroong-Troo, had been carried off by illness. One year later, on August 10, 1949, Kroong-Troo, who had been spitting blood for weeks, also died. A month and a half later, on September 29, Jôong-Wan breathed her last after long months of suffering. Troo-Kroong and her children left the far end of the house to live with Yôong-the-Mad, who, like herself, belongs to the Ntöör clan. Wan-Jôong was taken in by his sister and neighbor, Jieng-Taang, and thus, for all practical purposes, continued to live under the same roof. The still unmarried children of his wife's first marriage followed their elder brother, Mhoo-Laang, to the canton chief's house. By October 1949, therefore, Taang-Jieng's vast long house had shrunk from five granaries to two.†

Taang-the-Stooped was the tallest man in Sar Luk. Spare rather than actually thin, at this time he must have been over fifty, but he was so hale and hearty and had so few wrinkles that a European would have thought

---

* "Pseudo" because it is not official and is not paid. —*Trans.*

† See *b*, III, IV, and V on map, pp. 8–9.

him younger. However, now he traveled only rarely and when his Cil "brothers" had suggested he accompany them to Kudduu territory to sell little Mang, he refused, alleging great fatigue. When the Phii Dih affair broke into the open, Taang had been upset, and the trips to Poste du Lac, where he was summoned for interrogation, had worn him out. The purification rite he performed on returning from his last trip had not succeeded in putting him completely back on his feet. He was seen less and less often in the fields. He complained of his chest, and his condition worsened daily. On November 17, Bbaang-the-Stag rushed to Sar Lang to fetch the *njau* Ddöi. On this occasion, a hen and a neckless jar of *rnööm* were sacrificed. But on the twentieth, Jôong-Wan (of the Rtung clan), who was the other healer in Sar Luk, had to be asked to perform a major exorcism, with the execution of a dog and "the dispatch" of a chicken with its wings and feet broken. The following day, Ndoong, the male nurse at the Public Health Station, judged Taang's situation to be so serious that he had him brought in for treatment.

By November 22, the harvest period is at its peak, and some people continue to garner their crops despite the ban against it because of the dog's immolation two days earlier. The sick man's family observes the taboo but does pick cotton, which is not forbidden. Late in the afternoon, Bbaang-the-Stag comes to ask me to back him up on persuading Ndoong to authorize Taang's being brought home. I disagree with this plan and explain to Bbaang that his brother-in-law will be really well cared for only at the Health Station. Bbaang does not dare tell me that the invalid's condition is hopeless.

In the middle of the night—ten past eleven by my watch—cries and wails are heard coming from the Public Health Station. Soon torches bob along the track, and a cortege rapidly approaches. Taang-Jieng-the-Stooped is dead. His body, wrapped in a mat and bound with rattan thongs to a long wooden pole, is carried by his brother Kröng-Aang, Bbaang-the-Stag, and Wan-Jôong-the-Widower.

When he left me, Bbaang had gone to the Health Station to be with his brother-in-law. He had returned after his evening meal. Seeing that Taang was taking a rapid turn for the worse, he had run to the village to call the women. It was too late. By the time they got to the Health Station, Taang-the-Stooped had breathed his last.

Howling rather than crying, their chignons undone and their hair falling in disarray around their shoulders, Tôong-Mang-the-Cook and the women return home. They remove their necklaces and bracelets. Jieng dismantles her hearth. The bearers lay the corpse on the low platform, on the mat where Taang-Jieng-the-Stooped used to lie every night by his wife's side. He lies there now, his body stiff, his limbs straight, his open hands flat along his thighs; his feet are firmly tied at the ankles and base of the toes with two lengths of sturdy cotton thread. Tôong spreads a new white shirt over his father's chest, and Jieng wraps his entire body up to the neck in a fine Mnong blanket. Weeping, each member of the family brings one or more Vietnamese bowls and places them as offerings alongside the corpse. Taang's children are particularly generous. Tôong-the-Cook lays two hundred piasters on his father's chest, and Aang-the-Widow a length of black calico. The members of the family, men and women, crowd around the dead man's head, crying and chanting dirges. His widow strokes his uncovered face, or even presses her tear-drenched cheek against it. Their strident wails and lamentations, punctuated by sobs, fill the house with a feeling of desolation:

> "O you, O Father, O you,
>> one digs There Below,
>>> one digs straight and true.

> O you, O Father,
>> one enters There Below,
>>> one enters stretched out flat.

> O you, O Father,
>> one planes There Below
>>> as one planes a coffin with the axe.

> O you, O Father,
>> the path There Below
>>> winds like a column of black ants.

> O you, O Father,
>> the kite There Below
>>> soars like the eagle Ayaa.

> O you, O Father,
>> the watering place in the Underworld
>>> is like a great pointy winnowing basket.

>>>> O Father, O you."

   Villagers arrive one after another. Each woman who enters goes to the low platform, sets a Vietnamese bowl by the dead man, squats, and, covering her eyes with her hands, simulates sobs or really does weep. She calls out to the dead man, and intones lamentations, paying no heed to what her neighbors are chanting. The feigned or genuine grief expressed in all these varied chants creates a veritable cacophony; some chants are howled, others simply murmured, depending on the mourner's lung power. The din in no way detracts from the funereal, at times even lugubrious, atmosphere that reigns in the room. When a woman tires, she leaves the group of weepers to smoke a pipe and join in the conversation of others in the common room. At first, faces are impassive or sad; the talk is of the dead man and his illness; other such cases are recalled. But soon, and especially when the sacrificial jar is opened, people weary of these macabre topics, and laughter breaks out more and more frequently. Yet all the while the swarm of weepers hovering over the corpse pours forth a constant stream of laments. When a woman who has been resting feels her strength restored, she returns to weep for the dead man with the same wrenching sorrow she displayed the first time. She will continue to perform this service throughout the night until, utterly exhausted, she finally goes home to snatch some sleep. She will return to the house of death and spend most of the next day and night properly fulfilling her office. For until the body is buried, a group of female weepers must hold constant vigil.

For the nonce, the large room is almost empty. So far, relatively few visitors have come to pay their respects to the dead man. It is late, and all the racket the near relatives of the departed are making has not managed to rouse the nocturnal torpor of the village. At the moment, only Taang's widow, his son, and Bbaang-the-Stag are performing the rites.

Within ten minutes of arriving at the house, Tôong-Mang-the-Cook, assisted by Bbaang-the-Stag, offers the first sacrifice. Bbaang slits the throat of a hen Tôong holds by its beak. With his hand, Tôong spreads the dripping blood over his father's chest, which has been bared for this purpose:

> "The beer from a large jar,
> a hen . . . these I offer you.
> Show them to our mothers and fathers,
> to our uncles, the younger and older brothers of our mothers.
> Remain close by the Rainbow,
> be at peace in the Underworld. . . ."

The victim is then laid by the dead man's right side.

This chicken and the jar of *rnööm* that will be opened in a moment are called "the hen and jar of rice beer for anointment of the hand" (*ier rnööm mhaam tii*). Actually, had there been time to bring Taang-Jieng to the village before he breathed his last, his palm would have been anointed with wort mixed with chicken blood so that, while still living, he could verify with his own eyes that he would be refused nothing for his burial, that everything due him would be rendered unto him. This sacrifice is intended also for the Ancestors, the inhabitants of the Underworld, whom the dead man has gone to join.

Because Taang-the-Stooped died before the rite could be performed, it is simplified and only his chest is sprinkled with the victim's blood. The act endows the offering with a supplementary role—that of a sign. The bloodstain is considered to be indelible and will last forever, even if the dead man were to return to earth as a *koon maa;* that is to say, if he were to be reincarnated as a newborn child. But in the kingdom of the Shades, everything is topsy-turvy: "the stain turns around" then and is found not on the infant's chest but on its back. (It is what we term the Mongolian spot.) I should add that the sacrificed hen has another name that defines its third function: "the chicken that leads the dead man along the road to the Underground Places" (*ier lâm troong Phaan*).

The dead man's future life in the infernal world is carefully prepared for. At his feet, where twenty minutes earlier the hearth still stood, a make-believe one is set up: several spent, charred logs support a pot that contains a handful of hulled rice steeping in water; a smaller pot is propped against it, into which raw vegetables have been thrown. In the Underworld, these assume the appearance of a real hearth and of real rice and vegetables cooking furiously over a real resin fire (which in this world is flameless). Two gourds, one of soup, the other of water, round out the supplies. His family remembers to lay by the dead man's head his pipe and tobacco pouch, as well as a manioc tuber and the adornments he habitually wore in his chignon.

Tôong-the-Cook melts some beeswax in the shard of a pot. He dips a cotton thread in the wax and twists it into a spiral; he lets one end protrude upright above the edge of the shard. He lights this candle and passes it over the corpse, from head to foot and back to the head, while he prays:

> *"Show our uncles, the younger and older brothers of*
> *   our mothers,*
> *show the mothers and the fathers.*
> *Remain close by the Rainbow,*
> *be at peace in the Underworld.*
> *Make firewood,*
> *beat hearth wood,*
> *prepare rice beer.*
> *Sell supports for the jars,*
> *the Spirits eat the buffalo. . . ."*

This candle, I am told, lights the way for the dead man's soul as it journeys to join the souls of his ancestors. For the duration of the wake, the candle will sit in the "mouth" of a small neckless jar offered the dead man by his family and placed near his head.

Once the jar for "the anointment of the hand" is in position and ready to be drunk from, Tôong-the-Cook siphons off some *rnööm* into a bottle, which he then places on the low platform, against his father's feet. In announcing his offering to his parent, he addresses to him the same prayer as before. Then they all drink from the jar, while around the corpse a group of women continues to sing laments. Kröng-Aang, the dead man's brother, first pulls on the drinking straw. As the son, Tôong-the-Cook follows him. He cedes his place to Bbaang-the-Stag (husband of one of the sisters), whom Can replaces (his wife, Groo, is a Daak Cat and therefore "daughter" to Jieng-Taang). The sisters of the deceased, Brôong-the-Widow and Aang-of-the-Mincing-Step (with, in addition, the wife of the canton chief between them), drink only after Kraang-the-Bladder, a Daak Cat.

Brôong-the-Widow expresses her despair over this fresh loss by a lament:

> "I look about me: my father is no more.
> I look about me: my husband is no more.
> I look about me: my eldest brother is no more."

Leaning toward his father's body, Tôong-the-Cook enumerates for his benefit: "Two hundred piasters, a white shirt, eight large and two small Vietnamese bowls. . . ." He repeats this list several times.

Bbaang-the-Stag describes for us the embarrassment Taang-the-Stooped had caused him during one of Bbaang's last visits with Taang at the Health Station. The dying man wanted tobacco and asked his brother-in-law to get some for him: "All you have to do is pick it in my own field," he said. Now, Bbaang knew that Taang-Jieng had set out tiny bamboo spikes among his tobacco plants, so he did not dare venture into the field. In fact, when such spikes are artfully positioned, only the owner can risk entering a garden he has decided to protect in this way. Anyone else would be wounded and thus give himself away to the villagers, who would jeer at the poacher. Bbaang-the-Stag was not keen on arousing suspicions, however baseless, and no matter what explanations he offered, some trace of doubt would remain for people of ill-will to exploit.

Jieng-Taang and her daughter plant bamboo wands at either end of the dead man's body, one by his head on the low platform, the other in the ground by his feet, Taang being so tall that his feet extend beyond the platform. Between these two sticks and about twenty centimeters above the body, the two women stretch a string made of shreds of red and white cotton. To this they attach cotton pompons, red and white alternating. The decoration has great mythic significance. This string is "the small cord of the *kuulêel* sparrow hawk" (*rsei tlaang kuulêel*)—that is, of the sparrow-hawk-soul. Later, the cord will permit one to distinguish the *kuulêel* from the ordinary sparrow hawk. The *kuulêel* takes wing upon the death of a human body, but it is easily recognized by the threads it wears on its claws, whereas the ordinary species has none. (The threads are the reapparition of the string stretched the length of the dead person.) The moment one sees a sparrow hawk, one pours rice soup on the ground and

Women weepers cluster around the corpse, above which is strung "the small cord of the sparrow-hawk-soul"

prays to it in order to draw its attention to this quasi-symbolic offering.

Ngee-Truu, the canton chief's wife, drinking straw in hand, declares with firm authority that henceforth Tôong-Mang must not live away from home. He must give up his position as cook at the school. His mother is now a widow—indeed, only widows are left in this house, and his place is here. Squatting a few steps away, Tôong does not visibly react.

Brôong-the-Widow cries to someone who is about to bar the door, "It's taboo to bar the door during a wake! It must only be closed, propped shut with a stick." Can says to me, "Nothing of the sort! You don't bar the door simply because, with all this drinking, people have to go outside all the time." And, in fact, you do see weepers and drinkers go and come incessantly; they relieve themselves by the threshold, which by morning will have been transformed into a stinking quagmire. The women hardly dare go beyond the door at a time such as this, when the Spirits who prowl around the house of the dead are particularly numerous.

Jieng is weeping copiously, her cheek pressed against the dead man's. His face will not be covered until dawn, and a slit at the level of the nostrils will be made in the shroud only when he is placed in his coffin. Throughout the night, the Mnong blanket which envelops him is drawn only to his chin so that, they say, he can contemplate his possessions (albeit his eyes are closed). Jieng inundates the man who was her husband with tears; beside her, a woman chants:

> "Under the eaves, behold once again, O brother, the
> white goat;
> on the low platform, behold once again, O brother, the
> women weaving;
> under the sparkling sun, behold once again, O brother,
> the kids locking horns and, as evening falls, the
> spurred cocks fighting."

Throughout the night, village women press around the body to join their tears and laments to those of Jieng, her children, and her sisters-in-law. In the middle of the room, the men and those women who are weary from their lamenting sit around the jar and chat about a host of things, few of which have to do with the bereavement that has befallen this household. By sunrise, the laments have subsided, as if muffled, and most of the drinkers have disappeared. The house of the dead man drowses, now almost empty. Apart from the family, the few people still present are young men and women who have made it a point of honor to hold vigil until daybreak.

November 24

At eight-twenty, sixteen men armed with axes and heavy bush hooks leave the village. In addition to relatives of the deceased, the group

A rest during the building of the coffin

includes at least one man from each granary in Sar Luk. They strike
out along the wide track in the direction of Paang Döng. When they
near the grove, about two hundred meters from the villages, they plunge
into the bamboo forest, with a scattering of tall trees, which borders it on
the right. After walking perhaps fifty meters, they stop; numerous *tloong*
(*Dipterocarpus obtusifolius*) grow here. The men soon spot a suitable
one: trunk very straight and almost a meter in diameter. During this rapid
search, several men have prepared a fire, which they light with a brand
one of them has brought from the village. Around this fire, those men
who are not busy will sit, smoking and talking while they rest. Once the
tree has been chosen, the ground around it is cleared and two young men
vigorously attack the trunk. The tree is felled within a half hour of our
leaving the village.

With heavy axe blows, one man squares the base of the trunk while
another works on the opposite end of the future coffin. Its length, two
meters fifteen, has been marked off with a rattan measuring rod brought
by Tôong-the-Cook. Four teams of two men each spell one another, working fifteen minutes or so at a stretch; in an hour's time, they have finished. Now the log is rolled over so that its narrowest surface faces up.
This will be the coffin lid. First, the bark is stripped off: Bbaang-the-Stag
and Bbôong-Mang-the-Deputy, standing on either side of the log, with
vertical blows of their axes make cuts no more than a span apart; then,
shifting their aim, they make slanting cuts, so that the bark is chipped off,
rather like scales. After a quarter of an hour, Kraang-Drüm relieves them
and, using the same technique, chips off the remaining patch of bark.

Meanwhile, a three-man team has set out to cut down a sapling, which
will serve as a battering ram, and two young men have gone into the
forest in search of rattan lianas. Another, working with the large chips left
from squaring the trunk, cuts them into long pieces and chamfers the
ends; these will be used as wedges in cleaving the trunk. Several men
take turns at this task.

Once all bark has been removed, the upper part of the trunk is shaped
obliquely on two sides, giving it the semblance of a roof. This job and the
planing that follows are done with short, sidewise axe blows.

Bbôong-the-Deputy, squatting near the fire, uses his bush hook to split
a hollow bamboo lengthwise into four pieces; he takes each in turn and,
still with his bush hook, he pares away the extremely tough sapwood that
lines this hard bark. The strips of bark thus obtained he chops into tiny
sticks; these will be used to form "the barrier of Srae" (Srae is a mythical
Hero), which will be set up as a ritual decoration at the cemetery.

Nothing about this work is at all gloomy. The men resting around the
fire crack jokes or hark back to old times. A short while ago, Bbôong-the-
Deputy was describing the complicated coffins the Mnong Pröng make.
They do not hollow the bier to form a simple trough but shape it to

suggest the contours of the human body; on the outside, they carve a tail at one end of the coffin or, sometimes, even four at the head and three at the foot. The talk turns from the Pröng to the Cil (not the clan but the tribe perched on the mountain slopes where the river rises). Vast disdain is expressed for these people, who eat only vegetables and no rice—but then, what a variety of wild plants they use.

"Just listen to this. This is their favorite dish. They take some vegetables, add some cornmeal, and throw in some salt, putrid pig's blood, and a handful of hulled rice. Then they cook the mess. A dish fit for pigs! Disgusting! And what's more, they never wash their pots!"

"I know another dish of theirs—sour rice soup. They let it steep in a small neckless jar for six days. Then, according to them, it's just right!"

Hearty guffaws.

Bbôong-the-Deputy speaks of the ceremony of the Great Oath, for which all Montagnard officials in the Highlands assembled in Ban Me Thuot. This year, they took the oath of allegiance not only to the big French chief but also to "the Vietnamese king." What most impressed Bbôong was not the parade of elephants but the rifle presented to the wife of Ma Kham Suk, the Lord of Ban Don, the village that hunters and trainers of wild elephants come from. Nor can he get over how thin old Mor was (the Bahnar headman, whom he mistakes for the headman of Pleiku). He is full of admiration for the talents of the headman of Bbuon Hoo as interpreter. Can, on the other hand, was most astonished by the parasols: "They were like Rhade hats carried on the end of poles by those fellows who were following the Great Yoo and the King." Having made a visible impression with this, he adds, "They're to protect them against the heat."

At eleven-fifteen, Jôong-the-Hernia and Sôi-the-Tokélo arrive bearing a big pot in which they have prepared bamboo-shoot preserve. They set it down in a warm spot near the fire, and go back to the village.

Ten minutes after the teen-age girls have come and gone, the planing is finished. Bbaang-the-Stag and Bbôong-the-Deputy start from opposite ends of the trunk and, with a charred stick, trace a black line to mark where the lid and body of the coffin will be separated. Tôong-the-Cook then slits the throat of a fine brown cock and chops off its claws. Bestriding the head of the coffin, he presses the victim's claws against the black charcoal line at the heart of the tree. Then, holding one claw in each hand, he extends his arms to the width of the tracing and, pressing the claws against the two lines, he moves backward to the foot of the coffin, where he brings the claws together again over the center. As he carries out this rite, Tôong implores the Spirit of the *Tloong:*

> "O Tree,
> O Bamboo,
> *whether this does you harm,*

The future coffin lid is stripped of bark . . .

. . . then *"cut with chicken's feet"*

. . . and, lastly, split with a ram

whether this does you good,
be kind to me.
I have looked for meat
 and for rice beer
  to anoint you with blood.
My dead I must have borne away;
I, living, must build the house,
 I must build the granary.
Do not show your wrath,
do not become angry,
  O You, Spirit of the Tree,
  I offer you meat to eat,
  I offer you rice beer to drink."

He lays the cock's claws on the stump of the felled tree. He has performed the rite called "the cutting with chicken's feet" (*coor jöng ier*), and now the men may proceed to cut out the trunk with wooden wedges and axe heads.

The operation begins at the "head" (*bôok*) of the coffin. With a heavy club, a man pounds vigorously to sink the first axe head into a split in the trunk probably caused by the tree's fall. The aim is to lengthen this split more or less along the outline traced in black. A second axe head is placed beside the first, then a third; when the cut is judged sufficiently deep, the three heads are replaced by a long wooden wedge, which is reinforced on either side by two of the iron axe heads previously used. Six men lift the young trunk prepared earlier as a ram and, bending over, they pound the wooden wedges with powerful, cadenced blows. The "head" of the coffin splits across its full diameter. Two axe heads are then inserted at the start of the two lateral cleavage lines.

At ten to twelve, about ten minutes after the splitting operation commenced, Truu, Kröng-Jôong, and Choong-the-Soldier turn up. The moment the canton chief arrives, he takes over; deciding that three wooden wedges have been placed too close together, he orders them separated.

The coffin lid has been stripped only on the right side. On the left, the cleavage line passes over bark which is stoutly resistant; here the split is very difficult to make and it deviates considerably from the black tracing. As the men pound away, they implore the tree aloud: "We offer you a pig and rice beer. Split the way you should."

They pause for five minutes to replace one of the three wedges. Then it is decided to cut new ones, not using the heavy chips from the felling of the tree but some big branches. These wedges will provide cylindrical surfaces to strike, and the bark will make them tougher.

The split veers more and more to the side, unfortunately. Several of the men even speak of abandoning this trunk, but the others immediately object. In an attempt to bring the cleavage back into line, the trunk is rolled over so that the black tracing is on top. One man straddles the trunk and, following the design, hacks away with his axe. When the crack is deemed sufficiently deep, two axe heads are inserted. Then the trunk is rolled over again, and the same tactic is used to correct the line on the other side.

With powerful ramming blows, the men pound the wooden wedges into the parallel fissures. Since the trunk still seems to split more readily where it has been stripped of its bark, they work only on that side. To supplement the ramming, a heavy branch is driven into the crack, which now reaches to the foot of the coffin. Finally, at five minutes to two, there is a tremendous cracking sound, the trunk divides, and the lid separates from the body of the coffin.

The men gather around the fire for their midday meal. Only Truu, Bbôong-the-Deputy, and Krŏng-Jôong work on, hollowing out the coffin and its lid. They will eat later. One man works with an axe, the second with just a handle and its blade; the third uses an adze. The choice of tool is a matter of personal preference, actually; the teams that spell each other in this task do not always use the same ones. The important job that will occupy the men during the late afternoon will be to debark and smooth the outer side of the coffin; for this, they will use axes.

Bbôong-the-Deputy, who loves to show off his skill as a craftsman, carves the coffin's "tail" and "horns." Making the tail is easy; he takes a bamboo stick some ten centimeters long and slits it for about three quarters of its length into fine strips, so that it looks like a whisk—or a horse's tail. This will be attached to the narrower end of the coffin lid. Fashioning the horns calls for a larger measure of skill. He takes a lath of fresh bamboo about eighty centimeters long; he feathers both ends so as to leave perhaps ten centimeters in the middle intact. The flexible fibers at either end of this rigid section he twists into two loops firm enough for the tips of the fibers to stand upright. Starting at the base of the loops, he winds a length of supple rattan around each strand. Then he makes two small whisks similar to the tail, and inserts them in the tips of each horn. With rattan strips, he braids two small rings and hangs one from each loop. The two rings and the loops are, respectively, the coffin's "eyes" and "ears." When the casket is finished, the "horns" are fastened with wooden nails to the head, and the coffin will thus represent a stylized buffalo. (It will be recalled that the chief soul of every man is his buffalo-soul.)

The job considered to be the most delicate is sculpturing the four feet of the coffin—in this instance, "feet in the form of breasts." It takes Bbôong-the-Deputy and his nephew, Choong-the-Soldier, a full hour to carve the two pairs of half spheres.

By seven o'clock in the evening, the finishing touches have been applied with axe and adze, and the men proceed to paint the coffin. Not much time remains, so they settle for painting on either side of the lid parallel bands of identical motifs; they resemble two superimposed rows of saw teeth, each tooth a right-angled triangle with the point turned downward and its surface stained with an indigo dye. If a painter makes a slip, the uniformity of this double indentation is suddenly marred by what looks like a sort of incomplete Maltese cross. Had we not been running short of time, the body of the coffin would have been painted also, and the lid decoration would have been more elaborate; both sides of the head and the side panel would have been embellished with the "tiger cheek" motif so prized by the Mnong, which consists of a six-pointed star inscribed within a circle.

At seven-thirty, the men finally leave the forest, carrying coffin, rattan, tools, etc., and do not stop until they set their burden down by the private door of the bereaved house. When she hears their voices, Jieng-Taang brings out the gourd of water with which the interior of the coffin must be washed. But she is no longer sure what she has to do and stands stockstill, one hand on her head, the other holding the gourd. Four men slip a rope around either end of the coffin, ease it through the low door, and set it down on the ground near the granary. The lid is removed, and holes and irregularities in the wood are filled with mud mixed on the spot. The edges are daubed with mud, so that presently the coffin can be hermetically sealed. The women remove the Vietnamese bowls and one small neckless jar from the low platform to permit the men to position the coffin properly on it. Jieng is weeping, her head pressed against her dead husband's ear. Tôong-the-Cook picks up the beeswax candle and passes it over the open coffin from head to foot. Anticipating the next step, Jieng moves precipitately "to gather up the soul" (*doop hêeng*) in her cupped hands; first she pours it into a large harvest basket, then over herself. The men wrap the corpse in a mat, place the head on a tunic folded in four, and cover it with a large Vietnamese bowl.

The body is laid in the coffin. With a long-nosed gourd Aang-the-Widow "gathers up the soul" in the area of her dead father's heart, and pours it over her own belly. It is now the turn of Brôong-the-Widow to perform the same rite and thereby accrue benefit for herself, her niece Dloong, and her sister, Aang-of-the-Mincing-Step. Aang-the-Widow repeats the rite, but this time does as her aunt has done: she uses only her hand to pour the soul over herself, her daughter, Jieng, and her nieces. Each member of the family must recover his soul in this fashion, because out of affection for the dead man it clings to him and thus risks being dragged in his wake as he journeys to the Underworld.

The coffin is filled with as many of the Vietnamese bowls offered as it will hold. Just before the men place the lid on it, Jieng lays some clean shells near the dead man's head, announcing her gift to him: "Here are Vietnamese bowls." (Earthly shells become bowls in the Underworld.)

The interstices between coffin and lid are filled in with mud. At the height of the chest, the mud caulking is mixed with glutinous-rice paste— "to avoid the smell of putrefaction," I am told. The coffin is tied at three evenly spaced intervals with rattan rope. The dead man's belt, pipe and tobacco pouch are laid on the lid, together with "the knife for ripping the shroud at the level of the nose." By eight in the evening, the body is secure in its coffin and the second vigil commences. All the men who shared in making the coffin go down to the river for a thorough bath of purification.

The *njat*, the principal offering of sacrifices and libations to the dead man, takes place a half hour later, when the men have returned from bathing. Jars of rice beer are arranged in a row in the common room. The two largest, those of Tôong-the-Cook and Brôong-the-Widow, are tied to the same post in the middle of the row. Each person offering a sacrifice carries his jar stopper covered with wort to join the others in front of the private door. Here they will kill their victims together. Brôong-the-Widow and Tôong-the-Cook sacrifice a pig each (of three and four spans, respectively); Truu, Can, and Krông-Aang offer one young chicken each. Jôong-the-Hernia stands beside her mother; Groo-Can and Aang-Krông beside their husbands; the dead man's wife and daughters beside Tôong. With their hands resting on their heads, the women weep—or, rather, they howl. Some cry, "O father! O father!"; another, "O husband!"; and another, "O brother-in-law!" The din is deafening, for these harrowing cries and appeals are accompanied by the squeals of the pigs and the cackles of the chickens being killed. Each animal sacrificed in honor of a dead person must be killed with a club, although normal practice is to slit the throat. The victim's blood is collected by rubbing the wound with wort. Those who have killed a chicken tear off one wing and claw and lay them on the stoppers of their jars. Each then sets his offering down on the low platform, against the coffin. Tôong and Brôong "anoint [the coffin] with blood," using the blood-soaked wort. It is only then that Truu notices their oversight and bids them look for the "nails" of their victims. They go out to cut off the left fore feet of the pigs they have immolated, and these also they place on the stoppers of their jars leaning against the coffin.

Then each person makes his libation. He goes to the jar he is offering, sucks beer into the drinking straw, and as soon as it is filled, plugs the upper opening with his index finger. He returns to the coffin and sprinkles the foot with *rnööm*, which he allows to dribble from the straw. Each announces to the dead man what he is offering. Jieng feels she will be doing enough simply to take a mouthful of beer and spew it on the threshold of the private door, for her son, Tôong, has offered the drinking-straw libation in behalf of the entire household.

Once this rite is completed, people go to drink from the jars while the weepers continue to vociferate around the coffin. Each person must sip liquor from all the jars, in order to avoid being struck down by fevers inflicted by the Spirits of the paths and forests. Some anxiety is felt for the men who went into the forest to fashion the coffin and who have not yet come to drink, but they will appear shortly. The room is jammed, although the whole village is not present. Some households are represented by only one person, and some individuals have not put in an appearance the whole day long, among them Baap Can, his wife, and old Krah.

The wake which begins now is a repetition of last night's. The same weepers succeed each other around the coffin, the same laments and dirges are sung, the same kinds of stories are told around the jars. However, there is one difference: the women now weep over a coffin, not over a corpse. Also, the guests' fervor has greatly diminished since last evening, for despite the six jars of beer that have been opened, the fatigue of the first vigil has been aggravated by a day's hard work. A few will hold up until morning by dint of drinking steadily. By dawn, the steps up to the door have been transformed into a stinking mire, for throughout the night the drinkers, men and women, have gone out to relieve themselves exactly where they did the evening before.

November 25

At nine in the morning, "the chicken that pecks up the maggots" (*ier coh rhae*) is attached by its feet to the ridge of the coffin. Four men carry the casket through the private door and set it down a few steps beyond the threshold. They release the rattan ropes that have kept it shut, and remove the lid, which they lay on the ground. Brôong-the-Widow, the deceased's sister, undoes the top of the mat shroud and uncovers the face of the dead man, so that for the last time he may see his wife and children and contemplate the sun and the sky. They are amazed to find the face intact, with no trace of decay. Bbaang-the-Stag attributes this to the injections and the pills of "magic European plants" the nurse had administered. Brôong lays some charcoal beside the corpse; the coals will act as guides for the dead man on his journey toward *Yaang Boec*, the Spirit who rules the Underworld. With a knife, Bbaang-the-Stag scratches a fingernail of the dead man and gives a pinch of the powder thus obtained to Kröng-Aang. On the latter's return from the cemetery, he will beg illness to remove itself by applying a little of this nail dust over the heart of his wife, then of Mang-Tôong and of Bbaang-the-Stag himself. All these people are under an interdict forbidding them to touch the dead man because they are married to younger relatives of his (younger brother and sister, and son). However, in the course of the funeral rites, they have touched the corpse dozens of times and frequently sat on Taang's mat, if only to weep, thereby violating the taboo. With the same appropriate exorcisms in mind, Bbaang-the-Stag snips off a piece of Taang-the-Stooped's loincloth and gives it to the dead man's son. Lastly, Tôong-the-Cook spreads a fine white napkin, new and fresh, over his father's face. The shroud is pulled up and the lid replaced. While the coffin is being roped again, the women smear it here and there with glutinous rice "to prevent the maggots from getting inside."

Tôong-the-Cook has not stopped bawling since morning. Now he seems unable to see; he staggers and, all of a sudden, literally collapses on the coffin. The women of the family, seated on the ground, their heads pressed against the casket, are weeping. Several men help Bbaang-the-Stag as he ropes and ties the coffin firmly with rattan in handsome geometric patterns that follow those they painted on it yesterday.

The small girls of the house stand a bit behind the older group. All three have placed their hands on their heads, but only little Jieng, the daughter of Aang-the-Widow, is shedding real, warm tears. She alone seems to understand the meaning of what is happening—that her grandfather, whose favorite she has been, is going away forever. The two other girls are frozen in their ritual pose, but they cannot squeeze out any tears.

Tôong-the-Cook and Wan-the-Widower sink small wooden nails in the front panel of the casket so that the dead man "may abandon here below the soul of the Buffaloes, the soul of the Jars, of the Salt, of the Rice. . . ." Jieng-Taang plucks these various souls from the air and pours them into a small neckless jar. All are essential to one's well-being, and they must not be allowed to attach themselves to the dead man and follow him into the Beyond.

The rattan decoration is completed, and the portage pole—the young, straight trunk also brought back from the forest yesterday—is solidly affixed to the coffin ridge. All the gifts offered the dead man have been brought from the house, for they must accompany him on his subterranean sojourn. Finally, the mourners are ready to set out for the cemetery, but first all necessary precautions must be taken to protect members of the household and their material possessions. Tôong pours a few drops of rice soup from a gourd on the head of each member of the family to preserve his quartz-soul (*naar bôok*), which dwells behind his forehead. Then, seizing a bundle of *rhôong* leaves, Tôong gives the interior of the house, including the granary, a ritual sweeping. He places a *rhôong* branch by the granary entrance and another above the private door; the rest he stuffs under the rattan rope encircling the coffin.

The weeping women of the family lean against the coffin, while Bbaang-the-Stag puts the finishing touches on the rattan decoration

It is a quarter to ten when the procession sets out. The coffin is very heavy, for in addition to its own weight and that of the corpse, it has been filled with a number of Vietnamese bowls. Four sturdy men grasp the portage pole, lift their burden to their shoulders, and start off, walking in single file. Tôong follows, his pannier heavy with gifts for his father; then comes Jieng, who carries nothing. A host of relatives and friends brings up the rear. They carry additional gifts offered the dead man, which they have divided among themselves: a large Djiring jar, two *yang dâm* (one given by Bbaang-the-Stag), one shove net and one setnet, a ventral harvest pannier with seeds and tubers of various domesticated plants, a large harvest pannier containing a pot of soup and one of rice, a Mnong bowl and all the Vietnamese bowls that could not be fitted into the coffin, three bottles of *rnööm*, a gourd of soup and another of water, "the chicken that pecks up the maggots," and a broom. In a word, everything the dead man will need to live in the Beyond.

The cortege follows the track for some fifty meters and halts where a path turns off to the cemetery. The porters set their burden down. With his bush hook, Tôong draws a line in the ground at either end of the coffin. He pours a little rice soup on each tracing and says:

> "*I pour you soup;*
> *do not go about asking for rice,*
> *do not go about asking people for soup.*
> *Here is your rice soup.*"

In one of the tracings, he plants a forked twig he has picked up nearby. This is a signal to the sparrow-hawk-soul, which, although we cannot see it, at this very moment is flying in the vaulted sky high above us, and is observing everything we do. Thanks to the forked twig, the *kuulêel* will be able easily to locate the spot where food has been poured for it, and it will not go begging from others.

Jieng cuts off a lock of her hair and lays it down, together with some charcoal, at the entrance to the path. The hair will become lalang grass in the Beyond, and will be used to roof the house the dead man must build for himself there.

The bearers pick up their burden again. Now they advance with difficulty, for the path we are following is narrow and rarely used. It is obstructed by low branches, bamboo, and thorny lianas; also, it goes up and down over uneven terrain, and crosses numerous brooks. The porters must be spelled several times, because the coffin weighs so much: "The horns of the powerful are heavy to carry." Taang-Jieng-the-Stooped was a rich man—the form and the material of his casket attest to that—and his soul was a powerful buffalo with massive horns, and that is why his coffin weighs so much. Suddenly, the path runs into a clearing; at the far side,

Tôong-the-Cook detains the quartz-soul of his uncle by pouring rice soup over his head

OVERLEAF: *As the mourners leave the trail to follow the path leading to the cemetery, an offering of soup is applied to the ends of the coffin*

some lalang-grass shelters that have gone to rack and ruin, shards of jars, and dilapidated baskets indicate the presence of old graves. After a twenty-minute walk, we are nearing the cemetery.

Along the track, the women had intoned loud laments, but they had fallen silent when we turned into the cemetery path. As we approach the cemetery, they again launch into noisy crying. Jieng, however, weeps softly and sings her plaints in a faint voice. In the midst of this grief, the conduct of Aang-of-the-Mincing-Step is somewhat shocking. She is thoroughly drunk; along the way, she tripped over a liana and fell flat on her face in this high grass—she and the big jar she was carrying in a pannier on her back.

The men set to work at once. Some take turns digging the grave, while others prepare a small, two-sided thatch roof for the tomb. Tôong-Jieng and Tôong-Biing suddenly dart off, gesturing wildly; their panic is caused by a mere hornet. Thinking the danger has passed, Tôong-Biing stops; the hornet sees its chance and stings him, whereupon he howls with pain. Tôong-Jieng treats him by rubbing a dead leaf on the afflicted spot and, as he does so, he begs the sting to go away.

Work resumes. What they must do is dig a rectangular grave, with its main axis running east to west. As the work proceeds, talk also goes on apace. A cemetery is a favorite haunt for soul-eating sorcerers, which leads Tôong-Jieng to suggest they install a machine gun in the branches of a fine tree by the edge of the clearing. On one of his visits to Poste du Lac, he had been mightily impressed by the way this weapon works.

Digging is done in relays; while two men are working, the others stand around the grave and talk. The conversation turns to how stupid women are, and how stubborn. "All women are blockheads," the even-tempered Tôong-Biing declares. "This morning, mine never once stopped bawling me out for everything under the sun—pounding the rice, cooking. She never let up, not for a minute. . . . But once I did hit back with a vengeance. Every morning she was at me, every morning hauling me over the coals, and I never said a word. But one fine day, she was walking ahead of me on the way to the *miir,* and she was ranting on and on, until suddenly I let fly with my bush hook, and I split the openwork pannier she was carrying on her back." Laughter from the others. Choong-the-Soldier agrees. "All women are blockheads," he says, and goes on to tell us how he broke a length of heavy rattan on his wife's arms after she had a terrible fit of jealousy when they got back from Ndut Lieng Krak, where the Exchange of Buffalo Sacrifices had taken place between Baap Can and the former canton chief. Tôong-Jieng turns to me and asks whether we French have such family scenes. To avoid dwelling on the subject (or perhaps to leave them with some illusions, I'm not sure), I answer no. "That's pure bunkum!" Choong-the-Soldier cries. "French husbands and wives do so quarrel! And as for jealousy, they feel it quite intensely. Why, when I was a soldier, one day I saw two Frenchmen fighting over a woman. And they weren't privates, either; they were sergeants. One of them wanted to kill the other. He was running after him with a big dagger."

By eleven-twenty, the grave is dug. It measures two meters twenty in length and sixty-five centimeters in depth. The sides are very straight, the bottom flat and smooth.

Tôong-the-Cook makes a loose knot in a small blade of lalang grass. Holding it at either end, he straddles the grave at its foot. Bending forward, he tightens the knot as he moves backward, and by the time he reaches the head of the grave, the knot is firm. Tôong continues to pull on the grass until the fiber snaps. He throws it into the brush. With this gesture, he has gathered up the souls of the men who had dug the hole, for otherwise there was the risk of the souls' lingering there.

The coffin is brought over to the grave. Two lengths of rattan rope are slipped under the coffin. Two men station themselves on either side and grasp the ends of the ropes. The portage pole is carefully positioned lengthwise to rest on the head and foot of the hole. The ropes by which the coffin is affixed to the portage pole are severed with a hoe and bush hook. Then the four men holding the rattan ropes on which the coffin now rests, gently, with scarcely a jolt, lower the coffin into the grave.

Bbaang-the-Stag lays a piece of notched wood on the casket, near the horns and to the left of the head. This is "the ladder of the soul" (*ntuung hêeng*). While a few men fetch long logs to cover the opening, the dead man's hoe and bush hook are laid on the floor of the grave, together with the still live "chicken that pecks up the maggots." Care is taken to keep one end of "the rope to guide the sparrow-hawk-soul" (*rsei sieng ja' tlaang kuulêel*) free of the covering logs. The other end is attached loosely to the rope encircling the head of the coffin. This cord of heavy rattan must show the way to the sparrow-hawk-soul. The logs are covered with a thick carpet of freshly cut lalang grass. On this, three jars are set, the largest placed directly over the dead man's head. It is eleven-thirty. All the men gather around the grave and beg the dead man, now that he is buried, to remain peacefully in the Underworld. As they pray, they push back over the top of the grave the earth that had been heaped to one side when the hole was excavated; they make a sort of oblong mound, the top of which is flush with the mouths of the small jars. When the mound is finished, Tôong tugs on the guide rope; in a prayer, he indicates to the soul the path it must follow if ever it wishes to be reincarnated. Then he tosses the rattan cord into the bushes.

All the men pick up a few slender bamboo sticks. Returning to the grave, they pray as they plant them crisscross at regular intervals around the border of the grave. This is "the barrier of Srae," and it will protect the dead man and his tomb.

While the others place on the grave the various objects offered the deceased to assist him in establishing himself in the Beyond, Bbaang-the-Stag mutters a prayer, as he places on the head of the grave the first clod of earth to have been spaded when the hole was dug. It is called "the clod of earth of the sparrow hawk" (*uuk tlaang kuulêel*). Finally, the thatch roof is laid over two stakes, which are set at either end of the grave.

In one last gesture, each man slips his hand beneath this small shelter, and lays on the sloping side of the grave a few twigs he has broken into small pieces. He announces to the departed:

> *"Here is your firewood,*
> *do not then ask it of others. . . ."*

There is no lingering at the grave; we return immediately to the village. Because this is the first time Aang-of-the-Mincing-Step has set foot in the cemetery, her friend Tôong-Jieng has her step over the blade of his bush hook, its cutting edge turned up. Kröng-Aang, the dead man's brother, brings up the rear. As he leaves the clearing, he is careful to bar the path behind him with a broken branch he finds nearby, to protect us from any pursuing sorcerers.

We are back in the village by noon, and everyone goes directly to the river for a thorough purification. Each person not only washes his body but also dips his clothing and tools in the flowing water. So that the Spirits of the paths and forests will not invade the watering place, where they could attack children, the men plunge in downstream; the water here is too deep for the women, however, who bathe at the watering place. Before returning home, everyone passes by the bereaved house, but no one goes inside. Each person washes his feet, hands, and bush hook—or whatever tool he has taken into the forest—in hot water from a pot Mang-Tôong has set outside the private door. Thus purified, one may return to one's own hearth with no risk of contaminating one's family or of falling ill oneself. By now, it is time for the midday meal.

After everyone has eaten, at twelve forty-five, the second round in the series of sacrifices and libations offered the dead man begins. Last evening, pigs and hens were immolated "to anoint the coffin with blood" (*njat mhaam boong*). Now the sacrifice is for "the abandonment in the forest" (*njat löi laat mbrii*). Actually, it is a repetition of the earlier ceremony: essentially, the two phases have the same general denominator and follow the same ritual. Yesterday, Tôong-the-Cook and Brôong-the-Widow had each offered the dead man the sacrifice of a pig and a jar of beer. Today, Tôong sacrifices a chicken and the rice beer of one medium jar, while

Brôong brings only a small neckless jar of *rnööm*. An ally, Tôong-Jieng, and a friend, Tôong-Wan, offer the same. Lastly, Bbaang-the-Stag sacrifices a piglet and a medium jar of *rnööm* in honor of his brother-in-law. As yesterday, while the sacrificer kills the pig or chicken with a piece of wood or a club, his wife, sister, or daughter stands beside him, her hand on her head, and calls on the dead man, wailing her grief. He cuts off a wing and claw of the chicken—or the "nails" of the pig—and places them on the jar stopper, which is already covered with a handful of wort topped by a few bits of charcoal. The sacrificers go in a body to deposit their offerings at the entrance to the path leading to the cemetery. There, each squats behind the jar stopper he has brought and, gazing in the direction of the cemetery, he identifies himself by name, describes his offering, and beseeches the dead man:

> *"The Salt and the Paddy, leave them for us Here Below,*
> *the Buffaloes and the Jars, leave them for us Here Below;*
> *the Lawsuits and Debts, carry them with you there below,*
> *Fire and Water, carry them with you there below. . . ."*

They return in a group to the village. Each sacrificer goes to the jar he is offering, fills his mouth with beer, walks to the private door, and sprays it out. This libation will appear instantly in the Underworld in the guise of drink. As the new master of the house, Tôong-Mang repeats this rite with each jar his guests have brought to honor his dead father.

Then the drinking begins.

The atmosphere suddenly becomes relaxed. After two days and three nights of continual tears and lamentations, a great calm descends on the village. An irremediable event has indeed occurred, misfortune has engulfed a household, but none of this finds further external expression apart from the dress of the bereaved family. For some months to come, its members will be in mourning: no necklaces around the throat or bound around the head; no bracelets at the wrists; with chignons undone, they will allow their hair to fall in disorder down their backs. Today, their faces are puffy, their voices faint and hoarse from having so long rent the air with their grief. However, from now on there will be no more lamentations, no more piercing cries from weepers. It is the absence of noisy manifestations of sorrow that creates the sense of détente. To this one must certainly add the fact that finally we have emerged from the uninterrupted round of rites which followed on Taang-Jieng-the-Stooped's death. These rites were determined and dominated by fear of the dead man. The living had to protect not only their own souls but also the souls of their possessions against the peril of their being dragged into the Beyond by their attachment to the deceased—or by his own jealousy or avarice. For, they say, no man, however wretched, leaves the world of the living with-

Back from the cemetery, Can washes the blade of his wiah *in purifying hot water*

A final sacrifice is offered the dead man by his children

out a terrible wrench, and everything in this world that he can lay his hands on he tries to carry off with him.

Around the jars, conversation cannot settle on any one thing. The talk ranges from how chill the last nights have been to the fact that, thanks to the nurse's medications, Taang-the-Stooped's body showed no signs of decay. The tone of the conversation is neutral. People drink and smoke; Wan-Ngaa-the-Rabbit has even brought a dog's hide with him, out of which he is cutting a tobacco pouch Bbôong-the-Deputy has commissioned from him.

But all present are shaken out of their torpor by the offer of "the rice of the Spirits of the paths and the woods." The son and brother-in-law of Taang-the-Stooped take down from the back wall the jars that are to be shared between the dead man's clan and his wife's. This move acts as a signal for Aang-the-Widow and Mang-Tôong to utter piercing cries. Crockery and personal jewelry are also spread out.

On one side, Brôong-the-Widow, younger sister of the deceased, represents the Cil clan. On the other, Tôong-the-Cook, acting in behalf of his mother and sisters, represents the Daak Cat.

The ivory earlobe plugs had belonged to the dead husband of Aang, the eldest daughter, and therefore are left out of the accounting. The handsome necklace of large antique beads (*mae rbaal*) Taang-the-Stooped wore when he was a bachelor is given to his sister. Jieng retains a necklace given her before her marriage. As for the metal chokers the couple subsequently acquired, Brôong-the-Widow, who is no doubt very much pleased to have got the fine *mae rbaal*, declares that she will relinquish all the chokers to her brother's children. Aang observes, with some emphasis, that her aunt must not claim later on that the children had been unwilling to share. This strikes the first prickly note in the negotiations between the two clans.

Jieng-Taang has brought out six Vietnamese bowls, two pieces of iron, and two earthenware pots. She gives half of each group of objects to her sister-in-law and keeps half.

They proceed now to "the goods of value." All the jars belonging to the bereaved household are displayed. Tôong has divided them into two lots: on one side, those that belong by right to the children or to Wan-the-Widower; on the other side, those his parents acquired during their life together. Taking up the jars one by one, Tôong details the circumstances in which it was purchased and the price paid. "This large Djiring *taang sôh* I bought for sixty piasters I earned working on the Plantation. This one likewise, but I paid eighty piasters for it. This one here is the canton chief's 'pig's head.' For this antique jar I gave twenty-six hundred piasters, a pig of three spans, a blanket woven by my sister Aang, and one young pig. This 'hard' jar cost two hundred piasters and a pig of three spans. So much for my jars. As to these four, they belong to my uncle, Wan, and they come from the division of joint property made with the Jaa clan after his wife's death. These six here belong to my sister Aang. They represent her share in the division of goods made with the Rjee after her husband died."

Tôong then passes on to the jars purchased by his parents and owned by them jointly: an antique jar (*yang drang*) bought for a pig of three spans, a large new jar, and an old turban; a small old jar bought for only five piasters (but that was a long time ago); a large antique jar, repayment for the loan of twenty panniers of rice; a large medium-priced jar (*taang laa*) acquired for one pig and six panniers of rice; a medium-size jar that Ndür-Yoon gave against six panniers of rice he had borrowed from the deceased; lastly, one large *taang sôh*, equivalent in value to a dozen panniers of rice.

Next, the household debts are enumerated. In the category of "meat debts"—that is, gifts of meat received on the occasion of a buffalo sacrifice which must be returned in kind when the receiver in turn immolates a buffalo—the couple owes one breast to the headman of Sar Lang, who gave them a breast when he made his Exchange of Sacrifices with Krông-Jôong; one "shoulder" (actually, the entire front leg) is due Ddöi-the-Shaman; two sides, including the ribs, are owed Bbaang-Aang in return for gifts received at the last Great Festival of the Soil in Sar Lang. One further substantial debt is "the row of corn" borrowed from Ddöi-the-Shaman that, by agreement, was to be repaid in the form of a large new jar.

However, Taang and Jieng have credits as well as debts. Krông-Aang, the dead man's brother, owes them six panniers of rice, which he promised to repay with one medium jar; Chaar-Rieng owes twelve panniers of lalang grass, also to be repaid with a jar.

They move on to the consideration of livestock. Taang-Jieng's one remaining animal had been a pig, and it was sacrificed the day before yesterday. All the other pigs and the poultry belong to his son; ergo, no shares to be meted out in this category.

It is almost four o'clock when the weepers receive their portion of "meat of the Spirits of the paths and woods" (*poec Mâp nae nyiim*): for each, a strip one finger long and two fingers wide. This meat, taken from the sacrificed pigs, will enable each woman who has ritually wept for the dead man to cleanse herself of the taboo that contaminates her.

Almost immediately thereafter, the rites of "spitting on the foot" (*choh jöng*) commence. They are the most important of the funerary purification rites and are accompanied by quite substantial gifts either as payment for assistance given by the villagers these last few days or as reimbursement of animal and rice-beer sacrifices offered the dead man, or both. They begin with Brôong-the-Widow, whose common room is an extension of Taang-Jieng's. Such close proximity to a dead man makes for a high degree of vulnerability, and to banish it potent measures are called for. Tôong-the-Cook chews a few grains of rice and spits them out on the blade of a bush hook, which he passes over his aunt's left foot:

> *"Our homes are side by side,*
> *our granaries are back to back.*
> *May the tubes be filled,*
> *may the* caak *be blinded.*
> *It is to this end that I spit."*

Then he offers Brôong a pannier of rice, on top of which he has placed one shoulder of the sacrificed pig and a bush-hook blade—a symbol of strength. (I should point out that, for her part, Brôong has given her brother's wife and children the two hindquarters of the pig she sacrificed in his honor.) Now she takes a pinch of white rice, which she will chew and spit on the top of her two doors as an exorcism.

The same quantity of rice and one thigh are given to Bbaang-the-Stag. Bbôong-the-Deputy and Choong-the-Soldier, who carved the "feet" of the coffin, each receive a filet, as much rice as a small ventral pannier holds, and a bush-hook blade. Krŏng-Aang is presented with half a breast, one bush-hook blade, a small neckless jar, but no rice. (The small neckless jar is merely being restored to him; he had given it to Taang-the-Stooped as compensation for the sacrifice of one hen and one *rnŏŏm* the elder brother had offered in honor of Krŏng's first wife after her death.) The other half of the breast goes to Kraang-Drüm. The canton chief and Can receive similar shares: one ventral pannier filled with rice for both, plus half a thigh for the former and half a shoulder for the latter. A portion of meat is given to Mhoo-Laang, who had offered a jar of rice beer, and to each of the six other men who helped make and transport the coffin. Each is given also a pinch of uncooked rice, so that he may purify his doors. As each man receives his gift, he is blessed by Tôong's spitting hulled rice on his left foot.

The bereaved house is crowded. As always when there is a distribution of gifts, people flock to the scene, attracted by this sort of ceremony, during which material possessions change hands. First, there are the individuals who will actually receive something. This nucleus is enlarged by the families of the people on the receiving end; they are drawn not only by material interest but also by the more or less star role their representative will play. Also, a beneficiary's relatives want to see that he gets his due. None of this is ever expressed in so many words and is only vaguely present to people's minds, but the spectators' lively interest in such scenes speaks for itself.

When the distribution has been completed, Bbaang-the-Stag tells the dead man's family to search in their memories for earlier important celebrations during which possessions were "devoured." He himself enumerates three buffalo sacrifices the deceased had performed. Someone adds a fourth, which took place in Phii Srôony and which Bbaang had not attended. Krông-Aang recalls in detail every buffalo sacrifice his brother made. Jieng and her brother, Wan-the-Widower, and especially her son, Tôong-the-Cook, elaborate on each episode Krông has evoked. Another Daak Cat, Krae-Drüm, adds his two pins' worth to this re-creation of the past.

When the evocation of the dead man's prestige and sumptuous disbursements has been concluded, the jars comprising the inheritance are brought to the middle of the room. Several times, Bbaang-the-Stag reiterates that one must divide only possessions the couple acquired during their life together. Everything they owned before their marriage and everything that belongs by right to their children must be excluded. "The jars balance out the couple's 'transactions,' " he continues. "Old debts of meat that wife and husband, sisters and mothers have eaten will not be taken into account. Only recent debts of meat will be discussed. There is one corn debt, which equals the value of a large jar—"

Brôong-the-Widow breaks in quickly: "That debt is for the wife and children to settle."

"The lalang-grass credit," Bbaang-the-Stag continues imperturbably, "will pay off the corn debt."

"How so? One is worth only a medium jar, whereas the other is worth a large jar!"

"The family will assume the debt for the corn and for the shoulder of buffalo, too, and you"—addressing Brôong—"for the breast and ribs. They will be given credit for the lalang grass, and you for the value of the rice."

Brôong-the-Widow is furious. Her face is contorted, and she begins to shout. The distended lobes of her ears reach almost to her shoulders, and as she angrily tosses her head they bounce back and forth. . . . No! She will not hear of the corn debt's being made a part of the inheritance. No! She rejects indebtedness for the breast. They are trying to cheat her because she is a widow and has only a daughter to stand by her. But she is resolved not to be swindled.

With his habitual good sense and gift for conciliation, Can tries to explain to her that the corn was eaten by the same communal group that accumulated the jars. She would be agreeable to sharing the jars but not the debts?

"It is not correct," he says, in conclusion.

In a rage, Brôong shuts him up. "What are you interfering for? Mind your own business. You're only a Bboon Jraang."

Can is dumbfounded by this sudden attack, and his cousin Tôong-Jieng answers for him. "You forget that Can is married to a Daak Cat. So this does concern him."

But Brôong-the-Widow stalks off, muttering against all these men who are hard on a poor, miserable widow. Even the ever so discreet Bbaang-the-One-Eyed, although he has the interests of the Cil at heart (his sister, Aang, is married to Kröng, Brôong's brother), reproaches Brôong for her unjustifiable behavior.

Troo-Jôong, who has no personal interest in the transaction, tries to mend matters. He crosses the common room to propose to the belligerent widow that she accept the debt of the shoulder and leave the breast, ribs, and corn debts to Tôong-Mang. She will receive credit for the lalang grass, her nephew credit for the rice. However, if she prefers the rice credit, since her brother, Kröng, is the debtor, she need only relinquish the other to Tôong-Mang. The Daak Cat promptly protest.

In the end, Bbaang-the-Stag's terms carry the day: the Daak Cat assume responsibility for the reimbursement of the corn and shoulder, and Brôong will have to repay only the breast and the ribs. The Daak Cat will get the rice credit, which Kröng promises to settle in kind after the harvest, and Brôong will collect the lalang-grass credit.

The atmosphere eases. Jieng gives her sister-in-law two bush-hook blades and keeps one complete bush hook. Brôong advances the idea of dividing the house. Bbaang-the-Stag interrupts. He is against this. Can, who is still recovering from his consternation, insists that it will have to be divided; otherwise, later on, "sisters and mothers" will find it food for gossip. Jieng, meanwhile, continues partitioning the inheritance. She keeps the openworked pannier of freshly picked cotton and relinquishes to her sister-in-law the cotton still standing in the field. Tôong-the-Cook tells his aunt to take a few tufts from the top of the basket to seal her claim to the cotton still in the field. Before the argument broke out, Jieng had added a Vietnamese bowl taken from her own share to the three she had already given Brôong.

Lastly, "the goods of value" are divided thus: Brôong inherits the two large Djiring jars and the *taang laa,* which is worth two Djiring—or, in all, the equivalent value of four Djiring. Tôong-the-Cook's share adds up to two Djiring jars, one large and one medium-sized, plus an antique jar that, because the bottom is cracked, is worth only one Djiring jar. (Were it in good condition, it could be exchanged for a buffalo.)

Additionally, Brôong is promised a woven side-wall panel for her *miir* granary. And finally, the two households divide equally between them four pots, two water gourds, and four soup gourds.

These last steps have been taken amid general calm. All of a sudden, a good half hour after he has been rebuffed by Brôong, Can erupts furiously. The widow's outburst had left him speechless, had literally rooted him to the spot near the door where he remained squatting. Now, with the incident seemingly closed, here he is, bellowing with anger. But instead of taking it out on the person who vexed him, he directs his wrath against his friend Bbaang-the-Stag.

"It's true I am a Bboon Jraang, but this business does concern me because I married a Daak Cat, and I've the right to speak. Bbaang-the-Stag married a Cil, so he has the right to speak. Yet I, who am married to a Daak Cat, I am supposed not to have the same right! I sleep with a Daak Cat woman, just as he sleeps with a Cil woman."

Can is as red as a cock about to spring. Bbaang-the-Stag answers him, laughing: "Why are you taking it out on me? I've already been insulted once tonight. This makes it twice in one day. I'm not the person who chewed you out. Why pick on me?"

"It was a Cil woman who insulted me, and you're married to a Cil," Can retorts. "Husband and wife are one, they are the same. As the French say, they are *même*. [*Même* is one of the few French words Can has picked up from his contacts as a runner with whites or their subordinates.] And a Cil husband and wife have taken it out on a Daak Cat husband and wife.

"You're being smart because you are a *kuang*," he goes on. "But someday I'm going to be a powerful man, too. You're a *kuang* because you have performed the Exchange of Sacrifices with other men. But when I'm living apart from my father, I'll become a *kuang*, too, and I'll perform the *Tâm Bôh*, too. . . ."

Bbôong-the-Deputy is laughing as he intervenes: "He's letting loose a volley of insults and abuse because that's his way of leading up to an Exchange of Sacrifices!"

Hilarity on all sides. Even Can calms down.

It is growing late. After this spectacular outburst, people who have drunk enough or for whom the jar holds little appeal are going home. The little girls of the stricken long house go to Jieng's private door and, without saying a word, throw out handfuls of sand. They are driving off the Spirits and Divinities whom misfortune has drawn to this house and to whom children easily fall prey.

Troo-Jôong and Krae-Drüm, who arrived rather late, each receive a portion of meat. Outside, Aang-of-the-Drooping-Eyelid and Aang-the-Long are seen returning from the cotton field, where they have been working late. Mbieng remarks that tomorrow no one will be permitted to harvest. If one were to, the rice would lose its nourishment.

The rice beer in the jar is by now much diluted. Also, there is little enjoyment to be had in dragging out funeral rites that have already lasted several days. Since the inheritance has been divided, the guests see little point in remaining. All those foreign to the house go home. It is now seven in the evening. The room, so filled with noise a short while ago, shelters only a few weary people, bruised by grief and worn out by the exhausting succession of rites they have had to perform. Their appearance only intensifies the feeling of oppression—compounded of sorrow and dejection—that has invaded their house. Their hair flows in heavy, untidy waves over their shoulders and backs. Their heads, throats, and arms are bare of jewelry. Their faces are streaked with tears, their voices hoarse or cracked. However, not one wail, not one groan is to be heard, for after leaving the ceremony it is unseemly to weep or lament.

Tôong sets out a fresh jar of beer in the common room. Beside it, he places an empty *yang dâm* and an armful of *rhôong* leaves, on which he lays an axe blade. The entire family gathers around these objects for the rite known as "the fanning of the body" (*prah sak*). Tôong fetches a hen and slits its throat over the axe and leaves, allowing the blood to drip on them. He seizes the bloody axe head and touches it eight times to the foot of each member of the family, counting aloud and asking the dead man:

> "*Leave with us the Salt and the Paddy,*
> *the Tobacco and the Pepper,*
> *but take with you the Debts and the Lawsuits. . . ."*

When this series of anointings is completed, everyone crowds around the leaves. Tôong raises the small neckless jar and revolves it eight times above their clustered heads. He addresses the same request to the deceased. Setting the *yang dâm* down on the ground, he passes his finger over it, immediately places that finger over the heart of the person next to him, saying "One," then "Two," and so on up to eight, and again utters the same prayer. He repeats this rite for every member of the family. Then, grasping the armful of blood-stained leaves, he brushes them over the walls of the granary, the mound of rice stored there, and over all jars, baskets, shelves, etc. In conclusion, he fans the air above the members of his family, who have remained squatting in their tight circle. His maternal uncle, Wan-the-Widower, then gets up and performs for Tôong all the rites of purification he has carried out for the others: "wiping with the axe," "revolving the jar above the head," placing the pinch over the heart," and "fanning the body." Then he throws the leaves of exorcism to the rear of the house.

Lastly, everyone sips more *rnööm.*

On the same landing, as we might put it, Brôong-the-Widow performs a simpler rite. In her case, it is less a matter of purifying than of blessing—in a way, she is adopting the goods she has just inherited. She sacrifices a chicken together with a *yang dâm* of rice beer. She passes the victim's gaping wound over "the rice for spitting," then over every jar included in her bequest, then over her own jars. Her concern now is not for her dead brother, and accordingly, this is the prayer she recites:

> "*Soul of the Salt, Soul of the Paddy,*
> *Souls of the Buffaloes, Souls of the Jars,*
> *fear nothing, do not flee. . . ."*

Both ceremonies unfold in the strictest privacy in the adjoining households. No outsider, except for the ethnologist, is present. This evening, the village can once again go early to bed.

December 2 (*The Taboo of the Seventh Day after Interment*)

For the first time since Taang's death, the women have resumed pounding rice in the morning.

Jieng, her daughter Aang-the-Widow, her son Tôong-the-Cook, and Tôong's wife, Mang, have assembled in front of their door, ready to set out on "the visit to the cemetery" (*coop môoc*). Brôong-the-Widow and Bbaang-the-Stag arrive to join them. Wan-the-Widower would like to go also, but his sister tells him to remain behind. "You are feverish, so stay at home. There are enough of us."

She tells him this several times, but Wan is determined to go. He accompanies the group a few steps, but then turns back and goes home to lie down.

It is a quarter to nine when we set out. Bbaang-the-Stag says we are to watch out for big monkeys. For this ceremony, it is forbidden to take a pannier, so they are carrying the final offerings to the dead man in their hands: a piece of manioc tuber and pepper, eggplant, and tobacco seeds. These will be placed on the grave together with symbolic objects that also must be laid on it: a miniature coop containing bits of burned wood (in the Beyond, these will look like chickens); some *rchah* nuts (these will be Vietnamese bowls in the Underworld); and a miniature blanket of woven banana leaves; accompanying these are the pieces of charcoal that, as always, will serve the others as scouts and guides.

As we near the cemetery, Bbaang-the-Stag recommends that we examine the ground to see if there are any "tracks of sorcerers and Spirits." Actually, one looks only for *caak* tracks, because the Spirits leave none. On the other hand, the sorcerers, who come to feed on the corpse of the man they have killed, leave "tiny footprints, like a suckling's, no wider than two fingers." What's more, the *caak* completely demolish "the barrier of Srae"—the collection of tiny sticks the men plant around a grave just before they erect the roof over it. If one does find tracks, this means that the *caak* have shared in killing the man one comes to mourn for the last time. One has a chance to save him by bargaining with the *caak* for his head through the mediation of the shaman. But if one sees nothing, then it is the Spirits who have killed him—killed him the way we here below immolate a buffalo—and in these circumstances, there is nothing that can be done. At least this is the explanation Bbaang gives me. We find no tracks.

When Jieng is within a few meters of the grave, she breaks into sobs, and all the other women follow suit. Weeping and lamenting vociferously, they set their offerings and the charcoal on the grave.

Soon Brôong-the-Widow gives the signal to depart. She and Bbaang-the-Stag start off and have almost crossed the clearing, but Jieng and her children linger by the final dwelling of Taang-the-Stooped, which they will never again be permitted to approach.

Brôong yells back, "Are you coming? If you don't, they'll catch our souls!"

The others come on the run. As Tôong leaves the clearing, he has his wife straddle his bush hook, the blade turned up, for this is her first visit to the cemetery. On the way back to the village, he cuts off a *rchah* branch to exorcise Troo-Jôong's baby, who has not stopped crying since his father helped transport the coffin. Once back in the village, a purifying bath in the river is required for all.

When they get back home, they find a huge lemon lying on the low platform; it comes from the School garden. For the moment, it may not be eaten, because the seven days during which all fruits, eggplants, rattan hearts, and the vegetable *pae sei* are forbidden have not yet passed. The taboo will not be lifted until tomorrow.

There is one final sacrifice of a hen. As in the earlier instances, the animal is slaughtered with a club a few steps from the private door. One wing and one claw are broken off and placed on the jar stopper, which is carried out to the cemetery path. But this sacrifice differs in important details: no one stands shouting lamentations by the side of the sacrificer; Tôong is alone and he weeps, but he assumes no ritual stance. Also, the jar is opened without an initial mouthful of *rnööm* being sucked up and spat out by the door. People drink from the jar but do not offer the first sips to the dead man. Now the ritual drinking is no longer an offering to the dead but rather a purification of the living, a token of their emerging from the suffocating round of funeral rites. "It is essential for the rest of us who are living to anoint our bodies with blood," Bbaang-the-Stag tells me.

It is a melancholy scene: people drink without relish, and many fewer are present. For that matter, there is almost no one in the village. Normally, the only people who may harvest today are those who took the precaution of sleeping in the forest last night. By so doing, they escape the grave taboo of the seventh day which rests upon the village. In fact, only Bbaang-the-Pregnant-Man, the holy man of the Fire Sticks, and his son-in-law, Kraang-Drüm, took this precaution. Truu spent the night in the village, but the canton chief has ignored the taboo and led the team of his niece, Aang-of-the-Drooping-Eyelid, out to his field. Most people, however, on this day when work with rice is forbidden, have gone to pick their cotton or dig tubers.

The jar is abandoned after two hours. Thus, amid general indifference, passes this seventh day, the last during which Taang-the-Stooped will mark the life of the community with his "presence." He has been buried according to the rules, he has been honored with numerous sacrifices, as befits a *kuang*, a man whose buffalo-soul wears heavy horns. Everything has been done to ensure that he will not return to disturb the repose of the living: he has been showered with gifts and sacrifices that will help him live suitably in the Underworld. In making each offering, people have taken care to point out to him the esteem in which he is held and the generosity that is being shown him. (Here modesty would have been out of place.) The presentation of gifts was seized as an opportunity to beg him to be reasonable, and not to return to challenge the living for the things of this world. For that matter, substantial precautions have been taken against any eventual return on his part.

And lastly, today one has "visited the cemetery" and paid a final visit to his tomb, which now is abandoned forever. Taang-Jieng-the-Stooped has henceforth ceased to exist as any entity whatsoever in the economic, social, or religious life of the village. He has rejoined the cohorts of the ancestors of his house where, as with all Gar families, male forebears play only a meager role until such time as they are reincarnated in a newborn child. Only then, when this new life begins for them, will they regain a place in the bosom of society.

· 🌵 · 🌵 · 🌵 · 🌵 · 🌵 · 🌵 · 🌵 ·

10
The Year of the Stone Spirit Gôo Ends.
We Shall Next Eat the Forest of Phii Ko'

December 3, 1949

SINCE "knotting the Paddy" (*muat Baa*), a rite which each household celebrates individually, the entire village has been working furiously to bring
in the harvest. The weather has proved favorable, for the most part. Except for a short stretch, from November 18 to 21, when intermittent rain
kept the teams inactive for one entire day, one morning, and one afternoon, the workers have enjoyed fine, sunny days. The only interruption
in this period of dogged labor was the death and funeral of Taang-Jieng-
the-Stooped, and the third and seventh anniversary days of the sacrifices
his passing had entailed. Some people took advantage of these ritually
obligatory abstentions from working with rice to pick their cotton or thin
their tobacco. Others went foraging for firewood or gathered wild vegetables. Time diverted from the rice harvest was held to a minimum, however, and some people even violated the taboo.

Villagers who got their grain in first have not been idle since, for they
immediately offered their services to neighbors.* Although the work force
concentrates on ever fewer fields, the work rhythm does not abate in the
slightest and, just as when the season opened, all day long Sar Luk is a
deserted village.

When all the grain has been gathered and deposited in the *rdae*—temporary granaries built by the border of the *miir*—the pace perceptibly
quickens, for now it must be transported from provisional storage to the
granaries in the village. This morning at dawn, seven families were

---

* See G. Condominas, "L'Entr'aide agricole chez les Mnong Gar (Proto-Indochinois du
Viêt-Nam central)," *Etudes Rurales,* Nos. 53–56 (1974), pp. 407–20.

engaged in the final transfer of their paddy. Baap Can's people set to work early enough for his team to complete two trips before the first meal of the day. At no other time do you see such activity along the path to the *miir*. The *rdae* are built at the entrance to the fields, and you pass between two rows of them before entering the enclosure. Traffic back and forth between *miir* and village is incessant. Of six teams, comprising forty-one people in all, at least one team is always in the process of loading. The master or mistress of the house stands in the *rdae* and fills each porter's pannier (sometimes a child helps out). The grain is tamped down by foot so as to fill each basket to the maximum. Only when all have been filled does the team return to the village, single-file as usual. Some men carry two panniers, one laid on top of the other. Back in the village, each bearer sets his burden down at the foot of the owner's granary. It is the master of the house who climbs up to empty the panniers.

The *miir*, meanwhile, is not deserted, for quite a few people are still harvesting. Mhoo-Laang had elected to have the bulk of his crop brought in yesterday; he engaged five people for the job, paying each one large pannier of paddy. He had a hundred and forty-two panniers of grain from his own field to be transported, plus thirty-five grown in the half field he had inherited from his mother, Jôong-Wan, now deceased. This morning, he had still to reap (with a sickle) and tread an area of glutinous rice and to harvest by hand a small area of ordinary rice, so he asked two people to come help him. By eleven-fifteen, only a few square feet of "real" rice are left, and Mhoo-Laang lets his co-workers return to the village. Still wearing his *khiu*—his ventral pannier—around his waist, he hand-harvests the last stalks in his field. He prays as he works, asking the soul of the Paddy to return to the village, to fear nothing, and not to flee; doing this, he "gathers up the soul of the Paddy" (*dôop hêeng Baa*). In point of fact, this is not the last of his standing grain. He has not yet touched the sacred square—the first area he sowed, at the base of his ritual Paddy post. Generally, people harvest this "to gather up the soul," but Mhoo-Laang prefers to reserve it for "the taking of the Straw" (*sok Rhei*), the rite which is performed the evening before the big sacrifice. Mhoo-Laang leaves his field and walks to the *rdae* he inherited also from his mother. The temporary granary has not only been emptied of paddy but also the woven mats serving as floor and side walls have been removed. Only the frame and the bamboos that supported the floor remain. Mhoo sets down his *khiu* and kneels; fanning the air under the skeletal flooring, he pours the air into his ventral pannier and asks the soul of the Paddy to follow him to the village, and not to shy away. Then he proceeds to his own *rdae*. Here only the woven walls have been removed. Mhoo-Laang climbs up to sweep the grain still lying on the floor into a half-filled pannier that had been left behind. He squats down and, reciting the same prayers, collects

In the temporary granary, panniers are filled with rice . . .

. . . and carried back to the village by a team of men and women

Mhoo-Laang harvests the last rice stalks in his field

the last small heap of grain in his *khiu*. Eight times he gathers up the air above the spot where this grain had lain, and pours it into his *khiu*. Then he imprisons the soul of the Paddy by stuffing into his first ventral pannier a smaller one left in the *rdae* for this specific purpose. He rolls up the woven floor matting, which a helper, walking behind Mhoo, will carry back to the village. Lastly, Mhoo attaches his two *khiu* crosswise on top of his large pannier and leaves the *miir*. Back home, he will complete the rite of "gathering up the soul of the Paddy" (*dôop hêeng Baa*), which is crowned by the sacrifice of a hen and a jar of rice beer.

It has been a particularly tiring day for the village, but little by little people relax. This evening, five households will drink to their *dôop Baa*. They are by no means the first to do so. Choong-the-Soldier performed the rite on November 22, but because only he was ready, he had to drink his jar all by himself, for no other villager had the right yet to sip from the straw. In effect, the *dôop Baa* lifts the taboos that prevail during the harvest season, and prominent among them is one that forbids drinking from the jar. The number of authorized drinkers increases as the rice crops are progressively harvested and stored, and by now other households have also performed their *dôop hêeng Bala* and thus freed themselves of the taboo. The opening of five jars this evening creates a festive atmosphere the village has not known since ritual Paddy posts were anointed and sacrifices were offered to the bodies of Truu and Bbôong-Mang a month ago.*

December 4

If the work rhythm was brisk yesterday, today it is almost frenetic. The hope is that the entire crop may be in by this evening, so that tomorrow rites may be performed to close the harvest—which for Sar Luk means, of course, to celebrate the end of the year. Of nine households which have not yet brought in all their grain, four have rice still standing. Even the poorest among them resort to outside aid. This morning, Kroong-the-One-Eyed came from Sar Lang to help his sister, Aang-Kröng, transport her crop. This afternoon, he helps his brother, Bbaang-the-One-Eyed, with his harvest. Villagers who have already brought back the soul of the Paddy hire themselves out to work for richer folk, like Kröng-Jôong or Bbaang-Jieng-the-Pregnant-Man. Truu absorbs the larger part of the available labor force. Twenty-seven people have gone to work in his field, so that, counting himself, his wife, and his adopted daughter, thirty individ-

---

* These rites were performed to purify the two men after their stay in the Poste du Lac prison. —*Trans.*

uals are laboring in one *miir* plot. It is this large cohort which accounts for the impression of frantic pace that marks the day.

Truu led his team out to the fields early this morning. The grain still covers a wide expanse, but, of course, the more numerous the workers, the faster the job is done, and by noon his field is entirely harvested. Ngee, the canton chief's wife, and Jaang Bibuu serve the workers their midday meal. At twelve-thirty, the twenty-eight panniers of paddy gathered in the course of the morning are carried to the village together with two others filled at the *rdae*. Eight are emptied into a wicker silo, where they will be kept for the next sowing. The others are carried to Truu's granary. At two o'clock, after the third trip, Truu doles out the day's wages: twenty-one panniers of paddy, which people immediately take home to empty into their own granaries.* Bbaang-the-Stag and his wife have not accepted any pay. During the rice shortage, they borrowed from the canton chief, and have reimbursed him for a portion of that loan by their labor today. Also the deputy and his wife and the two Rjee of the adjoining household have refused any payment. They allege their family bond as the reason, but it is likely that they, too, are settling a debt. Truu pays for a full day's work, although the job is not finished. If one were to wait for the last trip, one would risk running short of paddy to make these payments, and it is forbidden to climb up to one's granary today and remove grain that is to be given to another.

Kraang-the-Dogtooth has finished his team stint, and joins the crew of his foster father. Of thirty-one panniers carried in, Truu has eleven poured into the collective granary, an institution that has been re-established by the Commissioner. The canton chief is hereby paying off a debt to the community. (He realized I had been told a while ago that the buffalo immolated for "the sacrifice to his body" was paid for by his selling grain the community had placed in reserve. So he came to assure me that he had merely "borrowed" this rice and would be replacing it when his crop was brought in.) With maximum fanfare, the canton chief oversees the storage of the restored paddy, and is at the height of his eloquence in extolling his great honesty in doing so.

On the last trip from the *miir*, his remaining paddy fills only fourteen panniers. Truu does not return to the village with his team, but leaves his *rdae* to go back alone to his field with two *khiu*. Now he harvests the sacred square he sowed at the base of the ritual *dôong* bamboo on the day the *gun Baa* was planted. He reaps everything but the stalks tied to the sacred post during the ceremony that opened the harvest. Then he

---

* One pannier pays a couple for a day's work. A few single workers had already put in a day's labor for the canton chief yesterday.

squats, gathers up the air above the stubble, and pours it into his ventral pannier:

> *"Paddy of the marshlands, Paddy 'light,'*
> *Paddy jraang, Paddy 'mother,'*
> *return, all of you, to the village there below.*
> *Lest the roedeer eat you, return;*
> *lest the wild boar eat you, return;*
> *lest the monkey, the parrot eat you, return.*
> *Fear nothing,*
> *do not flee. . . ."*

He takes the second, smaller *khiu* and slips it into the first to imprison the Paddy:

> *". . . I place in the ventral pannier,*
> *I wedge in the ventral pannier,*
> *I place in the granary,*
> *I place in the house.*
> *Do not flee upstream,*
> *do not run off and get lost,*
> *do not sleep in foreign villages. . . ."*

Still praying, he ties knots in several stripped rice stalks and returns to his *rdae*. There, he opens the ventral pannier containing the holy grain. Eight times he gathers up the air beneath his temporary granary and pours it into the *khiu*, which he closes as before. He secures his holy burden sideways on the large pannier that holds the last paddy remaining in the *rdae*. Back in the village, he hoists all of this into his granary, and pours the contents of the pannier over his immense mound of rice. Praying, he does the same with the grain from the holy square, which he has brought back in his *khiu*. His wife sets one Mnong bowl of salt and a gourd of rice soup by the door of the granary. Truu pours a little soup over his heap of stored rice, and lays gourd and bowl on the top of it. The ventral pannier is left there, too. Then he climbs down for the last remaining panniers of grain and empties them in his granary.

Sar Luk's entire harvest is in, except that Bbaang-the-One-Eyed has been unable to finish transporting his paddy today. In all households—except his—the harvest taboo has been lifted by the *dôop hêeng Baa* ceremony. So, this evening a large crowd has gathered in the three houses where people will celebrate the crowning event of "gathering up the soul of the Paddy." This is the *mpan Baa* ("wreathing the head of the Paddy"). The master of the house climbs up into his granary and slits the throat of a chicken over his pile of rice—his entire crop of the year, apart from his seed reserve. Like Truu, on returning from his field he had poured rice soup on it and set down on it the soup gourd and bowl of salt. Now he lets the blood of the fowl flow freely over his stored paddy, the future food and drink for his whole household. He climbs down to consecrate a jar of rice beer at the foot of the granary ladder. Now he can rest, free of anxiety, for all his grain has been brought in; and he can drink and enjoy himself, since, for him, all the taboos that weigh on harvesters have been lifted.

As of this evening, a period of leisure begins for the village. No more grain need be harvested and transported, since Bbaang-the-One-Eyed has recruited none of his neighbors to help him. People are going to drink at the houses of the three *kuang,* who will be gathering up the soul of the Paddy, and no one will have to give a thought to going early to bed. Truu has brought out his set of flat gongs, and Wan-Jôong his set of bossed gongs. It is no exaggeration to say that as of tonight the biggest party of the year begins.

For all that, Kröng-Jôong is lamenting the damage wild animals have caused to his rice. Last night, some boar ravaged his field, a considerable part of which he had not yet been able to harvest. This morning, after transporting grain already stored in his *rdae,* his team had amassed in all only five panniers of paddy. Drink and conversation soon make Kröng forget his troubles—and for that matter, his granary is one of the fullest in the whole village.

In Truu's house, people are drinking steadily, and I take refuge at Wan-Jôong's. (He belongs to the Mok clan, and is married to Sar Luk's third healer.) Last evening, Wan had started to sing some "gong sayings" for me, and I am hoping to take further advantage of his good mood. Tonight he is even more favorably disposed, because he has opened a jar in honor of the Paddy and people are flocking to his house. But, quite late, Truu erupts on the scene, followed by his deputy, Bbôong-Mang, and one of his runners, Bbaang-the-Stag. From Truu's smart military salute to me, it is clear that he is drunk. Our host interrupts his recital and, modest man that he is, offers the drinking straw to the canton chief, who sets himself down before the jar. From then on, no one but Truu is to be heard. He asks Wan-Jôong to sell him some tobacco. He will pay three piasters for a packet of dried leaves, as he paid his long-house neighbor, Troo-Jôong. Wan replies that, unhappily, he has no more. "Too bad" is the retort, whereupon Truu undertakes to tell me the life story of our host. According to him, Wan-Jôong was very poor when he arrived in Sar Luk. He came from Düng Jrii, where, although he was village headman, he did not even have enough food to eat.

"Just think, Yoo, down there he was *khoa bboon,* but he was able to sacrifice only one buffalo during a Festival of the Soil." And Truu points to the pair of horns fastened to the edge of the granary.

Jôong-Wan catches him up: "Not for the *Nyiit Döng*. For the Blood Anointment of the Paddy," she says.

And Truu repeats after her, "For the Blood Anointment of the Paddy."

In a lower voice, she corrects him further: "The horns from the *Nyiit Döng* are hung above the door."

This Truu does not hear, and he goes on: "Every year a famine, nothing to eat, no rice. Then Wan comes here to live, near me. He brings in some fine harvests, he's got rice—every year. He eats as much as he wants, and he can even buy jars. He becomes a *kuang*."

Then he drops the subject of Wan-Jôong to speak of his own village. "Once upon a time, Sar Luk was a tiny village—it had just one house. Today it has become a big village. I advise all the coolies. 'Don't stay out in the fields to sleep,' I tell them. 'Work! You've got to clear a field and burn the brush and hoe and harvest. . . .' In the whole village there are only three people who don't produce—Yôong-the-Mad and Wan-the-Rabbit [he forgets the third]. . . . Next year, people who don't do a stroke of work I'm going to throw in jail."

When he tells me confidentially that he is a bit tipsy, I tell him it is because he has been drinking *alak* (Vietnamese rice aquavit, which Europeans call "choom-choom"). He protests vehemently. A thousand times over he has heard me warn how harmful this adulterated alcohol is, added to the fact that the Montagnards are not accustomed to it.

"I've been drinking only from my jar," Truu says. "But the beer is terribly strong and acid."

I make a skeptical face, so he sends Bbieng, the son of Bbaang-the-Pregnant-Man, to siphon off a bottle. I take a swallow; the *rnööm* is not excessively strong. I pass the bottle to Jôong-Wan, who takes a mouthful and makes a dreadful face. Her husband drinks next, and does the same. He returns the bottle to his wife, and she sips from it absently, quite forgetting to grimace.

At my request, Wan returns to the story of Jieng-Laang, the wife of the middle of the sky. Instant, attentive silence on all sides . . . until Truu falls into a discussion with his neighbors, but without losing the thread of Wan's tale. When Wan comes to the part where the hero is afraid to go up into the sky with the Female Spirits, Truu cuts him short: "Why doesn't he take a plane?" But he allows Wan to pursue his story, and when he has almost finished, Truu says to him, "The man's name [Wan was pretending that the name of the hero is unknown] is Ddöi-Naang. Naang is the woman-boar. And as for the tale of Jieng-Laang, that's the story of Nduu Buat, the son of Dlaang."

Whereupon he picks up the recital of this story in dazzling style. As always when Truu is drunk, he becomes an incomparable storyteller, and

now he breathes extraordinary life into the legend, making it come alive
for everyone. He also scatters allusions to current events through his account. This leads him to digress now, and to speak of the first Frenchmen
to explore the country:

"One of them used to have himself carried around in a sort of rope mat.
It was suspended on a long, transverse pole men carried on their shoulders. Can you imagine! He would have himself carried like that, on men's
shoulders, as far as Yön Dlei. He had four sons. And one of them was
handsome—ah, was he handsome! Back in those days, people called
Frenchmen *Pötoo* and Vietnamese *Tei*.* When a Frenchman appeared in
a village, people used to say to their children, 'Watch out! The King is
going to shoot at you!'—and all the children would run off. People were
very much afraid of Frenchmen. Our grandparents were idiots. If a fellow
owned three *yang dâm*, an iron bar, and a couple of panniers of paddy,
that was enough to make him a *kuang*. The Vietnamese used to strike a
hard bargain when they sold us a red vest. And when a Frenchman came
to a village, people would hurry to put things in order to make a clean
place for him."

The conversation shifts to other matters, and presently dies. It is late.
And when people have taken their fill of *rnööm*, they go home.

December 5

For several days, an extremely strong wind has been blowing from the
east. It is "the upstream wind," which is normal at this time of year.

As always on the eve of an important festival, men have spent the
morning cutting back the brush in the immediate vicinity of the village.
Afterward, Bbaang-the-Tin took it into his head to have Maang-the-Thin
cut his hair. A veritable epidemic of hairdressing broke out, infecting not
only all the young men but also the village headman and the canton chief.
A minor incident occurred in the course of the coiffure session: three letters arrived from Bbaang-the-Schoolboy in Ban Me Thuot, which briefly
re-established me in my role as public reader. Bbaang (he belongs to the
Bboon Jraang clan) was writing—in Gar—to settle a squabble between his
lover, Aang-the-Widow (daughter of the late Taang-the-Stooped), and his
"sister," Aang-of-the-Drooping-Eyelid, who had not behaved too well in
the affair. In his third letter—in Rhade—the student requested his
"brother" Can to send him some tobacco.

All in all, a day of great relaxation for Sar Luk. Only Bbaang-the-One-
Eyed, late in bringing in his paddy, had to work. Everyone else is getting

---

* *Pötoo* is the deformation of a Cham word meaning "king." *Tei* is the word by which Vietnamese denote Frenchmen, and the Gar of Upper Donnaï use it currently in the same sense.

Dressed with care, some men set out for the fields to perform "the taking of the Straw"

ready for the great festival of the year, and the one that marks its end: "the Blood Anointment of the Paddy" (*Mhaam Baa*). The festival actually commences this evening with a preparatory ceremony, "the taking of the Straw" (*ṣok Rhei*). Before one can bless the Paddy, one must first seek for it, and the importance, the preciousness, of such a Being requires one to set about the search with both care and style. "The taking of the Straw" is like a more impressive performance of "the gathering up of the soul of the Paddy," which, as we have seen, is reserved for the square of land that contains the sacred rice stalks and is the last to be harvested. Accordingly, as the first celebrants strike out along the path to the *miir* around five o'clock in the afternoon, one can only admire the pains people have gone to to deck themselves out suitably. Every man wears a *khiu* and a handsome blanket. Truu has donned a spotlessly clean blue shirt and a Basque beret. Ndür-the-Lame sports a spanking new undershirt. And Can! This is the first year Can has cultivated his own separate field, and he is eager to convoy the soul of the Paddy in properly splendid attire. He has put on a white vest, wrapped his head in a large black satin turban, and girded his father's saber around his waist. He has, furthermore, appointed his "brother," Maang-the-Thin,* who is dressed in a khaki shirt, over which he has slipped an undershirt, and an Army kepi, to carry the *khiu* and blanket Can will require for the rite.

When Truu reaches his field, he first tears off some leaves or stalks of pepper, tobacco, gourd, and beans. Then he walks to the sacred post of his crops and pulls up a foot of magic plant of the Paddy as well as the small sacred sickle which, when the harvest opened, he had stuck in the stalks wound about the ritual post. He pulls the post up. He detaches from the little "Paddy hut" the minute bamboo tube in which *rnööm* and bits of chicken had been stuffed during the rite of the Paddy posts. With his bush hook, he chamfers the tube opening on two sides to fashion a sort of whistle. Then he pulls up the *dôong dlei* planted when the field was sowed and the stake that has supported it, and he throws both away. He then hand-harvests the last stalks from "the knotting of the Paddy" and gathers up the grain, which he puts in his *khiu*, asking the while that the soul not flee but follow him to his house in the village. He then uproots a stalk of straw, which he adds to the various plants he had collected on arriving.

Lastly, he places the little whistle against his lower lip and, taking a long breath, blows into it once, twice. . . . At the eighth whistle, he stands up. The *khiu* containing the post paddy and the sacred sickle he attaches to his shoulder by its strap, and wraps it in his blanket, which he

---

* Maang-the-Thin has been living with his "brother" (first cousin), Can, since the death of his mother, Mae-Kroong, last October.

knots over his chest, as if he were carrying an infant. He collects all the
leaves and stems, including the straw, that he has pulled up, binds them
in one sheaf, and, lastly, shoulders the Paddy post and his bush hook. He
whistles at length into the erstwhile offering tube and, as he leaves, he
calls:

> *"Paddy straw,*
> *early Rice,*
> *behave well and be strong.*
> *I bring you back from the fallow land, from the lost field,*
> *I bring you back from the rushes and the reeds,*
> *I bring you back from the perch of the swallows, from*
> *   the perch of the birds;*
> *I bring you back from the fallow land and from the lost field,*
> *I bring you back from the cord of the fluttering scarecrow,*
> *I bring you back from the cord of the sounding scarecrow.*
> *Return to the village and there remain.*
> *I pull you up as did Sieng Nôor,*
> *I lift you up as did Sieng Nung,*
> *I bear you on my shoulder from the heights of the tall grove,*
> *O Spirit of the Paddy.*
> *Paddy coming from the Sky, I order you to take root;*
> *Paddy coming from the Earth, I order you to spring up from the soil;*
> *the pig at his trough, I order you to fatten him;*
> *Paddy in your granary, I order you to be firm for eating;*
> *Porcupine Tôong, I order you to see that I find wild beasts;*
> *my belly sated, I order you to see that I obtain goods of value.*
> *Paddy coming from the Rhade,*
> *Rice coming from the Rlâm,*
> *Animals, Jars, coming from the Kudduu,*
> *hasten hither. . . ."*

As Truu walks, now and then he blows on the whistle and repeats several of these verses. Every time he comes to a pool of water, which he
wades through or walks over on a log, he cuts a length of bamboo or of the
tieng kau rush—whichever comes first to hand—and places it on the
water to serve the soul of the Paddy as a bridge. At the same time, he
blows on his whistle and calls,

> *"Paddy straw,*
> *   early Rice . . ."*

All along his way, he whistles and begs the Paddy to return to the
village. At one point, he pulls up a *krae* root (*Memecylon scutellatum*),
which he adds to his sheaf, but he can find no "white horn." At last, he
reaches the village and his own house. Before entering by the main door,
he again whistles eight times into his tube and summons the Paddy.

Truu summons "the soul of the Paddy" that he will be transporting to the village

He whistles for it once again before leaving his field

Crossing a patch of water, he holds a stalk of the tieng kau *reed that will serve as bridge for "the soul of the Paddy"*

Inside, Truu goes directly to his granary. Before climbing up, he aligns his Paddy post with the ladder and attaches his sheaf of cultivated plants and sacred grasses to one of its rungs. He clambers to the top of his enormous pile of grain, unslings his blanket and ventral pannier, and pours the contents over the pile. He launches into a long invocation. He asks the soul of the Paddy to remain in the village and in his granary, "to fear nothing, not to flee." He enumerates all the beings, actions, and situations that could frighten it away—foraging of chickens and pigs, men's need of food for themselves and their livestock, the noise of pestles and of drinking bouts, and so on—and as an excuse for each, he adduces the example given by the Ancestors. He concludes by blowing eight times on the former tube for offerings, and plants this whistle at the top of the rice pile, the mouthpiece turned upward. Careful to avoid the whistle opening, he pours rice soup over the paddy and sets down the soup gourd and bowl of salt, imploring the soul of the Paddy to remain in his house.

Meanwhile, Kraang-the-Dogtooth has attached a jar of *rnööm* to the foot of the ladder. When Truu climbs down, he goes to fetch a leaf of the ritual *sraa* palm, pulling it from the floor of the granary, into which it had been stuck; this leaf he ties to the sheaf of grasses affixed to the rung of the ladder.

Truu smokes his pipe, leaving to his adopted son the task of filling the jar. Once it is full, he goes to the door of his house and whistles eight times. After the eighth whistle, he recites a long invocation, asking the soul of the Paddy not to run away. Then he climbs back up to the granary and on the top of his pile of grain he pours a little beer that has been siphoned from the jar into a long-nosed gourd:

> *"Eat this rice soup taken from the head of the stone,*
> *eat this cooked rice taken from the top of the pot,*
> *drink this tasty beer, taken from the top of the jar."*

And now Truu drinks. I take advantage of there being only a few people with us to persuade Truu to tell me the story of Nduu Buat, the son of Dlaang, and of his love affairs with the daughters of the middle of the sky. But Truu's sworn friend, Bbaang-the-Pregnant-Man, turns up, and Truu is only too happy to change the subject. He would rather talk about the people from Daa' Mroong who came to invite me to their Blood Anointment of the Paddy (which I cannot attend), but especially about his brother, Baap Can. With a satisfaction he finds hard to conceal, he confides that Baap Can is loaded with debts: he owes six buffaloes in all (Truu is able to name only four creditors owed one buffalo each), whereas he, Truu, owes nothing to any man.

We have a full moon this evening, so the time is right for the great sacrifice. A waning moon is not indicated for fear that the rice would likewise shrink and disappear. By eleven o'clock, Bbôong-the-Deputy is already busy grinding white paste, which will be his ritual paint. This may not be done out of doors, so a mortar has been set on the ground near the private-door post. In the mortar Bbôong places fermented rice flour —the same ingredient used to prepare *rnööm*—and a bit of magic plant of the Paddy and some sacred grasses (*krae*, "white horn," and "quail bone"). Adding rice beer occasionally, he grinds this mixture for a long time, until it becomes a very soft white paste. Then, without benefit of prayer, he slits the throat of a chicken and lets the blood drip over the concoction. With his pestle, he blends it a second time. The addition of the blood does not noticeably change the color of the paint.

It is growing late, and the whole village finally goes to sleep.

December 6

At four this morning, Baap Can's whistle awakens me. I hurry over to his house. Perched on the mound of rice in his granary, the old man is praying. Down below, old Krah holds a Mnong bowl (an imported porcelain bowl would not do, for the rice would slip) containing the ritual paint, and has already begun to decorate by hand the enormous upright that supports the granary floor. He paints simple geometric motifs—an unbroken series of large Greek key patterns; he spreads white paint over all the granary posts, large and small, and daubs some on every utensil in the house.

Baap Can whistles eight times, climbs down, and stands on the beaten earth floor of his house. Replying to a question of mine, the old man gives me the exact formula for his paste—similar to what I saw Bbôong-the-Deputy prepare—and explains that *rnööm* is substituted for medicine water (magic water, we might say) taken from the whirlpool in the rapids. It will "fix" the rice; that is, the rice will always return, just as the water in the whirlpool revolves continually and never flows away. Very hardy plants are chosen, he adds, so that the rice may grow in their image and be resistant. But Kröng interrupts:

"All these explanations are beside the point. We act in the way of our ancestors, who taught us."

Kröng has painted the upright supporting his own granary. He has drawn a line of Greek key patterns, and embellished the empty areas inside with crosses of various shapes and with dots. Also, he has painted the rungs of his ladder, the posts, stakes, and woven granary walls, and all household utensils—jars, panniers, pots. Lighting his way with a pitch faggot, he climbs up into his granary. From the top of his heap of rice, he takes the small sacred tube and whistles through it as he stands by the entrance to his storage space, mindful not to step outside. He launches into the long prayer that will be offered again and again during these days: may the Paddy now remain in the village, in the granary; may it not rove about in foreign parts; may the noises of daily life and the actions of men and animals not frighten it; may it remain among us; it will be given food and drink; may it fear nothing and may it not run away. Kröng clambers back to the top of his rice pile, where he whistles twice on his little tube and repeats several verses of the prayer. Then he climbs down from his granary and from the back wall of the house removes a large jar of beer, which he fastens to one of the front granary posts. He daubs some sacred paint on the throat of each member of his household, not forgetting himself, and asks the while:

> *"May one not choke while eating soup and cooked rice."*

The establishments of the two brothers-in-law have now been completely readied for the great Blood Anointment of the Paddy, which closes the year in which we have eaten the forest of the Stone Spirit Gôo. The two holy men are clearly well ahead of other villagers. Baap Can goes to summon Bbaang-the-Pregnant-Man. He comes back to announce that Bbaang is arriving. We wait. . . . No one comes. Again Baap Can goes out and calls him. A second wait. Baap Can is displeased. He inveighs against the master of the *Rnut*, who twice inconveniences him and still does not appear, although here everything is ready. He deflects his anger and picks on Bbaang-the-One-Eyed and Krae-Drüm: they took no part in yesterday's clearing chore, although he, Baap Can, had gone out to work. Impatiently, he proposes that his brother-in-law open the rite without Bbaang-Jieng. Kröng refuses: "I don't want to slit the hen's throat without Bbaang-Jieng. He is the holy man of the Fire Sticks, and he is the person who must lead us." So we wait. At last, the *croo weer Rnut* arrives in high spirits. Baap Can does not reproach him. It is six-twenty: the first sacrifice in the village circuit begins.

Baap Can leads his two colleagues to his granary. Bbaang-the-Pregnant-Man climbs up, holding the jar stopper on which he has placed some wort. Kröng-Jôong is carrying a hen and a cock. The three holy men pause at "the head of the Paddy"—the top of the mound of rice. Baap Can prays to the Spirit of the Paddy, while Kröng holds the two victims firmly and Bbaang, taking up his knife, severs their heads over the jar stopper. The latter two move to the back of the granary, squat, and there deposit the victims' heads—Bbaang the head of the cock, Kröng the head of the hen, as they pray in unison:

> *"Even if I eat, may your level sink no lower;*
> *even if I scoop, may no hollow appear;*
> *even if I open my hand, may you not flow onto the ground.*
> *I dig as one plants. . . .*

> *Coil yourself like the serpent,*
> *bring forth young like the bitch,*
> *grant me this, O thou, O Spirit of the Paddy."*

Baap Can and his brother-in-law climb down the ladder. Bbaang-the-Pregnant-Man stations himself by the granary door, against the edge of which the ladder rests. Before quitting his granary, Baap Can has said to his colleague, "There are ten panniers here" (which is to say, a hundred harvested pannierfuls).

But, as we will presently see from his prayer, the master of the Fire Sticks finds this quotation low.

Holding the decapitated cock in both hands, Bbaang-Jieng prays to the Paddy:

> *"Fear nothing,*
> *do not flee.*
> *Summon the buffaloes,*
> *summon the jars belonging to others to come here;*
> *summon the iron bar,*
> *summon the axes belonging to others to come here;*
> *summon the hoes that are used for weeding,*
> *summon the knives that are used for paring,*
> *summon the Vietnamese bowls that are used for meals.*
> *One hundred and seventy, conceal nothing."*

From the top of the ladder, he throws the cock down, but the victim falls in the wrong position. It is picked up and returned to the holy man, who does not stir from his place but repeats his prayer and throws again. A fresh failure is followed by several more. This persuades Bbaang-the-Pregnant-Man that the figure he has been advancing is inadequate. He continues his efforts, but this time he declares that two hundred pannierfuls of paddy have been stored. The Spirits approve, and the cock falls properly—in front of the ladder and with its claws turned toward it. An ovation greets this success, and the master of the *Rnut* concludes by turning toward the mound of rice:

"This is correct. There are in fact two hundred pannierfuls."*

This pseudo-divining operation of throwing the fowl is called *rla' ier*. When he has descended from the granary, Bbaang-Jieng receives from Baap Can a tube of beer, which Baap Can has him drink while he recites a series of wishes. Kröng, meanwhile, has concluded his prayer. Now people drink from the jar fastened to the granary post.

---

* An estimate closer to the truth than that of the master of the house. Actually, according to my own tally based on a daily count of the quantities brought into storage, Baap Can's granary is holding two hundred and ten pannierfuls, of which only three come from Can's field.

In Kröng-Jôong's house, a pig, its neck measuring four spans around, is sacrificed. A bit of blood is collected and, together with some wort, placed in a Mnong bowl. The master of the house hands the bowl to Bbaang-the-Pregnant-Man before the two men climb up into the granary, carrying a chicken. The holy man of the *Rnut* says to Baap Can, "You summon the Spirits from the ground. I will summon them from the tree."

Baap Can remains below. Bbaang-Jieng slits the hen's throat over the Mnong bowl, which he has placed atop the pile of rice. He buries the victim's head at the back of the granary; his invocation is seconded by the master of the house. Kröng climbs down from the granary with the bowl, which he hands to his brother-in-law, after having him drink a tubeful of beer. Baap Can goes "to summon the Spirits in the belly of the Paddy," while the master of the Fire Sticks drops the headless carcass of the chicken from the top of the ladder. He perseveres until he achieves the correct position. Triumphant, he climbs down and receives the tube of *rnööm* from his host. People gather around the jar.

We move now to the adjoining hearth of Tôong-Jieng (born of Jôong-Kröng's first marriage), who shares his common room with Mbieng, the lame husband of Grieng. (Grieng is his mother's younger sister.) Tôong-Jieng immolates a young pig measuring more than two spans in girth. His *kôony*, Baap Can, accompanies Bbaang-the-Pregnant-Man up to the granary to bury the chicken's head. His father-in-law, Kröng-Jôong, summons the Spirits in the belly of the Paddy.

Kröng tells me that the evening before last, shortly after I left, Wan-Jôong (of the Mok clan) asked Mbieng-Grieng to "anoint [him] with blood" because he had had an unpropitious dream.

Kröng spells it out for my benefit: "It was not just a simple anointing, the kind that involves giving goods of value in exchange. It was a matter of anointing the drumsticks, anointing for an exchange—for a real *Tâm Bôh*, not just a 'singeing of the pig by sisters and mothers.' "

I turn to Mbieng-Grieng and urge him to perform the anointment with blood that opens the whole cycle of sacrifices culminating in the sworn-friend alliance. I explain how much it would mean to me to be present at such a ceremony. But Mbieng protests. "I have no intention of making an Exchange of Sacrifices! My body has not grown enough [he means that he is not a *kuang*]. I refuse. Even if I were normal, but I'm lame. How do you expect me to go looking for a buffalo!"

With that, he leads the two holy men to his granary to sacrifice his two chickens.

The people from Upper Donnaï who came yesterday to invite me there now join us at Mbieng-Grieng's. The conversation turns to the plantations and the role of the administrative chiefs in recruiting field hands. The number of work days that must be furnished outside Gar territory is alarming. Seeing that their account of this state of affairs has troubled me, Truu says to the foreigners, "You're more afraid of your *kuang* than of the Commissioner."

They all protest.

"Then why don't you go and complain to him?" Truu demands.

His condescending, holier-than-thou tone annoys me, and I say sharply, "You're no one to talk like that, Truu. When the sector chief was pressuring your coolies, you didn't open your mouth. If I hadn't realized what was happening, no one would have known a thing about it!"

Then, after a pause: "Just the way he fattened himself on the sorcery affair in Phii Dih and Bboon Khaang."

"He knows, he knows about it!" they all chorus in surprise. (Because I had been told in strictest confidence of Bbaang-Dlaang's participation, no one here had realized I was aware of it.)

Seeing that he has nothing more to conceal, the canton chief blurts out, "As for the Phii Dih massacre, Bbaang wanted a large male buffalo rather than the ancient *rluung* jar they had intended to offer him. And he also received as 'a vegetable to be eaten' [that is, an animal sacrificed at the conclusion of a sale and eaten on the spot] one pig of five spans. Actually, no one got to eat the animal. Bbaang kept the pig to fatten it up."

Then, as regards Bboon Khaang, he informs me that the sector chief himself led people in the massacre.

"It was he and the two Choong, helped by Njruung, who killed people. And it was Mboong who inherited the set of flat gongs."

By way of excusing his own silence about the Phii Dih massacre, the canton chief goes on to tell me that the organizers of that mass killing had threatened him: " 'Don't forget that some Rjee, your own two *kôony*, the brothers Ddôol Bbaang, were killed for sorcery in Nyôong Rlaa by the Ntöör and Cil clans. And the Nduu and Ryaam, too.' So I was afraid and I held my tongue. I went to Phii Dih only in the morning," Truu continues. "Bbaang-the-Stag was running away from Phii Ko'. He came to take refuge in my house, and it was he who took me to Phii Dih in the morning."

Bbaang-Jieng-the-Pregnant-Man and Wan-Jôong had known Ddôol Bbaang, the murdered brothers. They themselves were only children at the time.

Thereupon, I am told that a long, long time ago, villagers from Bboon Dlei, Bboon Sar, and elsewhere had set out to exterminate the sorcerers of Daa' Mroong: "A hundred people . . . They wiped out the whole Nduu clan. . . ."

Truu has had a goodly amount to drink, and has stretched out on the low platform. The common room of Tôong-Jieng and his aunt is filled to the bursting point, for the two households are ready to offer the communal meal—the *biet coot,* or "meeting for the wort." The second jar of the day has been attached to the foot of the granary ladder. In Tôong-Jieng's quarters, a winnowing basket has been set nearby; it contains a pot of *rnööm* siphoned from the jar attached to the foot of the ladder, a serving basket of still steaming glutinous rice, and a pot of *pae lah tuh* (a dish of pork and beans over which broken rice is scattered). There are other dishes, notably cornets fashioned out of *tloong* leaves that hold the quasi-ritual food for this day—glutinous rice, ginger, and *pae lah tuh*.

The holy men squat around the winnowing basket with the master of the house, who offers them drink by lifting the cup to their lips.

Baap Can is served first, then Kröng, then Bbaang-the-Pregnant-Man, and, lastly, the ethnologist. Truu is half asleep and declines to drink. Baap Can takes the ancient buffalo horn from the winnowing basket and fills it with beer. He tosses in also some glutinous rice, *pae lah tuh*, bits of ginger, chicken, and pig's heart. Then he climbs up into the granary, followed by Bbaang-the-Pregnant-Man carrying a cornet of food, and by Tôong-Jieng. Kröng picks up the Mnong bowl of blood-drenched *coot* and a cornet of *pae lah tuh*. He will summon the Spirits in the belly of the Paddy, while his two colleagues nourish the Paddy itself.

Baap Can makes a small hollow in the top of the mound of grain and with short, jerky motions pours the contents of his horn into it. His companion has set his cornet of food beside this indentation. Jieng-Tôong, the mistress of the house, hastens under the granary with a blanket and a handful of glutinous rice. Above her, the three men chant:

> *"Fear nothing,*
> *do not flee,*
> *eat the chicken within,*
> *eat the pork within,*
> *drink the rice beer within.*
> *Do not go seeking the soup of another,*
> *do not go seeking the rice of another,*
> *do not go seeking the house of another,*
> *do not go seeking the granary of another."*

Presently, the rice beer seeps through the enormous pile of grain and drips from the granary floor. Jieng-Tôong holds out her blanket to catch it. The holy men are informed that the operation has been a success. The mistress of the house offers a prayer as, with glutinous rice, she tamps the place where the *rnööm* was seeping through. The three men descend from the granary, and Bbaang-the-Pregnant-Man inserts a drinking straw in the jar tied to the foot of the ladder. Tôong-Jieng offers each of the two holy men a large Vietnamese bowl of rice beer, and to his *kôony*, Baap Can, he gives a Mnong bowl of hulled rice topped by an upturned imported bowl. (The receiver always returns the Mnong receptacle.) When Kröng returns from his prayer, he also receives *rnööm*.

Tôong-Jieng gives the *croo weer* a cornet of food as they prepare to go officiate at the house of Mbieng-Grieng. Once he has served the adults, Tôong tells the children that they may help themselves. There is a rush of small bodies as the children, each supplied with *tloong* leaves, fall upon the quasi-ritual food.

At the lame man's house, it is Bbaang-the-Pregnant-Man who pours the libation to the Paddy. He expends a good part of the horn's contents with no results. When he shouts, "Is that it?" several voices reply, "No."

Now he is afraid he has poured too much. The operation may end with a flood beneath the granary, so he pours slowly. "All right now?" But the answer is "No."

"Phew! . . . It's cross!" To me, his voice sounds truly concerned.

He has entirely emptied his horn. He hands it down from the granary, so that it can be refilled. At last, the beer does trickle down into the blanket Grieng is holding, and the master of the *Rnut* can plant his half-emptied horn on top of the heap of grain. Climbing down, he joins Mbieng-Grieng and inserts the drinking straw in the latter's jar. The host presents Bbaang with a Mnong bowl of hulled rice, topped by an imported bowl. Each of the holy men has drunk a cup of *rnööm* lifted to his lips by Mbieng. He then gives them cornets of food. Two young men circulate among the guests, one carrying a *khiu* of glutinous rice, the other a pot of bamboo preserve cooked with chicken meat and ginger.

As always when people drink, they chatter. Sometimes the talk turns to trite matters or recent trivial happenings, but then some banal word suffices to bring an old story to mind. This is how Choong-Kôong-the-Soldier happens to tell us how he recovered his father's four flat gongs.

While his father was on a commercial trip, he left his gongs with Yaang-Dae, the father of Ngkoi, who is the present district councillor and lives in Phii Gur. Yaang did not make up his mind to buy the gongs, but he kept them without paying for them. The father of Choong died. At the time, Choong was an infantryman with the First Battalion,* garrisoned in Cam Ranh. In his absence, an uncle, Bbaang-Mae, and two other relatives from Paang Döng, where his father had lived, went to Phii Gur to reclaim the dead man's property. Yaang administered a severe thrashing to two of the travelers; the third escaped unscathed.

One day, Choong-Kôong's superior officer, a Captain Boutelleux, sends for Choong and reads him a letter: " 'Your father is dead, and your possessions have been stolen by foreigners.' " The infantryman requests and is granted a twenty-day leave.

The moment he arrives in Paang Döng, he goes to his uncle and asks what's been going on. Bbaang-Mae, Choong tells us, "pours me a little

---

* Of the Colonial Infantry. —*Trans.*

round jar" and explains the situation and says, "If you manage to recover the *cing*, we will divide. If not, that's the end of the matter.".

Choong-the-Soldier asks his maternal uncle, Bbôong-the-Deputy, and his friends Can, Bbür, and Tlam to help him. They get on their horses and ride downstream toward Phii Gur. In Rhaang, Choong-Jieng (of the Rjee clan) gives them food but refuses to accompany them.

At Yaang-Dae's house, there are no flat gongs to be seen. However, the elderly *kuang* pours them a drink from an ancient *ngoong* jar, and they discuss the matter. Their host refuses to return the four *cing*. He claims he has bought them. Choong replies that he has not been paid. The old man retorts that, yes, he has. His game is so well camouflaged that the visitors cannot make it out.

They sleep over at Yaang-Dae's. The next morning, Can shakes Choong awake: the Phii Gur are preparing to sacrifice a pig and have already brought out another *ngoong* jar. Choong leaps up and tosses five piasters to his hosts for the rice beer. Showing them fifty piasters, he declares, "If you accept this money for the pig, I agree to your killing him. If not, I refuse." *

The Phii Gur people demur, but faced down by the adamant young infantryman, in the end they give in.

Then one of the travelers discovers the four flat gongs hidden beneath the low platform. He brings them out and distributes them to his companions, "to play," he says, "and just enjoy the sound of their music." He hangs them around his friends' shoulders, and they beat a rhythmic cadence. When the concert is over, Yaang puts the flat gongs back beneath the platform. The young men ask to play again. The second concert ends, and Yaang slips the *cing* back into the same place. This maneuver is repeated several times. Finally, Can, Bbür, and Tlam pick up the gongs once more (Tlam taking two), but instead of playing them, they wrap them in their blankets and go out. As Choong describes it, "Yaang is furious. He throws the young men's pandanus mats and night effects in the urine." He yells, dons war garb, thrusts a saber in his *suu troany*, and threatens them. But Choong stands up to him: "You can hit me, you can kill me. But just remember that you will have to return my effects to the First Battalion."

Realizing that his bluster is just that, the old man begs him, "Take my ordinary jars, take my ancient jars. Just leave me the set of flat gongs. . . ."

But the young men jump on their horses and gallop off, Choong-the-Soldier and his *kôony*, Bbôong-the-Deputy, covering their flight.

"Do you imagine that Bbaang-Mae paid me with a jar of *rnööm* and a

---

* The sacrifice would have meant he accepted the old man's claim and was making his peace with him. —*Trans.*

chicken?" Choong asks me, in conclusion. "Nothing of the sort. He made the division of property, and that was that."

Choong-Kôong, who is our village headman, is proud of the effect his story has produced. He now tries to convince young Ngee, whose father is in prison in Poste du Lac, to go up to Poste du Lac and get himself a job on a construction site. He tells Ngee that they are building the palace of "the Vietnamese King." Despite the enticing prospect of a salary that would amount to a hundred piasters and two meters of white calico, the young man does not seem exactly enthusiastic.

Truu must be roused to attend the *biet coot* of his brother and brother-in-law, Baap Can and Krông-Jôong.

His strength restored, the canton chief consents to continue his account of the adventures of Nduu Buat, the son of Dlaang. His audience is all the more receptive, because people have had something to eat and are continuing to drink. Four households are offering four winnowing baskets of food and eight jars; to circulate among them, little moving back and forth is necessary, for all four families belong to the same long house. Alcohol loosens tongues but beclouds minds. In high spirits, Bbaang-the-Pregnant-Man wants music, and interrupts Truu to ask for the loan of his giant flat gong and his set of bossed gongs. He badgers Truu several times before the canton chief obliges with a drinking song. The master of the Fire Sticks returns to his place and tells his son Bbieng-Dlaang to go to Truu's house and fetch his gongs. The young man is very busy lighting his pipe with a live ember. Like his father, he is a good sort, and amiable when he is sober, but tonight he has drunk more than he can carry and he answers the old man rudely: "Why tell me to go get them?"

"Look here, don't you talk to me like that! We must get the gongs so we can play tonight."

A puppy wanders by and clumsily butts into the young man's legs. Bbieng hurls the live ember he is holding at the poor animal and hits it. The puppy howls with pain. Old Bbaang-Jieng, the only man here whom so far I have seen show any friendliness toward a dog, is outraged. He upbraids his son: "Dirty animal! Treating a dog like that, a little dog no bigger than that!"

He is choking with indignation. Bbieng, who is a sad drunk, bursts into tears. "Why are you jawing me? . . . I'm going to kill myself, I'll hang myself, like Tieng!"

And he rushes out.

His mother has been watching this scene all a-tremble. She runs, moaning, after her son, imploring him not to do anything rash. His *jôok*, Tôong-Wan (nephew and adopted son of Mbieng-Grieng), chases after and, luckily, manages to catch him. All three return, not to Krông's hearth but to Mbieng-Grieng's, Tôong supporting his friend around the waist. Mbieng himself is not entirely sober, and he welcomes the two young men in an unexpected fashion: "You behave like this to me because I'm lame. . . . You, who are my own nephew, have got him as drunk as this. . . . . If he did kill himself, I would kill you. . . ."

Tôong is a mild man and not in the habit of bringing trouble down on his own head. He is panicked by his best friend's behavior, and the shouts of his uncle, who is habitually quite restrained, only upset him more. So he wants to open a jar in honor of Bbieng-Dlaang to erase what has just happened. The latter has recovered some of his wits, and refuses: "I really am too drunk."

To calm Mbieng down, I say to him, "It's splendid that you and your nephew are going to make two *Tâm Bôh* together—you with Wan-Jôong and Tôong-Wan with Bbieng-Dlaang."

But Mbieng replies, "*Beng!* Taboo! Piling things up like that is not good, not good at all. The Spirits don't like to look in several places at the same time. So we have to make the *Tâm Bôh* one after the other. The nephew before the *kôony*, even. That wouldn't matter. But together— no."

My having mentioned two *Tâm Bôh* carried out simultaneously in the same family makes the others laugh, and throws the two young men into confusion.

It would seem that tonight the *rnööm* has hit particularly hard those people who are normally calm. For example, ordinarily Mang-Tôong, the wife of the cook, is not at all talkative and is never heard to complain. This evening, she brings up the question of how the inheritance was shared. She insists vehemently that Taang-Jieng-the-Stooped always wanted his antique collar of *rbaal* beads to go after his death to his son, Tôong-Mang. "He gave five piasters for it," she say stubbornly, "and when he died, his sisters and mothers took the necklace back."

December 7

Only four households were able to carry out their *Mhaam Baa* yesterday. This morning, everyone gathers at the house of Bbaang-the-Pregnant-Man, who will inaugurate the second series of sacrifices. He is immolating a fat pig four spans and one fist in girth. The holy man's younger son, Kroong-Sraang, holds the beast. With a single saber blow to the heart, Wan-Jôong kills it. Bbaang-Jieng sets a bowl of *rnööm* at the rear of his house for the benefit of the Spirits, then offers drink to his two colleagues as well as to Wan-Jôong and Troo-Jôong. It is Krông-Jôong who "summons the Spirits in the belly of the Paddy" and Baap Can who climbs up into the granary to officiate there in company with the master of the house. The offering of *rnööm* passes through the heap of grain and is caught up by Jieng-Bbaang. Baap Can tosses the beheaded fowl from the top of the ladder, and announces that two hundred pannierfuls have been stored. On his first throw, the *Yaang* confirm the estimate. Astonished and joyful, Baap Can exclaims, "They proclaim two hundred! They proclaim two hundred!"

Bbaang-Jieng offers a gift of rice to Baap Can for "having poured the beer," and gives a drink to him and to Kröng-Jôong, who has completed his prayer. Then the first drinking bout of the day begins. The men gather around small neckless jars and sip *rnööm* siphoned from the jar attached to the granary post. The women remain beneath the granary floor, where the mistress of the house brings each a large Vietnamese bowl of rice beer taken from the men's little jar. People drink and chatter until Bbôong-Mang comes to rouse the holy men and drag them off to his house. For Kraang-Drüm, Bbaang's son-in-law and immediate neighbor, is deferring his sacrifice; he intends eventually to immolate a goat.

By the end of the morning, we find ourselves in the tiny hut of Poong-the-Widow, after having drunk at the house of Choong-the-Soldier and of Troo-Jôong. The latter has sipped from every jar offered, and is feeling enormously expansive. I take advantage of this to switch the conversation to the massacres of sorcerers. On his own, Troo-Jôong describes for me the ordeal in which he took part in Romen, after the death of Jieng-Chaar, the mother of Broong-Dür, the canton chief. For me, the account is lively and colorful. However, Baap Can and the others (only a few people are present, fortunately, because Poong-the-Widow is too poor to receive on any scale) take scant relish in Troo-Jôong's exploit.

We move on to Bbaang-the-One-Eyed's. His neighbor, Tôong-Biing, is not opening a jar, which earns him vehement reproaches from Can—like Tôong's wife, a Bboon Jraang. Can points out that although Tôong's friend and neighbor is just as poor, he has nonetheless made the necessary effort.

In the early afternoon, each household that has sacrificed this morning proceeds to the *biet coot,* or sacramental meal. Troo-Jôong, not Bbaang-the-Pregnant-Man, opens the series. Troo has not stopped drinking, and rice beer has both loosened his tongue and swollen his pride. Troo had a hard youth. After a massacre of sorcerers, his mother had been sold into slavery, and as her son, he had lived in this miserable situation, in the house of unkind, tight-fisted masters. Nevertheless, he hoped to win his freedom by working furiously. His owners' bad faith forced him to run away, and he took refuge in the house of his "brothers," Taang Truu (Rjee and Rlük are associated clans). The work habits he and his wife had acquired when young permitted them, once they were free, to augment their possessions year by year. Thus, Troo-Jôong was in a position to perform the exchange of sacrifice of a pig with his friend Tôong-Jieng.

On my way to Troo's house, I had heard a tremendous noise. Troo had fallen at the top of the ladder to his granary as he was climbing up with the holy men. The Spirits "having proclaimed eighty pannierfuls" this morning, he is full of confidence and he comments, "This year eighty. Next year a hundred, and then I will kill a buffalo."

His wife, more astute than he, perhaps, and fearing the anger of the *Yaang*, scolds him: "Now, now, that sort of talk is taboo."

"*Khiep!*" Troo retorts. "Never mind. First, I will sell your white jar to get the buffalo for the Festival of the Soil. Then my giant flat gong for the Blood Anointment of the Paddy. . . . My children will grow up and become powerful. In my own lifetime, they will eat buffalo. . . ."

Spoken by a man in his cups, perhaps, but spoken with the pride of a man who is strong in both mind and body.

Troo-Jôong is not the only person to be thoroughly drunk. Truu now breaks into coarse talk such as I have never heard from a Mnong Gar. Among the Gar, the well-known "mother-in-law taboo" extends to the elders of the spouse (this is what is called the *tâm köih* relationship). By "elders" one should understand not only "sisters and brothers" (i.e., cousins) who are older than the husband or wife but also all persons belonging to the generation of the parents, grandparents, etc. One may have no physical contact with and make no impolite remarks about any individuals in this category. If you want to score devastating success in chaffing someone, it is enough to say that So-and-so intends to marry his mother-in-law or the elder sister of his wife (or, in the case of a woman, her father-in-law or the elder brother of her husband). The Mnong to whom such a remark is addressed is completely at a loss. Despite the fact that this form of banter is frequent, he becomes tongue-tied, and the most he can muster up to say is "You're lying, you're lying!"

Even a man as intelligent as Kroong-Biing, whose mind is so quick and resourceful, can find no other rejoinder. And obviously, everyone always laughs. Today Truu—and he had to be drunk to do it—has spun out this joke, embellishing it as surely no other Mnong Gar ever dreamed of doing. Singling out Can, who is a ninny at best and whose silliness increases in proportion to the amount of *rnööm* he imbibes, Truu says to him, "A letter's just arrived from Poste du Lac. It's an order. It says that at the party Yoo is going to give us here, all runners must take off all their clothes with the women they *tâm köih* to greet the Commissioner."

"You're joking, you're joking."

Truu is imperturbable. "I am not joking in the slightest. Ask Yoo. He translated the letter for me. The runners will walk up to their *tâm köih*, who will take hold of their things—like this!"

"I won't, I won't! I'll stay in bed."

"It's an order. You'll have to go along with the others. You'll be tied with two ropes. One will be held, like a halter, by your older sister-in-law walking in front, and the other by your younger sister-in-law following behind you. You'll be in the middle, and you'll buck and kick—like this."

Can is genuinely panic-stricken. "But I won't, it's impossible! . . . I'll pretend I'm sick. . . . I'll have Ndoong put me in the Health Station. . . . I'll hide in the forest. With one's *tâm köih!* With one's *tâm köih!* Completely naked! . . ."

The laughter is raucous but also somewhat constrained. Can must be calmed down and told that it's all just a joke his uncle has concocted, and finally he is reassured.

Everything settles down. People continue to drink. But all of a sudden, Kraang-Drüm rushes outside to vomit and is soon thereafter followed by Can.

Most drinkers now move on to the house of Bbaang-Jieng-the-Pregnant-Man, who initiated the first phase of the sacrifice this morning but who in the second phase is last. Bbieng-Dlaang comes to squat by his father's main door when he hears the flat-gong orchestra approach on its "circuit of the *cing*" through the village. He does not go outside, for the musicians walk through the interior of each house. When Maang-the-Thin, the first player in line, holding the "mother" instrument (the thickest and the one which establishes the beat), comes abreast of him, Bbieng seizes the *cing* by the rim. He sings a "saying of the gongs" while trying to make his partner-opponent sit down. An ovation salutes this lyric exploit. Maang-the-Thin squirms and makes no reply. On the contrary, he turns to the player behind him, who proves to be no more stouthearted than he. Krae-Drüm comes forward to take over the mother *cing* but does not manage to sing one full couplet. Emboldened by rice beer, Can enters the sacred contest. With difficulty, he struggles to the end of the second verse but then, amid general laughter, he gets all mixed up.

Faced with this multiple failure, the orchestra re-forms with the same players. This time, however, Kroong-Sraang, the younger brother of Bbieng-Dlaang, heads the group. By grasping the rim of the *cing mei*, Bbieng forces his brother to sit down, while he sings of Bbieng Coh Lêe's emerging from the subterranean world to become the leader of men. He is applauded by the drinkers, as is Kroong-Sraang when he squats and essays to chant a reply. He has less breath and assurance than his older brother but he wins equal acclaim. Is it because he is so handsome or because he has shown courage in venturing to perform when others considered more knowledgeable than he have failed?

This interlude is both lyrical and religious in nature, and as always when sacred old hymns are sung in their traditional form, the atmosphere is transformed. Everything is calm now. Also, people have drunk too much, and they seem groggy. At the suggestion of a man near me who

wants to liven up the party, I ask Bbür (Kroong-Big-Navel's brother, who
has come down from Nyôong Brah) and Bbaang-the-Stag and Can to form
a fresh group and play to wake people up. Bbaang-the-Stag seizes the
mother gong and begins a rhythmic beat, whereupon his wife, Aang-of-
the-Mincing-Step, jumps up and insults him. Her ugliness and her shrew-
ish temper, which contrast so sharply with her husband's strength, youth,
and perennial good humor, win her no sympathy. Bbaang-the-Stag bats
his eyelashes the way he always does when he is drunk; he stops playing
and without a word submits to the tirade of his ill-tamed termagant. Can
comes to his friend's defense, careful to strike a light note: "Why won't
you let him play?"

This serves only to unleash greater fury from the old virago: "That's
none of your business!"

Can explodes in turn: "Do I devour what belongs to you? Do I?"

"And do I devour your buffaloes?"

"Yes, you do devour my buffaloes!"

Red as a fighting cock, Can dredges up the affair that pits Cil against
Bboon Jraang, a story that eats away at him like a cancer. He recalls how
Krae-the-Widower killed a clan brother, a Cil like himself, who had been
married to Can's "little mother"—Jôong, of the Bboon Jraang clan. Not
satisfied with having killed the firebrand husband and contrary to all law,
Krae had sold the wife into slavery down south. And because of a Cil's voracity, his—Can's—"little mother" is a slave still. So no one can reproach
him, etc., etc. . . . Made both fierce and eloquent by drink, Can shouts
himself hoarse as he tells the story, and thanks to his digressions and reca-
pitulations it is interminable. His face is crimson; he jumps up, then sits
down, bellowing the while. Aang, standing near the main door, watches
him venomously. The wrinkles in her ugly face deepen, and her distended earlobes swing above her shoulders as she looses a fresh stream of
insults.

The two adversaries are no longer alone: other people enter the fray.
With her grande-dame air, Ngee intervenes for no very good reason—
simply because her niece and adopted daughter, Jaang Bibuu, belongs to
the same clan as Aang-of-the-Mincing-Step. Can silences her in short
order. Aang-of-the-Drooping-Eyelid is terrified by her brother's uncon-
trolled violence. She seizes his arm and tries to drag him away and begs
him to be quiet. She says to Ngee, by way of excuse, that her husband
was not aware of the affair, that Truu was soldiering at the time. But Ngee
replies slyly, "That makes no difference. I know quite well what the Rjee
think privately. . . ."

When I ask her, "Why do you say things like that?" she stops.

Old Troo, matriarch of the Sar Luk Rjee, claps her hand over her
grandson's mouth. To no avail. Can inundates us in a typhoon of words.

His father, who has been drinking at the other end of the long house, heaves into sight, delivers a resounding slap to the cheek of his son, who is much the taller of the two, and flees. Can comes over to show me the weal on his face, but en route continues to insult Aang-of-the-Mincing-Step, likening her to a rotted vagina and saying over and over, "Now you go so far as to cause me to be struck by my own father."

Happily, Bbür is on hand. He picks up the big flat gong and manages to lure Can, Bbaang-the-Stag, and three other young men into playing. The music gentles the manners of all and sundry. Aang-of-the-Mincing-Step and Ngee, her partisan, take off for Bbôong-the-Deputy's house. After playing four airs, the musicians abandon their instruments, and to tease Bbaang-the-Stag, Bbür not too accurately sings the latter's favorite song, to which Bbaang owes his nickname:

> "The stag is on the mountain, may the shaft of the
>   lance be quick, so says Bbaang, son of Mang.
> The stag is in the water, may the handle of the cast net
>   be quick, so says Bbaang, son of Mang.
> The wind blows hard, so says Bbaang, son of Mang. . . ."

It is growing late, and the clusters of drinkers are shrinking. Talk languishes. From the house of Bbôong-the-Deputy comes the voice, broken by noisy sobs, of the beautiful Laang-Mhoo, who is weeping: ". . . Poor . . . shameful . . . The memory of it breaks my heart. . . . My children have no fat to eat. . . . Whether I die or not makes no difference. . . . But my children, Sraang, Kroong, Mang . . ."

Truu is by the jar, only a few steps away from his "sister." Other Rjee are nearby also, mostly women—old Troo, Sraang, Mang-of-the-Jutting-Jaw, and her husband, Bbôong-the-Deputy. From where I am sitting, I ask what is distressing Laang. "No one disputes her," they tell me. And they all laugh.

I ask her, "What is wrong, O Laang?"

"No one disputes me," she says, which makes the others laugh again.

I walk over to the group. Discreetly, Truu makes himself scarce. Laang, whom I have never seen so drunk, cries harder than ever and now is fairly bawling out her secrets. I try to make her laugh by gently chucking her under the chin. I win one smile. Then, interrupted by occasional showers of tears, she tells us her woes. It is her "older brother," Truu, whom she is vexed with. When he comes home after drinking in other houses or villages, he rails at his "sisters and mothers." His wife, Ngee, is the same, Laang says. " 'You're nothing but orphans, paupers,' she tells us. 'My husband is a *kuang*, he works with the white men, he is canton chief, sector chief. Yours is nothing but an orphan.'

"She boasts about the meat she preserves in her jars, but we have no meat. She boasts about her *rnööm,* and the two of them drink, but they look down on us and we are ashamed. It breaks my heart. . . . My husband is covered with mycosis, with *tokélo.* He can't make fine talk, he has no sister, no mother. It breaks my heart. . . . She scolds us. . . . I have no brother any more. My brother is dead. . . ."

Each time Laang moans "It breaks my heart," her mother, old Troo, explains to me: "It's because she has lost her brother, your *jôok,* Kraang." (Actually, I knew Kraang slightly, having met him only on my first trip to Gar country.)

"And we do not borrow her paddy, either," Laang says, with emphasis.

Whereupon Bbôong-Mang observes, "They don't ask her for her paddy for fear she will refuse. You don't dare borrow from a *kuang* for fear he will refuse, and then you will feel too ashamed." What Laang said is correct, however: she never has borrowed rice from Ngee-Truu, only from Mang-of-the-Jutting-Jaw.

Laang continues through her sobs: "My shame is greater every day. . . . It breaks my heart, and that's why I'm crying. My daughter, Sraang, has no fat to eat. My son Kroong-the-Hernia has no fat to eat. . . . I suffer just from being alive. . . . Truu wants Kroong to marry Jaang Bibbuu so he can inherit the boy's jars, his flat gongs, and his rice. I don't want that. We'll stay poor. . . . It's Ngee. . . . She scolds us all the time. And so does Truu. . . ."

By now, she is quite calm. "I'm drunk, so I say what I feel—all the things I don't dare say when I'm sober. But when I am sober I am just as ashamed, because the attitude of Ngee and Truu toward us is so scornful."

Then, pointedly noting to me how Truu took off when I came over to speak to her and her family, Laang goes back to her quarters with her mother. I am left alone with Bbôong-the-Deputy and Mang-of-the-Jutting-Jaw.

They have been drinking a lot, too, and are in the mood for confidences. "Truu is proud," Bbôong says to me, "but he is not as hard as Baap Can. All the Rjee are ferocious." (His wife, Mang, is a Rjee but not from the same branch as the brothers Taang Truu.)

Then he starts to tell me the story of his wife, Mang-of-the-Jutting-Jaw.

Some Mnong Rlâm had sold a whole pressful of fish to Mang's parents. Her father had paid them soon afterward with a bush hook. But when the Rlâm heard he had died, they came back here and "sued," claiming that the bush hook had never been delivered to them. The Rjee then offered, and the Rlâm agreed to accept in settlement, an imported turban and red vest and a saber. The head of the family, Taang, the son of Mbrii Guu, contributed most of this indemnification; Ddoong-Mang, the father of Truu and Baap Can, supplied only a small part. When the enemies had taken themselves off, Taang Mbrii Guu informed Mang's mother that he would have to be reimbursed. The poor widow had nothing to her name, so to speak, so the Rjee sold her to Paang Pê' Nâm for five flat gongs. They likewise sold her sister, Jrae, who at the time was a little girl, to the Mnong Laac, in Bboon Döng, for twelve buffaloes. Later, Jrae married a Laac, and in due course her husband went to lodge a complaint with the Commissioner in Dalat, who set the couple free. Subsequently, the husband became rich. Their three sons are still living—Broong, Wal, and Krieng—but the parents are dead.*

The Rjee sold Jôong's children separately. The sale of Mang's older brother, Ndoong, to the Kudduu brought twelve buffaloes; Nar, her younger brother, was bought by the Düng Jrii clan in Sar Lang for five flat gongs. The proceeds of these sales went to Taang Mbrii Guu; Baap Can's parents received only one or two buffaloes.

As for Mang herself, she was kept as a slave by the Rjee of Sar Luk. She was still a very young girl when she was carried off by some Phii Kroec people, but she was later returned by her abductors. (An involved story has it that Phii Kroec was at odds with the village of the headman Chaar, and that Sar Luk played only the role of assigned intermediary in the affair.)

The Rjee treated Mang so harshly that one day she ran away to Phii Jjöt and appealed to Mbaam—a Rjee—who agreed to buy her for two buffaloes. This was when Bbôong came to know her, and presently he married her. But at the time of his death, Mbaam had not yet been able to hand over the full value of the two promised buffaloes. Baap Can and Taang Mbrii Guu come to Phii Jjöt to reclaim their slave. They seize Mang-of-the-Jutting-Jaw and her husband as well, saying to him, "You married our slave, so you become our slave." They bind the couple and drag them off to Sar Luk. There, with the sacrifice of a hen and a jar of beer, they "adopt" the couple. Bbôong remains in Sar Luk for a full year. Then, on the pretext of going with some other men to buy bush-hook blades and pandanus cloaks, he takes with him a small decorated basket filled with rice and escapes to Dalat. He enlists in the Garde Montagnarde. The Rjee do not dare prevent Mang's joining her husband. "And better still," Bbôong tells me, "since then, they have never dared remind me that Mang is their slave. They're afraid of me. But what *I* fear is that when I die they may come to claim her again. In front of me, they are afraid, but I fear that at my death they will come and take all my possessions, my buffaloes, and my jars. That's why I've sold my set of flat gongs. Now I'll be able to buy buffaloes, which I'll kill and in that way pay off my meat debts. And with my piasters, I'll buy fabric, clothing. I don't want to leave

---

* According to Kroong-the-Short, in a conversation of August 25, 1949, Mang-of-the-Jutting-Jaw became a slave after her maternal grandfather inadvertently set fire to a field.

them one single thing." And for further security, he wants to put a certain distance between himself and the Rjee "by going back to his 'sister's' house," in Bboon Dlei Daak Rhiu.

Unquestionably, Bbôong-the-Deputy's bête noire is Baap Can. In the course of his account, he has revealed that Baap Can claimed that Sieng-Dee-the-Cook's set of flat gongs belonged to him; at the time of the attack on Phii Ko', he stole them and has been keeping them until such time as the Phii Dih people come to take them back. Bbaang-the-Stag also claimed that the *cing* belonged to him.

Taking advantage of the deputy's bitterness, I attempt to learn in what circumstances Baap Can had shared in a murder in the Rlâm village before returning here to sacrifice his first buffalo. Bbôong-the-Deputy amends this: "No! It wasn't the Rlâm village, it was the Ndee."

But that's all I find out. It is two in the morning when I leave this unfortunate couple who, after extremely difficult beginnings, succeeded in winning recognition and a solid position in the "valley," only, alas, to lose all their descendants—daughter, son-in-law, and grandchildren—in the terrible epidemic that struck Sar Luk last year.

December 8

The Mhaam Baa rites resume this morning. Nine households must officiate today—those who occupy the four long houses on the north side of Sar Luk. But the village finds it hard to wake up. People are worn out by last night's heavy drinking, which followed on the heels of two previous days of celebration. The final phase of the ceremonial rounds opens with the four richest houses, which happen to be adjacent and which belong to Truu, Mhoo-Laang, Bbaang-the-Stag, and Jieng, widow of Taang-the-Stooped. The drink consumed here has not, however, kindled any zest whatever by the time the holy men approach the five remaining households, which are among the poorest in the village. There is a brief diversion when some people arrive from Ndut Lieng Krak to invite me to their Blood Anointment of the Paddy. However, the day promises to be anything but festive as rites follow on rites, jars on jars.

Then, in the afternoon, a sensational event occurs. A troop of Montagnard infantrymen, all of whom speak Mnong, appears, led by two French noncommissioned officers and two French soldiers. Their commanding officer in Dalat wanted them to take a look around Mnong country and, if possible, visit their home villages.

In an instant, Sar Luk shakes off its apathy. Wan-Jôong's son Nyaang is a member of this particular company, although he is not on the tour. However, his friends Par and Bbaang-the-Corporal are well known in the village. Once the infantrymen are quartered in the canton chief's house, they wander about. I am in a quandary. I do not have supplies on hand to offer decent hospitality to the Europeans. But presently a line of bearers appears at the far end of the track, carrying chests. A note from the Commissioner explains that he and the doctor have been held up at the first bridges, and so have entrusted my rations to the nearest village for delivery.

Around five o'clock, the French sergeant commanding the detachment offers the village a diversion in the form of grenade-fishing. Everyone—men, women, children, and oldsters—hurries to the river downstream from Sar Luk. Some are so eager that they want to jump into the water at the first detonation, and must be restrained. The dead fish float to the surface. There is much diving, shouting, laughing—a tremendous scuffle, for everyone wants to gather the largest possible share of this miraculous haul.

In the evening, as always when a special event gives him the opportunity, Truu proves to be a first-rate host. *Rnöom* and *alak* are in bountiful supply at his house—most of the *alak* contributed, it is true, by the soldiers, who are well supplied with imported products and always proud to display them. Two other householders, Kraang-Drüm and Wan-Jôong, offer hospitality to the two *kahan* in the troop who belong to the Rtung clan, which is their wives' *mpôol*, making these men the women's "brother and son."

And so the year in which we ate the forest of the Stone Spirit Gôo comes to a beautiful close. Its last day will remain engraved in the memory of all for having ended in such an exceptional way: a troop of soldiers came to drink in our homes on the final day of the *Mhaam Baa*, giving unhoped-for brilliance and luster to the greatest of annual ceremonies.

December 9

Shortly after the detachment took off—an unforgettable spectacle for Sar Luk—the crackle of a fusillade reaches our eats. With much brio, Baap Can presently describes for us the great event, which he happened to witness. Coming upon two peacock roosts, the soldiers opened fire with machine guns, and only two or three birds, quicker than the rest, managed to escape. The soldiers killed a monkey also. Heady spice, this, for future conversations.

Ngee, Rieng-Chaar's son, is leaving us. He has let himself be persuaded by the village headman, and will go with See-Aang, of Paang Döng, to work on the palace the Emperor of Annam is building on the hill that overlooks Poste du Lac.

The year in which we ate the forest of the Stone Spirit Gôo ended with the final day of the *Mhaam Baa*. Today, we begin a new year, the year in which Sar Luk will offer its Great Festival of the Soil. It is necessary that the villagers be solemnly reminded of the promise they made to the Divinities. Accordingly, in the early afternoon, the entire village gathers at the house of the master of the Fire Sticks, Bbaang-Jieng-the-Pregnant-Man. One must proceed to "the blood anointment of the flat gongs and the drum" (*mhaam cing mhaam nggör*).

Our host squats at the foot of an already prepared small purple jar with Wan-Jôong, the go-between, and Wan's deputy, Bbaang-the-Stag. The master of the Fire Sticks tells his son Bbieng-Dlaang to bring him a horn. He slits the throat of a hen over a Mnong bowl filled with *coot*, on which he has laid a few pieces of charcoal. They receive a share of the blood, the rest being absorbed by the beer wort. He passes the drinking straw to Wan-Jôong, kissing Wan's hand. In a brief speech, he relates the history of the imminent *Nyiit Döng:* how in the year the village ate the forest of the Daak Rmüt, the Saffron Brook (which is to say, 1946), it had decided to offer the Spirit of the Soil this great collective festival. During the celebration of the posts of the Paddy that year, when the holy men were drinking at his, Bbaang-the-Pregnant-Man's house, they had called in Wan-Jôong, who, at the time, was sharing his long house and lived on the other side of Kraang-Drüm. They had asked Wan to be go-between (*ndraany*) in the Festival of the Soil. They had then proceeded to "the uprooting of the Rattan" (*dok Reh*). Now, Bbaang says, the time has come for the village to carry out the promise it had made the year "when we ate the forest of the Saffron Brook."

When the master of the Fire Sticks has finished his speech, Wan-Jôong has Bbaang-the-Stag touch the drinking straw. Bbaang has been appointed second go-between because he is the main holy man in Phii Ko'. Then Wan inserts the *gut* in the jar, praying for the greatest possible success in this undertaking. The horn resounds in powerful, prolonged rolls. It falls silent when the principal go-between, having concluded his prayer, launches into a harangue of his own:

"O you, our village community. It is now time to perform our great sacrifice. 'We are coerced into it,' say the poor. But this is not so. It is our ancestors, our forebears, who have set us the example, and we only do as they did. We force no one to go to great expense, but tradition requires us to hold this festival. . . . For three years I have been telling people to set about getting ready, to find buffaloes, to prepare jars. But every year it has been necessary to wait for the year after. Now we can no longer delay, we must put ourselves to rights with the Spirits. Some say, 'You people begin looking for buffaloes, and we will follow you.' Well, speaking for myself, I am going to find a buffalo, for it is essential that this year we honor the Soil. . . ."

Bbaang-the-Pregnant-Man takes down the sacred winnowing basket that contains the Fire Sticks and other ritual implements. The go-between exorcises them by passing a handful of blood-drenched charcoal over them. Wan repeats the gesture over our host's drum and all the village's metal musical instruments, which have been assembled here for the occasion: two sets of six flat gongs, one set of three bossed gongs, and one giant flat gong. Then he goes outside to lay the charcoal on the path to the cemetery, asking the coals to beg the people in the Underworld not to grow angry and to protect the villagers.

Upon Wan's return, the three men together, using blood-soaked wort, anoint the Fire Sticks, the Rattan rope, and the contents of the sacred winnowing basket. Then Wan alone blesses the bossed gongs, the *cing*, the *chaar*, and the drum. Two young men, each armed with a pair of mallets, squat at either end of the drum, and for some minutes the house shakes as its deep voice sings a syncopated double roll.

Krŏng-Jôong takes his turn at the jar (I had begun to drink before Wan-Jôong finished his speech), and Baap Can speaks next:

"Let those who have goods of value set out in search of buffaloes. Let those who can search for buffaloes search for them. Let those who can afford to search only for pigs search for pigs. . . . But no one is forcing you to do this. I am a holy man in the forest and in the village, and I teach what it is proper to do in order to obey our ancestors. But I do not want anyone to come later and reproach me for ordering him to borrow!"

Krŏng-Jôong, who has relinquished his place at the jar to the go-between, speechifies in his turn:

"We say that in order to follow the teachings of our ancestors one must look for buffaloes. The poor say to us, 'You can do that because you are rich.' But if we are rich, it is because we rise early, we leave the village to sow, to weed, to watch over our fields. . . . That is how we get salt and paddy. But the poor do nothing and so they have no paddy. They let weeds, rats, peacocks, wild boar, and deer invade their fields. They never bestir themselves, and all the while the peacocks and wild boar lay waste to their *miir*. . . ."

Wan-Jôong passes the drinking straw to Bbaang-the-Stag and then distributes the instruments in the two flat-gong sets to various young men. Placing himself at the head of the procession, the go-between winds his way through the village, followed by the two *cing* orchestras playing in unison. They go into every long house, entering by the private door at one end and exiting from the private door at the other end. In each home they pass through, those present sprinkle at least the leaders of the *cing* groups with fresh water, "so that bodies may be cool, so that there may be no death and no debts." If the household owns a hanging drum, two musicians quit the orchestra, which stops playing, and beat it resoundingly in a double syncopated rhythm. In this fashion, Wan-Jôong leads his double orchestra into every dwelling, neglecting none. This is "the circuit of the flat gongs" (*rok cing*).

On our return, Baap Can, who drank after Bbaang-the-Stag and then gave his place to Bbôong-the-Deputy, reproaches the young men, saying that they have not sounded all the drums in the village. A brief controversy ensues. Having thus drawn attention to himself, the holy man embarks on some self-glorification as an "eater of buffaloes." He enumerates in detail the sacrifices of twenty horned victims that he has made since he set himself up in a separate household, and he describes the four animals he has sold since he became a *kuang*.

The drinkers follow each other at the jar. Bbieng-Dlaang passes among them with a large Vietnamese bowl containing chicken ground with squash leaves, pepper, and salt. Each person takes a pinch.

Kraang-Drüm, the son-in-law and neighbor of Bbaang-the-Pregnant-Man, circulates among us for quite another reason. He offers everyone a long-nosed gourd containing water and a few grains of white rice. In turn, each person dips his finger in the gourd, brushes it over his own belly, and again dips his finger in the water. He repeats this gesture seven times, offering wishes, of course, and in conclusion, cracks the joints of his fingers. Only Bbaang-the-One-Eyed, standing beside little Wan (for whom Kraang-Drüm gathers up the medication), brushes his finger first over his own belly and then immediately over that of the little boy, repeating the double gesture seven times. After Kraang-Drüm has progressed from the first person to the last—for people do not move from their place in order "to smear on the medication" (*mboong gun*)—he returns and over his son's belly repeats the gesture that all adults present have made. This magic operation is explained thus:

"Our buffalo-mother [that is to say, an adult's buffalo-soul, the young buffalo being the soul of an ailing child] is grazing, and the young buffalo comes up to nibble grass near his mother's muzzle. The female buffalo jostles him, and the baby buffalo falls down and hurts himself. Because she is tired, the cow has jostled the little one. That is why one takes something from the big mother buffalo to rub on the little one, so that he may get well. What comes from the belly of the buffalo-mother is called *gun*." *

I take this opportunity to ask Wan to clarify for me the *gun* allegedly possessed by the "voracious" canton chief of Daa' Mroong, in Upper Don-

---

* A difficult word to translate, and the term "medication" does not convey its sense satisfactorily. *Gun* denotes everything that, by virtue of its internal magic qualities, both causes illness and supplies the cure. However, some *gun* are purely beneficent forces. These are notably vegetables—most often, the Zingiberaceae—used in various rites; for example, the *gun Baa* (translated as "magic plant of the Paddy") and *gun Ik* ("magic plant of Coolness"). Western medicines are also called *gun*.

Wan-Jôong, go-between for the future Great Festival of the Soil, leads the gong players through the village

naï. "That's got nothing to do with buffaloes jostling or competing for the salina," he replies. "It has to do with the *gun* that 'eats' men. Bbaang-Jrae [not to be confused with old Troo's son] cultivates it. He rubs it on his palms, and if he just hits somebody he kills him."

People chatter and drink, and time passes. Presently, Wan-Jôong picks up the sacred winnowing basket containing the Fire Sticks, Rattan rope, and the Mnong bowl of beer wort and blood, and he goes out, followed by one flat-gong orchestra walking in single file as it plays. Pipe clenched between his teeth, the go-between at the head of this musical procession carries the sacred basket to his house and sets it down on his low platform. With the help of his sons, he prepares a jar while waiting for the other *kuang* still at Bbaang-the-Pregnant-Man's to bestir themselves. They finally arrive. Bbaang-the-Pregnant-Man and Bbaang-the-Stag join their host at the foot of the jar, by which Wan has placed the Mnong bowl with the *coot* and blood he brought in the sacred basket. After slitting the neck of a chick over the bowl, Wan passes the drinking straw to the master of the Fire Sticks, who hands it to the second go-between to hold for a moment, and then inserts it in the jar. The three men describe to the Spirits the offerings that are being presented to them now, and beg for their protection. Each man takes a pinch of the blood-drenched wort, and together they anoint the contents of the sacred basket, with particular emphasis on the Fire Sticks and Rattan. Lastly, while the master of the *Rnut* drinks from the jar, in the same fashion the go-between anoints his suspended drum and the flat gongs carried by the orchestra. Bbaang-Jieng is not actually drinking; he has merely tasted the *rnööm* and, finding it too bitter, he escapes under a shower of taunts.

Without question, today is the day for treatment by what we might call the "antibody" method. Tôong-Biing turns up, bearing a long-nosed gourd that contains water and grains of rice, a Vietnamese bowl of hulled rice, and a piece of iron. He has a terrible eye ache and wants Bbaang-the-Stag to treat him. Bbaang had suffered from the same trouble a few years ago. His condition had been so serious that he had had to call in a shamaness from Paang Pê', who had finally succeeded in curing him. As a result, Bbaang-the-Stag now possesses the *gun* for an eye affliction, and Tôong-Biing has come to take some from him. The bearer of the *gun* must moisten a tuft of cotton in the long-nosed-gourd water, brush it over his own eye, then over the eye of the sick man. He again moistens the cotton in the water with the grains of rice, etc.—seven times, plus one. But despite the offered remuneration of a bowl of rice and a piece of iron, Bbaang-the-Stag needs a lot of coaxing. Tôong stands there, looking miserable; both eyes are swollen, and I suggest to him that he go early tomorrow morning to the Health Station. But he answers, "*Weer!* Taboo."

For three days, foreigners are taboo for him (in the double sense that he may neither go to the house of a foreigner nor receive one), as are widowers and dogs (neither may enter his house). Likewise, he must not eat ripe peppers (green are permitted) or *pae sei* (a *Gnetum* that, when ripe, has the brownish-red coloration of pepper).

People do not linger at Wan-Jôong's; his jar is not renowned for its quality. Some are hoping to finish the day more agreeably at Bbaang-the-Stag's. As second go-between and master of the Fire Sticks in Phii Ko', he should rightly repeat in his own house the same sacrifice offered by Bbaang-the-Pregnant-Man and Wan-Jôong. But Bbaang declares that he has no *rnööm* ready, and there the matter rests.

December 10

After a night of wind and rain—the last stirrings of the wet season—the village shakes itself awake. The day's prospects are still uncertain, for the sky is darkened by a ceiling of low clouds. Contrary weather notwithstanding, an air of gaiety prevails, and even before the women have finished pounding the rice, a group of young men has completed "the circuit of the *cing*." They have made each dwelling resound with the powerful song of the six flat gongs and the houses of those who possess drums vibrate to their furious double rhythm.

Around eight o'clock, Krông, Jôong, and their daughter, carrying panniers and bush hooks, set out for Nyôong Brah, where they will spend a few days. They will be helping Bbür-Aang, Jôong-the-Healer's son by an earlier marriage, to bring his paddy from his *rdae* to his granary in the village.

Sar Luk stretches out to enjoy a day's respite that no special rite will disturb. A group of women goes to gather wild vegetables. Others bring their looms outside for the first time in a month to work in their yards.

The flat-gong orchestra executes a second "circuit of the *cing*" in midafternoon, and a third at sunset. In this way, one keeps the Spirits in suspense and also reminds the villagers of the promise they have made them.

Except for a brief visit from some Paang Döng people who come to invite me to their "taking of the Straw," an otherwise uneventful day for Sar Luk draws to a close.

December 11

Again the village awakens to the music of "the circuit of the flat gongs." A few women weave, others do odd jobs about the house; the men also remain in the village. Around nine-thirty, all heads of household gather at Bbaang-the-Stag's. The holy man in Phii Ko' has brought out a *yang dâm* of beer and placed it in the middle of his common room. His house must be the scene of the first phase of the *rwaang brii* ("the inspection of the forest"), for this year the village will eat the forest of Phii Ko'. Each head of household brings with him an ordinary Mnong bowl filled with white rice. As he places it in the big winnowing basket beside the small neckless jar, he announces, "Here is my rice," and sits down. Of the holy men, Baap Can is the only one to bring some. Truu, who is not a *croo weer,* has brought none. The hulled rice will be divided among the holy men. All those who want a field to cultivate to feed their families are on hand, except for Kröng-Jôong. But before leaving yesterday for Nyôong Brah, he had told Bbaang-the-Stag he would be absent, and today he is represented by Kroong-Big-Navel, one of his wife's sons by a previous marriage.

Bbaang-the-Stag passes the drinking straw to Baap Can, his brother-in-law, who hands it on to Bbaang-Jieng-the-Pregnant-Man, who inserts it in the jar. The three holy men recite:

> *"Today, I lead the village community, the community*
> > *of a single forest;*
> > > *I lead, of the teen-age girls, two,*
> > > *I lead, of the teen-age boys, one, two.*
> > *Gôih Tree, do not splinter,*
> > *Chah Tree, do not be abusive,*
> > *Branch of the Tloong Tree, do not scold us,*
> > > *do not heap reproaches upon us.*
> > *Prevent legs from being broken,*
> > > *arms from being cut,*
> > > *one's returning disabled.*
> > *Ward off the epidemic,*
> > *ward off the tarsier,*
> > *ward off the hanging beehive.*
> > *Devour, O Flame, O Spirit of the Fire."*

Baap Can pulls two stalks of lalang grass from the roof, breaks them into equal lengths, and arranges the pieces in parallel lines on the ground to represent the general configuration of individual parcels of land. In this instance, Baap Can is filling a double role—that of a holy man in Sar Luk (because he is head of the Rjee) and that of a holy man in Phii Ko' (because he is married to Aang-the-Long, sister of Bbaang-the-Stag). He lays out three parallel rows of sticks, thus outlining the disposition of plots that had been assigned to each head of household when a division was made two years ago. At that time, Sar Luk had already decided to "eat" this section of the forest of Phii Ko', a plan that was abandoned scarcely a month after the *rwaang brii.* The row nearest the old man serves only to mark off, for the record, the swampy area no one had wanted. Baap Can will borrow sticks from this row, as needed, to extend

The holy men (Baap Can, Bbaang-the-Pregnant-Man, holding the straw, and Bbaang-the-Stag) consecrate the jar opened for "the inspection of the forest of Phii Ko'," which we will "eat" next

the most important line, which indicates the fields cut from the side of the hill. The intermediate row designates fields at the foot of this hill, which border on the swampy zone.

First, Baap Can deals with the previous distribution, beginning with the field farthest upstream. He asks every man present whether he is still in agreement. The repetition is absolutely essential. Some people were not on hand before (Choong-the-Soldier, for example, who was discharged from the Army only last year); or they were not yet cultivating land separately (like Tôong-Wan) but now need a plot of their own; others have died (like Ndêet, the husband of the incestuous Aang) or have emigrated (like Taang-the-Widower after his wife's death). Also to be considered are those who are bound by recent friendship and wish to have adjoining fields, like Bbaang-the-One-Eyed and Tôong-Biing, who, starting this summer, occupy the same long house.

Several times, Baap Can reviews this map, which indicates the distribution of every plot of land, and he discusses it with the interested parties. Then he gives the signal for departure. It is about ten-thirty. Each man carries his bush hook and a small pannier containing a yam (*buum lô'*), some ritual grasses, and a little hoe. It is the first fine day after a week of, variously, drizzle and rain. The air has not yet dried the vegetation, which glistens in the full gamut of its varied greens. Now that the sky has cleared, it seems higher, deeper. We strike out along the French track. Bbaang-the-Stag tears off a *rkôong* leaf and, as he walks, waves it before his lips and blows on it to ask that the roedeer not bell and that the expedition be carried out under favorable auspices. Next, he breaks off the top of some lalang grass growing by the side of the track, and knots it around his propitiatory leaf. We cross Paang Döng territory, where, leaving the new track, which leads to Bboon Dlei, we continue along the old one, which runs along the river, twenty or more meters from the bank. We cross the Brook of the Salina-in-the-Shape-of-a-Snake's-Neck by means of a culvert, and the Saffron Brook by a more substantial bridge. Finally, at eleven-fifteen, still led by Bbaang-the-Stag, we leave the track and plunge into the bush, walking due north. For almost a half hour, we make our way through fairly dense jungle dotted with trees, before we come to our guide's future field, which lies at the foot of the hill. The vegetation is changing in appearance. Although almost as dense as the area we just left, it is less difficult to penetrate. Tall, sharp-edged grass growing thickly in a muddy soil is succeeded by bushy undergrowth. The ground becomes firmer underfoot, which makes walking easier. Now the trees are tall and close together. This twenty-year-old forest promises to yield fertile soil. Only its distance from the village accounts for the decision two years ago to defer exploiting it. But today everyone agrees that it is beautiful.

Bbaang-the-Stag points out his own land, then shows his *jôok*, Kraang-

Drüm, the field that will be his. An imaginary northwest-southeast line
separates them. Assisted by his two Sar Luk colleagues, the holy man in
Phii Ko' indicates to each man the plot destined for him. It is a little con-
fusing to try to locate on the actual terrain the rectilinear alignment Baap
Can had mapped out on the ground with twigs. Actually, for the moment,
it is not a question of mapping the entire *miir* but of suggesting the succession of fields, which will be visited one after another. And this is still
not too precise. Following the northwest line that separates the future
fields of Bbaang-the-Stag and his friend, we come to the plot of Yôong-
the-Mad. We cross this, and the holy men point out to Choong-the-
Soldier the land allotted to him, which lies to the west of the widow's. We
return to the center of Yôong's field. When Sar Luk abandoned the project of cultivating this area, the people of Phii Dih had asked Bbaang-the-
Stag to rent them this forest. They had even begun to cut it down, but
then an epidemic struck the village, and they deserted this forest, where
the trees were too big, for a shrub area easier to clear. To the east of
Yôong, Tôong-Biing immediately takes possession of his field. He lops off
a bush at the midpoint, and at the foot of the slender decapitated trunk
buries his yam and presses the loose soil down seven times with his
elbow. He is about to insert the bouquet of ritual grasses he has brought
with him, to which he has added the tip of a branch broken off on the
spot, into a slit in the trunk, but he is stopped and told that this is taboo.
So he piles some branches over his planted tuber, and throws two pieces
of wood to the east and to the west.

"The inspection of the forest" continues. Each proprietor "cuts a
stump" on his terrain. Some follow Tôong-Biing's example and immediately carry out the rite of taking possession. The outer borders of the future *miir* are marked by cutting back undergrowth, starting from a landmark—a large tree or a rock—indicated by the holy men; this is
unnecessary where there is a ditch, which suffices as a line of demarca-
tion. Lying on Krŏng-Jôong's field is a giant of the forest, a *nggeer* (*Hopea
odorata* Roxb.), which is highly valued as lumber for construction. The
tree is partly cut up. Bbaang-the-Stag does not hide his indignation. The
people of Phii Dih felled the tree and informed him only after they had
carved out a canoe. When such happenings occur, the Spirit of the Soil attacks the holy man. Had the Phii Dih people acted properly, they would
first have asked Bbaang's authorization, bringing him a bowl of white rice.
And once the canoe was dug out, they should have offered him the sacrifice of a chicken and a jar. (If the entire tree was to be consumed, these
gifts should be accompanied by a *yang dâm.*) "That is the normal conduct
that should be observed, but those people do as they please!"

By two o'clock, "the inspection of the forest" is completed. The men
who have preferred to remain with the group of holy men now scatter.
Each goes to his own field to perform the rite of "cutting the stump and

planting the tuber" (*sreh ngguu tâm buum*). I follow Bbôong-the-Deputy. When he reaches his land again, he kneels at the foot of the freshly decapitated bush and, with his hoe, opens two furrows. In the smaller, he "plants the grasses and the *ngör* bamboo." Actually, he has no bamboo but only two ritual grasses, *ül tlaa* (*Carex indica*) and *rboo* (a tree with alternate leaves). This morning, he "fed" this bouquet some head rice. In the second and much deeper furrow, he buries his yam, reputed to grow if the harvest promises to be good, or to shrink if the yield will be small. He places some pottery shards in the same furrow, together with some *kiep mêem* shells; they have an exorcising function. Same function for the strong-smelling ginger (*caa*) that accompanies them. Bbôong rubs the edge of his bush-hook blade with the ginger to prevent accidents; he chews and spits out a piece to drive off tarsiers, whose presence in a freshly cleared field obliges the proprietor to abandon it. Bbôong covers the furrow with earth, which he tamps down seven times with his elbow. This will prevent the roedeer and wild boar from later invading and laying waste to his field. He accompanies the performance of each ritual operation with the recitation of verses that state its purpose: to prevent the accidents that are frequent when cutting down trees; to forestall the arrival of harmful animals that would require his abandoning the field, or of pillagers that would ravage the crops. When each man has completed his ceremony of "cutting the stump and planting the tuber," which marks his ritualistic taking possession of his land, he joins a few others, and the men return in small groups to the village. By four o'clock in the afternoon, the last laggard—Kraang-Drüm—arrives home.

Now Sar Luk enters the one period of genuine leisure it enjoys in the course of a year. The women weave, the men look for bush-hook handles and forge tools. These few essential tasks leave much free time, which the villagers use to travel or to feast and carouse. This until the dry season sends them, armed with axes and bush hooks, out to the new forest that is to be felled, thus introducing a new annual cycle of toil and troubles. Then we will eat the forest of Phii Ko'.

The forest of the Stone Spirit Gôo has yielded all that men's labor could draw from it, and it is abandoned. It will live on in memory as a guidepost by which the villagers will date events occurring in the course of the year in which it was "eaten." After some years have passed and after all the other forests on the territory of Sar Luk and Phii Ko' have been cut down, they will return to slash it once again, burn it off, sow in the earth it will have renewed, and harvest the grain its soil will produce. And of the events that will come to pass in the course of these manifold labors, they will say again that they took place "the year when we ate the forest of the Stone Spirit Gôo."

Bibliography

Glossary

Indexes

BIBLIOGRAPHY

ABBREVIATIONS

B.E.F.E.O.: *Bulletin de l'Ecole Française d'Extrême-Orient*, Hanoi.
B.I.I.E.H.: *Bulletin de l'Institut Indochinois pour l'Etude de l'Homme*, Hanoi.
C.E.F.E.O.: *Cahiers de l'Ecole Française d'Extrême-Orient*, Hanoi.
F.A.: *France-Asie*, Saigon.
T.I.A.: *Travaux de l'Institut Anatomique de la Faculté de Médicine de l'Indochine*, Hanoi.

Canivey, J. "Notice sur les moeurs et coutumes des Moï de la région de Dalat." *Revue d'Ethnographie*, Vol. IV (1913), pp. 1–30, ill.
Condominas, G. "Le lithophone préhistorique de Ndut Lieng Krak (Darlac–Viêt-Nam–Indochine)." *Comptes-rendu de l'Institut Français d'Anthropologie*, Fasc. No. 4 (January–December 1950), Nos. 64–71 (conference of June 21, 1950), pp. 15–16.
————. "Le lithophone préhistorique de Ndut Lieng Krak." *B.E.F.E.O.*, Vol. XLV (1951), Fasc. No. 2, pp. 359–92, figs. 42–65 (map, drawings), 2 tables, bibliog., and pls. XLI–XLV.
————. "Rapport d'une mission ethnologique en Pays Mnong Gar (pays montagnards du Sud-Indochinois)." *B.E.F.E.O.*, Vol. XLVI (1952), Fasc. No. 1, pp. 303–13, fig. 38, maps, pls. XXIV–XXXV.
————. "Inceste à Sar Luk." *F.A.*, No. 73 (June 1952), pp. 263–69; No. 74 (July 1952), pp. 370–78.
————. "Ethnologie de l'Indochine et bibliographie ethnographique." *Ethnologie de l'Union française (Territoires extérieurs)*, Vol. II: *Asie, Océanie, Amérique*, by A. Leroi-Gourhan and J. Poirier, with the collaboration of A.-G. Haudricourt and G. Condominas. Coll. Pays d'Outre-Mer, 6th ser.: Peuples et Civilisations d'Outre-Mer, No. 2. Paris: Presses Universitaires de France, 1953.
————. "Chansons Mnong Gar." *F.A.*, No. 87 (August 1953), pp. 648–56.
————. "Le plus vieil instrument de musique du Monde." *Exploration Outre-mer*, pp. 58–65. Paris: La Documentation Française, 1953.
————. "Enquête linguistique parmi les Populations montagnardes du Sud Indo-chinois." *B.E.F.E.O.*, Vol. XLVI (1954), Fasc. No. 2, pp. 573–97, tables.
————. "Notes sur le *tâm bôh mae baap aa kuôn*, échange de sacrifices entre un enfant et ses père et mère (Mnong Rlâm)." *International Archives of Ethnography* (Leiden), Vol. XLVII (1955), No. 2, pp. 127–59, pls. V–VIII, photos, drawings, map, bibliog.

———— and A.-G. Haudricourt. "Première contribution à l'ethnobotanique indo-chinoise. Essai d'ethnobotanique Mnong gar (Protoindochinois du Viêtnam)." *Revue Internationale de Botanique Appliquée et d'Agriculture Tropicale*, 32nd Year, Nos. 351–52 (January–February 1952), pp. 19–27; Nos. 353–54 (March–April, 1952), pp. 168–80.

Dournes, J. *En suivant la piste des Hommes sur les Hauts-Plateaux du Viêt-Nam.* Paris: Julliard, 1955 (Coll. Sciences et Voyages), 253 pp., photos, maps, gloss.

Education, numéro spécial consacré aux Populations Montagnardes du Sud-Indochinois, No. 16 (June–August 1949), 205 pp., maps.

Haudricourt, A.-G. "Les voyelles préglottalisées en Indochine." *Bulletin de la Société de Linguistique de Paris*, Vol. XLVI (1950), Fasc. No. 1, pp. 172–82.

Huard, Captain P. "Les Mnong (contribution à l'étude des groupes ethniques du noeud des trois frontières: Annam, Cochinchine, Cambodge)." *T.I.A.*, Vol. III (1938), pp. 261–68, photos, maps, drawings.

———— and Lieutenant A. Maurice. "Les Mnong du plateau central indochinois, 1er série." *B.I.I.E.H.*, Vol. II (1939), Fasc. No. 1, pp. 27–148, photos, maps, drawings.

Humann, M.-R. "Exploration chez les Moïs (Indo-Chine), 1888–1889." *Bulletin de la Société de Géographie* (Paris), 7e série, Vol. XIII (1892), pp. 496–514, map.

Husmann, H. "Das neuendekte Steinzeitlithophon." *Die Musik Forschung*, 5th Year, Pam. No. 1 (1952), pp. 47–49.

Jouin, B.-Y. *La mort et la tombe, l'abandon de la tombe: Les cérémonies, prières et sacrifices se rapportant à ces très importantes manifestations de la vie des autochtones du Darlac.* Paris: Institut d'Ethnologie, 1949, pp. 260, ill., map, bibliog.

Kirby, P. "Communication on the 'Lithotone' discovered in Indo-China in 1949 by Mr. Georges Condominas, and described by Mr. André Schaeffner in 1951." *South African Journal of Sciences*, September 1952, pp. 48–50.

Lewis, N. *A Dragon Apparent. Travels in Indochina.* London: Jonathan Cape, 1951, 317 pp., photos, map.

Maitre, H. *Les régions Moïs du Sud-Indochinois. Le Plateau du Dar Lac.* Paris: Plon, 1909, 335 pp., ill., maps.

————. *Les jungles Moï, Mission Henri Maitre, 1909–1911. Indochine Sud-Centrale. Exploration et histoire des hinterlands moï du Cambodge, de la Cochinchine, de l'Annam et du Bas-Laos.* Paris: Larose, 1912, 578 pp., photos, drawings, maps, bibliog.

————. "Les populations de l'Indochine." *Bulletin et Mémoires de la Société d'Anthropologie de Paris*, 6e série, Vol. III (1912), pp. 107–15.

Maurice, Lieutenant A. "Recherches sur les Mnong, 2e série." *T.I.A.*, Vol. VI (1939), pp. 1–20, drawings.

————. "A propos des mutilations dentaires chez les Moïs." *B.I.I.E.H.*, Vol. IV (1941), pp. 135–39.

Monfleur, A. *Monographie de la province du Darlac.* Hanoi: Imprimerie d'Extrême-Orient, 1931 (Exposit. col. internat., Paris, 1931), photos, maps.

Ner, M. "Au pays du droit maternel (compte-rendu de missions)." *B.E.F.E.O.*, Vol. XXX (1930), Fasc. Nos. 3–4, pp. 533–76, photos.

———. "Compte-rendu de mission." *C.E.F.E.O.*, No. 28, 3rd Qtr. (1941), pp. 4–8.

———. "Les coutumiers moïs." *C.E.F.E.O.*, No. 30 (1942), pp. 14–15.

Saurin, E. "Etudes géologiques sur l'Indochine du Sud-Est (Sud-Annam, Cochinchine, Cambodge oriental)." *Bulletin du Service Géologique de l'Indochine*, Vol. XXII, No. 1; Hanoi: Imprimeve d'Extrême-Orient, 1935, 419 pp., pls., drawing, map, bibliog.

Schaeffner, A. "Premières remarques sur le lithophone de Ndut Lieng Krak." *Comptes-rendus de l'Institut Français d'Anthropologie*, No. 69 (conference of June 21, 1950), pp. 16–17.

———. "Une importante découverte archéologique: le lithophone de Ndut Lieng Krak, Viêtnam." *Revue de Musicologie*, 33rd Year, Nos. 97–98 (July 1951), pp. 1–19, photos.

Schmid, M., P. de la Souchère, and D. Godard. *Les sols et la végétation au Darlac et sur le Plateau des Trois-Frontières*. Saigon: I.D.E.O., 1951 (Archives des Recherches Agronomiques au Cambodge, au Laos et au Viêtnam, No. 8, 1951, 112 pp., photos, maps, tables, graphs.

Yersin, A., "De Nhatrang à Tourane par les pays moïs, 1894." *Indochine*, Nos. 137 (April), 146 (June), 150 (July), 1943, maps.

Supplementary Bibliography

IN this supplement, the principle followed in the main bibliography of citing all works that mention the Mnong Gar has been abandoned. Otherwise, it would have been necessary to indicate reviews of the first French edition of the present work and of *L'Exotique est quotidien*. Of all such, I do list here two essays because they are more largely concerned with the Mnong Gar than with the book under review.

Similarly, I have eliminated books and articles that, among data of diverse origin, mention only one Mnong detail in support of some argumentation or for purposes of comparison. I have noted one article in which the Mnong source plays a considerable role, and one study that rests in part on an analysis of the Mnong kinship system.

Also excluded is material relating to the Ndut Lieng Krak lithophone. This can be consulted in the new edition of *L'Exotique est quotidien*, listed below.

Most of the works cited below appear, of necessity, over my signature. I need scarcely say that I should have preferred a much shorter list, but to incorporate the material in a single large work requires time that has not been at my disposal.

Barber, M. "A Critical Evaluation of the Indo-China Ethnography of Georges
    Condominas." In partial fulfillment of the requirements for the degree of
    Bachelor of Philosophy in South-East Asian Studies. University of Hull,
    September 1971, iv + 79 pp., multig., bibliog.
Condominas, G. "Fête à Sar Luk." *Les Temps Modernes*, No. 194 (July 1962), pp.
    15–47.
———. "Minorités autochtones en Asie du Sud-Est." *Politique Etrangère*, Vol.
    XXVIII, No. 1 (1963), pp. 44–57.
———. *L'Exotique est quotidien, Sar Luk, Viêt-Nam central*. Paris: Plon, 1965,
    538 pp., figs., maps, pls., ind.
———. "Classes sociales et groupes tribaux au Sud-Viêt-Nam." *Cahiers Interna-
    tionaux de Sociologie*, No. 40, new series (1965), pp. 161–70.
———. "Commentaires sur l'étude du Prof. P. E. De Josselin De Jong: 'Agricul-
    tural Rites in Southeast Asia—An Interpretation.'" *Journal of Asian
    Studies*, Vol. XXIV, No. 2 (1965), pp. 291–93.
———. "Two Brief Notes Concerning Mnong Gar." *Lingua*, No. 15 (1965), pp.
    48–52.
———. "Some Mnong Gar Religious Concepts: A World of Forms." *Folk Religion
    and the Worldview in the Southwestern Pacific*, published under the direc-
    tion of N. Matsumoto and T. Mabuchi. Tokyo: The Keio Institute of Cul-
    tural and Linguistic Studies, 1967, pp. 55–61.
———. "Le Déluge, chant mythique Mnong Gar." *L'Ephémère*, No. 14 (1970),
    pp. 216–21.
———. "Le Tabou de l'aîné(e) du conjoint." *Echanges et Communications:
    Mélanges offerts à Claude Lévi-Strauss à l'occasion de son 60ème anniver-
    saire*, ed. by J. Pouillon and P. Maranda. Paris and La Haye: Mouton,
    1970, pp. 235–41.
———. "Vietnamiens et montagnards du Centre et Sud-Viêtnam." *Tradition et ré-
    volution au Viêtnam*, published under the direction of J. Chesneaux, G.
    Boudarel, and D. Hemery. Paris: Anthropos, 1971, pp. 135–46.
———. "De la rizière au *miir*." *Langues et Techniques. Nature et Société*, ed. by
    J. M. C. Thomas and L. Bernot. Paris: Klincksieck, 1972, pp. 115–29, figs.,
    4 pls. Translated into English by M. Fineberg under the title "From the
    Rice Field to the *Miir*," *Social Science Information*, Vol. II, No. 2 (1972),
    pls. I–V, pp. 41–62.
———. "Musical Stones for the God of Thunder," tr. by N. Stoke. *Crossing Cul-
    tural Boundaries*, ed. by S. Kimball and J. B. Watson. San Francisco:
    Chandler Publishing Co., 1972, pp. 232–56.
———. "Deux aspects de la civilisation du végétal en Asie du Sud-Est." *Etudes de
    géographie tropicale offertes à Pierre Gourou*. Paris and La Haye: Mouton,
    1972, pp. 120–26, pls. I–VII.
———. "Aspects of Economics among the Mnong Gar of Vietnam: Multiple
    Money and the Middleman." *Ethnology*, Vol. II, No. 3 (1972), pp. 202–19.
———. "Ethics and Comfort: An Ethnographer's View of His Profession" (Distin-
    guished Lecture 1972). *Annual Report, 1972 American Anthropological As-
    sociation* (1973), pp. 1–17.
———. "Schéma d'un *mhö*', séance chamanique mnong gar," in "Chamanisme et

possession en Asie du Sud-Est et dans le Monde Insulindien." *Asie du Sud-Est et Monde Insulindien, Bulletin du Centre de Documentation et de Recherche (CeDRASEMI)*, Vol. IV (1973), Fasc. No. 1, pp. 61–70.

————. "Rites de la reconstruction du village mnong gar (*dlang rngool et mhaam hih*)." *L'Homme, hier et aujourd'hui. Recueil d'études en hommage à André Leroi-Gourhan*. Paris: Cujas, 1973, pp. 365–82, 13 figs., bibliog.

————. "L'Entr'aide agricole chez les Mnong Gar (Proto-Indochinois du Viêt-Nam central)," *Etudes Rurales*, Nos. 53–56 (1974), pp. 407–20.

De Josselin De Jong, P. E. "An Interpretation of Agricultural Rites in Southeast Asia, with a Demonstration of Use of Data from Both Continental and Insular Asia." *Journal of Asian Studies*, Vol. XXIV, No. 2 (1965), pp. 283–91.

Lebar, F. M., G. C. Hickey, and J. K. Musgrave. *Ethnic Groups of Mainland Southeast Asia*. New Haven: Human Relations Area Files Press, 1964, 288 pp., maps, bibliog., ind.

Levy, P., "Les Mnong Gar du Centre Viêt-Nam et Georges Condominas." *L'Homme*, Vol. IX, No. 1 (1969), pp. 78–91.

Lounsbury, F. G., "A Formal Account of the Crow- and Omaha-type Kinship Terminologies." *Explorations in Cultural Anthropology: Essays in Honor of George Peter Murdock*, ed. by W. H. Goodenough. New York: McGraw-Hill Book Company, 1964, pp. 351–93.

Murdock, G. P. (ed.). *Social Structure in South-East Asia*. New York: Wenner-Gren Foundation for Anthropological Research (Viking Fund Publications in Anthropology, No. 29), 1960.

Papy, L., "L'agriculture sur brûlis chez les Moïs des Hauts Plateaux du Viêtnam central, d'après Georges Condominas." *Les Cahiers d'Outre-Mer, Revue de Géographie* (Bordeaux), Vol. XI, No. 41 (January–March 1958), pp. 79–83.

GLOSSARY

OF MNONG GAR WORDS AND TERMS *

Aê Diê (a Rhade term): the Lord of the Sky in the Rhade pantheon. Used by Western missionaries to denote the Christian deity.

alak: Vietnamese rice aquavit, as distinguished from rice beer (*rnööm*).

(tlaang) ayaa: the *ayaa* eagle, a large mythical bird of prey.

ba': to carry (a child) on one's back, wrapped in a blanket. By extension, to beget (construed in this sense in genealogies); to rear.

baap: father of. E.g., Baap Can.

beng: religious ban; taboo.

> *Beng nyiim!* "Crying is taboo!" *See weer.*

biet coot: "meeting for the wort." A communion meal in certain rites.

(Yaang) Boec: Spirit and group of Spirits governing the Underworld (*Phaan*), where they dwell.

bôh sür baap in: "to singe [roast] a pig in honor of one's father." The latter is expected to offer a series of gifts in return. A family rite corresponding to the *Tâm Bôh*, which, however, can be performed only by those who are not related.

böt daak: "[fishing by] damming the stream." When such fishing is done in the river, the entire village participates.

(Yaang) Brieng: Spirit and group of Spirits of Violent Death, residing in the Sky.

broo: to lead (someone) into all the houses of the village, especially in order to offer an object for sale.

> *broo rnôom:* the ritual procession of male and female servants of the sacrifice on the night of the *Nyiit Döng* (*q.v.*) preceding the killing of the buffaloes.

cae trôo': "resin from the Sky." Used by the shamans (*njau*) for their fumigations.

caak: soul-eating sorcerers.

> *caak Ddoong:* woodland sorcerers related to the evil Spirits *Mâp Mang, Phöt Puu,* etc.

---

* The reader interested in questions of language will find complementary information in the Plant Names and Subject Indexes. The alphabetization of Mnong Gar terms follows the author's preference for a phonetic transcription (the only possible one in 1949 on an ordinary typewriter). Thus, double (long) vowels and double (preglottalized) consonants are considered as one (thus, *ndrii* precedes *ndrieng*; *ng* (ŋ) and *ny* (ñ) are treated as separate units (thus, *ntuung* precedes *ngkook*); and diacritical marks over vowels affect their ordering (*o* precedes *ô*, which precedes *ö*—thus, *dööm* follows *dôop*).

caak nêet nêet: a nocturnal bird considered to be a sorcerer in search of victims.

caan: to borrow.

chaar: giant flat gong. *See cing; goong.*

choh jöng: "to spit on the foot." A ritual payment that is made after a burial.

chuu (or *suu*) *ntôih:* "to set fire to the slashed forest."

cing: flat gongs, six of which, in graduated sizes, form an orchestra. *See chaar; goong; rok cing.*

coop môoc: "visit to the cemetery." The ritual takes place seven days after interment and marks the permanent abandonment of the grave.

coor jöng ier: "cutting with chicken's feet." A work rite, performed in conjunction with felling a large tree.

coot: rice-beer wort. A ferment made mainly of rice flour (*ndrii*) to which a large quantity of bran has been added. The mixture is placed in a jar that is kept hermetically sealed for a few days, a month, or even longer. To obtain the *rnööm (q.v.)*, one need only fill the jar with water. But first one scoops out a bit of *coot* into a Mnong bowl (*kröö*); a pinch of this is used in anointing and praying.

> *coot mhaam:* "wort [impregnated with] blood"—that is, blood taken from the sacrificed animal. The anointment thus expresses the double offering that is the basis of all Montagnard religious ceremonies: the libation (the *coot* representing the jar of rice beer) and the blood sacrifice (the blood symbolizing the animal chosen as victim for the ritual).

croo weer tööm brii tööm bboon: "the holy men in the forest and in the village." Normally, there are three: the *Rnoh*, who is in charge of field allotments for planting; the *Rnut*, who guards the sacred Fire Sticks; and the *Rnööp*, "the holy man in the village" who is the final authority on questions relating to changes of site for individual dwellings, for a village as a whole (*rngool*), etc. In Sar Luk, the three roles are performed, respectively, by Baap Can, Bbaang-the-Pregnant-Man, and Kröng-Jôong.

cum tii: reciprocal hand kissing (actually, one blows lightly on the partner's hand). It takes place only at the foot of a jar that is to be consecrated, or around a winnowing basket when a ritual gift is about to be offered. However, *see* p. 174.

daak: water; river; brook; expanse of water. The word precedes the names of streams or lakes; *e.g.,* Daak Mei, Daak Laak.

> *daak mpaa:* watering place.

ding: bamboo tube. Generally denotes drinking tubes, which often have fire-worked decoration.

> *ding paa:* fire-worked bamboo tubes containing buffalo hide and bamboo-shoot preserve. In a group of *ding paa*, the two most important are the ones whose open ends are extended by a crook. They are indispensable gifts at betrothal and marriage ceremonies.

dlei: see *dôong* and Index of Plant Names.

dok Reh: "uprooting of the Rattan." A collective rite that opens a new cycle of *Nyiit Döng (q.v.).*

dôih: "legal case" or lawsuit; *e.g., geh dôih; kuang dôih; noo ngöi dôih.*

dôok braak!: "monkey-peacock!" Very coarse profanity and, if addressed to an individual, an insult.

dôong, or *dlei dôong,* or *dôong dlei:* a ritual post made of *dlei* bamboo that is planted in the sacred square on the occasion of the first sowing of the season.

dôop hêeng [*böh Yaang böh caak*]: "to gather up the soul [from the Spirits and the sorcerers]."

dôop hêeng Baa: an agrarian rite of collecting the soul of the Paddy.

dööm mbuu: "the corn season"; *i.e.,* August–September. *See jiik.*

(yang) drang: the name of a type of antique jar.

ê' loeh: "iron excrement"; *i.e.,* the clinkers produced in forging. It has magic protective powers.

Esoo geh dôih: "There is no case"; that is, no grounds for a lawsuit.

Geh dôih: "There is a case."

goec hêeng: "to tie [a piece of lalang grass] around the throat of the soul." A magic precaution to protect the souls of gravediggers.

goong: a gong with a raised boss in the middle. Played in a three-man orchestra, it is accompanied by the *chaar. See noo goong.*

gô' uiny: "to remain near the fire." The expression denotes childbirth and the related rites.

grôong: a sort of musical harness made of bracelets, necklaces, and small bells. (In Kudduu, *grôong* means "bell.") It is used in one kind of shamanist séance (*mhö'*).

gun: (1) Everything that causes illness by virtue of intrinsic magic properties and also supplies the means of cure. *Gun* is both "poison" and "medication." Those who have fallen ill possess the power (*gun*) that cures them of the illness. *See mboong gun; sam gun.* (2) Some *gun* (they belong to the genus *Curcuma*) are consistently beneficent; in these instances, *gun* has been translated as "magic plant." *See* Index of Plant Names.

gut: a drinking straw made of a reed. It is inserted into the jar so that one may suck up the *rnööm* it contains.

hêeng: souls, of which every individual possesses several, each of a different form. *See dôop hêeng; goec hêeng; (tlaang) kuulêel; mhö'; naar; tau bung.*

hii saa brii . . . . "we eat the forest [of] . . ." Followed by a proper name, the formula serves (1) to indicate the area of territory where the fields (*miir*) currently under cultivation are located; (2) to denote a given year. A year is identified not by numbers but by the name of the forest that in a given planting season was slashed, burned off, and brought under cultivation.

hih nâm: "house-granary." It is the part of a long house (*root*) where a married couple and their children live, including married daughters who do not yet have separate living quarters with their husbands.

hôol cae trôo': "fumigation [of the ailing person] with resin from the Sky." The operation precedes the shaman's departure into the Beyond. It may also be performed independently of a séance (*mhö'*).

ier: chicken.

> *ier coh rhae:* "the chicken that pecks up the maggots." The chicken, offered alive to the deceased, accompanies him into the grave.

> *ier rnööm mhaam tii:* "the chicken and the beer from the jar for the blood

anointment of the hand." This is the first sacrifice offered the deceased.

ier lâm troong Phaan: "the chicken that leads [the deceased] along the road to the Underworld." Another name for the same sacrificial fowl.

jiik: weeding. By extension, the period for weeding, which takes up the greater part of the rainy season.

joot mhaam: "to stamp on [a victim's] blood," which has been sprinkled on ritual leaves.

joot mhaam sür mhaam sau: "to stamp on the blood of a pig and the blood of a dog." A collective rite to purify the village after a violent death.

jôok: sworn friend. Specifically, a friend with whom one has made the Exchange of Buffalo Sacrifices (*Tâm Bôh*).

kaa: fish.

kaa jôt, kaa laang: varieties of very small freshwater fish.

kaa piet: fish press.

kaa sak: a fish suspended from a bamboo stake as an offering during the rite of "setting fire to the slashed forest" (*chuu ntôih*).

kahan: soldier. A Rhade word meaning "soldier" that denotes both a militiaman of the Garde Montagnarde and a rifleman.

Khiep!: "It doesn't matter!" or "All right!"

khiu: a small pannier strapped over the belly of a harvester (ventral pannier).

khoa bboon: village headman (*khoa* is a Rhade term).

khôop: a small rectangular metal box containing a mirror. An imported article.

khual Yaang: "to summon the Spirits." A chanted prayer in verse form. It is distinct from the *rec,* or the recitation of wishes in couplets, which does not require the blood of a victim.

khual Yaang ndül Baa: "to summon the Spirits in the belly of the Paddy." The prayer is chanted while applying a pinch of wort soaked with blood to the last granary post, the one facing the private door of the house.

kiep mêem: a small bivalve shell used in magic protection rites.

koon: child; son (or daughter) of.

koon maa: a child who is the reincarnation of a person recently deceased. *See njür koon.*

kôony: the younger brother of the mother; also, the son of this younger brother of the mother upon the father's death.

têng koon kôony: "to follow the daughter of the younger brother of the mother." A preferential marriage between cross-cousins. One instance: the marriage of Kroong-Big-Navel (son of Jôong-the-Healer) and Aang-of-the-Drooping-Eyelid (daughter of Baap Can).

kriet: an oblong wicker box for seed, with a narrow neck.

kuang: a rich or powerful person. Literally, "an adult male."

kuang dôih: a rich man recognized as a go-between in a lawsuit. The term could be loosely construed as "judge."

kuat (or *kat*) *rsei nang:* "to tie the thread of the days."

(tlaang) kuulêel: the *kuulêel* sparrow hawk, or the sparrow-hawk-soul of a human being. It appears at the moment of, or shortly after, the death of the host body.

lâm daak yang: "to lead to the water of the jars." At celebrations in which several jars of *rnööm* belonging to different people are assembled in one room where the contents will be drunk in the course of the same ceremony, every person present, led by the go-between (or holy men, as the case may be), passes in single file before the row of jars and tastes from each before the respective owners and their partners begin to drink.

löh (or *sreh*) *ruih:* "to chop or cut the incompletely burned felled wood." This farming chore follows immediately after burning the slashed forest (*chuu ntôih*).

mae rbaal: a large antique glass bead, cylindrical in shape; also, a necklace made of such beads.

Mâp Mang: evil Spirits who are forest dwellers and who prowl in the vicinity of paths and of places contaminated by death. *See caak Ddoong; Phöt Puu.*

mboong gun: "to smear on the poison-medication." *See gun* (1).

mbuung kriing: "hornbill beak." A motif carved at the top of the ritual pole used exclusively in buffalo sacrifices for sickness or death.

mhaam: blood. By extension, certain sacrifices that involve anointing with blood:
Mhaam Baa: of the Paddy.
mhaam jöng: of the foot.
mhaam rnôom: of the male and female servants of the sacrifice.
mhaam Rnut rsei Reh: of the Fire Sticks and Rattan rope.
mhaam sür: the sacrifice of a pig for a blood anointment.

mhö': a shamanist séance during which the shaman (*njau*) leaves for the Beyond to bring back the sick person's soul, held prisoner there by the Spirits and sorcerers. *See dôop hêeng; hôol cae trôo'; njau mhö'; tau bung.*

miir: swidden or slash-and-burn cultivation. (English-speaking geographers use the Malay term "ladang.") Denotes also the immense area cleared and cultivated by the village as a whole, or the plot of an individual household which constitutes one unit of the entire *miir.*
tum miir: field hut, generally built on very high pilings.

môih: to clear land of trees; slash; also, the season for slashing.

môong: large dark pebbles used in the boiling-water ordeal by which sorcerers are discovered.

möng ê' jju': "tobacco-excrement stick." A pipe cleaner fashioned of a thin sliver of bamboo. It is used in magic rites. The frayed end is greatly fancied as a kind of chewing tobacco by Mnong women.

mpan Baa: "to wreathe the head of the Paddy." Offerings are deposited atop already stored paddy in what constitutes the second phase of the *dôop hêeng Baa.*

mpôol: clan, or, more precisely, following Murdock's terminology, matriclan; the ensemble of individuals claiming descent from a common ancestor *through the maternal line,* the clan name being transmitted from mother to child. Members of the same *mpôol* are "brothers and sisters" when they belong to the same generation; "fathers-mothers and children" or "uncles-aunts and nephews-nieces" when they belong to two successive generations; finally, "grandparents and grandchildren" when the generations to which the clan members belong are separated by one generation or more. Members of the same clan may neither intermarry nor have sexual relations.

mprê': the aspersion of blood with a sprinkler during the purification sacrifices that follow on a violent death.

nal: the private quarters of the house (*hih nâm*) where the granary and that section of the low platform reserved as the sleeping area for couples and young girls are located.*

naang: a platform of woven bamboo.

 naang rah: ritual stall.

 naang röng: ritual veranda. These two *naang* may be built only before the house of those who are sacrificing a buffalo.

naar: magic quartz; a piece of quartz that is a pledge of an alliance (*tâm nta'*) with the Spirits. *See rtee.* The *njau* use their *naar* in treating their patients.

 naar bôok: "the quartz in the head," or the quartz-soul, which is lodged in the skull behind the forehead.

ndah: the bombax pole mast of the buffalo sacrifice.

 ndah yang: the stake for the jar in the same sacrifice. The stake is to the jar what the pole mast is to the animal being sacrificed.

ndraany: go-between.

ndrii: rice flour. When fermented, it is used in making *rnööm.*

 ndrii tâm triu: fermented pancake ceremoniously offered, on condition that the offering be reciprocated, during the Exchange of Buffalo Sacrifices. *See coot; weh phei.*

ndrieng: death by violence; or one who dies a violent death.

ndrööng Yaang: small altar hung from a purlin in the roof. It is built only for a buffalo sacrifice.

nhaa chii (or *sii*): "leaves of trees." A bundle of tree leaves (*see* footnote on p. 178 for its composition) used in setting fire to the felled wood on the site of the future *miir.*

nhaat sôor saa pae: "to chase away [the Spirits and] order [the patient] to eat vegetables." The rite is performed upon recovery from a long illness.

nhêel (or *töih*) *kec:* "announcement of the harvest," a social rite that precedes the harvesting.

 nhêel kec Phaan in: "announcement of the harvest to those dwelling in the Underworld." A religious aspect of the above (the beginning of an ancestor cult).

nier: bamboo split lengthwise and flattened to serve as a kind of carpeting or mattress, which is placed on the living platform. *See* Index of Plant Names.

njat: a funeral offering or, more especially, a sacrifice in honor of the deceased.

 njat löi laat mbrii: "funeral sacrifice for the abandonment [of the deceased] in the forest" following interment.

 njat mhaam boong: "funeral sacrifice for the blood anointment of the coffin," performed just before burial.

 njat rpuh: "funeral offering made to the buffalo." Objects are placed briefly on the body of the buffalo just sacrificed.

njau: magician. *Njau* are divided into two categories. The more common are mere

---

* Young boys (and guests) sleep on the section of the low platform that is in the common room (*wah*). —*Trans.*

healers (*njau proproh*), who are able to care for patients only by massage (*proproh*) or by simple magical ministrations. The *njau mhö'* are shamans or psychopomps; they have the power to travel into the Beyond during their public séances (*mhö'*).

njür koon: "to carry the child outside." The rite normally takes place seven days after birth.

noo: thing; word; lay; poetic forms defined by the words that come after.

 noo goong: "the saying of the gongs," sacred myths ritually chanted in alternate form.

 noo ngöi dôih: "the lay of justice," a poem on a juridical matter, recited during trials.

 noo pröö: "epic lay"; that is, an epic.

nool poec: "debt of meat." The receiver of a gift of meat during a sacrifice is obliged to repay in due course.

nôot: punishment, in the form of a general emaciation, for breaking the rules that govern relations with one's *tâm köih*—the elder clan "brothers and sisters" of the spouse and clan relatives belonging to older generations.

nsôom: tassel.

ntaang, or *taang:* the names of several types of jars.

ntöng ndah rlaa: "the raising of the giant-bamboo pole mast."

ntuung hêeng: "the ladder of the soul." A notched stick placed at the head of a coffin.

ngkook: the pandanus, or screw pine. By extension, mats or raincoats made of stitched pandanus leaves.

ngoong: the name of a type of antique jar.

nyiit: to drink. By extension, a celebration or festival.

 Nyiit Döng: Festival of the Soil.

 nyiit Keep: ceremony of the Pincers.

 nyitt ndah: rite of the [Paddy] posts.

paang daak: a semi-collective fishing expedition, for which a stretch of river is completely dammed by two dikes running from bank to bank.

pae lah tuh: "vegetable broken-rice bean." A dish prepared on the occasion of the *Mhaam Baa;* it is made of pork and beans, over which rice fragments are scattered.

Phaan: the subterranean abode of the dead; the Underworld.

phit!: an interjection uttered at the start of formulas of wishes (*rec*).

Phöt Puu: evil Spirits related to the *Mâp Mang* (*q.v.*).

pieng bôok: "cooked head rice." For certain rites, rice is skimmed from the surface of the first potful cooked that particular day.

plaa, or *keep:* a length of bamboo, one end of which is split to hold, stuffed in together (*keep*), ingredients that are intended to communicate certain qualities to the growing paddy. The *plaa* is planted in the field on the day of the *nyiit Keep.*

poal bôok ier: "divination by a chicken's head." The head is split in two, and the parts are cast, as in a heads-or-tails throw. Performed in marriage rites. *See* pool.

poec mâp nae nyiim: "meat [to protect] those who have wept from the *Mâp*

Mang." Here "to weep" means "to sing laments." The meat portion comes from the *njat* sacrifice and is distributed to each weeper.

pool: a genuine divinatory operation or a magic action designed to ensure the suitable realization of some desired event.

    pool ding boh: consultation by pressing hulled rice into a "salt tube."

    pool ding mhaam: consultation by the heads-or-tails manipulation of two longitudinal halves of a tube that has served to store blood.

    pool dlei: the same operation performed as part of the burning of the slashed forest rite.

    pool gun Ik: the same operation performed with the two halves of a cylindrical piece of the magic plant of Coolness.

    pool taak: "consultation of the lance." The lance is inserted, upright and balanced, in a covered Vietnamese bowl containing water and grains of rice. See *poal bôok ier; rla' ier; rblaang; rtlup.*

pôong rlaa: a special way of felling the giant bamboo chosen as a ritual pole mast. It is cut flush with the ground, rather than above its thorns, and is lowered with care, rather than, as usual, being allowed to crash down.

pötoo: corruption of the Cham word for "king."

Praang, or *Tei:* French.

praang baal: a harangue aiming to make harmony prevail during the drinking that precedes a buffalo sacrifice.

prah: ritual fanning.

    prah sak: "ritual fanning of the body."

proproh: therapy by massage.

    proproh uuk, or *proproh kiek:* "the treatment [by which one extracts the sorcerers'] mud, or sand."

rbii Baa: "to caress the Paddy." A marriage rite in which the father of the bride for the first time takes his son-in-law into the family granary.

rblaang (böh any): "the top facing [me]." In divining, this is the proper way for the split stick to fall; that is, the hollow side of the half nearer the heads-or-tails, *(pool)* consultant falls face upward. See *rtlup.*

rdae: the temporary granary built at the entrance to the *miir.*

rla' ier: "[to make] the hen roll [at the foot of the granary ladder]." A pseudo-divinatory operation performed in the course of the *Mhaam Baa.* See *pool.*

rluung: a very valuable jar.

rmuul: dibble. In sowing, long sticks used in pairs; the men make the holes into which the women drop the seed. See *tuuc; kriet.*

rnôom: the male and female servants for the sacrifice. A *kuang* who must make a buffalo sacrifice engages a young man and a girl—the *rnôom*—about a month before the ceremony. Their task is to prepare the celebration. The young man is responsible for fashioning all the ritual properties and decorations that every buffalo sacrifice requires. The girl's is mainly gathering fuel and cooking.

rnööm: rice beer. The jar, already prepared with wort, is opened only when one is about to offer the drink. The jar, stuffed with leaves to prevent the bran of the *coot (q.v.)* from rising, is then filled with water. The *rnööm* is sucked up through a drinking straw *(gut),* the lower end of which is inserted deep in the jar.

rnööm bööm phei: "rice beer in response to [invitation] rice."

rnööm prah rhaal ndraany: "rice beer to fan the sweat of the go-between."

Rnut: the sacred Fire Sticks. By rubbing them one sparks the fire that will burn the fallen wood and brush at the *chuu ntôih.* By extension, the holy man who is guardian of the Fire Sticks.

rngool: a village site.

rok cing: the procession of the flat-gong orchestra through all the houses in the village.

root: house; the long house sheltering several families, or house-granaries (*hih nâm*).

rplee nnaan: "change of name." This is done after a serious illness in order to mislead Spirits and sorcerers.

rsei sieng ja' tlaang kuulêel: "rope of thick rattan to guide the *kuulêel* sparrow hawk." The rope to guide the sparrow-hawk-soul is placed at the head of the grave before filling it with earth; the rope is later removed.

rtee: the egg-shaped pebble that, together with the shard of quartz (*naar*), is part of everyone's magic equipment.

(*süm*) *rtleh:* the name of a bird, probably the woodpecker.

rtlup (*böh Yaang*): "tails [toward the Spirits]." This designates the favorable (or necessary) way for the stick to fall in a heads-or-tails (*pool*) consultation; that is, the half farther from the consultant should fall with the rounded side up-turned. *See rblaang.*

rwaang brii: "the inspection of the forest." An agrarian rite and public ceremony accompanying the allotment to villagers of individual plots for cultivation.

rwec bôok: "revolving [the small neckless jar] above the head." A ritual gesture, one of many purification ceremonies.

sae: husband.

sah: pannier.

  sah kec: harvest pannier. The largest size in use.

sal: to reciprocate in kind. However, when sickness is involved, in *sal Muu* ("to give to the Bear") and *sal Yaang* ("to give to the Spirit of the tree"), because both are considered to be at the root of the illness, the gifts are accompanied by hostile actions.

sam gun: application of gun. *See gun* (1).

siam ê' sür siam ê' sau: "to feed with pig's excrement, to feed with dog's excre-ment." The principal phase in the sacrifice in expiation of incest.

sok Rhei: "the taking of the Straw." An agrarian rite performed on the eve of the big annual celebration that marks the completion of the harvest—the Blood Anointment of the Paddy.

sreh ngguu tâm buum: "to cut [a tree to make it into] a stump and plant the tuber." The rite that signifies taking possession of one's plot of land at the time of the inspection of the forest (*rwaang brii*).

suu troany: loincloth; or the langooty of the early travelers. The chief article of clothing for the Proto-Indo-Chinese man. It is a long band of cloth that is slipped between the legs and wound around the waist, the most highly deco-rated section of it falling in front.

  suu troany ding door: the loincloth woven especially for the *Tâm Bôh.*

taang, or *ntaang:* the name of several types of jars.

> *taang sôh:* the most widely used jars, in particular those called (from) Djiring.
>
> *taang laa:* medium-priced jar. *See yang.*

tâm (1): to plant; to place a plant in the earth.

> *tâm gun Baa:* "to plant the magic plant of the Paddy." An agrarian sowing rite. *See tuuc.*

tâm (2): the concept of exchange, of reciprocity.

> *Tâm Bôh:* "the Exchange of Roasting"; that is, the Exchange of Buffalo Sacrifices.
>
> *tâm bôok:* "to knock heads together." An action that occurs in marriage rites. The term also denotes marriage.
>
> *tâm ge':* "to fight." An expression used in speaking of buffaloes.
>
> *tâm köih:* a mode of address and of behavior that is observed, under pain of general emaciation *(nôot)*, vis-à-vis elder clan "brothers and sisters" of the spouse, and those relatives of the spouse belonging to older generations.
>
> *tâm nta':* an alliance with the Spirits.
>
> *tâm nyiit:* "exchange of drinks." Two partners, in turn, raise a drinking tube to each other's lips.
>
> *tâm rec ntii nae:* "exchange of formulas to instruct others"; that is, speeches made by the holy men.
>
> *tâm siam:* "exchange of food." The two partners lift a handful of food to each other's lips.
>
> *tâm triu:* the aggregate of gifts the two leaders of a *Tâm Bôh* offer each other.

tau bung: "to shake [the leaves in order to collect] the spider-soul." This is the final episode of the *mhö'* as it is currently performed. Very often, the term denotes the entire shamanist séance. Even when there is no séance, the *tau bung* may be performed by the spouse or near relative of the invalid in the course of exorcising the illness.

Tei (a word of Vietnamese origin), or *Praang:* French.

(süm) tei: the *tei* bird, which is considered responsible for pains in the shoulder.

tereh: small cockroaches (?).

Tlaa kap!: "May the tiger devour you!"

tlaang: a bird of prey; sparrow hawk. *See (tlaang) ayaa; (tlaang) kuulêel.*

tling tlör: a xylophone played in the fields. It is made of four horizontal bars hung by two rattan strings to a fifth bar, which, in turn, is attached to an upright support. The two other ends of the rattan strings are fastened to the ground by stakes. The bars of this musical "ladder" are struck by two players, one using two hammers, the other using only one. *See,* in the author's study of the pre- or proto-historic lithophone he discovered at Ndut Lieng Krak, Fig. 52 and Plate XLIV, 2; *Bulletin de l'Ecole Française d'Extrême-Orient,* Vol. XLV, No. 2.

tok: to extract; to draw.

> *tok möng:* "to extract the slivers." A magic healing rite that consists in sucking the sorcerers' arrows (minute slivers of wood), which are the cause of the illness, from the affected area.

tok yoo: "to draw [by lot the names of the] ancestors," in order to give the name of one to a newborn child.

tong: to sing; a song; a chant.

  tong rpuh: "buffalo song."

  tong yang: "jar song." Both are sacred hymns that recall mythic episodes; they are sung through the night preceding a buffalo sacrifice.

tuuc: to sow by dropping seed in holes. *See tâm* (1).

tuk mee lööt: "where you go," "Where are you going?"

tum: hut.

  tum miir. See miir.

  tum Nduu: hut of the Spirit Nduu. A ritual construction on stilts that, in miniature, is reminiscent of the field huts *(tum miir)* and is associated with the Great Festival of the Soil.

uuk tlaang kuulêel: "earth [of the] *kuulêel* sparrow hawk." The first clod of earth dug when a grave is being excavated; it is placed on the finished grave before the mourners leave the burial ground.

wah: the common room shared by two neighboring households. Also, the space that separates their two house-granaries *(hih nâm).*

waih mpôh: "to chase [the Spirits from the] abandoned field." A magic curative rite.

weer: sacred; forbidden; taboo. *See croo weer; beng.*

weh phei: "to weigh the hulled rice." A rite during which the guests invited to a buffalo sacrifice offer a bowl of hulled rice to the sacrificer in response to his invitation. In the course of the *Tâm Bôh,* there is a second "weighing of uncooked rice," this time offered by the *jôok,* who is the ranking guest, so to speak. His gift is reciprocated, his sworn friend immediately offering him a thick, hard pancake of fermented rice *(ndrii tâm triu).* This double operation is repeated in the second phase of the feast, but then the protagonists' roles are reversed.

wiah: the Mnong bush hook. The long *dlei* bamboo handle is curved at the knob where the shoulder of the blade is inserted.

wül: a large black hairy spider that lives in a hole in the ground.

Yaang: Spirits. *See khual Yaang; ndrööng Yaang; rtlup (böh Yaang).*

yang: jar.

  yang dâm: small neckless jar.

  yang drôh: medium-size jar.

  yang ke' it: neckless jar even smaller than the *yang dâm. See drang; ngoong; rluung; taang; ndah yang.*

yoo: the generation of grandparents; great-grandparents; the ancestors. It is a respectful form of address for Westerners. (The author's Mnong Gar name was Yoo Sar Luk.)

yôh bôok rpuh: "ritual deposit of the buffalo skulls." It takes place three days after the end of the Great Festival of the Soil.

INDEX

OF GEOGRAPHICAL AND ETHNIC GROUP NAMES

In this index, the names of ethnic groups are in italic; the names of places, rivers, etc., in roman. Words beginning with preglottalized consonants have been listed here in accordance with the method used in the Index of Personal and Clan Names.

INDEX

OF PERSONAL AND CLAN NAMES

MNONG usage has been followed in that an individual's surname appears before that of the spouse, to which it is linked by a hyphen; for example, Kroong-Sraang is the husband of Sraang-Kroong. In the case of two brothers, the two names are simply set side by side.

The clan name of each individual and of his or her spouse follows, italicized, linked by a dash, and enclosed in parentheses. It should be borne in mind that among the Mnong Gar an individual belongs to the clan of his mother.

For nonresidents of Sar Luk, the village where they reside has been indicated.

For an explanation of the alphabetization of Mnong Gar names, see the footnote appended to the first page of the Glossary (p. 361). However, while long (double) vowels are treated the same as short (single) vowels and alphabetized accordingly (thus, Kraang follows Krah), preglottalized (double) consonants, here and in the Index of Geographical and Ethnic Group Names, are considered distinct units and placed at the end of the alphabet group. Thus, Bbaang follows Brôong rather than Baap Can; Ddoong does not precede Drüm but follows Dür. And because Ng and Ny transcribe single phonemes (see footnote p. 361), names beginning with these letters are listed at the end of the "N" group.

378

Index of Personal and Clan Names

Brôong-the-Widow (*Rjee*) (*continued*)
Dwarf, and Jieng-the-Short; daughter of
old Troo; sister of Laang-Mhoo, with whom
she lives; "sister" of Truu and Baap Can,
23, 202–3
(Master) Bbae, the name of a buffalo, 70, 237
Bbaang (?), husband of Dloong, and ancestor
of the *Cil* clan, 88
Bbaang (*Ntöör*), an ancestor of Aang-the-
Long, 217
Bbaang (*Ntöör*), son of Yôong-the-Mad (and, it
seems, of Bbôong-the-Deputy), 62
Bbaang (*Ntöör*), of Sar Lang, son of Lieng
(*Rjee*) and of Jôong, deceased, 128, 131
Bbaang-Aang. *See* Bbaang-the-Stag
Bbaang-Aang (*Düng Jrii—Ryaam*), of Sar
Lang, holy man of the Fire Sticks in that
village; elder brother of Choong-Yôong, the
village headman; maternal uncle (*kôony*) of
Dloong (wife of the shaman) and father of
Jôong-Nyaang, Bok, and Kaar, 227–38,
241–9, 254, 297
Bbaang-the-Corporal, friend of Nyaang-the-
Soldier (*Rtung*), 340
Bbaang-Dlaang (*Daak Cat—??*), of Bboon
Dlei Laac Yô'; district chief, 86, 100, 170,
201, 221, 234, 327
Bbaang-Jieng. *See* Bbaang-the-Pregnant-Man
Bbaang-Jrae (*Rjee—Ryaam*), of Nyôong Brah,
son of old Troo; brother of Laang-Mhoo and
Brôong-the-Widow; former infantryman,
23, 111, 138–9, 346
Bbaang-Jrae (*Cil—Paang Tiing*), Daa' Mroong
canton chief, 60–1, 346
Bbaang-Lang. *See* Bbaang-the-One-Eyed
Bbaang-Mae (*Koon Yôong—Paang Tiing*), of
Paang Döng, paternal uncle of Choong-
the-Soldier; sworn friend (via the pig) of
Mhoo-Laang, 329–31
Bbaang-Mang, of Ndut Sar, friend of
Wan-Yôong, of Paang Pê' Nâm, 77
Bbaang-the-One-Eyed = Bbaang-Lang (*Daak
Cat—Nduu*), brother of Kroong-the-One-
Eyed, Aang-Kröng (who lives with him),
and Nyaang; son of Kraang-Laang
(*Rtung—Daak Cat*); friend of Tôong-Biing,
43–4, 97–9, 108, 116, 200, 203, 265, 300,
311, 313–14, 316, 324, 333, 344, 350
Bbaang-Poong, called the Laac (*Ntöör
—Rlük*), of Sar Lang, son-in-law of
Yaang-Dlaang, whose house he shares,
244–49
Bbaang-the-Pregnant-Man = Bbaang-Jieng
(*Düng Jrii—Rtung*), father of Drüm-
Kraang, Bbieng-Dlaang, and Kroong-
Sraang; sworn friend of Truu and of Kroong-
the-Short; holy man of the *Rnut:*

biographical data and character traits, 23,
25, 87–8, 140, 200–1, 327, 331–3; holy
man of the *Rnut*, 23–5, 48, 53–4, 87,
94, 139, 141–2, 154, 160, 177–85,
191–5, 198–201, 205, 241, 264, 305,
324–6, 328–9, 332–3, 342–3, 346, 348,
362; other, 55, 69, 141, 151, 186, 196,
205, 311, 315, 322, 325, 329, 335
Bbaang-the-Schoolboy (*Bboon Jraang*), of
Ndut Lieng Krak, "brother" of Srae-Jaang,
Can, Aang-of-the-Drooping-Eyelid; lover
of Aang-the-Widow (*Daak Cat*), 165, 167,
169, 173, 316
Bbaang-the-Stag = Bbaang-Aang (*Ntöör—
Cil*), younger brother of Aang-the-Long
(and *kôony* of her children by Baap Can);
"son" (nephew) of Yôong-the-Mad. Holy
man in Phii Ko' and canton runner. Substitute husband of Aang-of-the-Mincing-Step;
is raising one of her nephews; another
nephew of his wife, Wan-Rieng, married,
lives with him; sworn friend (April 1949) of
Kraang-Drüm:
biographical data, 20, 25, 103, 194–5,
209, 265, 327, 337, 340, 346–7;
brother-in-law of Taang-the-Stooped,
265–6, 268, 270, 283–6, 292–3, 298–9,
303–5; character traits, 87–8, 172–3,
194, 298–30, 303–4, 336; holy man in
Phii Ko', 20, 25, 35, 66, 155, 159, 161,
178–84, 274–5, 340, 342, 344–51;
kôony of the children of Baap Can (and
latter's brother-in-law), 35, 38–9,
41–2, 45, 69, 77, 167, 170, 172–3, 221,
265; runner, 20, 25, 138, 153, 161,
170, 265, 314; other, 17, 39, 97, 107,
137, 140–1, 146, 151, 178, 199, 201,
312, 314, 337
Bbaang-the-Tin (*Rtung*), son of Wan (*Mok*)-
Jôong, 316
Bbieng Coh Lêe, the mythic Hero, who led
men from the Underworld to live on the
earth, 335
Bbieng-Dlaang (*Nduu—Rjee*), Laac Döng
canton chief; son-in-law of old Troo, 23, 25,
47, 156, 159
Bbieng-Dlaang (*Rtung—Paang Tiing*), son
of Bbaang-Jieng-the-Pregnant-Man, with
whom he lives; brother of Drüm-Kraang
and Kroong-Sraang, 24, 103, 108, 141, 315,
331–2, 335, 342
Bboon Jraang, 164n., 165, 206–7, 301
of Ndut = Biing-Kroong, her children
(Srae-Jaang, for one), her brothers and
sisters, 24, 27–8, 30, 34, 38–42, 48, 55,
71, 164–8, 170–5, 215–17, 220–1
the Paang Döng affair = Jôong, sister of

Luk; Wan-Tôong (of Sar Luk) is also a
member, 22, 203–4
in Sar Luk, 39, 109, 130, 140, 145, 148,
155, 164–8, 166n., 170–2, 205–7, 248,
333, 335, 348. *See also* Genealogical
Chart
main branch: descendants of the sister of Taang Mbrii Guu: Baap Can,
Truu, etc.; Troo, her daughters
(and their children) and sons;
Kroong-the-Short, who, together
with his half sister, lives in the
home of his wife in Ndut Lieng
Krak, 16, 19–26, 123, 312, 333–4,
338–40. In the narrow sense, "the
Rjee" denotes Troo and the households of her two daughters and her
granddaughter living with her in
the house she shares with her
"son," Truu, 22–4, 77, 138–9, 156,
202, 264–5, 297, 336–7
Mang-of-the-Jutting-Jaw, family of,
sold by the *Rjee* of the main branch:
24, 338–9
Rieng-Chaar, family of, 98–9, 102–3,
107–9, 341
Rlük, 130, 145, 148, 333
in Phii Ko': Sieng-the-Cook, whose
maternal niece, Drüm-Krae, lives in
Sar Luk with Tôong-Jieng, 208–9,
264, 340
in Sar Lang: Ddöi-the-Shaman, whose
maternal niece, Mang-Tôong, lives in
Sar Luk, 126–8, 130–5, 138–9, 142,
144–8, 153–6, 162–3, 203, 226, 229,
232, 237, 249, 266, 297
in Sar Luk: Troo-Jôong, 333–4
Rtung:
family of Jieng (wife of Bbaang-the-
Pregnant-Man); also Ndêh-Mang, of
Ndut Lieng Krak, 342
family of Jôong-Wan-the-Healer, 235,
265, 342–3
Ryaam, an important clan in Sar Lang and
Nyôong Brah; also in Nyôong Rlaa, where
it took part in the massacre of the *Rjee* (the
Ddôol Bbaang affair), 327

See-Aang (*Rjee—Ntöör*), of Paang Döng,
younger brother of Kroong-Mae; "distant
brother" of Baap Can, Truu, etc., 341
Sieng = Tieng-the-Widower (*Cil*); his first
name before his serious illness, 116–17
Sieng-Aang (*Paang Tiing—Ryaam*), of
Nyôong Brah, holy man in this village,
connected with the Sar Luk *Rjee* through
the sister of his wife; his father was sworn

friend of Truu, 34–5, 38, 62, 77, 191, 193–5
Sieng-Dee = Sieng-the-Cook (*Rlük—Sruk*),
younger brother of the father of Aang-the-
Long; maternal uncle (*kôony*) of
Drüm-Krae; murdered by the *Cil* of Paang
Döng after the Phii Dih massacre, 208–9,
340
Sieng-Dloong (*Bboon Kroong—Rlük*), of Sar
Lang, assistant to the village holy men, 228,
232, 234, 248
Sieng-the-Kuang (*Nduu*), of Nyôong Rlaa, 240
Sieng Laa, the name of a rock Spirit and its
brother, 130–1
Sieng-the-Little, a Rhade; a plantation over-
seer, 158
Sieng Nôor and Sieng Nung, the names of
mythic heroes, 319
Sieng-Rau (*Ryaam—Paang Tiing*), of Sar
Lang, 255
Sieng-the-Widower (*Cil*), becoming Sieng-
Ôot (*Cil—Phok*) through his remarriage; of
Little Sar Luk; elder brother of
Tôong-Biing and the incestuous Aang-
the-Widow, 82, 85, 88–91, 97, 157, 216
Sieng-the-Widower (*Daak Cat*), of Sar Lang,
235
Sôi-the-Tokélo (*Rlük*), orphan girl adopted by
Mang-Tôong (wife of Tôong-the-Cook), sis-
ter of her mother, 275
son of the American minister in Ban Me
Thuot, 160–1
Srae, mythic hero ("barrier of Srae"), 274, 292
Srae = Srae-Jaang (*Bboon Jraang—Ntöör*), by
virtue of his betrothal to the daughter of
Baap Can and Aang-the-Long in October
1948; son of the first marriage of Biing (wife
of Kroong-the-Short); brother of Jrae;
"brother" of Can, Aang-of-the-Drooping-
Eyelid (the half brother and half sister of his
wife); schoolboy in Ban Me Thuot, xviii, 24,
27–8, 30, 34, 38–42, 48, 55, 71, 121, 164–8,
170–5, 215–16, 220–1
Srae (*Ntöör*), maternal uncle (*kôony*) of Aang-
the-Long, 217
Srae-Jaang. *See* Srae (*Bboon Jraang*)
Sraang, ancestor of the *Cil* clan, 88
Sraang-Kroong (*Rjee—Rtung*), lives in the
same house as her mother, Brôong-
the-Widow, her grandmother, Troo, and
her "little mother," Laang-Mhoo; sister of
Kroong-the-Stag, Mang-the-Dwarf, Jieng-
the-Short; married to the son of Bbaang-
the-Pregnant-Man; has one daughter,
Poong, 23, 202–3, 212, 215, 337
Sruk, 20, 216–17; Phii Dih sorcery affair
aimed against members of this clan living in
Phii Dih and Phii Ko', 208–9, 216–17, 264

INDEX

OF PLANT NAMES*

baa: paddy, rice (*Oryza sativa* L.). *Baa* denotes both the cereal in the general sense of the term (rice), but mainly paddy (the growing plant, the grain of rice, and rough, or unhulled, rice)

standing paddy (*baa*), 64, 148, 179, 210, 252, 258–60, 306–7, 311–12, 367; early varieties of, 258, 307, 319; straw, or *rhei,* 307, 318–19, 369. *See also* Subject Index: Agrarian Rites (taking of the Straw); Agriculture (straw, or *rhei*)

grain (*baa*), 19, 35, 46–7, 64–5, 95–6, 107, 109, 147, 157, 167, 210, 254, 260–1, 264, 297–8, 301–2, 306–13, 315–18, 322–5, 338, 343, 365–6, 368–9 chaff of the Paddy (*nchiep Baa*) and bran (*lök*), 19, 214, 258–9, 362. *See also* Subject Index: Childbirth (rites); Food and Drink (wort [*coot*], winnowing and hulling of rice, rice beer [*rnööm*])

early varieties of, 157

seeds, 13, 188–9, 197–8, 209, 312–13 *See also* Subject Index: Agrarian Rites (belly of the Paddy, gathering the soul of the Paddy, head of the Paddy, Blood Anointment of the Paddy, sowing); Agriculture (sowing, harvesting, temporary field granaries, transportation); Housing (granary)

hulled raw rice (*phei*), 95–6, 178; ceremonial uses of (rice of invitation), 29, 36, 38–40, 46–7, 54–5, 74, 155, 193–4, 222, 231–4, 238, 241–2, 351–2, 368–9, 371; cooking water used as shampoo (*daak wii*), 41; as food (preparation of *pieng* and *poor*), 19, 40–1, 228, 275, 290, 328, 339, 367; magic use of, 116–17, 122–3, 135, 138, 140, 156,

172–3, 202–3, 212–13, 220, 252, 269, 297–8, 302–3, 344, 367; as offering to the *caak Yaang,* 128–33, 136, 142, 144–6, 150, 158; as ritual gift, 29, 167–9; saffroned (*phei rmüt*), 33, 57, 75, 128–9, 133–4, 142, 148–9, 158, 219, 241; simulacrum (represented by rice bran), 258–9; as wages, 129, 133–4, 136, 142, 144, 146, 148, 150, 155, 158–9, 205, 211, 348, 351

cooked rice (*pieng*): as everyday food, 46–7, 98, 102, 104, 106, 122, 145–6, 157, 163, 170, 210, 275, 286, 301, 328; as ritual meal, 170–1, 185, 296; as ritual offering, 38, 104, 106, 142, 144–5; "head rice" (*pieng bôok*), 197, 220–1, 253, 259–61, 322, 352, 367; simulacrum (represented by *phei*), 269

cooked glutinous rice (*pieng baa baar*): in sacramental meal, 52–3, 61, 66, 68–9, 71, 79, 230–3, 236–7, 242–3, 248–9, 328–9; as ritual offering, 33–4, 66, 68, 104, 106, 229–33, 253–4, 328; magic use of, 44, 64–5; as (more or less ritual) caulking, 282, 284, 328

rice soup (*poor*): as food, 102, 104, 106, 122, 145–6, 155–6, 159, 197, 217, 275, 328; as ritual nourishment, 167; as ritual offering, 104, 106, 107, 213, 270, 272, 284, 286, 313–14, 319, 322; "head soup" (*poor bôok*), 259–61

(rice) flour (*ndrii*), 17, 54–5, 74, 81, 135–6, 141–2, 145–6, 224, 322–3, 362. *See also* Subject Index: Agrarian Rites (Blood Anointment of the Paddy); Food and Drink (rice beer [*rnööm*])

gun (*gun Baa*). *See below*

bamboo, kinds of. *See dlei, ngkaar, ngör, rlaa* in ritual constructions, 7, 30–1, 45, 47–8, 58, 70–1, 89, 91, 110, 114, 129, 135–6,

---

*The identification of plants is based on determinations made by A.-G. Haudricourt for our joint study of Mnong Gar ethnobotany.

SUBJECT INDEX

Accidents: to human beings, 40–1, 119, 348, 352; to animals, 34, 39, 40

Acculturation and Cultural Contacts:
cash payments for farm labor, first instance of, 153, 161
eating manners and politeness, 236–7, 248–9
imported products, 341, 364; chromos, 161, 161n. *See also* Food and Drink; Jars; Receptacles; Weapons
locomotion (*rdeh*), Western means of: airplane, 150, 315; bicycle, 161; jeep, 200; truck, 157
punishment, affecting severity of, 99–100
rites: modification of, 38, 55–6, 240, 253–4; nonobservance of, 200–1
taboos: evolution of, 110–11; nonobservance of, 153
See also Army and Garde Montagnarde; Dress and Personal Adornment; Government; History; Medicine; Money; Plantation; Religion (Christianity); School; Trade

Administration. *See* Government

Adoption (*roong*): of children, 22–4, 157, 191, 311–12, 318n., 322, 336; consecration of newborn infant by village, 224; consecration of relatives joining a household, 97, 203, 257; of a slave, 339; of survivors of a bereavement, 107–9, 204

Adultery, 22, 62, 120–1, 126, 150–1. *See also* Divorce; Marriage; Sexuality

Agrarian Rites, xx, 14, 81, 192, 198–9, 202, 209–10, 226–8, 254, 256–64, 306, 307–13, 318–26, 340–2, 369
inspection of the forest (*rwaang brii*), 348–52, 369; cutting the stump and planting the tuber (*sreh ngguu tâm buum*), 351–2, 369
burning felled wood (*chuu ntôih*), 177–95, 362, 363, 366; post, 180–6; leaves (*nhaa shii*), 178, 178n., 180, 184–6; charred wood (*mal uiny*), 191–2
collective fishing and anointment of *Rnut* and leaves, 176–9, 180, 189–90; making the fire, 184–6;

Rnut anointment and drinking from gourds (*nyiit ndoh*), 191–3; sowing by women, 188, 198
sowing, or "planting the magic plant of the Paddy (*tâm gun Baa*)," 196–203, 312–13, 318–19, 363, 369; the post (*dôong dlei*), 196–8, 259–60, 307, 312, 318–19, 362–3
ceremony of the Pincers (*nyiit Keep*) and *plaa* stalk, 210, 258, 367
ceremony of the Paddy posts (*nyiit ndah*), 29, 227, 252–7, 311, 318–19, 342, 367; Paddy post (*ndah Baa*), 253, 257, 259–60, 318–19; tube altar (*ding poal yôot*), recut as ritual whistle (*ding hoot Baa*), 254, 318–19, 322–4
announcement of the harvest (*nhêel*—i.e., *töih*—*kec*), 29, 43, 258, 366; to people in the Underworld (*nhêel kec Phaan in*), 258–9, 366
knotting the Paddy (*muat Baa*), 259–64, 306, 312–13, 318–19
gathering the soul of the Paddy (*dôop hêeng Baa*), 307, 311, 313–19, 363, 365
taking of the Straw (*sok Rhei*), 34, 53, 81, 307, 318–22, 347, 369
Blood Anointment of the Paddy (*Mhaam Baa*), 34, 81, 84–5, 108, 147, 155, 191, 196, 249, 314–15, 323–9, 332–4, 340–2, 365, 368, 369
Festival of the Soil, the Great (*Nyiit Döng*), 38, 107, 179, 180, 193, 196, 204, 221–2, 225–8, 240, 242, 252–6, 297, 314–15, 334, 342, 361, 362, 367, 371; uprooting the Rattan (*dok Reh*), 342, 362; blood anointment of flat gongs and drum (*mhaam cing mhaam nggör*), 342–6; blood anointment of Fire Sticks and Rattan rope (*mhaam Rnut rsei Reh*), and raising of the pole mast (*ntöng ndah rlaa*), 228–40; feast (*Nyiit Döng*), 240–52, and ritual procession of sacrifice servants (*broo rnôom*), 242–5, 361; deposit of buffalo skulls (*yôh bôok rpuh*), 252–5, 371
See also Rites

393

---

*For the Mnong, the boundaries separating magic from religion are extremely fuzzy, and it is only for convenience that in this index any distinction is made. Actually, all the data included under the listing of Magic necessarily appear under Rites and also under Sacrifice (the latter being, obviously, a part of the former).

Sacrifice (*continued*)

consecration of persons and possessions, 26, 28, 97, 172, 203, 220–1,
228, 257–8, 302–3, 340, 365. *See
also* Adoption

contract. *See* Trade

exorcism. *See* Magic

expiation. *See* Law and Economy
(sacrifices as reparations)

funerary. *See* Death

for an invalid. *See* Magic (exorcism of
illness); Shaman and Shamanism

prestige (all buffalo sacrifices, of whatever category)

protection, 175, 214–15, 364

purification, 90, 95–7, 150–1, 215, 266,
302, 304–5

techniques used in (felling of trees,
construction), 32–4, 65–9, 228–40,
275

welcome, 53–5, 241–2

other, 121, 161, 189, 257, 302–3, 311,
332, 351–2

buffalo (*sreh rpuh*), 7, 13, 19–20, 25–6,
30–1, 33–4, 38–9, 76–80, 123–4, 128,
138–41, 158–9, 179, 191, 194–5, 199,
203–6, 222, 226, 228, 230–1, 238, 240,
242, 244, 253, 257, 269, 297–9, 304,
314, 334, 339–40, 344, 365, 366, 368,
370

simultaneous sacrifice of several buffaloes, 196, 233, 240, 245, 248

myths concerning the first, 58–9,
229–30

servants for (*rnôom*), 26–7, 30–1, 35,
38, 54, 58–61, 65, 70, 76–7, 79–80,
233–4, 242, 361, 368; engaging and
anointing of, 26–7, 43, 194, 228,
230, 365, 368; responsibilities of,
26–7, 30–5, 40–1, 44–5, 48–9, 68–9,
76–7, 79–80, 228, 230–1, 235–40,
242–3, 253, 368; wages of, 138. *See
also* Agrarian Rites (Great Festival
of the Soil); Index of Personal and
Clan Names (Dloong-the-Black-
Girl, Kröng-the-Stutterer, Nyaang)

victim in (*rpuh*), 25, 30–1, 33–4, 39,
48–9, 51, 53–5, 57–9, 62, 86, 91,
99–100, 149–50, 232–3, 237–8,
240–1, 243–4, 253–4. *See also,
above,* other victims (parts of body)
name of, 58, 70, 236–7; adornment
of, 48–9, 58, 60, 140, 240–1; song
to (*Tong Rpuh*), 58, 245 (*See also*
[Oral] Literature); execution of,
59–60, 62, 76, 79, 140, 245, 361;
funerary gifts to (*njat rpuh*), 60,

76, 248, 366; cutting up and shar-
ing of, 60, 62, 64, 76–7, 141, 147,
205, 248–9, 252. *See also* Animal
Husbandry; Division of Activities
by Sex; Food and Drink; Law and
Economy (meat debt); Money;
Social Status; Souls and Body;
Trade

constructions and decors for, ritual,
30–1, 148, 228, 252–3, 365, 368. *See
also* Rites (places where rites take
place that are anointed, and in village, field, etc.)

inside the house: jar post and barrier
(*ndah, nggaar yang*), 30, 41, 49, 55,
69, 228, 235, 252–3, 366; second low
platform (*ndrôong,* or *lôong, jöng*),
30, 49, 151–2, 228, 236; small suspended altar, 30, 229, 233, 254, 366

outside the house:

giant-bamboo pole mast (*ndah
rlaa*), 7, 19, 31–4, 45, 65–9, 80,
199–200, 202, 228, 230–3,
240–1, 243, 366, 367, 368

bombax posts (*ndah blaang*), 7,
13, 30, 43, 45, 52, 57–8, 60,
68–9, 72, 74, 80, 221, 235–8,
240, 252–3, 366; halter,
68–69n., 70, 238, 240, 252–3;
hut of Spirit of the Paddy, 30

stall, ritual (*naang rah*), 31, 57,
74, 77–8, 248, 366

veranda, ritual (*naang röng*), 7,
30, 52–3, 61, 64, 69, 71, 74, 76,
78, 162, 228, 230–2, 236–7,
240–1, 243, 248–9, 366

hut of the Spirit Nduu (*tum
Nduu*), 227–8, 253

hornbill-beak post (*mbuung
kriing*), 139, 148, 203, 365

Sanitary Conditions. *See* Medicine (illnesses
and infirmities)

School, Frontier, xx, 6, 41, 121–2, 138, 209,
264, 272

cook, 208–9, 264, 272, 332. *See also*
Index of Personal and Clan Names
(Sieng-Dee, Tôong-the-Cook)

Groupe Scolaire Antomarchi, in Ban Me
Thuot, 24, 27, 165–6, 174–5

schoolboy(s), and former schoolboy(s),
24, 27–8, 71, 165–6, 174–5, 221, 316.
See also Index of Personal and
Clan Names (Bbaang-the-Schoolboy,
Kroong-the-Stag, Ndür-Yoon, Srae-
Jaang, Taang-the-Schoolboy)

teacher, 41, 121, 138, 205. *See also* Index
of Personal and Clan Names (Baap Nô')